THE
POLITICS OF
MISCALCULATION
IN THE
MIDDLE EAST

Indiana Series in Arab and Islamic Studies

Salih J. Altoma, Iliya Harik,
and Mark Tessler,
GENERAL EDITORS

THE
POLITICS OF
MISCALCULATION
IN THE
MIDDLE EAST

RICHARD B. PARKER

INDIANA UNIVERSITY PRESS
Bloomington and Indianapolis

The paper used in this publication meets the minimum requirements of American National Standard for Information Sci-
ences—Permanence of Paper for Printed Library Materials,
ANSI Z39.48-1984.

♾ ™

Manufactured in the United States of America

Library of Congress Cataloging-in-Publication Data
Parker, Richard Bordeaux, date.
The politics of miscalculation in the Middle East / Richard B.
Parker.
p.   cm.—(Indiana series in Arab and Islamic studies)
Includes bibliographical references and index.
ISBN 0-253-34298-8 (alk. paper).—ISBN 0-253-20781-9 (pbk.)
1. Middle East—Politics and government—1945–1979.   2. Israel
—Arab War, 1967—Diplomatic history.   3. Israel-Arab Border
Conflicts, 1949-   —Egypt.   4. Lebanon—History—Israeli
intervention, 1982–1984.   I. Title.   II. Series.
DS63.1.P383   1993
956.04—dc20   92-23947

1 2 3 4 5   97 96 95 94 93

CONTENTS

Maps

Acknowledgments

I would particularly like to acknowledge the generosity of the Wilson Center for International Scholars of the Smithsonian Institution for the fellowship given to me in 1989–90 to work on this project and of the Earhart Foundation of Ann Arbor, Michigan, for a travel grant that permitted me to travel to Moscow to interview Soviet scholars and officials about the origins of the June War of 1967. Thanks are also due to the Fulbright Commission in London for granting me the John Adams Fellowship, which permitted me to do interviewing in Britain, and to the Royal Institute of International Affairs for giving me a place to work at Chatham House.

I am grateful to friends and former colleagues who gave me interviews about their own views of the cases studied. Special thanks to those who read the manuscript or portions of it and gave me advice and counsel: L. Carl Brown, William Quandt, Donald Bergus, David Korn, Morris Draper, Philip Habib, Brian Urquhart, and General Indar Jit Rikhye. They bear no responsibility for errors to be found herein. Those are all mine.

Added thanks to William Quandt for his generosity in letting me use the Abba Eban letter about the 1967 green light.

Finally, a vote of thanks to my wife for putting up with it all and not asking when it was going to be over.

Introduction

This is a study of three serious policy failures in the Middle East: the June War of 1967; the War of Attrition, or Canal War, between Egypt and Israel in 1968–70; and the abortive May 17, 1983, peace agreement between Israel and Lebanon. All three involved serious miscalculations by one or more of the parties involved. My purpose has been threefold: to establish and record what actually happened, to explore what lay behind the decisions taken in order to see whether there are useful lessons to be learned, and to illustrate the universality of the miscalculation phenomenon—everybody does it.

By the term *miscalculation* I mean a policy decision which goes awry because those making it did not foresee properly what the results would be. The results can range from bothersome misstep to national disaster. I exclude mistakes caused by physical or mental incapacity (as some have argued was the case with Anthony Eden in the 1956 Suez affair) but not by personal idiosyncrasy. I originally determined to exclude mistakes caused by lack of information but concluded that this was a legitimate factor in the War of Attrition case, although it should not have been in the other two cases.

The classic example of miscalculation is Israel's failure to react to visible Egyptian preparations for an attack in 1973 because such an attack did not fit the "concept" of what the Egyptians were likely to do, given Israel's air superiority. This miscalculation has been described and analyzed in considerable detail by various writers; see, for instance, Avi Shlaim's "National Intelligence Failures: The Case of the Yom Kippur War," in *World Politics* (April 1976). But there has been little else written on the mechanics of the phenomenon in the Middle East, except with regard to Israel. Little has been written about what happened on the Arab or Soviet or even American sides in terms of the decision-making process, and almost nothing from the point of view of the diplomatic practitioner.

This absence of studies on the subject has not been for lack of examples, going back to the beginnings of history. In the modern period we find the Russians under Catherine the Great, the French under Napoleon, the British under various governments, the Soviets under Brezhnev, the Americans under both Democrats and Republicans, the Israelis both Labor and Likud, the Iraqis both royal and Baathi, the Iranians both imperial and Khomeiniite, the Moroccans, the Libyans, the Jordanians, the Lebanese, and every other people of the region making repeated errors of judgment as to the reaction a particular decision will provoke.

Given the explosive nature of most of the disputes in the Middle

East, the results have rarely been simply bothersome. They have usually been tragic. The short list since World War II is impressive. I would include at least the following: the Arab misreading of Jewish capabilities in 1948, the multiple miscalculations of the Aswan-Suez affair in 1955–56, the Arab rejection of the Eric Johnston proposals for unified development of the Jordan waters in 1955, the 1957 Eisenhower Doctrine, the United States involvement in the Lebanese election of 1957, the Egyptian misadventure in Yemen starting in 1962, the Soviet-Egyptian miscalculation leading to the 1967 June War, the Jordanian decision to enter that war, the U.S.-Israeli misreading of Soviet intentions during the War of Attrition in 1970, the Israeli misreading of Egyptian intentions in Ocotober 1973, the Moroccan and Algerian miscalculation of each other's capabilities and determination with regard to the issue of the Western Sahara in 1975, the American misreading of Menachem Begin at Camp David in 1978, the Iraqi invasion of Iran in 1980, the multiple Israeli-American-Lebanese miscalculations of 1982–83, Qadhafi's miscalculations in Chad, the Moroccan error in seeking a unity agreement with Libya in 1984, the Sudanese government's attempt to impose the shari'a law on non-Muslims in the south, the U.S. involvement in the Lebanese presidential election in 1988, and Saddam Hussein's invasion of Kuwait in 1990, certainly one of the most spectactular misreadings of recent times.

Why do these things happen, and are they inevitable? We expect individuals to make mistakes in their personal decisions as they go through life, but we expect governments composed of rational leaders to do better, multiple heads theoretically being better than one. Indeed, I find Arab audiences and student audiences in the United States generally skeptical that a government such as that of the United States, with all the technological wizardry and information at its fingertips, could stumble blindly into a policy error. Many Arabs in particular are unwilling to believe that a government which can put a man on the moon may not know what it is doing in, say, Lebanon, and they conclude that what we describe as an error of judgment is an attempt to disguise a diabolically clever ploy to attain a conspiratorial goal.

Yet in each case studied here it is evident that the crucial decisions were not diabolically clever but the result of failure to appreciate the full impact of given courses of action. Nor were the failures inevitable. The actors could have followed different courses which would have yielded different results had they known what the outcome would be. If that is so, can something be done to prevent or at least diminish recurrence? Before we can speak intelligently to that question, we need to know more about why people reacted as they did.

In 1967 the crisis was set off by the Soviets' telling the Egyptians that the Israelis were massing troops on the Syrian border. The report was plausible, given the tensions then current between Israel and Syria, but as far as I can tell it was untrue, and the Soviets should have known that. Why did they choose to pass this report to the Eygptians, and why did the Egyptians choose to overreact to it, bringing catastrophe down upon themselves?

Three years later, in 1970, why did Washington refuse to take seriously a Soviet warning, in a letter from Premier Aleksei Kosygin to President Richard Nixon, that if the Americans did not restrain the Israelis from their air attacks on targets in the Nile Valley, the Soviets would have to do something? The warning was dismissed by U.S. and Israeli Sovietologists as a bluff, but six weeks later the Soviets had committed troops to the air defense of Egypt, something they had resisted doing in the past. This development had serious, unanticipated consequences for the Israelis when war came in 1973.

Finally, why did the United States persist in pushing through the May 17, 1983, peace agreement between Israel and Lebanon in spite of clear warnings that Syria would oppose it and was capable of blocking it? The end result was a humiliating policy failure for the United States and the emergence of Syria as the dominant foreign power in Lebanon.

I have no definitive answers to any of these questions. I can provide partial answers and some illumination of the circumstances, but mysteries still remain about the motivations of the actors in each case. Some of the mysteries may eventually be clarified when the official archives of all the states involved are open to public scrutiny, but even the full official record is likely to be incomplete under the best of circumstances. I speak as one who contributed to this record and who recalls how much he left out.

Nothing like the full record is available at present. After over two years of requesting, I received from the U.S. Department of State roughly two-thirds of the pertinent telegrams regarding the June War; about three-fifths of those sent are of only marginal interest. Because of time and space limitations I have not even attempted to retrieve the documents for the War of Attrition and the Lebanese affair, but have relied primarily on my own notes, on the recollections of persons involved, and on published accounts, hoping that future historians will complete the job when the archives are open.

I chose the three cases in question because they illustrate the universality of the miscalculation phenomenon and because I had direct personal knowledge of at least some aspects of each case. I was political counselor at the U.S. Embassy in Cairo at the time of the 1967 war and was the officer in charge of Egyptian affairs in the Department of State for three years immediately thereafter, during the War of Attrition. I was ambassador to Lebanon in 1977–78 and served as adviser to the U.S. Businessmen's Commission on Reconstruction in Lebanon in 1983. I know personally most of the actors on the Lebanese and American sides of the negotiations leading to the May 17 agreement. Although my recollections and those of other survivors will not always be completely reliable, they may be a useful adjunct to the official record, which is often indecipherable without them.

While the three cases are similar, there are obvious differences. They have in common a Middle Eastern setting, a context of war, and a misreading of the probable consequences of a given course of action. Among the differences is one of scale. The June War was a multinational catastrophe which changed the map of the Middle East and raised the threat of U.S.-Soviet confrontation. The War of Attrition caused serious casualties on both sides and had serious military consequences for Israel, but the damage was limited to the combatants, no changes of territories resulted, and there was no realistic threat of U.S.-Soviet armed confrontation over the issue. The Israel-Lebanon fiasco of 1983 was a national tragedy for the Lebanese, but damage to the United States and Israel, the architects of the failure, was minimal.

As the gravest and most complex of the three crises, the June War has received the fullest treatment in this study—five chapters. The primary questions concerning this crisis relate to why the Soviet Union and Egypt reacted as they did, and I have examined their roles separately and in detail in order to fix the sequence of cause and effect more firmly. Separate treatment inevitably led to a certain amount of repetition, but I feel that the repetition is necessary to help the reader follow the events as viewed from different perspectives.

The United States merits a chapter not because Washington miscalculated (although some would argue that it did in its handling of Israel) but because Soviet and Egyptian suspicions and doubts about the U.S. role were an important factor in the Egyptian miscalculation. I have not gone into Israel's role except tangentially because it has been well covered by Israeli writers. Questions remain about Israel's actions or nonactions early in the crisis, and I have been unable to answer them, but they will eventually be dealt with by Israeli authors as the archives for that period are opened.

Part of my effort has been directed at interviewing Egyptian and Soviet survivors of the period who can comment intelligently on what happened. The survivors are fewer than one would like for a comprehensive study. The leading actors in the tragedy are gone. While those still with us have thrown some light on what happened and why, Soviet and Egyptian motives remain moot. I hope the information presented here will lend new substance and vigor to the debate.

The War of Attrition is treated in two chapters. Most of what happened in that war is already well known, and there are few questions to be answered about the events. For the most part I am recording the atmosphere in which the U.S. decision was taken to dismiss Kosygin's message of January 30, 1970, as not being serious. While the precise reasons for the decision may be debatable, certainly it reflected the limitations of Eurocentric expertise about the Soviets. That there are lessons to be drawn from this experience is clear, but there is unlikely to be agreement about what they are.

The agreement of May 17, 1983, between Israel and Lebanon and the events leading up to it are given three chapters. This agreement was the result of a prolonged negotiation which in retrospect was doomed from the start. The question is why more people did not realize earlier that it was hopeless and why negotiation continued even after those involved knew (according to their current recollections) that it was going nowhere. While the recollections are incomplete and must eventually be corrected and amplified by the official record, they offer unusual insight into the tragic dilemma which confronted Secretary of State George Shultz in the spring of 1983.

The conclusion sums up the findings of the case studies and my own views as to why people acted as they did. I discuss but do not attempt to answer in detail the question of what should be done to prevent future miscalculations. That is for the reader to reflect on and for the behavioral scientist to elucidate.

Readers should bear in mind two observations. First, the cases studied relate to a particular geographic area which has its own peculiarities and problems and its individual diplomatic and rhetorical styles. In the Middle East, rhetoric often obscures truth, and it reflects mindsets that differ from those in other areas of the world. Lessons learned there are not necessarily applicable elsewhere. Second, with the benefit of hindsight we can claim that we would have acted differently had we been the decision makers, but they had to deal with a different set of realities. They were rational and intelligent people making decisions which they believed were in the national interest. They guessed wrong, but misjudging the outcome of a decision is a common human failing. It happens to all of us often, and life would be rather dull if it did not. Individual mistakes are one thing, however; those by governments are something else.

It seems reasonable that if decision makers were more aware of the true nature of past mistakes and what caused them, they would be more likely to avoid repeating them. While experience is an inefficient teacher, there is no substitute for it, and a clear appreciation of why a policy failed in the past, coupled with a realistic understanding of the differences between the circumstances then and those today, should lead to wiser choices. If we are to profit from the past, however, we must rely on what actually happened, not on myths.

PART ONE

———

THE JUNE WAR

CHAPTER

1

THE SOVIET WARNING

Gross miscalculations based on gross misinformation.

Dr. Mahmoud Fawzi, vice-president for
foreign affairs, United Arab Republic[1]

The 1967 June War, a brief but violent conflict between Israel and three
of its Arab neighbors, permanently altered the political landscape of the
Middle East. Although Israel began the shooting, Egypt initiated the crisis
that led to the war. Egypt in turn was responding to a Soviet report that
Israel was concentrating troops on its border with Syria, preparatory to
an attack. There were no such concentrations, but the report was believ-
able because tension between Syria and Israel was high as a result of a
long series of incidents along the border. These incidents had provoked
a number of threatening statements by Israel's leaders to the effect that if
Syria did not stop sponsoring cross-border sabotage activities by Palestinians, Israel would have to take strong measures.

According to former Egyptian officials, the Soviet report was given to
them on May 13.[2] Similar reports had been received earlier from the Syrians, but the Egyptians had not taken them seriously because they did
not trust the Syrians. They took the Soviet report seriously because it was
plausible and because the Soviets were serious people. They responded
by mobilizing their forces and sending them into the Sinai Peninsula bor-
dering Israel. A few days later they demanded withdrawal of the United
Nations Emergency Forces (UNEF), which had been keeping the peace
along their border with Israel, and followed the withdrawal with a declaration on May 23 that they were closing the Gulf of Aqaba to Israeli
shipping.

Israel had already said that closure of the Gulf would be taken as casus belli, and it kept its word. In spite of efforts by diplomats and politicians to find a way out of the crisis, Israel struck on June 5, destroying
most of Egypt's air force in the first hours and eventually routing the
Egyptian army and roundly defeating the Syrian and Jordanian armies,
which had also entered the fighting. By the end of the week Israel was in

control of all of the Sinai Peninsula, the West Bank of Jordan, and the Golan Heights of Syria.

An unmitigated political and military disaster for the Arabs, this short war was a turning point for the region. How important it will appear in the long record of history remains to be seen, but some direct and indirect effects can be listed immediately: the rise of the Palestinian guerrilla movement to prominence and the emergence of terrorism as a fact of life for Westerners as well as for Arabs and Israelis, the collapse of Nasserism as the leading ideology of Arab nationalism, the partial dismantling of Jordan and the creation of Greater Israel, the temporary eclipse of Lebanon as a viable state, the consolidation of the special relationship between Israel and the United States, the October 1973 war, and the *intifadah*, or uprising, in the territories that Israel occupied. It has long been evident that there will be no permanent peace in the area until a settlement regarding these territories is reached, and the popular Arab response to Iraq's demand in August 1990 that Israel withdraw from them as a condition for Iraq's withdrawal from Kuwait illustrates the continued vitality of the issue.

Furthermore, the political and social currents in Israel and the Arab world that were stirred up by this conflict have been working their way to the surface ever since. They include an Islamic fundamentalist revival and a corresponding fundamentalist-rightist upsurge in Israel, the strengthening of local as opposed to Arab nationalism, the delegitimization of the leadership in both Israel and Egypt which brought about the war, and the long turmoil into which Palestinian society and politics have been thrown.

Some observers will argue that in the long run the results will prove to have been beneficial, either because they have made (or will make) the Arabs accept Israel or because they will eventually be seen to have strengthened Arab resolve against that state. In any case, it is clear that things did not turn out as the Soviet Union and Egypt expected and that the crisis resulted from one of history's classic miscalculations. This chapter and the next focus on the role of the Soviets in helping to precipitate the crisis. Succeeding chapters deal with Egypt's reaction and the role of the United States.

THE IMPORTANCE AND NATURE OF THE WARNING

None of the parties to the conflict seem to have anticipated war in the spring of 1967. There was tension along the Israel-Syrian border, but that was normal. Egypt was thought to be too involved in Yemen, where the best third of its army was tied down, to undertake any military initiatives. Jordan wanted peace along its border, and so did Lebanon. Syria was being troublesome but was too weak to attack Israel, and the Israelis had no interest in a major war with anyone.

In retrospect it is clear that the political-military solution was supersaturated and all that was required to make it precipitate was for someone to drop in a crystal of solute. That act was performed by the Soviet Union. There are several versions of how the Soviet warning was delivered.

According to Ahmad Hassan al-Feki (al-Fiqi), the Egyptian undersecretary of foreign affairs, the report was delivered to him by Dimitri Pojidaev, the Soviet ambassador, on May 13. Pojidaev called on al-Feki in his office and through an interpreter read out a message from Moscow which gave numbers and types of forces and their location. It was not a vague warning but a detailed report. (Nine days later, in a speech at the Bir Gifgafa air base in Sinai, Egyptian President Gamal Abd al-Nasir (henceforth Nasser) said that on the thirteenth the Egyptians had received "confirmed" information that "Israel was concentrating huge armed forces of about 11 to 13 brigades . . . divided into two fronts, one south of Lake Tiberias and the other north of the lake. The decision made by Israel at this time was to carry out aggression against Syria as of May 17."[3]) Also present at the meeting on the Egyptian side, according to al-Feki, were Ashraf Ghorbal, al-Feki's chef de cabinet and later ambassador to Washington,[4] and Salah Bassiouny, then a middle-grade officer with the rank of counselor in al-Feki's office. The Soviet report, taken down by Bassiouny as it was read, was sent immediatley by telex to the office of Sami Sharaf, Nasser's secretary for information, i.e., intelligence.[5]

On the same day Anwar Sadat, then president of the National Assembly, or parliament, was transiting Moscow en route home from a visit to North Korea. According to Sadat's account, he was seen off at the airport by Vladimir Semyenov, the Soviet deputy foreign minister, "who was accompanied by the speaker of the Soviet Parliament [apparently Nikolai Podgorny, chairman of the Presidium of the Supreme Soviet]. The plane was more than an hour late, which gave us a chance to talk at length, mostly about the Syrian situation. They told me specifically that ten Israeli brigades had been concentrated on the Syrian border. When I arrived back in Cairo [later that day] I realized that the Soviet Union had informed Nasser of this."[6]

Mohamed Heikal, Nasser's confidant and publisher of *Al-Ahram* newspaper, reported that Sadat arrived at Nasser's home shortly after midnight on the thirteenth as Nasser and Marshal Abd al-Hakim ʿAmr, first vice-president and deputy commander-in-chief of the Egyptian armed forces, were discussing their possible response to the Soviet warning.[7] Sadat gave them a firsthand report on his Moscow conversation, which had already been reported by telegram from the Egyptian Embassy in Moscow.[8] Heikal's version of the Moscow talk has some details different from Sadat's version. Heikal writes that according to the minutes of the conversation, Podgorny was preoccupied with the Israeli concentrations on the Syrian frontier and said, "Syria is facing a difficult situation and we will help Syria in the situation which it faces. We have informed President Nasser in Cairo of the information we have." Podgorny then turned suddenly to a discussion of petroleum prospects in Egypt.[9]

A second version of the delivery of the warning in Cairo comes from Bassiouny, al-Feki's special assistant, who told me that Pojidaev had originally asked to see Muhammad Shoukri, the chef de cabinet of Mahmoud Riad, the foreign minister, who was out of town. The Egyptians had decided that it would be more appropriate for al-Feki to receive him and he did so in Mahmoud Riad's office. Bassiouny was not present, but al-Feki came back from the meeting with five or six pages of paper he had been given by Pojidaev and instructed Bassiouny to write a description of the meeting to be sent to the presidency. After Pojidaev's call the Egyptians sent their chief of staff, General Muhammad Fawzi, to Syria to look into the report. Fawzi went on the fourteenth and returned on the fifteenth. As related in his memoirs, he reported to 'Amr that there were no abnormal Israeli troop concentrations. (Fawzi's trip is described in more detail below.) According to Ashraf Ghorbal, both Riad and Shoukri took the report with a good deal of salt because it was not supported by evidence from other quarters.[10]

Yet a third version of the Cairo events comes from Heikal, who has written that the warning was delivered on the thirteenth by a Cairo representative of Soviet "intelligence" (mukhabarat, presumably the KGB) known as Sergei, who had the official rank of counselor in the Soviet Embassy.[11] Sergei had requested an urgent meeting with the director general and intelligence, Salah Nasr, to give him a message that an Israeli concentration of eleven brigades was gathered on the Syrian frontier. Heikal gives no source for this account.

The three versions are not inconsistent. Diplomatic missions in Cairo at that time often delivered messages through more than one channel hoping to improve the chances that someone responsible would see it. It was not customary for the Soviet ambassador to carry such messages to the Foreign Ministry, however, and former Soviet Foreign Ministry officials maintain that there is no record of his being instructed to do so, which raises perplexing questions about why Pojidaev did it.

It appears, then, that the Soviets gave the warning to the Egyptians three times. That it was done at a very high level in Moscow on the same day it was done at a lower level in Cairo would seem to indicate a deliberate and concerted effort, but the former Soviet officials just mentioned say there is no record of such concertation. Much remains to be clarified about the operational mechanics on Moscow's side.[12]

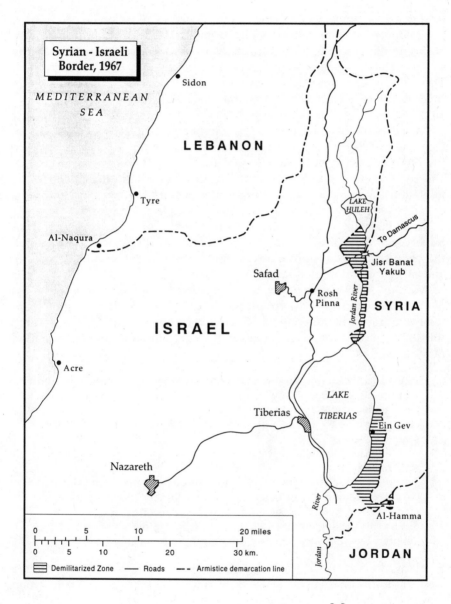

Syrian - Israeli
Border, 1967

MEDITERRANEAN
SEA

Sidon

LEBANON

Tyre

Al-Naqura

Safad

Rosh
Pinna

LAKE
HULEH

To Damascus

Jisr Banat
Yakub

SYRIA

ISRAEL

Acre

Jordan River

Tiberias

LAKE
TIBERIAS

Ein Gev

Nazareth

River

Al-Hamma

Jordan

JORDAN

| 0 | 5 | 10 | | 20 miles |
| 0 | 5 | 10 | 20 | 30 km. |

Demilitarized Zone — Roads - - - Armistice demarcation line

MAP 1

TRUE OR FALSE?

In spite of the Soviets' earnestness, the report seems to have been untrue. No evidence has been made public to date to support it, and there have been enough credible denials from a variety of sources to make it highly unlikely that the Israeli troop concentrations actually existed as claimed. The mystery ever since has been why the Soviets said they did. Even in Moscow there seems to be a general realization that the report was not true.

While both the Soviets and the Egyptians asserted at the time that they had intelligence to back up the report, they did not produce it. When the Israelis learned of it they invited the Soviets to tour northern Israel and see that there were no concentrations. They reportedly extended the invitation three times and each time the Soviets refused it, saying they already knew the facts and did not need to go to the area.[13]

In addition to Israel's denials, observers from the United Nations Truce Supervision Organization (UNTSO) stationed in the region reported that they had seen no concentrations. Similar reports were received from U.S. and other foreign military attachés in Israel.

Various Arab sources also confirmed that there were no visible signs of such concentrations. In an interview with *Al-Hawadith* magazine (September 2, 1977), Shams Badran, Egypt's minister of war at the time, had this to say about his conversations on the subject in Moscow in the period May 24–28:

> When I met with [Premier] Kosygin he said to me, "You have obtained a big political victory. Now we must work to calm the situation. We have helped you with arms and information."
>
> I interrupted him, saying, "That information is what moved us to send troops into Sinai."
>
> He understood what I was referring to and said, "That information was true."
>
> I did not reply to him, but I had a session after that with [Marshal] Grechko [the minister of defense] and said to him, "We sent Muhammad Fawzi to Syria and the airplanes made a reconnaissance and they did not find a single Israeli soldier. . . . a Syrian delegation under the deputy prime minister is arriving tomorrow. Ask them."

Similarly, Jordanians at the radar station at Ajloun, which commands a view of northern Israel, reported no visual sightings of Israeli troop movements, according to Samir Mutawi, author of *Jordan in the 1967 War*.[14]

General Fawzi, in his memoirs, states that

> on May 14, 1967, Marshal Abd al-Hakim 'Amr ordered me to go to Damascus to investigate and to learn the truth about the information we

had received from Damascus and the Soviet Union about the Israeli concentration of troops on the Syrian border. I went the same day and
stayed there twenty-four hours, during which I inspected the Syrian
front command and asked questions of responsible officers in the Syrian
staff and at the front about the truth of the report. The result was that I
did not get any material proof confirming these reports. To the contrary,
I saw two aerial photographs of the Israeli front, taken by the Syrians
on the twelfth and thirteenth of May, which showed no change from
the normal military situation.[15]

Al-Feki confirms Fawzi's account. He told me that the report was
checked with the Syrians, who denied it and even sent an emissary to
Moscow to tell the Soviets it was untrue, but by then it was too late.[16] If
that was the case, why did the Syrians report the concentrations in the
first place? Or did they? That is but one of the puzzles concerning the
origins of the crisis.

Returning to our original question, if there were no troop concentrations, why did the Soviets say there were? Israel is a small country, and
the Soviets should have had intelligence assets there which would have
enabled them to know immediately if a military movement of the size
alleged had or had not taken place. Their embassy had no military attachés and had not had since the opening of diplomatic relations in 1948.*
That could have hampered their access to military information and, more
important, denied their ambassador the sort of professional advice he would
need to evaluate what he heard, but the embassy presumably had KGB
personnel who had some competence in military matters (something the
Soviet military may dispute), and it would not have taken a military ge-
nius in any event to learn that the report was untrue.

Or so it would seem. But gathering military intelligence in Israel was
not an easy matter for foreigners. The Americans apparently relied on
their assistant naval attaché, Lieutenant Lynn P. Blasch, who was resi-
dent in Haifa and made almost daily reconnaissances of northern Israel,
for their conclusion that there were no concentrations. Blasch describes
Israel as an Iron Curtain country as far as information about military matters was concerned and says that even the friendly Americans had to dig
everything out. He maintains, however, that there were absolutely no
signs of troop concentrations before May 23 and only a slight augmenta-
tion thereafter.[17]

Not only did the East Europeans have no service attachés; they also
had small embassies, and they and the Israelis regarded each other with

*Neither did the other East European countries. I was told by a former Soviet diplomat who
served in Tel Aviv from 1948 to 1956 that the Israelis had never asked for an exchange of
attachés. I have been unable to get an official explanation of this but assume it was because
Israel did not want East European military personnel poking around.

deep suspicion.* With few friends and resources in a state considered to be in the imperialist camp, it is understandable that the Soviets and other East Europeans would be reluctant to accept at face value anything the Israelis did or said and would be prey to any rumor or conspiracy theory that came their way. They would certainly regard with suspicion any Israeli offer to give them a tour of the area to see that there were no concentrations, and they would be afraid to tell Moscow it was mistaken if they made such a tour and found out the report was groundless. It was perhaps better not to know, and certainly better not to quarrel with Moscow. Besides, if the report was not "stenographically true," as one Soviet official remarked at the time, that was just a detail.

At this remove, without access to the Soviet archives, I have been unable to ascertain whether the Soviets made any effort to confirm the story on the ground or by quizzing diplomatic colleagues. My sources in Moscow, however, surmise that no effort was made.

In *An Autobiography* (p. 318), Abba Eban, who was Israel's foreign minister at the time, says the Soviet ambassador in Tel Aviv, Dimitri Chuvakhin, protested to Israel about concentrations on the Syrian border on May 11. According to Michael Brecher in *Decisions in Crisis.* (pp. 46–47), Chuvakhin protested on the twelfth. Neither Eban nor Brecher cites a source, and it is not clear whether there were two protests or whether there was confusion about dates. It seems as though there were two conversations, however. (Eban says Chuvakhin saw Israeli Prime Minister Levi Eshkol on May 11 and Eshkol invited him to send his military attaché to the north in search of the "eleven to thirteen brigades." Chuvakhin responded that his function was to communicate Soviet truths, not to put them to a test. Brecher says that Chuvakhin talked to the director general of the Israeli Foreign Ministry, Arye Levavi, on May 12. Levavi called his attention to the tense situation on the Syrian border. When Chuvakhin protested about Israeli troop concentrations in that area, Levavi invited him to see for himself that there were none and Chuvakhin declined.)

It is also not clear how Chuvakhin's protests were related to the warning delivered in Cairo. Were the two actions conceived of as a coordinated, tandem approach, or were they separate in Soviet minds? In any event, Eban's account indicates that the Soviets had the information in question at least two days before they gave it to the Egyptians.

Soviet allegations of Israeli troop movements directed against Syria were not new. Heikal reports that as early as April 28, Sadat, during a stopover in Moscow en route to Pyongyang, was told by Vladimir Semyenov that "Kosygin had given the Israeli ambassador a sharp dressing down about Israeli troop concentrations against Syria. The ambassador had replied that he could deny the existence of such concentrations and

---

*The Israeli diplomatic list for 1967 shows seventeen Soviet, eleven Rumanian, six Polish, and four Bulgarian diplomats. The U.S. Embassy had thirty-five persons on the list, including six service attachés.

that Eshkol had asked the Soviet ambassador in Tel Aviv to go see for himself that there were none. Kosygin had rejected this invitation, as the Soviet ambassador in Tel Aviv had rejected Eshkol's."[18] This is probably a reference to a Soviet note delivered to Israel's ambassador in Moscow, Katriel Katz, by Semyenov (not Kosygin) on April 25, which said in part: "The Soviet Government is in possession of information about Israeli troop concentrations on the Israeli-Arab borders at the present time. These concentrations are assuming a dangerous character, coinciding as they do with the hostile campaign in Israel against Syria."[19] Heikal reports that Semyenov added to Sadat that the Soviet Union did not need to send anyone to the northern front because "it had the means to know the truth without anyone visiting the site." That was to become a familiar refrain.

Indeed, the Soviets appear to have had an obsession about such troop concentrations. As far back as May 25, 1966, Semyenov had called Katz in and read an official statement warning about troop concentrations on Israel's frontiers with the Arab states,[20] and on October 12, 1966, Chuvakhin had delivered a diplomatic note to Eshkol saying "there are at present renewed concentrations of the Israeli army on the Syrian border." Eshkol had invited Chuvakhin to go with him to see for himself and Chuvakhin had declined.[21] One Israeli researcher has recorded eight occasions on which the charge was raised officially or in the Soviet press before the crisis.[22]

Be that as it may, on May 13, 1967, did the Soviets believe the story or had they invented it?

THE INVENTION THEORY

For years conventional Washington wisdom has been that since the Soviets could not possibly have believed the report, they must have fabricated it for one or more of a variety of reasons. Some observers argue that it was done in an effort to manipulate Egypt into supporting the leftist regime in Syria, which had come to power in February 1966 and was following an adventuresome policy on the border that risked a violent Israeli response. Alternative versions maintain that the Soviets were trying to make the Egyptians more dependent on them or to get Egypt out of Yemen by making it withdraw troops in order to confront Israel. There is also a wide-ranging master plan theory which relies on various remarks by Soviet leaders on the need for Arab unity to conclude that the Soviets were trying to forge an alliance of radical forces in the area that would take over South Arabia and the Gulf of Aqaba, which were the real targets of Soviet policy in the region.

The earliest expression of the invention-manipulation theory which I have come across is in Michael Bar Zohar's *Embassies in Crisis* (p. 2), but it has been repeated and amplified by many others since that book was published in 1968. A rather persuasive exposition of the thesis can be found, for instance, in Winston Burdett's *Encounter with the Middle East* (pp. 162–209). I have always been troubled by it, however, not just because it rests on plausible supposition rather than direct evidence but also because it would have been extraordinarily imprudent of the Soviets to have fabricated the report and used it as they did at a time of great tension along the Syrian border. That would have been out of character with their previous and subsequent rather cautious behavior in the Middle East.

Certainly the uncooperative and obstructionist attitude of the Soviets at the United Nations and in Moscow at the time could justify the conclusion that they were determined to use the crisis to discipline Israel. Their private, as opposed to public, statements, however, make it clear that by the second week they were anxious to prevent a war which they feared would lead to a confrontation with the United States. We have direct evidence of that from three participants in the May 1967 visit of Badran, Egypt's war minister, to Moscow: Badran himself (in his *Al-Hawadith* interview) and Feki and Bassiouny, both of whom told me that the Soviets preached for hours about the need for restraint "now that you [Egyptians] have made your point."[23] Similarly, the fact that the Soviets made parallel demarches in Cairo and Tel Aviv in the early morning hours of May 27, when the respective Soviet ambassadors got Nasser and Eshkol out of bed to urge them not to start hostilities, showed a high degree of concern that things had gotten out of hand.*[24]

One can argue that the Soviets' actions two weeks into the crisis had little to do with their reasons for starting it in the first place and that they had begun urging restraint only when their maneuver went awry and they feared the consequences. This argument is hard to rebut in the absence of direct evidence to the contrary from the Soviet side. If it is correct, it implies a high degree of irresponsibility or incompetence, or both, on the part of the Soviets, who should have been well aware of the possible fatal effects of their action.

Yet another explanation seems to be rather widespread in the Arab world. I have heard it from a variety of educated, well-informed Arabs, including Egyptians. It argues that the Soviets invented the report hoping to draw Nasser into a trap in order to be rid of him, because they saw him as an obstacle to the spread of communism in the area. An abbreviated version of this theory appears in Ali Abdel Rahman Rahmy's *The Egyptian Policy in the Arab World* (pp. 232–35). This explanation is hard to take seriously, but it illustrates the lengths to which people will go to find

---

*The Soviets were responding to an American report of representations made by Abba Eban in Washington on May 25, that the Egyptians were about to attack. Eban was dubious about the report but was following instructions (see Eban's *Autobiography*, pp. 348–52). The order to make these representations may have been a ploy to smoke out the U.S. position, as suggested by Brecher (*Decisions in Crisis*, p. 131), but in fact it seems that Marshal ʿAmr and the air force commander, General Sidqy Mahmoud, were planning an air strike for May 27 until Nasser put a stop to it. This development is discussed in more detail in chapter 3.

a plausible, conspiratorial explanation for miscalculation or incompetence, particularly when a defeated hero is involved.

DID THE SOVIETS BELIEVE IT?

Hard as it is to swallow, given the lack of evidence that there were troop concentrations, the Soviets may have believed what they were saying. We have seen that Kosygin told Badran in May that the report was true. He repeated the allegation to the U.N. General Assembly on June 19: "On May 9 the Israeli parliament empowered the Government of Israel to carry out military operations against Syria. Israeli troops began to advance to the Syrian borders and mobilization was effected" (U.N. Document 6717, June 19, 1967). Similarly, the deputy chief of mission in the Soviet Embassy in Damascus in 1967, Evgueny Nersessov, who was my ambassadorial colleague in Rabat in 1978, told me that there had been intelligence from more than one source supporting the report and that it had been "confirmed."[25]

One may argue that that was simply an example of Soviet cynicism about the truth, but the Soviets' belief in the report apparently was convincing to senior Egyptians, at least initially. Al-Feki told me that he did not believe the Soviets were lying, "because they were very correct with us at the time."[26] Indeed, none of the former Egyptian officials with whom I discussed the report seemed to believe it was a deliberate Soviet fabrication. These officials include Mahmoud Riad, who was foreign minister at the time;* Zakaria Muhieddin, then vice-president; and Sayyed Marei, Sadat's deputy.

Over against that is Eban's observation:

> It is quite impossible that Moscow could have believed what it was saying. The mobilization of "eleven to thirteen" Israeli brigades, to say nothing of their concentration in the north, would have had a conspicuous effect on our national life. The disruption of normality in so many families would have resounded across the chanceries and newspapers of the world.[27]

To illustrate what Eban was talking about, the total mobilized strength of the Israeli army in the 1967 war was twenty-five brigades more or less, of which ten were infantry, nine were armored, two mechanized, and four paratroop, according to Trevor Dupuy in *Elusive Victory* (p. 231). Only two brigades were on active duty when the crisis began. Mobilizing ten more would have meant 30–40,000 men and 2–3,000 vehicles.[28] Moving this mass of men and vehicles around an area as small as Galilee would

*Riad expressed this belief to me in spite of Shoukri's comment, reported above, that Riad was skeptical of the Soviet report.

inevitably attract attention from a variety of observers, including those of the Israel-Syrian Mixed Armistice Commission who were stationed, and some of whom were residing, in the vicinity and the Jordanians at the Ajlun radar station as well as the Syrians on the Golan Heights.[29] Furthermore, the sudden withdrawal of reservists from civilian jobs for mobilization would be so obvious that the mobilization would be apparent to an intelligent observer in Tel Aviv or Jerusalem as soon as it began.

That the Egyptians and the Soviets would be unwilling to discuss the source and nature of the unspecified "intelligence" which supported their charges was understandable. What was remarkable in this instance was their apparent lack of interest in independent confirmation. While the Soviets were refusing Israel's offers of a tour of Galilee to see for themselves, the Egyptians were turning a deaf ear to warnings that they were making a dreadful mistake, even after hearing from their own chief of staff that there were no Israeli troop concentrations. At that time the Americans had regular and frequent intelligence liaison with the Egyptians. The CIA station chief was identified to Salah Nasr, the director of general intelligence, the Egyptian equivalent of the CIA, and met with him frequently. Regular channels of diplomatic communication were also open between the U.S. Embassy and Egypt's Foreign Ministry and Presidency. These channels were used to tell the Egyptians that the report was untrue, but the Egyptians seemed uninterested.[30]

When I asked al-Feki why the Egyptians did not believe U.S. denials, he said, "Because we trusted the Soviets more than we did you."[31] Similarly, Nasser and Riad told U.N. Secretary General U Thant on May 23 that the U.S. chargé d'affaires, David Nes, had given them assurances that there were no Israeli troop concentrations.[32] But they noted that U.S. Ambassador Raymond Hare had given them a similar denial of Israeli troop concentrations in 1956, and the Israelis had attacked anyway.[33] The implication was that 1967 was a repeat performance. Hare denies that he gave any such assurance.[34]

Riad's explanation given to me can be summarized in three words: nobody was lying. What counts is intention, and the Israelis clearly intended to attack Syria. The actual presence or absence of troops on the ground was not all that important, given Israel's ability to mobilize in a matter of hours. The Soviets had their own sources inside Israel and knew what they were talking about, according to Riad. The proof of Israel's intentions, if any was needed, was a statement by Yitzhak Rabin, Israel's chief of staff, on May 12 threatening to occupy Damascus and overthrow the Syrian regime.[35]

RABIN'S STATEMENT

The statement by Rabin is another of the mysteries surrounding the 1967 miscalculation. Even the date is uncertain; it is variously given as May 11 or 12. The statement is thoroughly established in the minds of many Arabs and Israelis as the starting point of, or at least a major contribution to, the crisis. Indeed, one Israeli explanation of Rabin's well-publicized but brief bout of depression or nervous exhaustion a few days later, on May 23–24, was that he was overcome by guilt because he had precipitated the crisis by his statement.

The text of Rabin's statement, according to the Arabs, was "We will carry out a lightning attack on Syria, occupy Damascus, overthrow the regime there and come back."[36] The Syrians referred to it immediately in a statement issued by their Foreign Ministry (FBIS Daily Report, May 15, 1967, p. G-2), and Nasser referred to it in his speech at Bir Gifgafa on May 22: "On 12 May the first statement was made, a very impertinent one . . . that the Israeli leaders had announced they would undertake military operations against Syria to occupy Damascus and bring down the Syrian regime."

Rabin has denied making such a statement, and there is no verifiable published text. According to the Israel-produced *Middle East Record* (vol. 3, p. 187), no such statement was made and the notion that it had been made was the result of a misquote in United Press International's coverage of an Israel Defense Forces (IDF) press briefing held May 11. UPI had reported that "a high Israeli source said today Israel would take limited military action designed to topple the Damascus army regime if Syrian terrorists continued sabotage raids inside Israel. Military observers said such an offensive would fall short of an all-out war but would be mounted to deliver a telling blow against the Syrian government."[37]

A related comment by Rabin appeared in the Israeli newspaper *Lamerhav* on May 14. It quoted him as drawing a distinction between retaliation against Lebanon and Jordan, whose governments opposed infiltration, and retaliation against Syria: "In Syria the problem is different, because there it is the authorities who send out the saboteurs. Therefore the aim of action against Syria is different from what it ought to be against Jordan and Lebanon." That may have sounded ominous, but it was not a threat specifically to overthrow the regime.

A final and perhaps authoritative version of what was actually said on May 11 by an unidentified IDF spokesman (apparently the chief of military intelligence, General Aharon Yaariv[38]) is given in *Middle East Record* (vol. 3, p. 187). Referring to a document in the archives of the Shiloah Center at Tel Aviv University, it states:

> [The IDF spokesman referred to] an Israeli answer that will convince the [Damascus] regime that the profit they had from what they call the "popular war of liberation" will turn into a loss. He also stressed, however, the connection between the border incidents and the politics of the Damascus regime, whose popular base he described as "very narrow." As to the size of the military action against Syria, the officer expressed his personal opinion that "the only sure and safe answer to the

problem is a military operation of great size and strength. But not everything that is sure is possible, and I think there are reasonable chances to find a solution of the problem by military action short of this kind of action." He said that Israel needed a type of action that would warn the Syrians of the dangers of a "probable or possible or imminent all-out military confrontation" with Israel, but that there were alternatives between the extremes of counter-guerrilla war and an "all-out invasion of Syria and conquest of Damascus."

Whatever Rabin or Yaariv or someone else may or may not have said, there were enough verifiable statements by Israeli leaders during the period in question to create an impression that they were about to take serious military action. Various commentators have argued that the statements should be understood in the context of Israeli politics and sensitivities to border incursions and that they were not all that different from previous utterances by Israel's leaders. That may be true, but nevertheless they were taken seriously by the Arabs and others and they helped make the report of troop concentrations easier to believe in Cairo and Moscow. As Eban remarks in *An Autobiography* (p. 318), "If there had been a little more silence, the sum of human wisdom probably would have survived intact. The same is true of the briefing of foreign military attaches on May 11, in terms which they understood to augur a major assault by Israel in the coming days."

Granting that no unusual troop concentrations or movements on Israel's side of the line had actually occurred, the political climate in Israel was such that the Soviet Embassy, if it had heard about the IDF briefing, would have been derelict if it had not reported that Israel was about to strike at Syria. Everyone else in Israel seems to have reached that conclusion. Public attitudes in Israel, statements by Israeli officials saying clearly that Israel would have to resort to force if the Syrians did not reform, and Israel's continued belief in the doctrine of retaliation as a means of keeping the border quiet all disposed Israeli and foreign observers to suspect that a strike was imminent. The question was not whether Israel was going to strike, but when and how.

On May 13 the *New York Times*, for instance, carried a front-page dispatch by James Feron with the headline "Israelis Ponder Blow at Syrians—Some Leaders Decide That Force Is the Only Way to Curtail Terrorism." Datelined Tel Aviv, it read in part:

Some Israeli leaders have decided that the use of force against Syria is the only way to curtail increasing terrorism. Any such reaction to continued infiltration would be of considerable strength but of short duration and limited in area. This has become apparent in talks with highly qualified and informed Israelis who have spoken in recent days against a background of mounting border violence. They tend to believe that Syria cannot be dissuaded from her infiltration tactics except by direct action from Israel. According to the view prevailing here, the Soviet Union, which supplies arms to Syria, is unwilling or unable to temper Syrian actions, while Western powers have little influence in Damascus. . . .

Premier Levi Eshkol warned yesterday in a published interview that Israel would not hesitate to use air power in response to continued border harassment from Syria. He spoke of the "gravity of recent incidents" and said there had been 14 of them in recent months. The nature of the operations, he said, suggested the work of Syrian Army commandoes rather than the mercenaries previously employed for infiltration and sabotage. . . .

One qualified observer said it was highly unlikely that the United Arab Republic, Syria's closest ally in the Arab world, would enter the hostilities unless the Israeli attack were extensive.

SOMETHING TO GO ON?

Concluding that Israel is going to strike somewhere sometime soon is one thing; reporting that it has X number of brigades in positions A and B and is going to move by D day represents a major escalation of the intelligence finding from reasonable presumption to categoric assertion. What made the Soviets take that leap if they did not invent the report? What did they take as evidence? Were they victims of an intelligence failure or an intelligence fabricator? Or were they reacting to something specific and concrete which has not yet been divulged? The following hypotheses suggested to me by Israelis and Egyptians in private conversations in the summer of 1989 indicate the range of possibilities.

Fabrication

One hypothesis is that someone fabricated the story and sold it to the Soviets. Obvious culprits would be the Syrians. The suggestion is that the Syrians fed the story not only to the Soviets but also to the Egyptians in an effort to attract their support. Then the Soviets, concerned about the security of the Syrian regime, also passed the report to the Egyptians, never dreaming they would react as they did. The Egyptians saw the Soviet report as supporting the Syrians' story—a textbook case of false confirmation.

In looking at such a scenario, one would expect the Soviets to have been cautious about accepting at face value a Syrian report of this nature. They were experienced enough in dealing with Damascus to have wanted confirmation. Indeed, one former Egyptian official with an intelligence background believes that the Soviets' giving of the report to al-Feki rather than Nasser meant that the Soviets did not take it all that seriously because it had come from the Syrians; they were simply passing it on for the record. To him the report had "smelled Syrian" at the time.[39]

If the Syrians were the source of the report, it is noteworthy that although the May 13 statement by the Syrian Foreign Ministry speaks of "mercenaries and agents of Jordanian intelligence with the imperialist weapons massed along Syria's borders," the May 15 complaint (S/7885) by Syria's permanent representative to the Security Council about Israel's aggressive intentions makes no mention of troop concentrations. Expressions of concern were made to U.N. officials by Syrian officials, however. These are discussed in chapter 3.

Misinterpretation

A second hypothesis is that there were minor troop movements by Israel which the Soviets misinterpreted. The movements were rotational, were connected with the May 15 Independence Day parade in Jerusalem, or were both. Brecher reports in *Decisions in Crisis* (p. 45) that "some tank units were sent there [northern Israel] as reinforcements after the 7 April flareup." Any such movement would have involved only a limited number of troops, and considerable inflation would have been required to arrive at a figure of ten or more brigades. Nevertheless, is it possible that this movement of armored units could have been given more importance than it deserved? More precision on exactly what constituted "some units" would perhaps enable us to decide.

One variation on this hypothesis is that the Soviets were in fact worried that Israel might be planning to attack Syria and wanted to have Egypt solve the problem for them. They did not want to get involved themselves. Someone gave them a false report which fit with their preconceptions, and they passed it on to the Egyptians as something to be taken seriously. Another proffered variation is that the Soviets thought war between Israel and the Arabs was inevitable and wanted it to occur sooner rather than later. The Syrians did not want to face Israel alone, and that disposed the Soviets to accept the report, which came to them from one of their intelligence agents or a similar source.

Disinformation

According to Brecher, Israel's cabinet decided on May 7 that if Syria did not heed its public warnings and all other noncoercive methods failed, Israel would launch a limited retaliation raid.[40] It is conceivable that, as one such "noncoercive" measure, Israel engaged in a disinformation effort using any of a number of possible channels, such as the Beirut rumor mill or Israel's own intelligence assets in Cairo. In this way, Israel may have floated information indicating that a large-scale raid was in preparation and pinpointing the units which would participate and when. The purpose would have been to intimidate Syria, not to alarm the Soviet Union and Egypt. The report could have been picked up by the Soviets, however, who could have taken it seriously, perhaps because it was specific and detailed and fit with their perceptions.[41]

This hypothesis is certainly the most attractive. It would explain everything. In particular it would explain why the Soviets would believe the report—they thought the original source was Israeli. I have found no direct evidence to support it, but I have also found none for the other hypotheses, including the invention theory.[42]

Anthony Nutting, in *Nasser* (pp. 397–98), argues that Israel was trying to draw Nasser into a fight. The Israelis, he writes,

> appear to have deliberately set out to persuade the Russians, and hence the Egyptians, that a major assault on Syria was imminent. By a clever combination of leakage, for the benefit of the Soviet Embassy in Tel Aviv, and fictitious radio messages which they rightly assumed would be picked up and relayed to Cairo by Russian ships patrolling in the Eastern Mediterranean, they made sure that Nasser would be immediately informed that his Syrian ally was about to be invaded.

Although Nutting obviously was drawing on conversations with many senior Egyptians, he gives no sources, and one cannot tell whether this report was an exercise in imagination or whether there were some facts to back up his thesis.

This explanation was first suggested to me by an Israeli scholar in 1987, but I have been unable to find another Israeli who will accept it. Two bits of information support the thesis to some extent. First, on leaving Israel when relations were broken in 1967, Soviet Ambassador Chuvakhin reportedly accused Israel of waging a disinformation campaign.[43] Second, when I asked General Aharon Yaariv, who was director of Israeli military intelligence in 1967, about the possibility of such a campaign, he said, "Not at that time. There had earlier been discussion of taking some Syrian territory and holding it . . . the Soviets might have gotten wind of that."[44] The Soviets had gotten wind of the May 7 Cabinet decision at some point; in their statement of May 23, discussed below, they said Israeli's decision to attack Syria was taken on May 9. If they held such a belief before May 11, it, along with the statements of Israel's leaders, would have inclined them to accept readily anything purported to be the details of what everyone knew was about to happen.

Contingency Plan

In *From War to War* (pp. 276–77), Nadav Safran has the following explanation:

> The Russians sought to compromise Egypt into a closer, overt, and dramatic identification with Syria's security. The opportunity to try to do

so came in May 1967, when they apparently got hold of an Israeli contingency plan for a large-scale attack on Syria. They conveyed the substance of the plan to the Egyptians without indicating to them that it
was a contingency document, with the object of inciting them to make
a military demonstration that would express their identification with Syria
and hopefully deter any type of Israeli action, large or limited. The Russians succeeded in getting Nasser to move but could not prevent him
from going beyond the token demonstration to which they hoped he
would confine himself.

This contingency plan could be what General Yaariv was referring to
when he mentioned a "discussion of taking some Syrian territory." Jacques
Derogy and Hesi Carmel, in *Untold History of Israel* (pp. 213–15), assert
that the contingency plan in question was prepared in 1957 by Yuval Neeman, then assistant director of army intelligence, and "the Soviets merely
had to update the document to turn it into one that would convince Nasser and make him move." These authors maintain that the Soviet Union
wanted to start a war. A former senior Israeli intelligence officer in a position to know informed me that the Neeman plan actually dated back to
1952; he doubted very much that the Soviets would have been able to
obtain it.

There is, then, no shortage of explanations of how the Soviets might
have been persuaded that their report was true. Some hypotheses are
more plausible than others, but none is supported by hard evidence. All
require a certain element of faith and imagination.

At this point, we can summarize what we do know. We know that
the report was delivered on or about May 13 at least twice, in Cairo and
Moscow. The report was plausible and was taken seriously by the Egyptians. And as far as we can tell, the report was untrue.

We can also summarize what we do not know. We do not know
whether the Soviets believed the report. If they believed it, what were
they reacting to? We do not know the Soviets' motive in passing the report to the Egyptians. And we do not know what the Soviets expected
the Egyptians to do or what the Soviet estimate was of the military balance between Israel and Egypt.

CHAPTER
2

MOSCOW'S EXPLANATIONS

The pipeline was full of remarkably crude
intelligence.

Soviet official, September 11, 1990

In an effort to answer some of the questions posed in the first chapter, I
made a two-week trip to Moscow in September 1990 at the invitation of
the Institute of Oriental Studies to interview present and former Soviet
officials and journalists about their recollections of the events of 1967. The
principal problem the Institute and I faced was to find survivors of the
period who were both knowledgeable and able to talk. We assumed, perhaps incorrectly, that no purpose was to be served by trying to talk to the
KGB or the military, because neither would speak frankly. The two ambassadors most directly involved, Pojidaev and Chuvakhin, were both
dead. Pojidaev's deputy, Alexander Semiochkin, was reportedly too ill to
be interviewed, and we never managed to locate Mikhail Yakushev, who
had been Chuvakhin's deputy, or Evgueny Nersessov, who had been the
deputy chief of mission in Damascus (although I had spoken with Nersessov twelve years earlier, as noted in chapter 1).

I was, however, able to interview Anatoly Barkovsky, the Soviet ambassador in Damascus at the time, who gave me useful insights into the
view from that capital. I also had a useful interview with Georgiy Kornienko, recently retired deputy foreign minister, who had been head of
the American department in the Foreign Ministry in 1967 and subsequently a member of the working group which prepared a detailed study
of the 1967 crisis for the Central Committee of the Communist party of
the Soviet Union, during which he had access to all the relevant papers
on the subject.

I received valuable insights into the intelligence environment in 1967
from Oleg Bykov of the Institute of World Economy and International
Relations (IMEMO) and Vitaly Naumkin, deputy director of the Institute
of Oriental Studies. I also had useful comments from Alexander Kislov,
deputy director of IMEMO, who was the Tass correspondent in Cairo in
1967; Igor Beliaev of *Literaturnaya Gazeta*, a well-known commentator on

Middle Eastern affairs and a frequent interviewer of Nasser; Anatoly Egorin, the *Novosti* correspondent in Cairo in 1967; Tatiana Karasova, head of the Israeli department at the Institute of Oriental Studies; Leonid Medvedko, who was the Tass correspondent in Damascus; Mikhail Popov, who served in the Soviet Embassy in Tel Aviv from 1948 to 1956 and was researching the history of USSR-Israel relations; and Georgiy Mirsky of IMEMO.

Unfortunately, none of these people except Barkovsky was a principal actor in the drama we are discussing, and none of them, including Barkovsky, could provide details about Pojidaev's demarche in Cairo (see chapter 1) or the source of his report. We are unlikely to have such details until Soviet researchers burrowing in the archives come across them, and even then we are unlikely to learn much about intelligence details. What that means in effect is that we may never have a definitive and satisfying answer to the questions posed in chapter 1. We may have to be content with a mix of incomplete written records (we have none from the Soviet side at this point) supplemented by personal recollections, which are often unreliable.

This chapter summarizes the results of my efforts to begin recording recollections on the Soviet side. The harvest is thin, but it is more than we had before.

ORIGINS OF THE SOVIET WARNING

I found my Soviet contacts generally unwilling to accept the thesis that Pojidaev's report sparked the conflagration. They argued either that Israel was trying to provoke Egypt or that Egypt was bent on taking the initiative but that the report itself was not very important. Several interviewees repeated Mahmoud Riad's argument that whether or not Israel actually had troops massed on the border was irrelevant because it could have had them there in a matter of hours; there was no question but that it intended to attack Syria soon in any event.

While no one in Moscow was able to provide the details of what Pojidaev said or did, all but one of my contacts maintained that the Soviet Union had not fabricated the report of May 13 and would not want to jeopardize its relations with Egypt, the anchor of the Soviet position in the Middle East, for the sake of Syria, no matter how leftist the latter's government might be. The exception suggested that there were two explanations. One was that the Syrians were behind it and had fooled the Soviets into believing the report without checking it. The other was that the political leaders in the USSR had falsified or doctored an intelligence report in order to provoke a crisis with the hope that it would "give a boost" to Nasser, who was in trouble domestically and in Yemen. The leaders had not expected their action to lead to war but thought that Nasser, who was very important to Moscow, would take some bold step that would enhance their position as well as his. This interviewer admitted that this scenario was pure speculation; he had no personal knowledge of the decision-making process in this case.

Several of those interviewed suggested that the report might have originated in Egypt rather than in Syria or Israel and that it might have come via either KGB or military channels. One suggested that an Egyptian military officer could have been the source. (As mentioned earlier, in note 25, chapter 1, General Murtagi maintained that the source of "confirming reports" was the Soviet military attaché in Beirut.)

My contacts generally agreed that the report was not taken very seriously in Moscow, where it was not expected to provoke a war. Kornienko, the retired deputy foreign minister, commented that the Soviets had no motive for fabricating the report and there was no basis to the allegation they had done so; they certainly would not have wanted to risk their relations with Egypt for the sake of Syria. Kornienko thought that the Soviets had passed information to the Egyptians as a friendly gesture. He did not remember the source of the report, but it had come from somewhere; the Soviets did not invent it. He did not remember whether Moscow believed it "100 percent," but governments often passed to other governments intelligence reports for which they could not vouch entirely, but which they thought should be called to someone's attention. In this instance, he could recall no debate about whether to pass this particular information to the Egyptians, which meant to him that it had been done routinely, as the natural thing, and that it had not been taken terribly seriously.

One Soviet official said he had discussed the matter with an unidentified "intelligence official" in preparation for our discussion. This source had said the report was genuine and had not been invented. My source speculated that some KGB colonel trying to score points in the career game had been eager to report something he knew the political leadership would find congenial. An unfortunate aspect of the Soviet system was that people tended to report what they thought their superiors wanted to hear. This tendency had also been a factor in the Soviet decision to intervene in Afghanistan.

Another official commented that the leaders wanted to believe the report because it fit their perceptions of the situation and of Israel's role in the area. The Soviets had been prepared to cut relations with Israel since 1966. They saw the area as divided between pro-U.S. and pro-USSR forces and wanted to believe that Israel had aggressive designs on the Arabs. The idea that Israel was preparing to attack Syria was current.

A similar evaluation was given by an official with an intelligence background who had been a consultant to the Central Committee at the time. He described the fabrication-manipulation theory as "too plausible to be true." He had only been on the fringes of the problem in 1967 but thought it was a case of unreliable intelligence and a lack of time to check and recheck it. Several of my other contacts also commented on the time factor as an element in the Soviet miscalculation, noting that the Foreign Ministry had been slow to react and its instructions were often late in arriving.

The Central Committee consultant suggested what might be called the incompetence thesis—that the report had been given to the Egyptians without proper processing. This was a failure in the Soviet intelligence apparatus, not an act of deception. The Soviets had merely been sharing intelligence in a routine way. That the report had come from Moscow probably made the Egyptians think it was reliable, and they took it as a "smoke signal" for them to move. It had been unwise of them to do so. They must have had their own sources and should have checked the report before acting. They apparently thought they were working against time, however. (This was certainly the case if, as the Egyptians claim, the Soviets told them that Israel was going to attack Syria on May 17.) Furthermore, the whole Egyptian chain of command was dominated by a readiness to welcome what was expected and to reject what was not. Much of what ensued was the result of poor planning and operational shortcomings on the part of both the Soviet Union and Egypt.

Perhaps the most significant single comment on the operational factors at work came from Barkovsky, the ambassador to Syria in 1967. He did not know the origin of the report (which would seem to militate against a Syrian origin) and had been kept completely in the dark about what Ambassador Pojidaev and Chuvakhin were doing in Cairo and Tel Aviv. There was little lateral communication between posts in the field. Reporting went through Moscow, which decided what to pass on to other posts. The Foreign Ministry did not function well in this respect and rarely told posts what was going on next door. In Damascus, for instance, Barkovsky had no idea what the embassy in Beirut was reporting about events in Lebanon, although these events were of direct interest to Damascus.

On first hearing of this compartmentalization I thought it might explain the Soviet failure to realize that the report was false, because it raised the possibility that Chuvakhin in Tel Aviv was unaware of Pojidaev's demarche of May 13 in Cairo and that had he known what was being said to the Egyptians he might have warned Moscow that it was wrong. Unfortunately for this theory, Chuvakhin evidently had heard the allegation about troop concentrations by May 11 at the latest, when he spoke to Eshkol about it. He would have had plenty of time to correct the record before Pojidaev went to the Foreign Ministry, and we cannot blame compartmentalization for his not doing so.

Compartmentalization, however, might have been a factor, along with ideology and tactical considerations, in the bizarre remarks Chuvakhin was making to the effect that oil interests and the CIA rather than the regime in Damascus were behind the trouble on the border. (For an example, see Eban's *Autobiography*, p. 318.) Barkovsky said that in Damascus he at least knew that Syria was sponsoring infiltration and sabotage along the border. According to him, Syria was well aware of the risk of forceful Israeli retaliation and had no illusions about the disparity between their two forces. It was concerned about what was likely to happen but was hoping to enflame the Arab world. On one hand Syria was trying to bring the Palestinians under control through the mechanism of Saiqa, a Syrian-controlled Palestinian paramilitary force, and on the other was sponsoring fedayeen activities. In short, Syria was behaving irrationally.

A senior Syrian officer, for instance, told Barkovsky that Syria was planning large-scale guerrilla operations in the Jerusalem area along the lines of Soviet operations behind German lines in World War II. When Barkovsky pointed out that the Russians had woods to hide in, whereas there were none around Jerusalem, the officer replied that the Syrians would hide in the "gardens."

If Barkovsky reported on Syria's behavior to Moscow, it either did not register or Moscow chose to ignore it for tactical and ideological reasons and to continue to maintain that imperialism, oil interests, and the CIA were causing all the trouble along the border. Chuvakhin would naturally follow Moscow's line, but he might have been more cautious about pressing it on Israel had he known the truth about Syrian behavior.

What conclusions, if any, can we draw from the remarks just summarized? The fabrication hypothesis remains a possibility, but I found no convincing evidence to support it. The argument that the Soviets were responding to what they thought was a genuine intelligence report is plausible, and there is some Soviet testimony to support it, even though it does not come from people who were at the center of the drama in 1967.

I had the impression that my Soviet contacts were speaking truthfully. In the atmosphere of glasnost, which was strong in September 1990, people in Moscow were free with their comments about the shortcomings of the Soviet system and critical of the leadership that had been in control in 1967. No one appeared to be trying to protect the record of that government or to conceal facts, and there was none of the ideological double-talk which characterized Soviet diplomats over many years. People were open and at times surprisingly frank. Several scholars at the Institute of Oriental Studies remarked that the Soviets also would like to know the truth about 1967.

There are serious problems with the incompetence thesis, if we may call it that. The first is the continued repetition, over the space of a year, of the charge that Israel was concentrating troops on the Syrian border. In each case these charges were unsubstantiated. Their repetition raises the suspicion that the Soviets were simply engaging in a disinformation effort and that they knew the report was untrue but kept repeating it in an effort to harass and isolate Israel. It is possible that they actually believed what they were saying, of course. That would indicate that Soviet intelligence was a good deal worse than most of us thought at the time.

The second is that the Soviet assertion that the information was not considered particularly important and was passed routinely is not supported by the way it was passed. For the ambassador of a major power to go to a foreign ministry and read off a report of this nature, particularly in a place like Cairo where the most innocent act can become a major portent, is to give it an importance which goes well beyond the routine. To make the same point to a senior official passing through Moscow is to further emphasize that importance.

We may find in time that there is a satisfactory, and banal, explanation for all of this and that no great significance should have been attached to the Cairo or the Moscow demarche, because the former was done at a subordinate level and the latter was a matter of happenstance (because Sadat's plane was late). But until then it is difficult to escape the conclusion that the report was passed deliberately as a priority matter requiring immediate attention. Given the prevailing tensions in the area, that action would not have been unreasonable on the part of the Soviets, but it implies that they expected Egypt to do something about it quickly.

THE NATURE OF THE SOVIET MISCALCULATION

We are left with two alternative hypotheses: that the Soviets fabricated the report or that they believed it. If the Soviets fabricated it, their miscalculation was enormous. While the Russians have often used disinformation as an instrument of national policy, it is one thing to plant a rumor or fabricate a document and another deliberately to give a close partner who is the key to one's position in the Middle East detailed information, known to be false, about imaginary troop concentrations in a situation as tense as that of May 1967.

Whether the Soviets believed it or fabricated it, what did they expect Egypt to do? In 1960 a similar case had followed an incident at Khirbet Tawafiq in the Israel-Syrian demilitarized zone. The Egyptians and Syrians had convinced themselves that Israel had taken a licking at Khirbet Tawafiq and was planning to retaliate with a strike against Egypt. Nasser had quietly sent troops into Sinai and had suddenly confronted Israel with their presence. He had not asked UNEF to move and had not talked about closing the Strait of Tiran.[1] He had simply let Israel know that Egypt was prepared to fight if necessary. Israel had reacted prudently, and the Egyptian troops had been withdrawn. The whole affair had been kept quiet, and both sides had deliberately avoided publicity or escalation.

Did the Soviets expect a similar performance in 1967? Perhaps, but it would have been highly risky and irresponsible to provoke Egypt in the rather different circumstances of 1967 without carefully exploring the likely reaction. I have found no evidence that the Soviets took the latter step, and it is clear from their behavior and from the comments of my contacts in Moscow (as well as from Soviet comments at the time) that they did not expect Egypt to react as it did.

Since the crisis, a recurrent question has been to what extent the Soviets were involved in Egypt's decision-making process. Signals in this respect are mixed. At the time there was little comment from the Soviets, but their uncooperative stance at the United Nations led many to conclude that they must have been a party to decisions of the United Arab Republic, at least in the beginning. Journalists reported, however, that unidentified Soviet diplomats were saying that the Soviets were not consulted about the decisions regarding UNEF and the Strait of Tiran, although one diplomat said that the Soviets had approved the decision to mobilize and send troops into Sinai.[2]

In "The United States and Egypt" (p. 11), William Quandt reports that a leading Soviet expert on the Middle East confirmed to him in 1988 that the Soviets had encouraged Nasser to mobilize his armed forces in 1967 in order to deter Israel from striking at Damascus. But I spoke to the same source in 1990 and was told that the Soviets had merely passed the intelligence report to Nasser to alert him. I was told by Kornienko that the Soviets were not consulted in advance about any of the decisions taken by Egypt—mobilization, sending troops into Sinai, the withdrawal of UNEF, the closure of the Strait of Tiran—"and were concerned by them." This assertion is borne out in the account by Heikal in *1967—Al-Infijar*. He makes no mention of Soviet participation in the decision to mobilize and to send troops into Sinai; this decision was made by Nasser and 'Amr alone. He also reports (p. 509) that on May 18 Nasser, concerned that he had had no reaction from Moscow to Egypt's request for the withdrawal of UNEF, instructed his ambassador there, Murad Ghaleb, to inquire about the Soviet view. Ghaleb saw the Soviet deputy foreign minister, Semyenov, the same day and asked for his views. Semyenov apologized, saying he was not the Soviet government and "did not have all the information" (p. 612). Nasser did not receive a response until May 22, when Pojidaev called with a message of "complete support" from the Soviet government, the Central Committee, and the Communist party for the decision to withdraw UNEF. Pojidaev described this tripartite assurance as the strongest possible message which could be given because it had been taken by all three bodies. Nasser took the occasion to inform Pojidaev that he had just announced the closure of the Strait of Tiran. Heikal writes that "Pojidaev's astonishment was apparent on his face and he asked for details and about the reasons for announcing it before the arrival of the Secretary General [of the United Nations]" (pp. 522–23).

Two things seem clear from this account. One is that the Soviet leaders had to assemble and consult after the fact in order to decide what their position was going to be on the withdrawal of UNEF. The other is that they had no advance warning that the Strait of Tiran was going to be closed. It was at this point, perhaps, that the Soviets became concerned that the situation was getting out of hand.

SOVIET ESTIMATES OF THE MILITARY BALANCE

Judging by comments made by Soviet leaders to Shams Badran, Egypt's minister of war, in Moscow in late May, they did not expect war to occur.[3] But they seemed to be confident that Egypt was strong enough to confront Israel if it came to that. Their miscalculation in this respect was serious, and it illuminates the problems of highly centralized, authoritarian systems when it comes to intelligence of this sort.

In fairness to the Soviets, Egypt's military capabilities were difficult for outsiders to assess, given the restrictions on access to the military, even by Egyptians. As we will discover, Nasser himself seems not to have known the true state of affairs within the army. To a certain extent, all foreign intelligence agencies had to guess, but thanks to the Soviet Union's large military aid program in Egypt, the Soviets had numerous advisers at various levels in the UAR armed forces and should have been familiar with their deficiencies.

There was little informal or social mixing between the Soviet advisers and the Egyptians, however. The Soviet establishment in Egypt had its own clubs and schools and even its own doctors, and the Soviets largely kept to themselves. The Egyptians encouraged this state of affairs because they did not want foreigners to learn much about their armed forces or to form close personal ties with their military personnel. The lack of informal contact would not necessarily prevent a competent foreign observer from noting deficiencies, but it would limit access to information about military politics and personalities (e.g., the Nasser-ʿAmr rivalry) and would make the observer overly dependent on the official Egyptian line, which was often divorced from reality.

My Moscow contacts were divided about how accurately the Soviet military advisers judged the situation. Some maintained that the advisers had an accurate picture but were overriden by their superiors. One contact reported, for instance, that a Soviet colonel of his acquaintance had told his commander in Cairo that Egypt was in no shape for a contest with Israel but the latter had told him to shut up because such views were unpopular in Moscow. That would indicate a familiar gap between what the line officers knew and what the division commander thought.

Other contacts maintained that there was a general overestimate of Arab military capabilities by the Soviets. Medvedko, for instance, who was the Tass correspondent in Damascus, said that the Soviet military had no illusions about the Syrian air force, whose pilots were sitting in coffeehouses instead of their cockpits, but thought the Arabs in general were capable of confronting Israel. He and his colleague from Tel Aviv, when they met on neutral territory, would debate the respective merits of their host countries' military establishments, each of them confident that his own would triumph.

Whatever the Soviets in the field may have known or thought, the upper echelons in Moscow appear to have thought that Egypt was strong enough to confront Israel militarily. One of my contacts in Moscow said that the Soviet leaders had made a number of irresponsible statements to the Egyptians to the effect that Egypt had the strongest army in the region, thanks to Soviet equipment. Leonid Brezhnev, then first secretary of the Communist party, and Marshal Grechko, minister of defense, had been particularly careless in this respect in their conversations with Nasser and other Egyptian leaders. Premier Kosygin, more careful, had tried to play a restraining role. As a result, the Egyptians considered him less sympathetic than Brezhnev and Podgorny, the Presidium chairman, and had tried to play off the different Soviet factions against each other.

These remarks are borne out, with a somewhat different twist, by Heikal's account in *1967—Al-Infijar* (pp. 609–25). Heikal contrasts what he imagines to be a unity of views and planning between Israel and the United States with the lack of clarity in the Soviet-Egyptian dialogue:

> Podgorny, Kosygin and Brezhnev were talking three different languages. Brezhnev was enthusiastic and oratorical, Kosygin was wary and calculating, while Podgorny was miserly with his words, and when they emerged his listener would have to have them repeated in order to try to understand what he was saying. These differences were not a question just of accent, but could give contradictory meanings to their utterances.
>
> At the political level below the summit, ministers like Gromyko spoke so that one was unable to discern exactly what their opinion was, official or personal. The party leaders, like Suslov, Ponamaryeev, Shelepin and Mazarov, were always agitating for resistance to the end in the name of revolution, but no one outside the corridors of the Kremlin could identify precisely the source of their confidence that the decision-making process was dependent on their ideas.
>
> As for the military, they were even more complicated. Given the importance of the military supply relationship and the prominence of the military leaders in the power structure, their words carried particular weight with the Egyptians, but it often appeared that the circuit was closed. Grechko, a ground forces officer, liked the atmosphere of crisis, while Rodenko, the Air Marshal, was taken by the good flying weather all year long [in Egypt], while Admiral Gorshakov had eyes only for straits and gulfs connected with the three colored seas: the Black, the White [Mediterranean] and the Red.

Nasser, feeling a need to clarify Soviet attitudes and wishing to ask for more military equipment, sent Badran to Moscow for that purpose on May 25. Referring to the notes of conversations between Grechko and Badran, Heikal quotes Grechko as saying that

> he knew the United Arab Republic [Egypt] armed forces today were not what they were ten years earlier, and there was no one who wanted to provoke or pick a fight with them. The Soviet Union was pleased to see Egypt strong because it felt it had had a role in forming that strength, not only with arms but also with work and ideas. He had been most happy with the maneuvers during his last visit. This was why the enemies of Egypt and the agents of imperialism feared its strength and put their tails between their legs like frightened dogs.

In Heikal's account Grechko goes on to say that he does not think the imperialists will resort to war because the Arab people are strong and united and ready for war. Nevertheless, he thought it preferable to avoid an armed clash. He saw the Gulf of Aqaba as the center of the crisis and did not think Israel would try to remove Egyptian forces from the gulf unless pushed to do so by the West, particularly the United States. The latter might attempt to force the strait, and it, not Israel, was the real danger. The United States should not be given any pretext to start a fight; "all of us are ready to die for just causes, but we must think about *how* we are going to die." Imperialism would resist and would continue to resist for a while longer; what Grechko feared was that the Syrians, who were "flying in the air," would begin the attack and bring about a political loss. In short, even Grechko was urging caution at this point, but he seemed to admit no doubts about Egypt's military capabilities.

SOVIET COMMITMENTS OF SUPPORT

All of my interviewees in Moscow were agreed that there had been no Soviet commitment to go to the defense of Egypt with military force, even in the event of U.S. participation in an Israeli attack. There was also agreement, however, that the Egyptians thought they had a commitment of some sort from the Soviets, although its nature was not clear.

Belief that the Soviets would come to their aid if they got in trouble, and particularly if the United States was involved in the fighting, appears to have been an important factor in the Egyptians' miscalculation of their situation in the event of war. While there may have been some semantic confusion, perhaps related to the three different "languages" Heikal attributes to the Soviet triumvirate, it is evident from his account that the Egyptians had reason to expect more than they received. The Soviets were too free with their apparently unequivocal statements of support.

According to Heikal's account, when Pojidaev called on Nasser on May 22 with the message of support from the Soviet leadership, Nasser said it was very late in coming: "In the first days we were expecting a word from you, and we didn't hear anything until we asked for it ourselves." Pojidaev responded that had it been simply a matter of issuing a statement from the government it would have been a matter of hours, but this message came also from the Central Committee and the party. That had required a meeting of the committee and contact with party secretariats in all the republics, causing the delay.

Nasser responded that he didn't want to spend much time on these details because events were going beyond the withdrawal of UNEF. He had been unable to see Pojidaev earlier in the day because he had been off announcing the closure of the Strait of Tiran. After a discussion of that event, Nasser returned to the question of Soviet support and said he wanted Pojidaev to tell Moscow that the Soviets had played a principal role in the current confrontation with their confirmations *(ta'kidat)* regarding Israel's troop concentrations. The Egyptian response had made Egypt the target of Israeli troop movements. He wanted Moscow to keep that in mind.

After saying that the Soviets had given the Egyptians the information they had at the time, that they did not think the situation was all that tense, and that Israel would not be acting as it was without the support of the United States, Pojidaev replied, "You and the rest of the Arab world must know that the USSR stands decisively behind the independent Arab states. . . . And if the situation develops into an aggression by imperialism and its 'straw child' Israel, we will take the necessary measures" (*Al-Infijar*, pp. 522–24)

The following day the Soviet government issued a statement supporting Cairo's request for the withdrawal of UNEF, explaining that the Egyptians considered that its presence gave Israel a military advantage and declaring:

> Let no one have any doubts about the fact that should anyone try to unleash aggression in the Near East, he would be met not only with the united strength of Arab countries but also with strong opposition to aggression from the Soviet Union and all peace-loving states."[4]

The most categoric assurance, however, came from Marshal Grechko. It was given to Badran as he left Moscow for Cairo on May 28. There is a difference of opinion about exactly what was said, but Heikal quotes from the Egyptian memorandum of the conversation (which was prepared on the aircraft returning to Cairo, I am told, by al-Feki and Bassiouny, who were present at the conversation). Heikal provides the text of the memorandum on page 625 of *1967—al-Infijar* and also has a barely legible photocopy in the appendix. The document is signed by Shams Badran and consists of two paragraphs. The first recounts an exchange about the

Egyptian request for arms during the farewell ceremony at the airport. The second reads:

> After the ceremony we went to the aircraft and before we boarded it he [Grechko] drew me to one side and said, "Rest easy about all your requests. We'll give them to you." Then he added, *"I want to make it clear to you that if America enters the war we will enter it on your side. Do you understand me?"* [Emphasis supplied.] Then he went on to say, "We received information today that the Sixth Fleet in the Mediterranean returned to Crete the marines it had been carrying on landing vessels. Our fleet is in the Mediterranean, near your shores. We have destroyers and submarines with missiles and arms unknown to you. Do you understand fully what I mean? . . . I want to confirm to you that if something happens and you need us, just send us a signal. We will come to your aid immediately in Port Said or elsewhere."

In an earlier version of this exchange published in *The Sphinx and the Commissar* (pp. 179–80), Heikal quotes the Egyptian ambassador in Moscow, Murad Ghaleb, who was present, as saying to Grechko, "That was very reassuring, Marshal." Grechko laughed and said to him, "I just wanted to give him one for the road." Heikal goes on to say that the Badran mission produced three conflicting views on the Soviet attitude: al-Feki reported a clear impression that the Soviets wanted Egypt to de-escalate; Badran, given Grechko's parting words, had a different story; while Ghaleb sent a private letter to Nasser telling him Grechko's assurances should not be taken at face value (it did not reach Nasser until after the fighting had started).

By May 28 the Soviet attitude was of secondary importance. Certainly Moscow still had influence in Cairo, but the forces leading to war were already too strong to be stopped, and Egypt no longer had them under control. The die had been cast with the closure of the Strait of Tiran on May 22, and war was all but inevitable unless Egypt backed down, something which was not politically possible for Nasser or ʿAmr at that point. Badran's report, however, was probably a factor in Nasser's increasingly belligerent stand, as exemplified in his remarks to the National Assembly on May 29: "When I met with Shams Badran yesterday he handed me a message from . . . Kosygin saying that the Soviet Union supports us in this battle and will not allow any power [meaning the United States] to intervene until matters were returned to what they were in 1956."[5]

In their repeated assurances of support, the Soviets apparently meant that they would supply arms, not intervene with military force, although the Egyptian account of Grechko's remarks has him clearly promising the latter. The Soviet leaders had much to learn about communicating with the Egyptians, but the latter were also hearing what they wanted to hear. Kornienko commented to me in Moscow that none of the Soviet leaders could commit the USSR in advance to military intervention. He could well imagine Marshal Grechko making the remarks to Badran, but Grechko had been on the job only a few months; his lack of caution reflected his bureaucratic inexperience and did not mean anything. When I told Kornienko that as early as January 1967 the Egyptian ambassador in Moscow had hinted to his American colleague that Egypt had some sort of security commitment from the Soviet Union, Kornienko said he could imagine the Egyptians saying that, but there was nothing to it.

THE SOVIET PERFORMANCE

I was told in Moscow that Nasser asked the Soviet Union to intervene in the fighting and it refused. We now have details about this exchange in Heikal's *Al-Infijar*. Heikal reports (p. 728) that ʿAmr summoned Pojidaev urgently on the morning of June 6, after it became clear how badly the Egyptians had been hit the day before. According to Heikal, ʿAmr lost his nerve to the extent of asking whether what he saw was the result of a U.S.-Soviet conspiracy. He then tried to lessen the shock which showed on Pojidaev's face by saying it was not he who was saying that, but it had come to him as a general opinion among his officers. ʿAmr then asked, "Where are the promises which Marshal Grechko gave to . . . Badran? The Americans have entered the battle on the side of Israel."

Pojidaev asked if ʿAmr meant that U.S. forces were participating in the fighting. ʿAmr replied affirmatively. Pojidaev said if he received confirmed and reliable information to that effect he would transmit it immediately to Moscow, "confident that the Soviets would appreciate its importance and react accordingly." In response, ʿAmr complained that the Americans gave Israel better equipment than the Soviet Union gave Egypt, but Heikal does not say whether ʿAmr presented any evidence of U.S. participation. Heikal does not indicate his source for the account.

Heikal goes on to say (pp. 728–29) that Nasser learned of the meeting and summoned Pojidaev later the same day. (In this instance Heikal is quoting from a record of the conversation in the Abdin Palace archives.) Nasser asked Pojidaev to send a message to Kosygin saying: (1) The UAR and he personally appreciated all the efforts the Soviet Union had taken and was taking. (2) The UAR was facing an exceptional moment in its history, a moment which could affect the entire region. It was in such moments that true friendship showed its metal and its essence. These were the moments that were not forgotten. (3) It was clear that the United States was behind Israel with all its weight. There was irrefutable evidence that the Sixth Fleet and the American bases near the region were making a big effort in the operation, and in any event, the course of events, as the USSR knew and as he knew, confirmed that Israel was executing an American-Israeli plan. (4) Up to that time the UAR ground forces were still holding, but this could not last for long, given the impact of Israel's air strike on capabilities for providing air cover. (5) Any cease-fire in light of the current balance would be a clear victory for Israel. (6) The loss of Egyptian aircraft fortunately was not matched by a loss of pilots, because most of the planes were hit while on the ground. Now there was an urgent need for aircraft to replace those lost in the first strike. With replacement aircraft, Egyptian pilots in forty-eight hours at the most would be able to return to the skies over the battlefield and affect the war's outcome. (7) He expected a quick response to his request and expected the ambassador to use all available means to speed the message to Kosygin and the Soviet leadership.

Nasser was surprised to receive an answer a few hours later saying that the Soviet leaders had decided to supply Egypt with a large quantity of aircraft, the types of which would be decided in a matter of hours. To avoid provoking a reaction from the United States, however, the Soviets preferred to send the aircraft in boxes to Algeria, from whence the Algerians could send them to Egypt either crated or assembled. Heikal comments that this would have meant the loss of a week at least, while the situation on the front was changing every minute. So much for Grechko's promise.

CONCLUSION

If we accept the thesis that the Soviets believed the report, or at least thought it was plausible enough to warrant their passing it on, it is hard to see how they could have done otherwise. Not to have informed the Egyptians that Israel was about to strike Syria would have opened them to charges of at least incompetence and bad faith.

Accepting that they had no alternative, however, they made two serious miscalculations. First, they misjudged Egypt's reaction. They may have expected a repeat of 1960, or they may have thought Nasser would just put his troops on alert. It seems certain that they did not expect what happened. Second, they misjudged Egypt's military capabilities. Their relaxed attitude and their dismissal of appeals for urgent action at the United Nations in the early stages of the crisis were evidently related to their confidence that Egypt was in a position to take care of itself if it came to war.

In neither miscalculation were the Soviets entirely to blame. Egypt's reaction was disproportionate and out of character, the result of the Egyptians' own miscalculation of their state of military readiness. It could not have been predicted, except possibly by some insider who knew Nasser's and ʿAmr's minds very well.

As noted, Egypt's military capabilities were difficult for outsiders to assess. The Soviet Union had an advantage over its Western counterparts in terms of access, thanks to the presence of Soviet military advisers, but that does not seem to have done them much good. Indeed, their role as suppliers and advisers may have clouded their vision. Like other aid administrators around the world, Soviet officials in Egypt wanted their programs to be seen as successful by the people at home, and that would incline them to project an optimistic view of the progress being made, thanks to Soviet help and equipment. The Westerners, with more limited access and a lack of vested interest in the Egyptian performance, had a much more accurate appraisal. They had no doubt from the beginning that Israel would win hands down and went on official record as saying so.

Those two Soviet miscalculations are at least understandable. But the Soviet error in accepting the false report of Israeli troop concentrations, if that is what occurred, is less so. As a Soviet official commented to me in Moscow, "The acid test of intelligence in times of crisis is assessment." The Soviet Union failed this test in May 1967.

Ideology was undoubtedly a factor in that failure. Reading accounts by eyewitnesses such as Heikal and Abdul Majid Farid (see the annotated bibliography), one is struck by the extent to which both the Soviets and the Egyptians had become prisoners of their conception of the relationship between Israel and the United States and of their stated conviction that the United States was out to destroy the Egyptian revolution. Both the Soviets and the Egyptians were unable to take U.S. actions at face value, and their vision of Israel as a puppet of the United States made them seriously undervalue Israel's independent military capabilities.

Operational and bureaucratic factors were also at work. Time constraints, an overly centralized communications network, overzealousness by intelligence personnel trying to please the home office, and competition between the different services may have been as important as mindset in making the Soviets accept the report and pass it on. The time constraint may have been particularly important. If it was only a matter of five or six days before Israel was to attack Syria, this possibility was something the Egyptians should know about immediately if they were to have time to take countermeasures. Checking the report would have taken another twenty-four hours or so, and the creakiness of the Soviet diplomatic apparatus probably meant that even more time would be required. One can imagine that, whether the report was true or not, the Soviets thought they could not take the risk of not informing the Egyptians immediately.

None of that excuses the incompetence of Soviet intelligence personnel if they believed the report, or of their leaders who created a climate in which reporting had to fit with perceptions at the top. But it does bring us to the next question: why did the Egyptians react as they did?

CHAPTER

3

THE EGYPTIAN REACTION

Actually, I was authorized by the Supreme
Executive Council to implement the plan at
the right time. The right time came when
Syria was threatened with aggression.

Gamal Abdul Nasser, May 26, 1967

Much writing has been done on the causes of the June 1967 War and the
reasons for Egypt's reaction to the Soviet report, but until recently little
direct evidence has been available about the motives and thoughts of the
Egyptian leaders. The two principal figures, President Nasser and his first
vice-president, Marshal ʿAmr, died not long after the event, apparently
without leaving any memoirs or written explanations of their actions.

A number of senior members of the Nasserite establishment, however, have since spoken out in one way or another. Memoirs have been
published by, among others, Anwar Sadat; Mahmoud Riad, the foreign
minister at the time; Sayyed Marei, who was Sadat's deputy in the National Assembly; General Muhammad Fawzi, the chief of staff; and General Abdul Muhsin Murtagi, commander of the Sinai front in 1967. Mohamed Hassanein Heikal, the one-time publisher of *Al-Ahram* and Nasser
confidant, has not published his own memoirs but has written extensively on the period, drawing on his private collection of official documents, which seems to be vast and comprehensive, as well as on Egyptian government archives and other sources. While he had unparalleled
access to Nasser and is uniquely qualified to comment on the latter's state
of mind, he tends to be selective in his use of the material he has and is
not as careful as he should be about checking facts. As a result, while he
has given us the most fascinating insights to date on what went on in
Egypt during the Nasser period, it is sometimes impossible to know what
to believe. The most important of his revelations to date appear in *1967—
Al-Infijar* (1967—The Explosion), from which I have already quoted extensively. Published in Arabic in 1990, it is over one thousand pages long
and contains photocopies of various documents that Heikal uses to support his contention that Egypt fell into a well-laid U.S.-Israeli trap that

was the work of a pro-Zionist cabal. He posits a triad of intelligence, oil, and the arms industry, subsequently expanded to include the Israelis, being directed by the "hidden government" run by U.S. National Security Adviser Walt Rostow, with Robert Komer being the man immediately responsible. Their primary purpose was to destroy the Egyptian revolution, which was an obstacle to U.S. influence in the area.

Another important Arabic source, although it is concerned more with the postwar than the prewar period, is Abdul Majid Farid's *Min Mahadir Ijtima'at Abd al-Nasir* (From the minutes of the meetings of Abdul Nasser). Farid was secretary general of the Presidency from 1959 to 1970 and participated in most of the formal meetings which Nasser had during that period. His commentary on the Nasser-'Amr relationship is particularly useful.

Testimony has also come from various notables of the period in newspaper and magazine articles and at trials after the war, and books have been written by Egyptian authors on particular aspects of the war. While these accounts often do not agree, they give us considerably more insight than we had in 1967 and immediately thereafter. Egypt under Nasser was a closed society, and it is remarkable how little even the Egyptians in Cairo knew about what was really going on at the top of the pyramid. A partial unburdening of minds has taken place, but there is still much to learn before we can be certain what actually happened in 1967.

To date, no official history of these events has been published by the Egyptian government, although during the Sadat period Husni Mubarak, then vice-president, was charged with compiling a history of the revolution, including the 1967 war. This work has not yet seen the light of day, and according to one of the people interviewed by the compilers, the latter have had difficulty finding key documents. Thus we are not yet in a position to write a definitive history, but Heikal's quotations from the record show that there is more in the Egyptian archives than many scholars thought.

Here I make an attempt to reconstruct the Egyptian decision-making process based on interviews with survivors of the Nasser regime and the Lyndon Johnson Administration, on published memoirs, on the official U.S. government record, and on the writings of others who have already surveyed the field. The written sources used are listed in the annotated bibliography. On some points I have also relied on my own recollections and notes.

EGYPTIAN INTENTIONS

Agreement is general in Egypt today that Nasser made a terrible miscalculation when he reacted as he did to the Soviet warning. But there is little agreement on why he did so. Those Egyptians who are trying to preserve Nasser's image tend to put the blame on Marshal 'Amr, the armed forces commander, and on the minister of war, Shams Badran. Some argue that Nasser was misled by his own conceit, others that he fell into a trap set by Israel and the United States. Some argue that he was the victim of Soviet manipulation.

A relevant question posed from the very beginning of the crisis was whether the Egyptians were following a plan or improvising as they went along. At the time it looked to the U.S. Embassy in Cairo as though Nasser and 'Amr had decided their army was ready to take on Israel and were looking for a pretext, which was given by the Soviet warning (see Cairo's telegram no. 8080 of May 27, 1967, document 12 in the appendix). The intelligence community in Washington, however, rejected this thesis and argued that Nasser was improvising. Before we try to sift and weigh the evidence for or against these propositions, we need to look in greater detail at the events leading up to June 5.

PHASE I: THE BUILDUP

Of the five distinct stages we can discern in the crisis, the first is the irregular, and sometimes imperceptible, buildup of tension. It began before 1964 with mounting Arab concern about Israel's plans to divert waters of the Jordan River out of its watershed and over into the coastal plain. The Arabs resolved to do something about it and began planning, and eventually started preliminary work on, a diversion of their own to deprive Israel of the Jordan headwaters, which rise at Banyas in Syria. This work eventually fizzled out when it became clear that Israel would go to war over it and that the Arab states were not ready to face that challenge. More important, agitation over this issue led to the first Arab summit (i.e., a meeting to which all the Arab heads of state or government were invited) in January 1964 and to the formation of the Palestine National Council. Little else happened at the time because Egypt, the most influential Arab state, was preoccupied with its involvement in the Yemen revolution and with its own economy. The Palestine problem was, the Egyptians and Americans agreed, "in the icebox." That was the actual term used by officials at the time.

One reason it could be in the icebox was that Egypt was insulated from the problem to some extent by the presence of UNEF. This force was stationed along the 1948 armistice line, which demarcated the Gaza Strip from Israel; along the international border, which ran from the southern end of the Gaza Strip to the Red Sea just southwest of Eilat; and at Sharm al-Shaykh, on the southern end of the Sinai Peninsula at the narrow entrance to the Gulf of Aqaba (see map 2).[1] Ras Nasrani, a headland twenty kilometers north of Sharm al-Shaykh, overlooks the Enterprise Channel through the Strait of Tiran, which is the regular passage

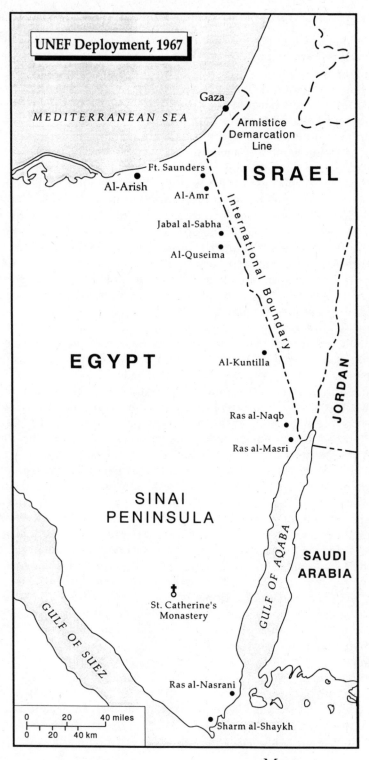

UNEF Deployment, 1967

MEDITERRANEAN SEA

Gaza

Armistice
Demarcation
Line

Ft. Saunders

Al-Arish

ISRAEL

Al-Amr

Jabal al-Sabha

Al-Quseima

International Boundary

EGYPT

Al-Kuntilla

JORDAN

Ras al-Naqb

Ras al-Masri

**SINAI
PENINSULA**

GULF OF AQABA

**SAUDI
ARABIA**

St. Catherine's
Monastery

GULF OF SUEZ

Ras al-Nasrani

Sharm al-Shaykh

0	20	40 miles
0	20	40 km

MAP 2

for large vessels entering the Gulf of Aqaba. Another, more difficult route, the Grafton passage, is closer to the Saudi coast, but it is little used. Beginning in 1951, Egypt, with a coastal battery at Ras Nasrani, had closed the strait to Israeli and other ships carrying strategic cargo for Israel. Israel had occupied Sharm al-Shaykh along with the rest of Sinai in 1956 and reopened the strait to its shipping. It had agreed to give up Sinai in 1957 in exchange for a U.S. commitment in writing to exercise the right of free and innocent passage through the strait.[2] The Americans were spared the necessity of doing anything about this commitment as long as UNEF occupied the post at Sharm al-Shaykh, allowing Israeli ships and cargo bound for Israel to pass freely through the strait.

The Palestinians, however, did not want their cause to be left in the icebox. One result of their frustration with the inactivity of Arab governments was the emergence in the mid-1960s of a number of increasingly active Palestinian paramilitary organizations which engaged in cross-border operations against Israel from bases in neighboring states, principally Syria and Lebanon. These operations became more ominous after a radical leftist government came to power in Syria in February 1966, proclaimed its support for the concept of a popular war of liberation, and permitted, even sponsored, increased cross-border sabotage operations directed against Israel. That led to a notable escalation of incidents and tensions in the spring of 1966 and into the fall.

Although Jordan's government, in contrast to Syria's, made a determined effort to prevent cross-border operations in its sector, it was not entirely successful. As a result, and perhaps because Israel hesitated to attack Syria, which it regarded as its principal danger at the time but which had become an important Soviet client, Israel staged a major reprisal raid on November 13 against the Jordanian village of Samu^c, near Hebron on the West Bank. Eighteen Jordanians were killed and fifty-four wounded, while 125 houses and other structures were destroyed. The largest operation of its kind since 1956, it was a serious black eye for the Jordan government and its army, which was caught in an ambush when it responded to the raid. In part to deflect criticism from itself, Jordan launched a campaign of invective against Egypt for failing to come to its aid and for hiding behind UNEF while Jordan was bearing the brunt of Israeli violence. Egyptian officials shrugged that off and explained that under the rules of the United Arab Command they were not obliged to respond to local actions of this sort, but they were more bothered by the Jordanian criticism than they admitted. (For an insight into the attitudes and forces at work here, see Malcolm Kerr, *The Arab Cold War*.)

On November 4, 1966, Egypt and Syria had signed a mutual defense agreement obliging each to come to the aid of the other in the event of war with Israel. Syria had been anxious for such an agreement because it was concerned that Israel might retaliate in strength to dissuade it from sponsoring cross-border sabotage and terrorist operations. At the time, the U.S. ambassador in Cairo, Lucius Battle, asked Foreign Minister Riad in my presence if he was concerned that the irresponsible Syrians would drag Egypt into a war with Israel. Riad replied in effect that the Egyptians knew what they were doing and had no intention of letting that happen to them; we should not worry.

By the end of 1966, as a result of continued incidents in border areas, tensions between Syria and Israel had mounted to the extent that U.N. Secretary General U Thant called on the two sides to meet within the framework of the Israel-Syrian Mixed Armistice Commission (ISMAC) to settle their differences. In response, the Syrians and Israelis met in the MAC three times in early 1967, but there was no agreement on the agenda and further meetings were suspended as pointless. The border was relatively calm in February and March, but there was a serious escalation of tension on April 7, leading to an air battle in which Israel shot down six Syrian aircraft over Syria.

Syria immediately asked for help from Egypt under their defense pact, but none was forthcoming because, the Egyptians said, it was a local action, not a full-scale war. That was seen by diplomats in Cairo as confirming Riad's assertion that Egypt was not going to let Syria drag it into a war with Israel. Unfortunately, Egypt's continued prudence was strongly criticized by conservative Arab states, notably Jordan and Saudi Arabia. Again, while the Egyptians replied in kind with their own invective and explained that they were not obligated to respond in such cases, it seems clear in retrospect that the criticism was getting under their skin more than was generally realized at the time.

According to various published reports (e.g., Bar Zohar's *Embassies in Crisis*, p. 10), the Egyptian prime minister, Sidqi Suleiman, went to Damascus on May 5 to tell Syria that Egypt would come to its defense only in the event of a general Israeli attack on Syria, not because of any localized incident. Whether or not the report is true, that was certainly the Egyptian formula at the time, and the Syrians must have known it.

There were two more incidents along Israel's northern border in April and three in early May. Israeli leaders began to make ominous remarks about retaliation, and on May 11 Israel's delegate to the United Nations warned in a note to the secretary general that unless Syria altered its "unrealistic and aggressive policy," Israel would feel itself "fully entitled to act in self-defense."[3] The secretary general condemned the incursions into Israel.

PHASE II: ALERT AND DETERRENCE, MAY 12–15

This phase begins with the alleged Rabin statement of May 11, published on the twelfth, about occupying Damascus and overthrowing the regime. Prior to that, at some point during the period May 5–11, Syria reportedly told Egypt that Israel was concentrating troops on its northern border for an attack on Syria.[4] According to French journalist Eric Rouleau that occurred on May 8, when two Syrian intelligence officers arrived in Cairo to inform Nasser that Israel was preparing a large-scale military operation designed to overturn the regime in Damascus and to ask that Egypt come to Syria's aid. Nasser is supposed to have responded that he could not give an undertaking to do so unless his own intelligence services confirmed the report. The Syrians responded that their information came from two sources: "the Lebanese, whose prudence you know, and our own [intelligence] services, which sent officers into Israel. They observed troop concentrations there and informed us by radio." Rouleau asserts that "Nasser then tasked his own intelligence services with making an inquiry and asked Moscow if it thought Israel, incited by the Americans, was preparing an offensive against the Syrian regime."[5]

Rouleau gives no source for this account. The date may be correct, but there are problems with some of the other details. For one thing, the Lebanese intelligence services were hardly known for their "prudence" with regard to matters such as this. They had a respectable capability for following internal political developments but almost none for developing reliable information on events outside Lebanon.[6] Beirut itself was a notorious rumor mill, and any competent intelligence service would be suspicious of a report of this nature if it came from a Lebanese source, official or otherwise. It is also doubtful that Syria was capable of the kind of reconnaissance described. On the other hand, something of the sort may have happened, and it raises the interesting possibility that on May 13 the Soviet Union's Pojidaev was responding to a query by Nasser rather than taking an initiative. That would explain much.

It is striking how rapidly the crisis progressed thereafter. As noted, the Soviet Union passed its report to Egypt on May 13. Nasser later told U Thant that his cabinet met the same day and took a decision to react by sending troops into Sinai.[7] Also on that day, a UNEF supply convoy from Port Said was unable to cross the Suez Canal at al-Qantara because the ferry was being used by UAR troops. These troops may or may not have had something to do with the decision to react,[8] but certainly the military began to move in a big way the following day.

On the morning of May 14 at 11:30 there was a meeting at Marshal 'Amr's headquarters attended by senior commanders and staff. (The account in this paragraph and the next two is taken from General Murtagi's *Al-Fariq Murtagi Yarwa al-Haqa'iq*. It is similar to the account in General Fawzi's memoirs but more detailed.) The director of military intelligence, Major General Muhammad Ahmad Sadiq, confirmed the presence of Israeli troop concentrations on the Syrian front, information he had already passed to the High Command at 9:30 the previous evening. He listed the sources of his information, which included the United Arab Command (a paper organization under the command of an Egyptian general and headquartered in Syria), the Lebanese army, the Egyptian Embassy in Moscow, and the Syrian general staff. The intelligence indicated that Israel intended to strike on (or between?) the seventeenth or twenty-first of May.[9]

After the director of intelligence spoke, Marshal ʿAmr issued a number of orders, the purpose of which was to firm up the armed forces preparatory to entering a fight for which they were quite unprepared. The orders raised the state of readiness of the air force to the maximum and announced a state of emergency in all of the armed forces and the sending of front-line units to Sinai. (General Fawzi says the armed forces were "surprised" by these orders, which raised the level of readiness from permanent *(daʿim)* to full *(kamil)* as of 2:00 P.M. the same day and called for the mobilization of units to be sent into Sinai within forty-eight to seventy-two hours. These deadlines were not met because of the military's low state of preparedness.[10])

According to Murtagi, ʿAmr also spoke for the first time of undertaking limited offensive operations against Israel, something which had not entered into the calculations of the operations planners before, at the level of either the High Command or the Command of the Eastern Sector (Sinai). Murtagi says the Egyptian defense plan (al-Qahir) had provided for no such operations. ʿAmr also ordered Fawzi to go to Syria and to assure the Syrian leaders that Egypt was observing its mutual defense agreement, that it would intervene in the event Israel attacked Syria with a "full raid" *(ghazu shamil)* and occupied its territory or destroyed its air force, and that this intervention would be complete, with land forces participating. Fawzi was to make clear to the Syrians the extent of Egyptian preparations to this end.

Whatever their state of readiness, troops began moving quickly and ostentatiously through Cairo and out toward Sinai. Advance units began moving on the fourteenth and the main body on the fifteenth. One armored division had crossed the Suez Canal on the fifteenth,[11] and as the crisis developed the line of trucks on the Suez road stretched as far as the eye could see. At the Cairo end it looked like a well-planned and well-executed operation (as taught by the Command and General Staff School at Fort Leavenworth, according to the U.S. Army attaché's office). The movement had somewhat the air of a parade at first and as a result was dismissed by Israelis, Americans, and many Egyptians as an exercise in saber-rattling.

No one expected a war. Certainly, given his repeated statements about not being ready for war, no one expected Nasser to precipitate one, particularly with the best third of his army tied down in Yemen. On May 16 Feki, the undersecretary of foreign affairs, received U.S. chargé David Nes and told him that the purpose of the movement was to permit Egypt to respond militarily if Israel attacked Syria; in other words, it was purely defensive. As noted in chapter 1, Nes told Feki, on instructions, that U.S. intelligence indicated there were no Israeli troop concentrations on the

Syrian border, but the Egyptians noted to U Thant that Nes gave no "guarantees for the prevention of the outbreak of hostilities."[12]

United Nations Assurances

The classified cable traffic between the U.N. Secretariat and the chief of staff of UNTSO in Jerusalem shows that assurances that the U.N. observers had seen no Israeli troop concentrations on the Syrian border were given to Syria and Egypt as early as May 15. The cables are laconic and do not mention a systematic inspection of the border or how much observing had actually been done. The sequence of exchanges was as follows.

On May 13 the Syrian Foreign Ministry issued the statement mentioned earlier regarding Israel's aggressive statements and intentions. It was followed by a forty-five-minute meeting that evening between the Syrian permanent representative, George Tomeh, and U Thant, during which the two discussed the secretary general's May 11 remarks to the U.N. Correspondents Association in which he spoke of the increase in border incidents carried out by Fatah. Tomeh presumably complained about those remarks, which implied Syrian sponsorship of Fatah. The Syrians had steadily denied responsibility for such activities by Palestinian groups.[13]

On May 14 Tomeh saw Ralph Bunche, the U.N. undersecretary general for special political affairs, on instructions from the Syrian government and conveyed its "very serious concern" about what it considered to be an imminent threat of attack by Israel. Bunche assured him that UNTSO was fully alert to the danger and would do what it could to avert any military action. He did not say what sort of action it might be able to take (Bunche cable to Bull, no. 396, May 14).

On May 15 the chairman of ISMAC met with its senior Syrian delegate at the latter's request. The Syrian officer "expressed great concern about the alleged buildup in Tiberias area and sought comments." The chairman replied that his observers were confined to observation within the area of the demilitarized zone and "did not report any buildup within the defensive area or the demilitarized zone" (see map 2). The U.N.'s chief observer, General Odd Bull, in forwarding this report to the U.N. Secretariat, commented, "We have no reports, thus far, of any build-up. I should point out, however, that Israel does not have to concentrate her forces in any one area in order to mount an attack. I will keep you informed of the situation" (Bull cable to Bunche, no. 803, May 15).

Also on May 15, Bunche met with Israel's permanent representative, Gideon Rafael, who said Israel had noted the press reports, particularly in Cairo, about troop movements and "wished to emphasize that there has been no concentration of Israel troops on the Syrian border." He gave assurances that there was "no reason for anyone to be concerned about military action by Israel so long as the other side took none." He said this information might be conveyed to the government of the UAR with the condition that it not be publicized. Bunche told Bull that the information had been conveyed (Bunche cable to Bull, no. 398, May 15). In a second cable, also dated May 15, Bunche said the representatives of Syria and the UAR were clearly relieved to be informed of the Israeli assurances (Bunche to Bull, no. 399).

Thus, by the fifteenth the Syrians had received denials of the report from the ISMAC chairman and both Syria and Egypt had been informed of Israel's denial. It is not clear from the record when and how General Bull's affirmation of the chairman's denial was passed to the Syrians and Egyptians in New York. It may have been done informally and orally on the fifteenth or sixteenth, but there is no mention of it in the cables. The denial was communicated in writing at 5:30 P.M. on May 17 in a letter from the secretary general to Egypt's permanent representative, Muhammad Awad al-Kony. The message is buried in the text of a discussion of the Egyptian request for the withdrawal of UNEF, which had been presented the previous day:

> The Secretary General also wishes to inform the Permanent Representative of the United Arab Republic that as of now, on the basis of the fully reliable reports received from the Chief of Staff of the United Nations Truce Supervision Organization, there have been no recent indications of troop movements or concentrations along any of the Lines which should give rise to undue concern.[14]

On May 18 the Syrian delegate again expressed concern to the ISMAC chairman and seemed convinced there was an Israeli buildup near the armistice line. The chairman passed on to him assurances the senior Israeli delegate had given on May 16 (I have found no other record of them), that there was no concentration or buildup of forces on the Israel side of the border (Bull cable to Bunche, no. 820, May 18).

A slightly different formulation was used in the secretary general's report of May 19:

> There have been in the past few days persistent reports about troop movements and concentrations particularly on the Israel side of the Syrian border. These have caused anxiety and at times excitement. The Government of Israel very recently has assured me that there are no unusual Israel troop concentrations or movements along the Syrian line, and that there will be none and that no military action will be initiated by the armed forces of Israel unless such action is first taken by the other side. Reports from observers of the Truce Supervision Organization have confirmed the absence of troop concentrations and significant troop movements on both sides of the line. (22 UN SCOR, Supplement for April–June)

Read twenty-five years later, these messages and assurances sound remarkably anodyne and skimpy. One detects no note of urgency in them or any determined effort to give Syria ironclad assurances nothing was going on. Persistent Syrian suspicions in the circumstances are understandable. Egyptian doubts are less easy to explain, given General Fawzi's report that there were no concentrations, but there was not much substance from the United Nations to support his findings. A more vigorous U.N. effort might have been more convincing to the Arabs, who could not be expected to rely on Israel's denials, given the record of deceit on both sides.

PHASE III: UNEF WITHDRAWAL AND
THE PRELUDE TO TIRAN

The secretary general's letter of May 17 had been overtaken by the events of some twenty-five hours before. At 10:00 P.M. local time on May 16, a letter from the UAR chief of staff, General Fawzi, was delivered to the commander of UNEF, Major General Rikhye, in Gaza. It noted that Egyptian troops were moving into Sinai and said that "for the sake of complete security of all the UN troops which install OP's [observation posts] along our borders, I request that you issue orders to withdraw all these troops immediately." Rikhye said that he must refer the request to the secretary general; he did so immediately.

On receipt of Rikhye's message late in the day on the sixteenth, U Thant consulted with al-Kony, who was unaware of Fawzi's request. Thant asked whether the UAR would consider withdrawing the request and reviewing the situation before any further action was taken. Al-Kony queried Cairo and then informed Thant that UAR authorities would not be willing to entertain a request to change the content of Fawzi's letter. According to Bunche, Thant had informed al-Kony that he was about to send a direct appeal to Nasser to reconsider the demand for withdrawal and within an hour al-Kony returned to say that he had been on the telephone to Cairo and been instructed by Foreign Minister Riad to urge Thant most strongly not to make such an appeal because Nasser was fully determined on this matter and any such appeal would meet with a strong rebuff. This report on Cairo's attitude was one of the principal bases for Thant's decision to go along with the Egyptian request (Bunche note for the file, July 11, 1968, U.N. Archives, DAG-1/5.2.2.1.2, box 1).

Later that evening Thant asked al-Kony to inform his government that Fawzi's letter needed clarification. If it meant a temporary withdrawal of UNEF from all or part of the line, that would be unacceptable and would be considered as amounting to a request for complete withdrawal. If that was the intent, the letter should have been addressed to the secretary general and not to the commander of UNEF. He gave al-Kony an aide-mémoire expanding on these points at 5:30 P.M. the following day. This is the same aide-mémoire referred to earlier in which Thant conveyed the UNTSO report that there were no Israeli troop concentrations.

The UAR's response, signed by Riad, was received at noon on May 18. It said Egypt had decided to "terminate the presence of UNEF from the territory of the UAR and the Gaza Strip." U Thant accepted this response as definitive, and UNEF received orders from him the following morning to cease operations immediately and start a withdrawal.[15]

The termination of UNEF put a new and serious light on the crisis. While the force was too small to be an effective military barrier if either side really wanted to fight, it had been an effective psychological and political restraint, and it had absolved Egypt of the necessity to be belligerent for ten years.[16] Lifting that restraint greatly increased the likelihood of war. Nasser is variously reported to have said that it increased the expectation of war by 20 to 80 percent. The latter figure comes from Hussein al-Shafi ʿi, who was present at the meeting at which Nasser reportedly said it.[17]

Egypt's moves were no longer just a show of force; the situation on the ground had changed significantly. Nevertheless, war could still have been avoided if Egypt could have been persuaded to take no offensive action and to withdraw its forces once it was satisfied that Israel did not in fact intend to attack Syria on the scale alleged by the Soviets. It is not clear, however, what scale of Israeli retaliation against Syria the Egyptians would have been able to tolerate without making their own military response. Removing UNEF as a barrier greatly reduced their room for prudent maneuvering. Thus if Israeli retaliation on a large scale was inevitable, so perhaps was war, once UNEF was removed.

Among the actions which Israel would consider offensive was closure of the Strait of Tiran to Israeli shipping or cargoes. Although few Israeli vessels actually transited the strait (none at all had done so in the previous two and one-half years, according to the U.N. Secretariat at the time), it was important to the Israelis as part of their lifeline to the outer world, and in particular as the route used by tankers delivering Iranian oil to them. That Israel would consider interference with traffic through the strait as casus belli was well known in both Cairo and Moscow. Abba Eban made the position explicit when he informed the Soviet ambassador on May 19, after the decision to withdraw UNEF was known, that "there will be no war if the Egyptians do not attack and do not interfere with Israel's right of navigation."[18]

On May 21 the Yugoslav contingent of UNEF withdrew from the post at Sharm al-Shaykh and Egyptian troops moved in. The stage was now set for the next act. The big question in Cairo was whether the UAR would close the Strait of Tiran, as various critics, notably the Jordanians, were taunting it to do.

PHASE IV: CLOSURE OF TIRAN TO MAY 28

On the afternoon of May 22 Nasser addressed air force officers at the Bir Gifgafa (Abu Suwayr) base in north central Sinai. He told them that reoccupation of Sharm al-Shaykh was a reaffirmation of Egyptian sovereignty and "under no circumstances can we permit the Israeli flag to pass through the Gulf of Aqaba. The Jews threaten war. We say they are welcome to war, we are ready for it; our armed forces, our people, all of us are ready for war, but under no circumstances shall we abandon any of our rights. These are our waters. Perhaps war will be an opportunity for the Jews, for Israel, for Rabin, to try out their forces against ours and find out that all they wrote about the battle of 1956 and the occupation of Sinai was a lot of nonsense."[19]

The speech, broadcast over Cairo radio shortly after midnight on the twenty-third, became front-page news, with photographs, in the Egyptian papers that morning. The broadcast and the press made it clear that the strait would be closed to strategic cargo for Israel as well as to Israeli flag vessels, and during the day the Egyptians further clarified this by saying oil was considered strategic cargo.

The same morning, Richard Nolte, the recently arrived U.S. ambassador-designate (he had not yet presented credentials), delivered to Mahmoud Riad a rather general and conciliatory message from Lyndon Johnson to Nasser in which Johnson suggested sending Vice-President Hubert Humphrey to talk with Arab and Israeli leaders once the crisis had died down (The text of Johnson's message can be found in the appendix, document 3.) Earlier that morning, Nolte had sent a flash telegram to the Department of State saying that the Johnson message, which had been drafted the day before by Undersecretary of State Eugene Rostow, had been overtaken by the announcement regarding closure of the Strait of Tiran. He suggested that delivery be delayed until the Egyptian position was clearer and the message could be redrafted and made more to the point. The department told him to go ahead and deliver it anyway.

In the same meeting Nolte also delivered a note verbale deploring terrorism, expressing concern at the hasty withdrawal of UNEF, calling for a halt to troop buildups on both sides, saying that interference with navigation in the Gulf of Aqaba could have the gravest international consequences, and reiterating U.S. opposition to aggression in any form. (The text of the note verbale appears as document 4 in the appendix.) Johnson made a more detailed and ringing statement on the subject in an address to the nation that evening. He made a particularly strong statement of U.S. opposition to aggression:

> To the leaders of all the nations of the Near East, I wish to say what three American Presidents have said before me—that the United States

is firmly committed to the support of the political independence and territorial integrity of all nations of that area. The United States strongly opposes aggression by anyone in the area, in any form, overt or clandestine. This has been the policy of the United States led by four Presidents . . . as well as the policy of both of our political parties. The record of the actions of the United States over the past 20 years, within and outside the United Nations, is abundantly clear on that point.[20]

As noted earlier, the Soviet Union on the same day issued a statement saying that any aggression in the region would be met not only by the united force of the Arab countries but also by the strong opposition of the Soviet Union. Both statements contributed to the Egyptian miscalculation. Neither was worth much to Egypt when the chips were down.

For his part, Prime Minister Eshkol made a public statement saying that interference with Israeli shipping in the Strait of Tiran would be considered an act of war.

Meanwhile, U Thant, who had announced on May 20 his intention to go to Cairo, arrived there late on the afternoon of the twenty-third. He had learned of the closure of the strait during a stopover in Paris. He met with Riad the morning of the twenty-fourth and with Nasser that evening. The Egyptians were cordial but firm. (Thant's memoranda of these conversations are in the appendix, documents 5 and 6.) Thant told Nasser he had been very surprised to learn of the closure of the strait while in Paris. Nasser replied that the decision to do so had been taken some time earlier, but there was a question as to timing. If the announcement were to be made after the secretary general's visit, it would be widely interpreted as a snub, so it was decided to announce it before he arrived.[21]

According to Rikhye's account, Nasser said closure of the strait was inevitable once UAR troops had moved into Sinai. He and Riad made it clear that they had wiped out the last traces of the aggression of 1956 by getting rid of UNEF and closing the strait and that they had no intention of backing down. They were willing, however, to accept a two-week moratorium of action in the strait provided Israel did the same, and they were willing to have the issue of passage through the strait referred to the International Court of Justice (which was unacceptable to Israel).[22]

Nasser's most important commitment, however, was not to fire the first shot. He said that his military commanders had urged on May 13 that Egypt should attack Israel immediately, but he was committed to peace and therefore did not agree. "It was finally agreed," Rikhye reports, "that the UAR would only fight if attacked by Israel."[23] This same commitment was reiterated privately to the Soviets and Americans as well as publicly. It is generally considered today to have been a fatal error, but Nasser reportedly reasoned that to attack would inevitably mean U.S. participation on the side of Israel, and it was better to accept the damage of a first strike than to risk U.S. participation.

On the following day, May 25, Badran, the minister of war, went to Moscow, accompanied by a group of military officers and by Feki and Bassiouni of Feki's office. In his *In Search of Identity* (p. 173) Anwar Sadat said their trip was at the Soviets' initiative, but Badran's own account (in the *Al-Hawadith* interview mentioned earlier) said it was Nasser's idea, that Nasser had thought it would be good for the Egyptian minister of war to be seen conferring with his Soviet counterpart, presumably because that would let people know the Soviets were behind the UAR. Heikal's version confirms that it was at Nasser's initiative but says the purpose was to ascertain the Soviet position and ask for arms.

Badran met with Kosygin, Gromyko, Marshal Grechko, Semyenov, and other senior Soviet officials. He appears not to have had any specific message to convey from Nasser other than greetings, but had been charged by Marshal ʿAmr with submitting a list of equipment the Egyptians wanted immediately.

The most important aspects of the visit were described in chapter 2. In brief, Badran described Egyptian military moves and asked for more military equipment. Kosygin instructed Grechko to discuss Egyptian requirements with Badran, then began lecturing the Egyptians on the need for restraint. This was kept up throughout the visit by other Soviet officials. The Soviets also were unresponsive to Egyptian requests for more equipment in a hurry. Kosygin's words of caution were undone, however, by Grechko's parting remarks at the airport, discussed earlier.

Abba Eban, meanwhile, had gone to Washington, where he met with President Johnson on May 26 to ask for assurances about U.S. intentions to honor the Gulf of Aqaba commitment and to ascertain what the U.S. attitude would be toward Israeli military action against Egypt. Johnson used the agreed-upon phrase coined by Secretary of State Dean Rusk: "Israel will not be alone unless it decides to go alone." That was intended to be a warning to Israel not to make a preemptive strike at Egypt and to give the United States time to work out a solution to the navigation problem. Johnson repeatedly assured Eban that he would do everything in his power to open the gulf to Israeli shipping. After Eban left the meeting, Johnson reportedly said, "I've failed. They'll go."[24]

The Israelis pondered Johnson's remarks and eventually concluded, correctly, that he would not interfere or punish Israel if it struck first. His remonstrations did, however, result in a significant delay in Israel's decision to strike. This question is examined more fully in chapter 5.

On the same day, May 26, apparently sharing Johnson's view, Heikal wrote in his Friday column in *Al-Ahram* that war with Israel was inevitable because the Israelis could not accept the Arabs' imposing their will on them in the way the Egyptians had by closing the Gulf of Aqaba and would have to strike. Heikal was generally thought to reflect Nasser's views, and this column convinced the U.S. Embassy that it had been wise to decide a day or two earlier to evacuate dependents. The decision to do so had been communicated to the director of European and North American affairs at the Egyptian Foreign Ministry, Salah Hassan, by me on May 25. The Egyptians did not have to learn of it through their intelligence sources, as Heikal implies in *Al-Infijar.*

Also on the same day, while Badran was still in Moscow, in a further display of their concern, as noted earlier, the Soviets sent urgent messages of restraint from Kosygin to Nasser and to Eshkol. The messages were not actually delivered until the early hours of the twenty-seventh. The message to Nasser asked that Egypt not be the first to open hostilities and said President Johnson had informed the Kremlin that Egypt was planning to attack Israel that day.[25] Nasser had already received a similar message from the Americans via the Egyptian ambassador in Washington, Mustafa Kamel, who was summoned to the Department of State by Eugene Rostow on the evening of May 25 to be informed that Israel had just delivered an urgent message to the effect that Egypt was on the verge of attacking. Rostow said the Americans did not believe the report but were taking no chances. Such an attack would have very serious consequences. According to Riad, the U.S. demarche was taken by the Egyptians as a threat.[26] The message to Eshkol said the Soviets wanted Israel to use all means to avoid the outbreak of hostilities and commented that it was easy to light a fire but not as easy to put out as those who were pushing Israel beyond the brink seemed to think.[27]

Israel's cabinet met late in the evening of May 27 and continued in session until the early morning hours of the twenty-eighth. Eban arrived at Lod at about the time the cabinet convened and hurried to Jerusalem to join the deliberations and report on his discussions in Paris, London and, in particular, Washington. According to most accounts,[28] the cabinet split evenly on whether to strike at Egypt immediately or to delay and give the Americans a chance to solve the navigation problem. Eban, in *An Autobiography,* denies this and says there was no vote, only a discussion. In any event, no decision was taken. The cabinet reconvened on the afternoon of May 28 and opted for a further waiting period of two to three weeks. Members were influenced by, among other things, further strong messages from President Johnson and Secretary Rusk urging that they not preempt U.S. efforts to arrange an international approach to the Gulf of Aqaba problem.

Meanwhile, the rhetoric was heating up in Cairo. On the same day Israel's cabinet opted to wait, Nasser gave a press conference to an enormous crowd of journalists from all over the world during which he called for Israel to withdraw from Eilat and the al-Auja demilitarized zone (which Israel had occupied in 1955, ejecting the Egypt-Israel Mixed Armistice Commission from its quarters there in the process). He exuded confidence that Egypt and the other Arabs were now going to dominate the game which Israel had largely controlled hitherto. He was buoyed by a number of things: the wave of enthusiastic support sweeping the Arab world, the message from Grechko which Badran had brought, a message that morning from King Hussein proposing to come to Cairo in two days, and indications that Israel's cabinet apparently was not ready for war.

Egyptian perceptions that Israel was afraid of war were typified by Marshal ʿAmr's reported remarks at lunch with Nasser that day. According to Mahmoud Riad, he "laughingly announced" that he had ordered two Mig-21s to make a reconnaissance flight over Beersheba that morning and the Israelis had panicked. Riad, who was present, was deeply disturbed.[29] Israeli officials alluded to this incident in a conversation with U.S. officials a day or two later as one reason they would have to take military action.

PHASE V: THE FAILURE OF DIPLOMACY, MAY 29–JUNE 5

After his return to New York on May 26, U Thant submitted a report to the Security Council calling for a breathing spell during which all parties would refrain from belligerence and actions which could increase tensions. Thant also suggested that the situation would be eased if Israel returned to the Egypt-Israel Mixed Armistice Commission and if Israel and Syria resumed meetings of their MAC. When the Security Council reconvened on May 29, the United States and others supported the call for a breathing spell. The U.S. delegate said that forgoing belligerency meant forgoing the blockade of the Gulf of Aqaba. The Egyptian delegate, on the other hand, argued that the gulf was national not international water and that Israel was not a legal riparian in any event because it had occupied Eilat in violation of the U.N.-arranged cease-fire in 1949. He called on Israel to honor its obligations under the armistice agreement with Egypt and for UNTSO to return to its headquarters in the al-Auja demilitarized zone.

Two days later the United States and Egypt submitted draft resolutions, one calling for compliance with the secretary general's call for a breathing spell, the other calling for restoration of the provisions of the general armistice agreement between Israel and Egypt. They were still up for discussion when the war came.

On the bilateral side, diplomats and their governments, all of which had been taken by surprise by the course of events, had taken a while to get organized. The first significant U.S. response was the Johnson message to Nasser of May 22. The Egyptians focused more on Johnson's public statement of May 23, particularly that part which said the United States believed the armistice agreements were the best guarantee of peace along the borders and remained firmly opposed, as it had for four administrations, to aggression in any form. Although not labeled as such, this statement amounted to a unilateral reaffirmation of the Tripartite Declaration of 1950, which the other signatories, Britain and France, had repudiated when they attacked Egypt in 1956.

Riad told Nasser that he interpreted this statement as meaning the United States would oppose military action by either side and thus an outbreak of hostilities was out of the question, since Egypt did not plan to start the fighting. Nasser responded that he doubted Johnson's sincerity, and that it was inconceivable that Johnson had suddenly become evenhanded, given his pro-Israeli record.[30]

The closure of the strait put a new complexion on the affair for the United States, which was formally committed in writing to exercise the right of free and innocent passage through the strait for itself and "to join with others to secure general recognition of this right" (i.e., on behalf of Israel). It was now called upon to honor that pledge. In theory it had several possibilities for doing so, including unilateral escorting of Israeli vessels and cargoes in defiance of Egypt, multilateral action of a similar nature, and a political solution, somehow persuading the Egyptians to change their minds, either through the mechanism of the United Nations or otherwise.

The third alternative appeared to be unrealistic, and attention focused quickly on the first two. The big question was whether Egypt meant what it said about closing the strait or whether it was bluffing. Would it fire on U.S. or other ships escorting Israeli ships and cargoes through the strait? Officials of the Department of State apparently believed Egypt was bluffing, but the embassy in Cairo had a different appreciation of the risk. It thought Egypt was serious and would not hesitate to shoot. (See Cairo's telegram no. 8093 of May 28 in the appendix, document 7.) In any event, there was enough fear that it might and enough concern for the impact of unilateral U.S. action on relations even if Egypt did not shoot that a multilateral effort was far more attractive to Washington than a unilateral one. But given the attitude of Third World members, most of whom were supporting Egypt, organizing such an effort in the U.N. context was hopeless, and the administration therefore opted to support a British proposal for joint action by the largely Western "maritime nations," who had an interest in upholding freedom of navigation. Thus was born the concept which came to be known jocularly as the "Red Sea Regatta."

The idea was simple enough. Like-minded states would band together, make a declaration of support for freedom of passage in the Gulf of Aqaba (the so-called Maritime Declaration), and create a multilateral naval force which would escort Israeli ships and cargoes through the strait in defiance of the Egyptians, who would hesitate to fire on the naval vessels of such a combination of powers. But only the Australians, Canadians, Dutch, and Icelanders had agreed to participate in the regatta by June 4, and the Americans felt they needed at least fourteen adherents to provide enough international character to assuage congressional opposition to yet another foreign military engagement on top of the Vietnam War.

Egypt warned that it would not acquiesce in such a maneuver, and even Israel was unenthusiastic about it, because it would mean a diminution of its gains from the 1956 invasion. The idea was still in its initial stages when Eban arrived in Washington on May 25, and it was soon obvious that recruiting participants was going to be difficult and time-consuming. France and Italy, for instance, refused to go along, and Germany was doubtful. Meanwhile the United States had made it clear it would not act unilaterally. That reinforced Israel's conviction that the United States would not force the strait but would instead seek some political compromise at Israel's expense. Egypt probably thought the same, judging from its defiant behavior. The coup de grâce to the concept should have been given by U.S. Ambassador Charles Yost's telegram of June 2 (Cairo's 8362; a copy is in the appendix, document 10), but people in Washington were still talking as though it was a live proposition when the fighting started.

On May 29 the temperature went up another notch when Nasser addressed the National Assembly, which had given him full powers to govern by decree. He said, "I have said in the past that we would decide the time and place, and that we must prepare ourselves in order to win. . . . Preparations have already been made. We are now ready to confront Israel." He also said that if Egypt had restored the pre-1956 position vis-à-vis Israel, "God will surely help and urge us to restore the situation to what it was in 1948," i.e., before the creation of Israel. As in his press conference the previous day, he said the problem was much larger than the Strait of Tiran; it dealt with the rights of the entire Palestinian people.[31] Nasser appeared convinced that he had the mandate and the capability to turn back the clock. In his press conference he had said that "we accept no coexistence with Israel. The rights of the Palestinians should be given back to them."[32] Israel and the rest of the world could be pardoned for believing, on hearing this, that Nasser had decided to force Israel to the wall.

On the same day, Riad asked Nasser about the efficacy of the air force and Nasser said that 'Amr had assured him of Egypt's preparedness.[33]

Also on the same day, Syria's President Atassi arrived in Moscow for a meeting with Kosygin. Did Atassi tell Kosygin that the report of Israeli troop concentrations was untrue, as Badran had said the Syrians would in his conversation with Grechko? We have no access to the record and can only guess. The fact that on June 19 Kosygin was still talking as if the report was true suggests that he did not.

According to Heikal, on May 30 U Thant sent a message to Nasser and Eshkol urging restraint on all parties and expressing the hope that there would be a moratorium on action in the Gulf of Aqaba for two weeks.[34] Heikal says this was the turning point of the crisis, because Nasser assumed that the contents of Thant's message had been agreed to by the United States and the Soviet Union and that this meant no offensive action would be taken by Israel before June 14. This belief, combined with an upcoming visit to Washington by Egypt's Vice-President Zakaria Muheiddin, contributed to an Egyptian relaxation of vigilance which was not justified by the real circumstances. Gideon Raphael, Israel's U.N. delegate at the time, reports that Thant's message was never delivered to Eshkol because the Egyptians had rejected it. In this case, it is difficult to see how Nasser could have been misled by it.[35]

Also on May 30, Eban was quoted by the press, wrongly according to the Israelis, as saying Israel would open the Strait of Tiran "alone if we must, with others if we can." The same day, Jordan's King Hussein arrived in Cairo and concluded a military alliance with Egypt, the essential text of which was the same as that agreed to between Cairo and Damascus the previous November 4. It bound the two governments to "use all means at their disposal, including the use of armed force to repel an attack on either nation. An Israeli attempt to break the Egyptian blockade would be considered an act of aggression."[36]

Meanwhile, the administration in Washington was making efforts to establish a dialogue with Nasser, or at least with senior Egyptian officials, in the absence of an accredited ambassador on the scene. Nolte had still not presented his ambassadorial credentials and therefore Nes, the deputy chief of mission, was still chargé d'affaires. Nasser did not normally receive chargés. Indeed, in his May 28 press conference he said there was no contact between the United States and Egypt. Strictly speaking, that was not true. There was still an Egyptian ambassador in Washington and regular and frequent contact at the working level between the U.S. Embassy in Cairo and various offices of the Egyptian government, including the Foreign Ministry and the Presidency. There was no direct access to Nasser, however, and that was a critical factor preventing effective communication with Egypt's leaders.

On or about May 25 a decision was taken by Washington to send former Treasury Secretary Robert B. Anderson, who had long had personal contact with Nasser and had been involved in secret negotiations with him in the past, to Cairo to listen and feel out the Egyptian position, but not to negotiate. Anderson saw Nasser on the evening of May 31 or June 1. Nasser, cordial and relaxed, said he hoped for improved relations, but he showed no interest in compromise or in backing down from any of his positions. In a separate letter to President Johnson, dated June 2, Nasser said he would welcome a visit by Hubert Humphrey and was prepared to send Vice-President Muhieddin to Washington immediately.[37] (Anderson's reporting telegram and Nasser's letter are in the appendix, documents 9 and 11.)

On June 1 Riad received Yost, the retired U.S. ambassador, who had been sent by Washington to give Nolte a helping hand and some guidance. Nolte was a political appointee and a protégé of Nicholas Katzenbach, then undersecretary of state. A student of the area who knew Egypt well, Nolte had no previous diplomatic experience and was quite unfamiliar with the operational culture of government. As the crisis deepened, Washington, and the White House in particular, had become concerned at the need for someone more experienced on the scene who would have more effective contact at the higher levels of the Egyptian government. President Johnson had wanted to send Lucius Battle, but Battle felt that would be unwise and suggested Yost instead.[38]

Yost, a senior Foreign Service officer with wide experience who had briefly been a colleague of Riad's at the United Nations and in Damascus in 1958, called on Riad at home on June 1. According to Riad, Yost told him he had been sent to say the United States would oppose any party which began armed aggression.[39] That was indeed the substance of the U.S. public position, but U.S. officials had tried to make it clear that they could not restrain Israel indefinitely. Yost's own description of what he said to Riad (as reported in Cairo's telegram no. 8349; see the appendix, document 8) is unsatisfactorily brief:

> Yost explained our apprehension of consequences and possible repercussions of war and our so far successful efforts to persuade Israelis to hold off, citing however Israeli fears of Arab mobilization against them, Nasser's references to return to 1948 status quo, and Israeli conviction of vital interest in free passage through Tiran straits, as well as US policy on this subject.

Yost had arrived in Cairo convinced that the Egyptians were bluffing and was surprised to find the embassy in disagreement with him. He was even more surprised by the vehemence of Riad's reaction, which is well described in the telegram. After talking to Riad and other Egyptians, Yost left on June 3 convinced the Egyptians were serious. He recommended (in Cairo's telegram 8362; document 10 in the appendix) that it would perhaps be more productive to concentrate on limiting the damage and referring the issue to the International Court of Justice rather than trying to force the strait.

Meanwhile, also on June 1, a "war cabinet" was formed in Israel, with Moshe Dayan replacing Eshkol as minister of defense (Eshkol held that post as well as the prime minister's post) in response to criticism of Eshkol as being indecisive and ignorant of military affairs. Menachem Begin, the Herut leader, was brought in from outer darkness and given a minister's rank without portfolio, and the same was done for Joseph Saphir of the right-wing Gahal party. These moves were taken in Cairo as further evidence supporting Heikal's thesis that war was inevitable.

Also on June 1, Eshkol responded to Kosygin's letter of May 26, which had been delivered to him in the small hours of May 27. He said that Egypt's actions had forced Israel to take security measures—to mobilize its forces and to order them to keep watch for the security of Israel's borders. The reply was given to the Soviet ambassador, Chuvakhin, by the director general of the Israeli Foreign Ministry, Arye Levavi. Chuvakhin said the outcome depended on Israel but hinted that there were grounds for optimism. This hint piqued Israel's curiosity, and there was speculation that Moscow had decided it had gained sufficient ground with the Arabs, was not keen on risking further steps, and hoped Nasser could be brought to reopen the strait.[40]

On June 2, according to a variety of sources, Nasser met with senior officers of the political and military leadership and told them Israel would attack on June 3, 4, or 5, depending on the source. Riad says June 5 (*Amrika wa al-Arab*, p. 43). Sadat says it was one of the three (*In Search of Identity*, p. 174). General Fawzi, who was there, quotes Nasser as saying he expected the war to begin in two days or three at the latest, that is, on June 4 or 5. Nasser, in his July 23, 1967, Revolution Day speech, remarked: "I said . . . we must expect the enemy to strike a blow within 48 to 72 hours and no later. . . . I also said . . . that I expected the aggression to take place on Monday, June 5. The Air Force commander [Sidqi Mahmoud] was present at the meeting." According to Sadat, Nasser told Mahmoud that the air force would be dealt the first blow and Mahmoud replied, "We have taken that into account, sir; we shan't sustain losses beyond the calculated ten percent."[41]

Much has been said about this meeting and the failure of the air force to be prepared when Israel struck on the fifth. The Sadat and Nasser versions, one explicitly and the other implicitly, accuse General Mahmoud of misleading Nasser about his ability to absorb the first blow. General Fawzi's account does not agree, however. Fawzi says that Mahmoud, visibly disturbed, had estimated losses from an Israeli first strike at 15 to 20 percent and had said "this would mean the loss of the initiative on our part, which may lead to the crippling of the air force." (He said "crippling" in English.) On the other hand, Fawzi says that ʿAmr and Mahmoud did not take Nasser's warning seriously and that although there was agreement in the meeting to redeploy aircraft for protection, it was not in fact done because of ʿAmr's skepticism.

On the same day, June 2, Gromyko received Israeli Ambassador Katriel Katz in Moscow and told him that Eban's alleged statement of May 30, that Israel would open the strait itself if necessary, was "confirmation of the policy of adventurist military circles in Israel" but added enigmatically, in the same vein as Chuvakhin the previous day, "We are working for peace." His meaning was not clear to the Israelis.[42]

On June 3 Yost asked to see Riad urgently and told him the U.S. government was ready to receive Vice-President Muhieddin at any time. Riad called Nasser, who suggested June 5, and Yost agreed on the spot. (That is Riad's version. Muhieddin says the date set was June 7, and the telegraphic record agrees.) There was an audible sigh of relief from officers of the U.S. Embassy in Cairo, who saw this development as the first indication of a meaningful political initiative to resolve the crisis peacefully. The following day, everyone in Cairo who could went out and relaxed (I went sailing on the Nile with Nolte and Slator Blackiston, the embassy's economic officer), hoping the war cloud would blow away, if only the Israelis could be persuaded not to act.

That hope was illusory. On June 3, after hearing from the head of Mossad (Israel's equivalent of the CIA), Meir Amit, that the Red Sea Regatta scheme was going nowhere and that the United States would not oppose Israeli military action against Egypt, Eshkol and his kitchen cabinet had decided to recommend to the cabinet the following day that Israel should go to war. In effect, the decision to do so had been taken and the wheels were set in motion before the full cabinet met. Israel successfully concealed its intentions from Egypt and struck on the morning of June 5, attacking Egyptian air bases at breakfast time, when all the aircraft were on the ground in spite of Nasser's warning. The Egyptian air force was all but eliminated in a matter of hours, and Egyptian ground forces were routed from Sinai before the week was over. Nasser's dream had collapsed. He never recovered fully from the defeat and died three years later.

CHAPTER
4

FROM DETERRENCE TO DISASTER

> When we concentrated our forces I esti-
> mated that the likelihood of war breaking
> out was 20 percent. Before we closed the
> Gulf of Aqaba, we convened a meeting of
> the Higher Executive Committee at my
> home. We discussed the closure of the Gulf
> of Aqaba. That meeting took place on May
> 22. At that meeting I told them that the
> possibility of war was 50 percent. At an-
> other meeting I said that the likelihood of
> war was 80 percent.
>
> Gamal Abdul Nasser, July 23, 1967

The brief account in the previous chapter does only limited justice to a complex chain of events. It will serve, however, as a backdrop to a discussion of the principal questions about Egypt's decisions. Why did Egypt elect to go from deterrence to confrontation? What made it decide it could risk war with Israel? Was it following a preplanned strategy or improvising as it went along?

FROM DETERRENCE TO CONFRONTATION

According to Zakaria Muhieddin, Egypt's vice-president at the time, no one alive today can tell why Nasser acted as he did. Nasser took the answers with him to the grave.[1] We can, however, define the extent of our ignorance more precisely, because we have learned a good deal about Egypt's decision-making process, thanks to the revelations of Heikal, General Fawzi, General Murtagi, Abdul Majid Farid, and others.

The Choices

It has long been clear that Nasser thought he was obliged to react in some effective way when he learned, or thought he learned, that Israel was about to make a major assault on Syria. According to Heikal, Nasser thought the threat to Syria was real and that the regime in Damascus was in danger. If it fell, so would Baghdad, and the reactionaries would take over. Egypt would then be isolated before Israel (*Al-Infijar*, pp. 448–51).

For Nasser, doing something effective meant going beyond political measures such as protests at the United Nations. It meant doing something physical which would restrain Israel. No conceivable political action would have that effect, given the attitudes of the powers and of the United States in particular. In the absence of any other sanction, this meant that Nasser had to do something military. Whatever reservations he may have had about the state of his armed forces, he at least would have to make a show of force. He could not do nothing. He had gotten away with that domestically, if not regionally, at the time of the Samu' raid and the April 7 dogfight over Syria, but his prestige and Egypt's could not afford another such failure to react. The question was not whether he would react, but how and when. He had several choices, including deterrence and upping the ante.

Deterrence

In a repeat of 1960 he could send troops into Sinai in a show of force, warning Israel that if it struck at Syria it would risk an attack by Egypt in the south. It is not clear how long this would have restrained the Israelis if the situation along the Syrian border was as intolerable as they kept saying it was, but it would at least make them think twice and perhaps modify the nature of their response to Syria so as not to trigger war with Egypt. "Think twice" was in fact the phrase used by Marshal 'Amr in his order to the troops on May 14.

A show of force would be a reasonable reaction. It would be popular politically, and the risk of war would be moderate. Indeed, that was what both Israel and the Egyptian military (according to General Fawzi's memoirs) thought was happening at first. It was 1960 all over again, with the important difference that this time the troop moves were much publicized, whereas they had been kept secret, even from the Israelis, in 1960. The public show made many Egyptians think they were witnessing a parade. Heikal (*The Sphinx and the Commissar*, p. 175) says the publicity was due to Nasser's concern that "the Israelis and others might think the Egyptian army was too involved in the Yemen to come to the aid of Syria." But the publicity unleashed a military and political dynamic which soon got out of control.

Upping the Ante

Nasser could attack Israel without waiting for it to attack Syria. That would be foolhardy, but the military were urging it, according to Nasser. Until (and even after) his assurances to U Thant and others that he did not intend to strike first, it had seemed a possibility to many diplomats and journalists in Cairo, who were impressed with the evident determination of Egypt's leaders to confront Israel. According to Heikal, however (*Al-Infijar*, p. 574), Nasser thought a first strike by Egypt would give President Johnson and Israel the pretext they were waiting for and he should avoid that.

Alternatively, Nasser could respond to Arab criticism that he was hiding behind UNEF and call for its withdrawal, something that had apparently been on his mind and ʿAmr's for some time. It was not on many other minds, however, and the decision to take this step came as a general surprise. It meant moving from deterrence to confrontation. With it, Nasser lost most of his freedom of maneuver, and the risk of war went up sharply.

Nasser also could eliminate the traces of 1956. Not only could he remove UNEF; he could also close the Strait of Tiran. Israel's gains from the 1956 invasion would then be eliminated. The situation would return to what it was before—Egyptian and Israeli troops confronting each other all along the line and no Israeli traffic in the Gulf of Aqaba. It would create a dangerous situation but would not necessarily be fatal, had Israel not made it clear that it would consider interference with its shipping in the Gulf justification for going to war. Israel's position was well known at the time, and by his own account Nasser realized the risk of war would escalate if this path was taken.

In the event, Egypt exercised three of these options. It did not elect to attack preemptively, but it did move troops into Sinai, called for the removal of UNEF, and imposed a blockade on Israeli shipping in the Gulf of Aqaba.

The Move into Sinai

According to Rikhye's account, Nasser explained his actions to U Thant in this way: Israel had embarked on changing the existing regime in Syria, Syria had asked for Egypt's help under their mutual defense agreement, and Egypt was committed to honoring that pact. Accordingly, on May 13 what Rikhye refers to as the UAR cabinet had met and decided to move troops into Sinai. Rikhye then gives this account of Nasser's description of the deliberations of the thirteenth:

> Once his [Nasser's] cabinet had decided to move the UAR forces to the Sinai, [and] deploy them along the International Frontier and at Sharm-al-Sheikh, they anticipated Israel's reaction. His military chiefs were of the view that instead of giving Israel all the advantages of taking the initiative, the UAR forces should invade Israel once and for all and put an end to the conflict. Nasser had asked, "Are you ready to attack Israel?" They replied, "We will never be in a better position than now. Our forces are well-equipped and trained. We will have all the advantage of attacking first. We are sure of victory. But if we lose then we

deserve to be the losers and will accept Israel as better than us." Nasser said that his whole cabinet was determined to undo the consequences of events of 1956 but were divided on whether the UAR should invade Israel. He himself did not favor war. He was committed to peace and therefore he did not agree to an attack. It was finally agreed that the UAR would fight only if attacked by Israel.[2]

Heikal, however, describes the meeting of May 13 as between Nasser and ʿAmr only, and later Sadat, as we saw in chapter 1. He says it lasted from 7:30 P.M. until well after midnight and claims to have been with Nasser until the latter went to bed at 2:30 A.M. on the fourteenth, but he does not say whether he participated in the discussion with ʿAmr. He says Nasser and ʿAmr agreed that Egypt could not remain silent; events demanded that it be prepared for all eventualities. They also agreed that the General Staff should be summoned to an urgent meeting with ʿAmr the following morning to discuss measures to be taken in order to be prepared. They discussed sending the chief of staff, General Fawzi, to Damascus to inform the Syrian command of the measures decided on and to consider a response to an anticipated escalation of the situation. Heikal makes no mention of a decision having been taken either to mobilize or to start moving troops.

After a few hours' sleep, Nasser went to his office early on the fourteenth, expecting ʿAmr at least to call on the telephone before meeting with his officers. Meanwhile, Nasser consulted with a number of senior figures: Vice-President Muhieddin; Sidqi Suleiman, the prime minister; Dr. Mahmoud Fawzi, vice-president for foreign affairs; Ali Sabri, secretary general of the Arab Socialist Union; "and a number of members of the Supreme Executive Council."

ʿAmr did not call before his meeting, however. Rather, he called shortly before it was over to tell Nasser that he and his commanders had decided to send designated units to Sinai and that he had issued instructions to this effect in his capacity as deputy commander-in-chief. Heikal comments that there is no record of what passed between the two men during this conversation and the only clue is the minor changes ʿAmr made by hand to the original draft of his general order, which had already been typed, judging by the photocopy Heikal produces.[3]

Heikal does not say it in so many words, but his account can be read to say that ʿAmr took the decision to send troops into Sinai and began issuing orders to that effect without informing Nasser, who learned of it only after the orders had been issued. That does not seem to be borne out by Heikal's account of the subsequent discussion of the UNEF question, but it would not be inconsistent with what we now know about the Nasser-ʿAmr relationship.

The accounts of the May 14 General Staff meeting with ʿAmr given by Generals Fawzi and Murtagi in their memoirs indicate that far from there being a discussion of alternative courses of action, these officers were simply given orders for implementing decisions already taken. ʿAmr and his staff must have stayed up all night preparing a briefing and cutting orders for troop movements and mobilization. Perhaps ʿAmr thought he was carrying out what had been agreed to, but perhaps he was trying to force the pace. Whatever the case, Nasser went along with it. He certainly spoke as though he had dominated and controlled the decision-making process and gave no hint of any problems of insubordination.

If Heikal's account is correct, Nasser did not consult with his "cabinet," as he claimed to U Thant. Use of the term *cabinet* may have been the result of a linguistic problem; he probably meant the Supreme Executive Committee of the Arab Socialist Union. Theoretically the highest executive body of the state, it was used largely to sanctify decisions already taken by Nasser, according to Muhieddin.[4] Its members in 1967 were Nasser, ʿAmr, Sadat, Muhieddin, al-Shafiʿi, and Suleiman, i.e., the surviving active members of the original Revolutionary Command Council plus the prime minister. Al-Shafiʿi is the only member not named by Heikal, and he presumably is included under "a number of members." Thus Nasser did consult with the council, but there appears to have been no meeting and those consulted appear to have had only a small role in the decision-making process, which remained the exclusive domain of Nasser and ʿAmr—and perhaps only ʿAmr in this case.

The Removal of UNEF

Rikhye states that Nasser told U Thant on May 23 that "his military advisers noted that if hostilities broke out UNEF would be caught in between the antagonists. UNEF should therefore be asked to withdraw from the Sinai, but they could remain in the Gaza Strip. He added, 'This is the advice I received from my military experts and so I accepted it. Since the military wanted UNEF to vacate the Sinai, being a military matter I told General Fawzi to write to Commander UNEF.' "[5] According to General Fawzi's account, it was ʿAmr, not Nasser, who gave him the order, and it was given on the morning of May 16. This implies that the decision to ask UNEF to move was not taken before the fifteenth, a day after the decision to move troops.

It is perhaps noteworthy that Nasser claimed to U Thant that the original decision to request partial withdrawal was dictated by military necessity rather than by some larger political purpose, such as removal of the traces of 1956. In any event, the decision appears not to have received careful study, and its implications not to have been fully understood at the time it was made. In particular the Foreign Ministry (as opposed to the office of the vice-president for foreign affairs, Dr. Mahmoud Fawzi)* claims not to have been consulted, and by Nasser's account the request

*Fawzi, the grand old man of foreign affairs, had an office off Tahrir Square, near the Kasr al-Nil bridge, a mile or two from the Foreign Ministry. His functions were not clear to foreign embassies at the time, but he seems to have been used as an adviser by Nasser more than they realized. He may not have informed the Foreign Ministry of all his activities.

was treated as a purely military matter between two commanders. There was more consultation than the above account would indicate, however, and Nasser did realize the political significance such a request would have, even if ʿAmr did not. Judging by the failure to mention it in the accounts we have, however, Nasser seems not to have considered the possibility that the United Nations would not agree to a redeployment or partial withdrawal. Its unwillingness to do so came as an unpleasant surprise to Egypt. Had Nasser realized that would be the reaction, he might have thought twice before agreeing to make the request.

According to Heikal (*Al-Infijar*, pp. 457–77), thinking about a withdrawal of UNEF began some time earlier. It came up during preparations for the third Arab summit at Casablanca in 1964. It was renewed late in 1966 as a result of a proposal by ʿAmr in response to propaganda campaigns by other Arab states (notably Jordan and Saudi Arabia) accusing Egypt of hiding behind the force. Then it appeared a third time in a proposal made by King Hussein to cooperate with the United Arab Command in the spring of 1967.

Heikal states that in the meeting between Nasser and ʿAmr on the evening of May 13, the subject of UNEF "imposed itself" on the discussion of plans and measures to support Syria. It was agreed that helping Syria required the armed forces to be ready to fight, that the intention to fight and its requisite mobilization were difficult to carry out if UNEF stood as a barrier between Egyptian forces and their freedom of operation along the front, and that accordingly, something would have to be done with regard to UNEF to give them this freedom. There was disagreement, however, about what should be done. ʿAmr thought Egypt should ask for the total withdrawal of UNEF. Nasser thought that asking for withdrawal of the entire force would create an international problem which would negate the psychological effects of concentrating forces in Sinai. Heikal writes: "Then it would lead to the placing of obstacles in the way of the [Egyptian] forces if they were required to move." (That may be a reference to unfavorable international reaction, but Heikal's meaning is not clear.) Nasser therefore thought that Egypt's request should be only for withdrawal of U.N. forces from the 1948 international border with Palestine. "This was the opinion on which the May 13 discussion . . . settled." Heikal states, "and it was the view which was known to the General Staff in its meeting of May 14, when the subject of UNEF came up in a discussion of the plan for movements in the Sinai."[6]

Nasser discussed the matter with Mahmoud Fawzi on the morning of May 14 and again at noon on the fifteenth. Heikal says he had the good fortune to be present. Dr. Fawzi brought a collection of background papers and confirmed Nasser's belief that he was free to demand the withdrawal of UNEF at any time; the request did not have to go to the Security Council or the General Assembly. Nasser then said that he did not want to end the work of UNEF entirely for at least three reasons. First, he did not want his objective to be lost in the confusion. His goal was to help Syria if it was attacked by Israel, not to terminate the work of UNEF. He did not want to create an international crisis which would divert attention from the matter of Syria. Second, Gaza would be Israel's first objective in the event of hostilities, and it was difficult to defend. Concentrating forces there would be a waste. It would be better to isolate it from the rest of the army from the beginning. And third, terminating UNEF entirely would lead, among other things, to the stationing of Egyptian troops at Sharm al-Shaykh, which would require closure of the Strait of Tiran to Israeli shipping. He was not sure it was the right time for that. Heikal notes that neither Nasser nor Dr. Fawzi brought up the U.S. commitment to Israel regarding freedom of navigation in the Gulf of Aqaba. It apparently did not occur to them, if they remembered the commitment, that it might complicate matters.

Nasser then said that given these considerations, he wanted the request to UNEF to be for withdrawal from the international border of May 14, 1948, which would permit him to come to Syria's rescue without raising the issues of Gaza or Sharm al-Shaykh. In fact, if possible he would like to concentrate all of UNEF in Gaza to protect it from an Israeli attack.

Dr. Fawzi had agreed that the request for the withdrawal should be sent to General Rikhye. Such a move would mean that from the beginning the matter was being treated as one of practical arrangements. Furthermore, the Egyptian request should be framed to make it clear that it meant withdrawal from the international frontier, not Gaza or Sharm al-Shaykh.

The following morning, May 16, Nasser found on his desk an envelope from ʿAmr containing the text of the proposed request for withdrawal. Heikal gives a text in Arabic which matches the English version given to Rikhye.* Except for the awkward phrase "to your information" in the opening sentence, there is no fault in translation except that the word *all* before "these forces" was not used in the original Arabic, which simply said "these forces" (*hadhihi al-quwat*).

The text seemed to meet Nasser's requirements, but he got in touch with ʿAmr and asked for the English text, which he had before him half an hour later. He noted the discrepancy about "all these troops" and called Dr. Fawzi, who said he was right to raise the question because the terminology might lead to a misunderstanding. Fawzi suggested that it could be taken care of by changing the word *withdrawal* to *redeployment*.

Nasser then called ʿAmr and told him of Fawzi's proposal, saying he was particularly concerned about Gaza and remained convinced that concentration of UNEF in Gaza would be the best course. ʿAmr replied that the message was already on its way but he would try to intercept it and change the terminology as requested. ʿAmr called back that evening, at

*English text follows.

about the time the message was delivered to Rikhye, to say that they had been unable to prevent delivery of the request in its original form. This statement is not credible to me. ʿAmr had plenty of time to stop the messenger between morning and 10:00 P.M. It sounds as though he did not want to change the message. Is this another case of ʿAmr's insubordination?

According to Heikal, nothing could be done, but Nasser thought the matter could be taken care of in subsequent contacts and the clarifications which the United Nations might ask from Egypt during the political contacts which would ensue. The problem was that there were no subsequent clarifications or political discussions, by Egyptian choice. They would have been academic in any event, because the U.N. Secretariat was not going to accept a partial withdrawal, even if it was called a redeployment, and the Egyptians should have known that.

It is too bad, nevertheless, that if the Egyptians were talking about a redeployment only, they did not make clear what they had in mind. Their position would have been somewhat more tenable at the United Nations and elsewhere, and the impression that they were hellbent on a military confrontation would have been softened. That might have affected attitudes in Washington in their favor. As it was, they made no effort to clarify their position.

The two days following the Egyptian request of May 16 were critical. If a way could have been found to divert or disarm the Egyptian demand, war could probably have been avoided. U Thant has been blamed by many for the rigidity of his response, which forced Nasser's hand, and, alternatively, for not referring the Egyptian request to the General Assembly, which had jurisdiction, or calling a meeting of the Security Council under Article 99, rather than acceding to the request unilaterally. His defenders argue that he had no choice, and the attitude of the Communist and nonaligned states, most of which supported Egypt unquestioningly, meant that any effort to use the U.N. machinery to divert Egypt was doomed to failure. Many Egyptians argue, however, that if UNEF had only had the flexibility to adjust to the UAR military presence on the border for a while, the crisis would have blown over and the troops would have been withdrawn.

Heikal blames Bunche for U Thant's rigidity and claims that Bunche and the U.N. Secretariat had information making clear the limits of the Egyptian request, but Heikal does not specify what that information was. The evidence available is contradictory. For instance, Rikhye's report of the Thant-Nasser conversation of May 23, which appears in *Sinai Blunder*, implies that the Egyptians had decided in their May 13 meeting to deploy troops "along the International Frontier and at Sharm al-Sheikh." On page 163 of the same book, however, we find a postwar conversation between Rikhye and Mohamed Riad, who was Mahmoud Riad's chef de cabinet. Riad asked Rikhye, "But why did you withdraw UNEF? We didn't want you to pull out . . . you left us with no option but to reply the way we did [with the May 18 request for a total pullout]. Besides, we never asked you to withdraw from Sharm al-Sheikh. We only asked you to withdraw your posts in the Sinai, your observation posts close to the international frontier."

Similarly, Mahmoud Riad told me on June 3, 1989, that the only official version of what was asked for by the UAR was the text of his note of May 18, which ʿAmr (not Nasser) had ordered him to send and which speaks only of withdrawal from "our borders," not Sharm al-Shaykh. He makes a similar statement on page 18 of *The Struggle for Peace in the Middle East:* "I did not ask for withdrawal of UN troops from Gaza and Sharm al-Shaykh; my request was restricted to withdrawal from our international border." He commented that U Thant's insistence on all or nothing was foolish, because once UNEF was withdrawn the UAR had no alternative to implementing the 1951 law forbidding passage of Israeli cargo.

Riad said Rikhye's account was not to be taken seriously because Rikhye had made an error and was trying to defend it. His account is nevertheless the fullest we have, and it is consistent with the record and with Egyptian attitudes as seen by U.S. diplomats in Cairo at the time. Let us look briefly at his account.

The original request for redeployment of UNEF was in the letter from General Fawzi to General Rikhye, discussed earlier in this chapter. It was delivered by Brigadier General ʿIzz ad-Din Mukhtar, accompanied by Brigadier General Ibrahim Sharqawy, chief of staff of the UAR-UNEF liaison staff, at 10:00 P.M. on the sixteenth. The letter read:

> Commander UNEF (Gaza)
>
> To your information, I gave my instructions to all UAR armed forces to be ready for action against Israel, the moment it might carry out an aggressive action against any Arab country. Due to these instructions our troops are already concentrated in Sinai along our eastern border. For the sake of complete security of all UN troops which install OP's along our borders, I request that you give orders to withdraw all these troops immediately. I have given my instructions to our commander of the Eastern Zone concerning the subject. Inform back the fulfillment of this request.
>
> Yours,
> Farik Awal (M. Fawzy) COS of UAR

The tone is just short of peremptory. Its meaning seems clear: UNEF should withdraw the troops maintaining observation posts (OPs) along Egypt's borders (plural). Where they were to go was not specified.

It is important to bear in mind that UNEF was stationed in three distinct sectors (see map 2): along the Armistice Demarcation Line separating the Gaza Strip from Israel, not considered an international frontier but a temporary truce line; along the established, pre-1948 international border of Palestine, which ran from the Mediterranean to the Red Sea; and at Sharm al-Shaykh. UNEF had a number of observation posts along the armistice line in the Gaza Strip, five along the international border, and one at Sharm al-Shaykh. The armistice line was manned by Indians, Scandinavians, and Brazilians, the Sinai and Sharm al-Shaykh OPs by Canadians and Yugoslavs.

Egyptians argue that "along our borders" referred only to the established international border. The plural *borders* was a direct translation of *hudud*, a plural meaning "bounds" or "limits" which is commonly used in that form to designate either a single border or more than one. Dr. Fawzi, at least, was literate enough in English to realize that the use of the plural could be interpreted to mean not just the international border but others as well, but he does not seem to have noticed in this case. That is just one instance of general Egyptian carelessness in handling this affair.

Sharm al-Shaykh is on the coast, and one could argue that border and coastline are different and that the Egyptians had never thought of Sharm al-Shaykh as being "along our borders." If such was the case, they should have made more of an effort to make that clear. That they did not do so raises serious doubts about the sincerity of their claims; or perhaps more precisely, it raises questions about how well Nasser reflected the total Egyptian position, assuming Heikal's description of his position is accurate.

Far from drawing a distinction between Sharm al-Shaykh and the international border, the Egyptians twice told Rikhye he would have to withdraw from Sharm al-Shaykh. On May 16, when he responded to Fawzi's letter by telling Generals Mukhtar and Sharqawy he would have to ask the secretary general for instructions, Mukhtar replied, according to Rikhye: "General, you are requested to order the immediate withdrawal of UNEF troops from al-Sabha [the principal OP along the international border] and Sharm al-Shaykh tonight. Our supreme command anticipates that when Israel learns of our request to you, they will react immediately. In anticipation of any action they might take, our army must establish control over al-Sabha and Sharm al-Shaykh tonight."[7] That is pretty precise. The following day Sharqawy conveyed a further request, apparently oral, from Fawzi asking for withdrawal of the Yugoslav detachments in Sinai within twenty-four hours. In the case of Sharm al-Shaykh, Rikhye was given "forty-eight hours or so."[8]

It is theoretically possible that Rikhye misreported these two events or that the two officers were exceeding their instructions or being officious. Misreporting is unlikely, since Rikhye was recounting the conversations to New York immediately after they occurred. For the officers to exceed their instructions is perhaps more likely, but not much. Discipline in the

Egyptian army did not encourage individual initiative. What we know of ʿAmr's attitude makes it seem more likely that they were reflecting what they thought he had ordered. In any event, the UNEF commander could not be expected to know that they were freewheeling, if they were. He was speaking to senior officers of the UAR army, who had just conveyed a written message from the chief of staff. They certainly knew more than Rikhye did about what the UAR position was, and it would have been dangerous to ignore or defy them.

When Rikhye reported the May 16 exchange, U Thant acted quite properly in seeking clarification from the UAR permanent representative, al-Kony, a dour and rigid fellow with whom the Americans and the U.N. Secretariat found it difficult to deal, although the Secretariat rated him less difficult than the U.S. delegate, Arthur Goldberg. The UAR request was news to al-Kony, and he immediately queried Cairo. Heikal reproduces the text of al-Kony's cable, which makes several points. Al-Kony states that Bunche had called him to meet with the secretary general. He notes that Bunche had issued the invitation, was present at the meeting, and was the official spokesman. Bunche had informed him of the receipt of a telegram from Rikhye reporting that the Egyptians were asking for the withdrawal of UNEF from the armistice lines *(khutut al-hudna).* The withdrawal of UNEF from any portion of the armistice lines would make its entire presence out of the question. The government in Cairo alone, not the chief of its armed forces, had the authority to request withdrawal. If such a request was presented, the secretary general would inform the General Assembly. Al-Kony interjects at this point that UNEF was present in Egypt with the agreement of the UAR government. The agreement in this respect was between the UAR government and the secretary general, not the General Assembly. Therefore the UAR government had the right to demand the withdrawal of UNEF at any time, and the secretary general had no option but to withdraw it, although he could inform the General Assembly what he was doing. Al-Kony says Bunche and U Thant agreed.[9]

Ambassador Kamel in Washington reported that he had been called by the Department of State late at night and informed that the Egyptian authorities had requested the withdrawal of UNEF to Gaza. Heikal comments that this means the Americans understood what Egypt's intentions were.

The following day, May 17, al-Kony sent a long telegram reporting agitation among U.N. delegations and a conversation he had with U Thant and Bunche in which the former asked if al-Kony had any response from Cairo. Al-Kony said it would take at least twenty-four hours. He suggested to Cairo that if it was decided to request the total withdrawal of UNEF, it should be delayed until the current special session of the General Assembly was over in order to avoid debate on the matter in that body. His recommendation was rejected by Nasser, and Mahmoud Riad recommended that Egypt head off any attempt by U Thant to seek a modification of the UAR request.

Accordingly, a telegram drafted by Riad was sent to al-Kony. Heikal gives this text: "Ask for a meeting with U Thant and advise him not to send any appeal regarding the emergency forces in order to avoid its being rejected by Cairo, which would lead to embarrassment for him, something we do not want at all" (*Al-Infijar,* p. 474). Al-Kony informed U Thant of this message on May 17, thus effectively closing off any search for clarification. Not that it would have made much difference.

Nasser meanwhile was meeting with ʿAmr, Muhieddin, Sadat, Sabri, Suleiman, Dr. Fawzi, and Mahmoud Riad to discuss their next steps in light of the reaction in New York. According to Heikal (*Al-Infijar,* pp. 474–77), Nasser expressed the view that Bunche was complicating the affair so that the Egyptians could no longer discuss redeployment but had to choose between all of UNEF or none. He was imposing on the Egyptians a choice: accept the fait accompli and withdraw their request or accept escalation of the situation by asking for total withdrawal. Bunche knew that the first choice would cause Egypt to lose all its credibility and the second would lead to danger. Nasser thought it would be best for Egypt to request total withdrawal; he did not think it could wait until the end of the special session as recommended by al-Kony because its request had not come out of the air but had been a reaction to the Israeli troop concentrations. The wheel of events was turning and left Egypt no choice but to request total withdrawal. Not to do so would enable Bunche to embarrass Egypt, and it was better that the decision be the Egyptians' and not Bunche's.

After discussion, the meeting agreed with these views, and Riad sent this message to U Thant on May 18:

> The Government of the United Arab Republic has the honor to inform your Excellency that it has decided to terminate the presence of the United Nations Emergency Forces from the territory of the United Arab Republic and the Gaza Strip.
>
> Therefore, I request that the necessary steps be taken for the withdrawal of the Force as soon as possible.
>
> I avail myself of this opportunity to express to Your Excellency my gratitude and warm regards.
>
> Mahmoud Riad, Minister of Foreign Affairs[10]

With regard to Riad's remark reported above that he had never requested withdrawal of UNEF from Sharm al-Shaykh, it is difficult to see how the phrase "territory of the United Arab Republic" can be read to exclude Sharm al-Shaykh. If that was nevertheless what the Egyptians still meant on May 18, it is surprising that they did not use any of the numerous channels they had available to them to send a message to that effect to someone. This would not be the last time, however, that the Egyptians thought they were saying one thing but conveyed something very different.

Reading Heikal's account of all this, one is struck by his assumption that Bunche is responsible for the U.N. Secretariat's hard-line position and that were it not for him, U Thant would have gone along with the original Egyptian request for partial withdrawal. Heikal seems to have convinced himself that this was part of an elaborate Israeli-American plot to get Nasser, and that Bunche was carrying out the orders of the U.S. government in this respect. The negative Egyptian impression of Bunche was generated to a certain extent by al-Kony, who thought Bunche was an agent of the United States and whose obsession with him even the Egyptians recognized as excessive.* The idea that someone else in Bunche's position would have recommended that U Thant go along with the initial Egyptian request, however, shows little understanding of the situation in which UNEF would find itself.

Where does all this leave us? Briefly, it seems evident that whatever Nasser may have wanted, 'Amr wanted total withdrawal of UNEF from the beginning. Nasser did not want to terminate UNEF but was unrealistic in thinking it would abandon most of its OPs and withdraw to Gaza. Even that proposition seems never to have been put squarely to the United Nations. More important, no thought seems to have been given in advance to the possibility that a request for partial withdrawal would be unacceptable to the U.N. Secretariat. There was a serious lack of imagination in that regard. Once they had plunged ahead, the Egyptians were unable or unwilling to back down, even though they had reason to believe the original cause for their actions no longer existed. They went ahead with the request for total withdrawal, knowing that it was a very dangerous, even foolish, step. In their view U Thant's response left them no choice. They did not consider whether they had given him any alternative.

Closure of the Strait

Up to this point Egypt was in control of the situation. Egyptian officials were making the decisions and issuing the orders in light of what they saw as Egypt's national interests. Once they called for UNEF's with-

*According to a former senior Egyptian Foreign Ministry official, al-Kony told Thant that Bunche was persona non grata in Cairo, which was untrue. He was persona non grata to al-Kony. When Mahmoud Riad realized what al-Kony had done, he instructed him to tell Thant that Bunche was in fact welcome; but it was too late, and Bunche refused to accompany Thant on his trip. I am told he was too sick to go, in any event. It is not clear how much difference his being there would have made, but one cannot help thinking that Thant would have been better off if he had had an experienced staff member, perhaps Brian Urquhart, with him when he met with Nasser, because he knew little about the area and its problems, according to the Egyptians.

drawal, however, turning back became difficult if not impossible. They had tapped into a current of popular reaction which eventually carried them away. The question posed immediately was what to do about the Strait of Tiran now that UNEF was gone. Cairo waited three days before deciding to close it, but by Egyptian officials' own accounts they had made that decision inevitable by sending troops to Sharm al-Shaykh to replace the UNEF troops there. Opinion seems to have been far from unanimous in favor of doing so, however, at least in the military.

It has been argued that Nasser was testing the waters, that he did not want war, that he was waiting to see what Israel's reaction to the removal of UNEF would be before deciding to close the strait, and that Eshkol's moderate Knesset speech on the evening of May 22 convinced him that Israel was not ready to fight and he "could now go on the warpath without having to fear. . . . he was greatly encouraged in this by the over-whelming confidence displayed by the Egyptian pilots at Bir Gifgafa . . . when [he] . . . visited them that day."[11] At one time this assessment sounded plausible, but Nasser took the decision to close the strait before going to Bir Gifgafa. And while Eshkol's speech may have been a factor in his increasingly uncompromising posture, Nasser had already decided to take the step well before Eshkol spoke. According to Nasser's speech of July 23, the decision was made by the Supreme Executive Council on May 22. But since Nasser announced closure at Bir Gifgafa on that day, the council must have met earlier. According to the Cairo press at the time, he went to Bir Gifgafa, accompanied by ʿAmr and other senior of-ficers, at "noon." Therefore the council must have acted that morning at the latest. According to Sadat (*In Search of Identity*, p. 172), Nasser told the council that if they closed the strait the chances of war were 100 per-cent. He then asked if the armed forces were ready. ʿAmr replied, "On my head be it, boss! Everything is in tip top shape." According to Hus-sein al-Shafiʿi, ʿAmr actually said *bi raqbiti*, "on my neck be it." Everyone but Suleiman then agreed that the strait should be closed.

Muhieddin confirms the substance of Sadat's account. He told me that those in the meeting felt there was no alternative. Not to close the strait would make them look foolish before the rest of the Arab world.[12] Al-Shafiʿi also confirmed this account, saying that Nasser "explained the question of closing the Gulf of Aqaba as the last remaining trace of the aggression of 1956 which could be removed and said this would increase the expectation of military confrontation from 80 percent to 100 per-cent."[13]

Heikal's account (*Al-Infijar*, pp. 514–19) says the meeting began at 9:00 P.M. on the twenty-first and lasted until 12:30 A.M. on the twenty-second. A limited number of ministers as well as military experts at-tended in addition to the members of the Supreme Executive Council. Heikal reports that Nasser said the chances of war would go up to 50 percent if the strait were closed and that given the increased danger, the essential issue was the state of readiness of the armed forces. If they were not ready, he could cover for them politically. It would be difficult, but he did not want to put an impossible burden on the armed forces. ʿAmr replied in effect that he saw no alternative to closure of the strait, that the forces were "ready for the situation and had both defensive and offensive plans." The military orders regarding the operation of the closure were issued on the morning of the twenty-second, to take effect at dawn on the twenty-third.

Heikal confirms that an important factor in the timing was U Thant's scheduled arrival on the twenty-third. The Egyptians wanted to have the decision announced before Thant came so he would not try to dissuade them from doing it. Nasser said as much to Thant himself when they met.[14]

Here was a point where the Egyptians could have temporized and let themselves be saved from the inevitability of war. It would have been difficult, given the emotions which had been aroused, but Nasser had said he could still cover for the military if necessary. Thant's coming could provide the mechanism for a graceful pullback from the abyss. Egyptian officials could have allowed themselves to be talked out of closure and into submitting the case to the International Court of Justice, but they appeared not to be interested in salvation; they seemed to feel that they were in control of the situation and could deal with whatever Israel might have up its sleeve, and they moved deliberately to foreclose the U Thant option.

These internally consistent accounts from political sources are at odds with the accounts from military sources. According to them, closure was not inevitable. General Murtagi writes that on May 16 ʿAmr announced in a meeting with his officers that the withdrawal of UNEF had become necessary because of the troop movements in Sinai. The force had come at Egypt's request and was on one side of the line only, and the Arab opposition was exploiting it in its propaganda battle against Egypt. Murtagi goes on:

> As for Sharm al-Shaykh and the Gulf of Aqaba, the Marshal's view, as he told us, was that there was no fear. Thought had not yet been given to it, but attention was focused on the importance of Eilat and the southern Negev, and a large force must be prepared to isolate it from land and sea and prevent reinforcements and supplies from reaching it. . . .
>
> May 17 . . . on this day Operations asked the Marshal to speed up the sending of troops to Sharm al-Shaykh, which the international forces were going to leave, in order to precede Israel in any designs she may have had on it. Since the Marshal persisted in not denying any request made to him, he ordered that the commanders meet to look into the request from Operations, with a decision to be taken on his return in the evening.

The meeting was held and opinion settled on the view that there was no need to send forces to Sharm al-Shaykh and that doing so would force us to do one of two things. The first would be to abstain from exercising Egypt's legal right to control its territorial waters and to close the Gulf of Aqaba to Israeli navigation. In that case our attitude would be characterized as weak and would be subject to political and propaganda attack by some of the Arab States whose relations with us were not all they might be, and this was something which should be avoided.

The second was to exercise our legal rights and close the Gulf of Aqaba from Sharm al-Shaykh, and this would mean cutting off the political line of retreat and make war inescapable. . . . Given the fact that our forces were not the best, particularly since the best of them were fighting in the Yemen, we should avoid that. As long as navigation remained open in the Gulf of Aqaba it was not expected that Israel would occupy Sharm al-Shaykh, since there would be no justification for that in either domestic or world opinion.

Thus, those in the meeting, and they included the commanders of the three forces (Land, Air and Sea) and the Chief of Staff, and the Directors of Intelligence and Operations, arrived at the decision not to sent Egyptian forces to the area but to designate appropriate forces to do so if developments required it. . . . the Marshal agreed to this decision on his return and even added that the idea of sending troops to Sharm al-Shaykh was improbable and it was not intended to implement it. Unfortunately, two days after the meeting what we feared happened, and the High Command ignored its decision not to send troops and sent them in a way which can best be described as improvisational and unwise.[15]

This account is interesting for several reasons. First, it seems to confirm that before the delivery of the initial request on the sixteenth, the Egyptian military expected UNEF to be withdrawn from Sharm al-Shaykh. Second, it gives an insight into the improvisational nature of the decision-making process and would seem to indicate that the Egyptians were not following a master plan.

General Fawzi's version maintains that the decision to close the strait was taken on May 17, five days before the date given by Nasser, but he seems to be confused about when the closure was announced, and that throws his reliability regarding timing into doubt. He asserts that Nasser told him in 1968 that he had called the Supreme Executive Council, together with the prime minister, Suleiman, to a meeting on May 17. After discussing the political and military situation, the withdrawal of UNEF, and Marshal 'Amr's report on the possibility of occupying Sharm al-Shaykh, Nasser had called for a vote, and everyone but Suleiman had voted to close the Gulf of Aqaba to Israeli shipping. Suleiman and one member of the Executive Council not named by Nasser had wanted to separate the question of occupying Sharm al-Shaykh from that of closing the Gulf of Aqaba to Israeli shipping. At this point 'Amr had interjected, "How can

my forces stationed there simply watch the Israeli flag pass before them?"
(Heikal reports essentially the same remark by ʿAmr in his account of the
May 21–22 meeting.) The meeting had ended after this with no debate or
study of the issue. Fawzi asked why there had been a vote, and Nasser
replied, "The importance of the decision and the unity of opinion."

Fawzi comments that Nasser wanted a show of force and hoped to
arrive at his goal by political means and propaganda, whereas ʿAmr wanted
to escalate the military confrontation, knowing full well it would lead to
a military clash with Israel. Fawzi cites the lack of clear instructions as to
what the force at Sharm al-Shaykh was supposed to do about shipping
and the obvious lack of any prior planning about what units to send there
as evidence that occupation of that post with closure of the Gulf was not
an original intention of the planners. He says there was no mention of it
in the original mobilization orders of May 14 and thinking about it did
not begin until May 17, when ʿAmr called him in and told him to assemble the commanders the following evening to arrange for reoccupation of
Sharm al-Shaykh.

Fawzi met with the commanders on the seventeenth, as described by
Murtagi, and there was agreement that closure of the strait was not in
Egypt's interest because it did not have the forces to spare for the wid-
ened confrontation which would result and because its forces in central
and eastern Sinai were sufficient to protect Sharm al-Shaykh if needed.
When Fawzi gave ʿAmr a report of this discussion minutes before the
meeting of May 18, ʿAmr said, "But the political decision to close the
strait was issued *(sudira)* yesterday, and now it's incumbent on us to arrange the forces [to implement it]."[16] Fawzi goes on to repeat elsewhere
that the decision was issued on the seventeenth. This date cannot be rec-
onciled with the date in Heikal's account, which includes the text of the
order he says was issued on the twenty-second.

Yet another version is provided by Abdul Latif Baghdadi in his *Mudhakkirat* (p. 274). According to him, he, Hassan Ibrahim, and Kamal al-
Din Hussein, three of the original members of the Revolutionary Command Council who had been put out to pasture, called on Nasser on May
28 and he told them that "the plan was based from the beginning on
withdrawal of UNEF and returning to Sharm al-Shaykh." This implies
that Nasser was in favor of the actions taken from the beginning but does
not eliminate the possibility that he was talked or maneuvered into it by
ʿAmr and then put the best face on it he could.

From these accounts it appears that, as in the case of UNEF, the decision to occupy Sharm al-Shaykh and close the strait was taken without
a great deal of study. The operation has the earmarks of something decided on quickly, even impulsively, without thorough regard for the consequences. In particular, if we are to believe Generals Fawzi and Murtagi,
it was taken in spite of the military, who recommended against it but
whose recommendation may not have gone beyond ʿAmr. We do not

know whether Nasser knew of the military's views. He may have realized that closure of the strait would make war inevitable, but contemporary accounts suggest that he was quite relaxed about the risks. He was not interested in compromise. At some point between the fifteenth and the twenty-first he seems to have abandoned caution.

RISKING WAR WITH ISRAEL

By May 23 the Egyptians had accomplished a good deal, and they were prepared to leave it at that, although they were perhaps willing to go to the International Court of Justice to discuss navigation in the Gulf of Aqaba and wanted to revivify the Egypt-Israel General Armistice Agreement. They had answered their Arab critics, who had accused them of hiding behind UNEF and conspiring in the supply of Iranian oil to Israel. Nasser's, and Egypt's, prestige had never been higher, and the entire Arab world was rallying around. The world press was coming to Cairo to report these startling developments. Even King Hussein, whom Nasser recently had labeled publicly as an adulterer (or fornicator or whoremonger, depending on how one translates ʿahr), had ceased his propaganda attacks on Nasser, and a new era in Arab politics seemed in the offing. Israel had been pushed into a corner and would take a terrible licking if it tried to fight its way out—or so it looked to the public in Cairo, judging by the tone of the press and other media.

Had Nasser gotten away with it, it would have been a famous victory. Had he stopped at the end of the first stage and not called for the withdrawal of UNEF, he would have accomplished his initial goal of deterring Israel and he would have gotten away with it. Had he stopped at the end of the second stage and not closed the Strait of Tiran, he would have increased the risk of war substantially and would eventually have regretted that he had lost his excuse for not taking a more active anti-Israel policy, but he probably would have gotten away with it, at least for the time being. Success bred an appetite for more success, however, and he pushed to the third stage, where war became inevitable.

None of Nasser's decisions makes sense unless he thought his armed forces were ready to take on Israel's. Here the evidence is contradictory again, and there is no agreement on this issue among the survivors from his regime. This matter is discussed more fully in the next section of this chapter. At this point it will suffice to say that Nasser's public actions were those of a man who seemed to be full of confidence in his armed strength.

The obverse of this confidence in UAR capabilities was a belief that Israel was weak and divided and afraid to fight without outside support. There is much anecdotal evidence of this belief: pamphlets issued to the troops showing the disparity between Israeli and Egyptian arms, a variety

"We shall impose by force." Poster which appeared on the streets of Cairo on the morning of May 23, 1967.

of remarks by Nasser and others, posters and cartoons showing Egyptians running over Israelis who are depicted as derby-wearing midgets in the worst anti-Jewish tradition, and the attitudes Egyptians took toward those counseling restraint, particularly toward Americans who were seen as trying to protect Israel from righteous Arab wrath. In Cairo in those days the only question was when the United States would intervene to stop the march on Tel Aviv. This attitude is reflected in a poster (see figure) which suddenly appeared all over Cairo on the morning of May 23.

Foreign intelligence agencies did not share the Egyptians' confidence. The Americans had for years been of the view that the Israelis could take on all the Arabs at once. Israeli military officers seem to have had few doubts, and their estimate of Egyptian capabilities was quite low. The Egyptians were considered to be good in defensive positions but likely to break if their flank was turned. As noted earlier, the Soviets, who had hundreds of military advisers in Egypt, should have had a fairly accurate picture. But the upper echelons of the Soviet leadership had a quite unrealistic view of Egyptian capabilities, and that may have influenced the Egyptians to make the same sort of misappraisal. Immediately after the war, many Egyptians came forward to say they had known all along that the armed forces were in terrible shape, but none of them had spoken that way before the war, at least not to U.S. diplomats.

The unanswered question is whether Nasser knew the true state of his armed forces. If he did, why did he rush into a confrontation he should have known he would lose?

What Did Nasser Know?

Among the survivors of his regime there are two schools of thought about whether Nasser knew the true state of his armed forces when he elected to confront Israel. For some it is an article of faith that he did not know and had been misled by Marshal 'Amr. Fascinating revelations have come out since 1967 about the rivalry between these two men, a rivalry which was unsuspected by foreign observers as well as most Egyptians in June 1967. It clearly was a factor in Nasser's miscalculation, but defining its impact precisely is difficult.

Other survivors doubt that 'Amr could have prevented Nasser from knowing that his armed forces were unready. In their view, Nasser knew the true state of affairs in his military establishment but was engaged in a gigantic bluff and did not expect war, even though he said he did.

A third explanation which can be joined to either of the above is that Nasser's calculation of his strength was skewed by his misjudgment of the positions of the United States, the Soviet Union, and Israel.

Representative Views

Here I present summaries of views expressed by former Egyptian officials in my conversations in Cairo in June 1989 (or earlier in one case) and in London in the fall of 1990.

Zakaria Muhieddin

A member of the original Revolutionary Command Council (RCC) and a longtime associate of Nasser's, Muhieddin was vice-president and theoretically the third man in the regime after 'Amr, who was the first vice-president. He felt that Nasser had acted in a very uncharacteristic fashion. The president had said repeatedly that war would come at a time of his, or Arab, choosing, not someone else's. This would be when the Arab military forces were ready. The UAR armed forces had not in fact been ready to take on Israel, and even though Marshal 'Amr had absolute authority over the armed forces, Nasser had his ways of knowing what was really going on.

The problem had been one of quality rather than quantity. The best third of the army had been tied down in Yemen, and the remainder was poorly trained and unprepared. That plus the economic situation made it a poor time to take on Israel. Nasser knew this. He had acted like a man playing poker. He was bluffing, but a successful bluff means your opponent must not know which cards you are holding. In this case Nasser's opponent could see his hand in the mirror and knew he was only holding a pair of deuces.

All of this was out of character. In the early days of the revolution Nasser had been the most cautious member of the RCC; that was why he was its leader. He was forever saying, after they had taken a decision, "Let's think this over until tomorrow." After he came to power he gradually changed. He ceased consulting his colleagues and made more and more of the decisions himself. His tendencies in this regard may have been accentuated by diabetes, which Muhieddin said sometimes leads people to make rash decisions. That was the only rational explanation for his actions in 1967.

Mahmoud Riad

A career army officer, Riad was foreign minister from 1964 to 1971. He was not a member of the RCC but was a member of the Free Officers and apparently was trusted by Nasser. Nasser told Riad after the war that 'Amr had misled him about the capabilities of the armed forces (see Riad's *Amrika wa al-Arab*, p. 39). 'Amr had assured Nasser he could hold off Israel with one-third of his strength. Riad had questioned this at the time and had raised in particular with Nasser the question of whether Egyptian air defenses were adequate, but Nasser was unable to contradict 'Amr's assurances in this regard. Unfortunately, ʿAmr was not qualified to be a senior military commander. Egyptian intelligence had correctly predicted the Israeli attack on June 5 and Nasser had said as much to the senior officers, but ʿAmr had dismissed it and closed down Egypt's air defenses on the morning of June 5 because he wanted to visit units in Sinai that day. It was ʿAmr who had invented the excuse of U.S. participation in the Israeli attack and Nasser had believed him.

Sayyed Marei

Sadat's deputy in the National Assembly in 1967, Marei comes from a landowning family and was jocularly described as the regime's token feudalist. A banker and agriculturist, he was one of a few such people in the upper reaches of the hierarchy. To understand Nasser's actions, Marei told me, we must go back to 1961 and the breakup of the union with Syria. Nasser had been preoccupied with his prestige in the Arab world ever since. (Muhieddin made the same point and said Nasser had seen the 1962 Yemen revolution as a godsend which would enable him to restore his prestige and influence. This too was miscalculation; Nasser himself acknowledged the mistake to a National War College class in 1966.) Nasser was under attack from other Arab leaders for hiding behind UNEF, and King Faisal of Saudi Arabia in particular had gotten under his skin in this regard. (Mahmoud Riad, referring to repeated broadcasts from "Islamic Pact countries" which started out with a recording of Nasser telling a group of Palestinians that he was not going to recover their homeland for them, said these broadcasts had been especially galling.)

There was also the rivalry with ʿAmr, who controlled the army and commanded the loyalty of the officers. Nasser was unable to interfere in the armed forces but made speeches in which he appeared to be fully in control. He was bluffing. He had not expected war in either 1956 or 1967. He wanted to refurbish his image, not have a war.

Nasser tried on one occasion to reduce ʿAmr's power by creating a council which would result in reorganizing the defense establishment and removing ʿAmr from it, but ʿAmr had resigned in protest and Nasser had backed down. From then on he had no control over the army, and that was a major factor in the crisis.

Mohamed Hassanein Heikal

Heikal said that in 1967 Nasser still saw the world in terms of 1956. He still believed the myths about 1956 (for an example, I refer the reader to his remarks at Bir Gifgafa), and he believed he could get away with it again. The events of 1967 were a big adventure which did not turn out right. Nasser had wanted to withdraw UNEF and close the Strait of Tiran because both represented an embarrassment to him in inter-Arab politics. There had been considerable discussion of Egypt's state of readiness and

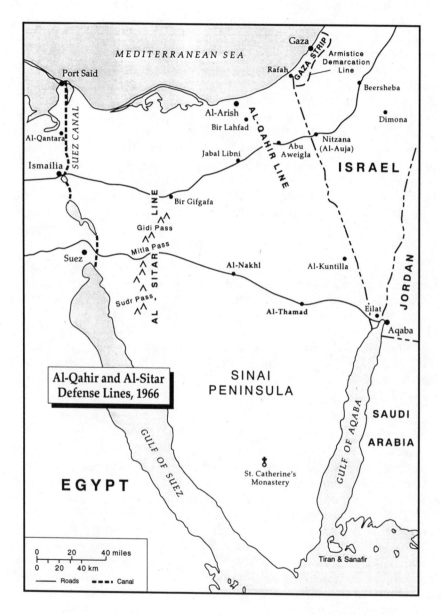

MEDITERRANEAN SEA

Gaza

GAZA STRIP

Armistice
Demarcation
Line

Rafah

Beersheba

Port Said

Al-Arish

Dimona

Al-Qantara

Bir Lahfad

AL-QAHIR LINE

Abu
Aweigla

Nitzana
(Al-Auja)

Ismailia

Jabal Libni

SUEZ CANAL

ISRAEL

Bir Gifgafa

LINE

Gidi Pass

Mitla Pass

Suez

Al-Nakhl

Al-Kuntilla

JORDAN

AL-SITAR

Sudr Pass

Al-Thamad

Eilat

Aqaba

**Al-Qahir and Al-Sitar
Defense Lines, 1966**

SINAI
PENINSULA

SAUDI

ARABIA

EGYPT

GULF OF SUEZ

GULF OF AQABA

St. Catherine's
Monastery

| 0 | 20 | 40 miles |
| 0 | 20 | 40 km |

Tiran & Sanafir

—— Roads   ▪▪▪ Canal

MAP 3

a decision had been taken not to make a preemptive strike. ʿAmr had assured Nasser that Egypt would be able to absorb an Israeli attack, even two waves, and then respond. There had been two plans of defense: al-Qahir (Mars, or the Conqueror) based on defense of the Rafa-al-Aweigla line, and al-Sitar (the Curtain), based on defense of the passes in central Sinai (see map 3). ʿAmr assured Nasser he could forget about al-Sitar, which was "just in case." Egypt would hold on the al-Qahir line and would have a capability for counterstrikes at Israel.

ʿAmr's assurances were based on the assumption that units would be where they appeared on the map and would be ready, but they were neither. Nasser had trusted ʿAmr because he was loyal and could maintain the loyalty of the army. He needed a professional soldier in that job, however, not a politician. (The remarks summarized here were made in a conversation in June 1983. Asked in 1989 whether Nasser knew the true state of the armed forces, Heikal said he did not.)

Ahmad Hassan al-Feki

Another ex-officer who apparently maintained good connections with the officer corps, al-Feki was undersecretary of foreign affairs and later ambassador to London. ʿAmr, not Nasser, had the loyalty of the armed forces, al-Feki said, and Nasser was not sure of them. He knew the state of the armed forces in 1967, however. He acted as he did because he was conceited. He had emerged successfully from earlier crises, particularly the crisis of 1956, and thought he could get away with challenging Israel. He was bluffing. He did not want war but thought that only he could make decisions.

Mustafa Abdul Aziz

Abdul Aziz, who was Muhieddin's special assistant in 1967, thought that Nasser did not know the true state of the armed forces. But Nasser was not alone; everyone was fooled. The Institute of Strategic Studies in London had issued a report saying that the Egyptian army was second only to Turkey's in the region, and it was widely believed. (I have been unable to find such a report. But the *Economist* of March 25, 1967, did report that "Egypt, which still has about 50,000 men engaged in the Yemen war, has the second strongest army in Africa," not the Middle East.) Abdul Aziz himself had believed that Egypt was ready to teach Israel a lesson; he had said as much to me at the time. If, however, Nasser had any doubts about the ability of his armed forces to fight Israel, he thought the Soviets would come to the rescue if his bluff was called, which he did not expect to happen. Nasser was not a gambler (there is wide disagreement with that proposition) and was wonderfully intelligent, but he was surrounded by people who were incapable of giving him good advice. After 1958 he had removed the naysayers from his immediate entourage.

THE RIVALRY WITH ʿAMR

A recurring theme in these remarks is the Nasser-ʿAmr rivalry. A good deal has been published in this regard since 1967, most of it in Arabic. Sources I have consulted include volume 2 of Baghdadi's *Mudhakkirat*, Riad's *Amrika wa al-Arab*, Fawzi's *Harb al-Thalath Sanawat*, Abdallah Imam's *Nasir wa ʿAmr*, and Farid's, *Min Mahadir Ijtimaʿat Abd al-Nasir*. The following is a brief summary of the main points in these accounts.

As young officers, Nasser and ʿAmr served in the army together and ʿAmr was Nasser's first recruit for the Free Officers Movement. They were the leading plotters and went together to see Muhammad Naguib on the night of July 19, 1952, to inform him of their plans for the revolution. Nasser and the RCC made ʿAmr the commander of the armed forces when the republic was declared in 1953, promoting him from major to brigadier over the heads of many better-qualified officers. ʿAmr remained in that position until 1967. He became the first Arab field marshal in 1958 and ever after was known as "the marshal."

The two men were very close to each other personally. ʿAmr's daughter married Nasser's younger brother, Hussein. Nasser named his son Abdul Hakim after ʿAmr. ʿAmr named his son Gamal. Their summer houses at Alexandria were next to each other, and Nasser referred to ʿAmr as "my brother" with apparent sincerity. Yet the two had been at odds since the early days of the revolution. ʿAmr was an effective politician, knitting together a clique of officers who controlled the military forces, doling out favors to friends and supporters, and punishing the recalcitrant or overly independent. He did not perform well in the 1956 campaign, however, and was held responsible by many for the break with Syria in 1961. He was then the vice-president in charge of the Syrian region of the UAR.

Nasser had tried to ease him out of command of the army on at least three occasions, in 1956, 1961, and 1962. This last effort is the best known. Nasser formed the Supreme Executive Council, which was to include all the members of the RCC with the stipulation that they would have to relinquish any executive positions which they held. ʿAmr, however, refused to surrender any of his prerogatives as commander of the armed forces and presented his resignation in protest at being asked to leave his position.

Subsequently, in a large meeting of officers, Nasser was taken by surprise by what amounted to a demonstration by those insisting that ʿAmr should remain in command. Nasser sensed that his own position was threatened and backed down. There was no stopping ʿAmr after that, and he consolidated his power and that of his clique of officers to monopolize control over all aspects of the armed forces, including the budget, which was untouchable. Officially he was the deputy commander-in-chief while Nasser was the commander, but that was a fiction.

There were many stories about ʿAmr and his officers. He was popularly alleged to be a hashish addict, and people made jokes about that. He secretly married a movie actress, reportedly scandalizing Nasser. His officers enjoyed a wide variety of *nomenklatura*-type privileges—importing cars and refrigerators for themselves in defiance of currency regulations and leading a life considerably more luxurious than that of their civilian colleagues. Both the Soviets and the Israelis commented later with some asperity about the preoccupation of Egyptian officers with their villas in Heliopolis and with material goods in general. The troops looked good on parade, but the officers were a would-be bourgeoisie. Too few of them were living in tents and working seriously on military preparedness. This became apparent on June 5.

It was ʿAmr's catering to these bourgeois tastes in a self-proclaimed socialist society, and the fact that he made the military a law unto itself, rather than his military competence, which earned him the loyalty of the officer corps.

To illustrate ʿAmr's belief that he was above the law, on one occasion, in the spring of 1967, he moved some of his men by force into a house in Giza which the U.S. Embassy had bought for an ambassadorial residence. He had decided to seize it for himself, even though the American purchase of the property had been approved by the UAR Foreign Ministry, the purchase price paid to the owner, and the property turned over to the Americans. Getting ʿAmr's men out proved a difficult task, requiring the intervention of the Foreign Ministry and the Presidency. Even then the Americans were never sure he would not try again.

ʿAmr also had absolute authority over what went on in Yemen. When, as the result of a violent incident in Taizz in the spring of 1967, the offices of the U.S. aid mission in that city were sacked by a mob, getting permission to send a team of Americans into the building to recover the classified papers left there required an extraordinary long-distance negotiation between Secretary of State Rusk and ʿAmr. No one but ʿAmr could authorize the entry.

Why did Nasser continue to tolerate ʿAmr? Speaking of the situation on June 7, when the magnitude of ʿAmr's incompetence had become evident, Sadat comments: "Militarily the situation was quite clear in Nasser's eyes. Why didn't he do anything about it? Why didn't he intervene—I must repeat this—dismiss ʿAmr on June 5, and take over command himself, or perhaps appoint another commander? We have no answers—only the huge question mark that looms large whenever Nasser had dealings with ʿAmr." [17]

It is clear in retrospect that even Nasser, whose authority people thought was absolute was afraid to confront ʿAmr because he was unsure of which side the officer corps would line up in the event of a struggle. He was in fact sharing power with ʿAmr, and neither was in total control. Mahmoud Riad comments:

It is hard to divine what was turning in Abdul Nasser's mind before June 1967. Did he fear that 'Amr would use his wide powers in the army to mount a coup against him? Or did he think the strong bonds of friendship between them would keep 'Amr from thinking in such terms? In either case, there is no doubt that there was a permament element of threat there. This was the influence which 'Amr's aides had over the army commanders, which had become apparent when 'Amr resigned from his position [in 1962].[18]

Baghdadi's memoirs are particularly rich in details of conversations on the subject with Nasser and other members of the RCC, who continued to have access to Nasser and 'Amr even after most of them had lost real power. Baghdadi reports Nasser as complaining, for instance, about 'Amr's refusal to get rid of officers who performed unsatisfactorily at the time of Suez (including Sidqi Mahmoud, the air force commander who was tried for incompetence after the June War) and in Syria, about 'Amr's failure to comply with Nasser's request for an enlarged presidential guard, about Shams Badran (who was 'Amr's leading hatchet man) for telling government companies that executive vacancies must be offered first to 'Amr's office, about officers who were plotting against him, perhaps with 'Amr's knowledge, and about his fears that 'Amr was creating a state within the state. At one point Nasser is quoted as saying: "You don't know Abdul Hakim. He has a southern character. He has been wounded. He will not forget that I told him to relinquish command." Nasser evidently feared 'Amr's control of the military and was unable to bring him to account.

And yet Nasser continued to play the role of the supreme commander, as in his address to the officers at Bir Gifgafa or his remarks to the senior commanders on June 2 that Israel would strike within the next three days and warning them to be ready. Asked why he did not take this warning seriously and why he insisted on visiting units in Sinai on the morning of June 5 and closing down the air defenses, 'Amr is reported to have replied that he did not know Nasser was a prophet or that heavenly inspirations had descended on him. Nasser had wrongly predicted no war in 1956 against the advice of his intelligence officers, and if he really thought Israel would strike on the fifth, why did he let an Iraqi delegation headed by the Iraqi prime minister and accompanied by Hussein al-Shafi'i go to Sinai on that day?[19]

General Murtagi describes how Nasser attended a meeting between 'Amr and his senior commanders on May 25 and ordered changes in troop dispositions to strengthen the defense of Gaza and augment the forces at Sharm al-Shaykh. It appears from this account that 'Amr accepted these changes, which were made at the expense of the overall defense plan. A shorter account, with no mention of troop changes, is given by General Fawzi. His account describes the two men meeting privately and taking decisions which were then announced to the assembled commanders, without discussion. Nasser obviously was playing a role in military decision making, and it sounds as though neither man could countermand the other. Certainly they could not do so in front of subordinates, and both obviously made an effort to keep their differences secret; otherwise everyone would have known about them. As it was, knowledge seems to have been confined to members of the Revolutionary Command Council and a few close associates, such as Badran. Riad comments:

> There is no doubt that the hidden struggle between Nasser and ʿAmr was among the principal reasons for the loss of the Sinai battle. It was a struggle of which no one knew the full extent. Nasser insisted on tolerating it in order to avoid a split in the regime. ʿAmr insisted on not disclosing it in order to keep his enormous power and total control over the armed forces and their budget, which made his command completely independent of the rest of the government apparatus.[20]

Riad illustrates the degree to which ʿAmr could conceal things from Nasser in his account of the progress of the fighting:

> In spite of all these weak points [which Riad has been discussing], a limited number of Egyptian units could have set up a defense line in the passes east of the Canal. This was the natural defense line. . . . this was clear to Abdul Nasser when he told Abdul Aziz Bouteflika, the Algerian Foreign Minister, in my presence, the afternoon of June 7, that the armed forces would retreat to this line and hold it to stop the Israeli advance. But it became clear to me the following day that while Nasser was talking about standing firm at the passes, ʿAmr had already issued orders the previous evening [June 6] for the withdrawal of all our forces to the west of the Canal. . . . ʿAmr's orders specified that the withdrawal was to be completed by the morning of June 7. . . . this was impossible, given the thousands of tanks and other vehicles and artillery units and the tens of thousands of soldiers in Sinai at the time.[21]

In other words, Nasser was apparently unaware of the chaos in Sinai at the time he spoke of defending the passes. It seems incredible that this could be the case, and Badran gives a different picture:

> On the sixth of June Israel was in control of the skies over the battlefield and the situation had become extremely difficult. . . . The Marshal called the President and informed him of the situation and the two agreed on withdrawing the forces west of the Canal. The President said to the Marshal, "Get the opinion of the senior officers and members of the RCC who may be there." (Some of the latter were frequenting the Marshal's office in order to follow the situation. I remember three of them: Hassan Ibrahim, Kamil al-Din Hussein and Abdul Latif Baghdadi. On that day there were only two of them. I can't remember which.) The Marshal asked opinions, starting with General Muhammad Fawzi, then

the Director of Operations, Anwar al-Qadi and General Ali ʿAmr, and all agreed. The two members of the RCC who were present also agreed. All this took place while the President was on the telephone. . . . And after the withdrawal was completed the President got in touch with the Marshal and ordered him to have the Fourth Armored Division return back across the Canal. It was considered a strategic reserve protecting the Egyptian state. He ordered him to send the division back across the Canal to occupy the passes and hold them. The Marshal reluctantly agreed and the rest of the story is known.[22]

General Fazwi gives yet a third account. It is worth repeating in some detail, because it illustrates the disarray which prevailed within the Egyptian military establishment and which was a major factor in Egypt's defeat. It does not say whether ʿAmr consulted Nasser on the withdrawal order, but Nasser plays no role in the account and elsewhere Fawzi quotes Nasser as chiding ʿAmr for not consulting him.

The first indication of the Marshal's intention to withdraw from Sinai came when a wireless signal from the High Command was sent to the commander of the Sharm al-Shaykh region at 05:50 on the morning of June 6, telling him to establish plans for complete withdrawal of his forces from Sharm al-Shaykh to the west of the Canal.

After noon on June 6, the Marshal said to me, "I want you to bring me quickly a plan for withdrawal of the forces from Sinai to west of the Canal. You have twenty minutes only."

I was surprised by this request. It was the first time an order was issued to me personally by the Marshal, whose psychological and nervous state was collapsing, in addition to the fact that the situation did not permit debate or discussion or to know the motives and thinking behind this order. The forces in Sinai, except for the 7th Infantry Division, were holding up to that time and there was definitely nothing which justified withdrawal.

I hurried to the Operations Room and called General Anwar al-Qadi, Chief of Operations, and Brigadier Tuhami, his deputy, and we sat for a short while thinking how to withdraw the forces . . . and we finished by setting down a very general plan . . . giving lines and times.

Then the three of us went to see the Marshal who was waiting for us behind his desk. . . . and Brigadier Tuhami began reading the plan, saying the forces will retreat to this line on this day, and to that line on the next . . . arriving at the final line west of the Canal on D-day plus 4, i.e. after three days and four nights.

When the Marshal heard these last words setting forth the time required for the withdrawal, he raised his voice a little and directing his speech to me, said, "Four days and three nights, Fawzi! I gave you an order to withdraw, period." Then he went into his bedroom, which was behind his office, in a state of hysteria . . . while the three of us stood astonished at his condition. Later, word arrived from Sinai via the Canal Command at Ismailiya that the Marshal had given orders to the commander at al-Arish to withdraw his forces, with their personal weapons only, beyond the Canal in one night . . . and that commander executed the order for himself, without informing his higher commander or adjoining units.[23]

Fawzi goes on to describe some of the communications problems which afflicted the Egyptians, with 'Amr giving orders without telling his staff, unit commanders calling up friends at the High Command to find out what was going on rather than going through channels, and General Murtagi learning of the withdrawal order from a passing military police officer, not from either of the commands above him. Murtagi asked the MP the source of the order and was told it was a personal order of the marshal, a phrase which had a magical effect in those days, and Murtagi withdrew to Ismailiya immediately. Fawzi also says that the Fourth Armored Division was told to defend the passes while other units withdrew. It did not make two crossings of the canal, as Badran alleges.

Which of these conflicting reports does one believe? Badran, 'Amr's faithful henchman, does not have a reputation for veracity. Fawzi's account is supported by others. For instance, Abdul Majid Farid told me that Nasser was not consulted about the June 6 withdrawal order. He had issued orders to his staff not to go to general headquarters once fighting started, and he personally did not go there until June 8 to avoid charges that he had interfered with the conduct of the war.[24] On the other hand, Sayyed Marei reports in his memoirs (vol. 3, p. 548), that Nasser told the Council of Ministers in Marei's presence, immediately after 'Amr's death, that he had been surprised at Egypt's unpreparedness when the battle began and that "the sudden collapse was what pushed him [Nasser] to issue the order for withdrawal of the Egyptian army from Sinai, but he had not expected the withdrawal to have the character of an exodus (irtihal)."

Whichever version we accept, it is evident that there was a high degree of impromptu, personal decision making, with little use of the formal command structure either for discussion and analysis of the options or for communicating the decision down the line.

It has long been evident to military commentators that the principal Egyptian failure in 1967 was one of leadership. Given their equipment and numbers, the Egyptians should have done better than they did. They had severe deficiencies in training and education, but properly led they should have given Israel a hard time. That was a reasonable expectation on everyone's part, including the Israelis, who were surprised at the ease of their victory. They had expected to win, but after a costly and bitter struggle.

Nasser's apparent belief that he was in a position to confront Israel did not seem entirely unreasonable at the time. He probably had more of the details of the armed forces' state of readiness than most chiefs of state, given his own military background, his status as commander in chief, the informal contacts he had with a variety of ex-officers who had their own contacts in the army, and the intelligence capabilities at his disposal (although Salah Nasr, the director of general intelligence, was reportedly an 'Amr man).

Or so it would seem, but the truth seems to be different. Abdul Majid Farid says that Nasser told him in August 1967 that, as Farid knew, he was a good chess player; had he known the truth, he would have played a different game. With regard to the utility of Nasser's longtime military associations, Farid says Nasser had tried to find out the truth using former military officers on his staff. They were to see their ex-colleagues in the military and sound them out on the readiness of the forces. 'Amr had learned of this and gone to Nasser demanding that it stop immediately, because it was contrary to a secret agreement between them that Nasser would not attempt to use his ex-officers in this fashion. Nasser, who always feared a clash between the military and the civilians, had acquiesced.[25]

The picture which increasingly emerges, then, is of a leader who was in effect the prisoner of an incompetent general. Whether Nasser realized how weak the officer corps was or whether he fully appreciated the weakness of the command, control, and communications aspects of the operation was perhaps irrelevant. He was not really in full control and had to contend with a commander who had the bit in his teeth and was determined to push through to an armed clash with Israel. Add to these problems the fact that 'Amr and Nasser were making last-minute changes in everything from tactical dispositions to unit commanders—often replacing commanders with some unqualified favorite who wanted his share of the glory—and it is small wonder that the Egyptians performed poorly. The argument can nevertheless be made that had 'Amr not panicked and given the order to withdraw, the Egyptians could have held for a while at the passes or at least done a more creditable job of defending them, although how long they could have done so without air cover was problematic.

That is a point for the military historians to argue. It suffices for our purposes to say that this part of Nasser's miscalculation was not as egregious as it seemed. He should have known better, but he was ill served. His problem was one of management rather than intelligence.

PLANNED OR IMPROVISED?

Were Nasser and 'Amr following a coherent plan, or were they improvising as they went along?* To foreigners in Cairo at the time, Egyptian

*A carefully reasoned argument that Nasser had not intended to seek a showdown with Israel can be found in "Nasser and the June War: Plan or Improvisation," by Leon Carl Brown, in *Quest for Understanding: Arabic and Islamic Studies in Memory of Malcolm H. Kerr* (Beirut: AUB Press, 1991).

actions looked preplanned and well organized. They were first of all inclined to view the Egyptian establishment as monolithic and to see Nasser
as an intelligent and sober leader who might get carried away by his own
rhetoric on public occasions but who was very careful in his private utterances and in his actions. It was inconceivable to most such observers that
the Egyptians would undertake a military movement on this scale without first putting some serious and detailed planning into it. The apparent
efficiency of the operation and the obvious élan and discipline of the troops
seen every day moving through Cairo were evidence of careful planning
and preparations—or so those of us sitting in Cairo thought.

There were also some minor phenomena that the U.S. Embassy ad-
duced as evidence to support the prior planning thesis. One was that a
large briefing book suddenly appeared on the desks of Foreign Ministry
officials, who would consult it when certain questions came up. Putting
such a book together was not the work of a couple of days. The Egyptians
later revealed that it was a briefing on the status of the Gulf of Aqaba and
the Strait of Tiran which had been prepared in the event of a referral of
that issue to the International Court of Justice. Salah Nasr, Egypt's director of intelligence, told the CIA station chief in effect that referral to the
court was the Egyptian ace in the hole, to be played at the right moment.
It seems to have been unconnected with the military movement, but the
Egyptians had obviously been giving serious and coordinated thought to
how they could restore their control over the Gulf of Aqaba by political
and legal means.

Another phenomenon was that military vehicles, previously marked
with minimal signs and symbols intelligible only to the initiated, suddenly blossomed out with elaborate insignias and unit designations, as
though the military, after years of anonymity, wished to advertise its
presence and the competence it had developed in secret. Judging by their
smiles and gestures, the drivers of these vehicles were delighted by the
general surprise at their existence. Some advance thought, although perhaps not too much, must have gone into the design and application of
the insignias. One morning I found myself alongside a truck that had
been so decorated. It evidently belonged to an artillery or missile unit,
because its insignia was a devil in the pharaonic-Baal pose, with a missile
of some sort in his upraised right hand, but the artist had painted the
hand backward. The missile could not be effectively launched forward
from that posture. In retrospect, that symbolized the entire operation.

Most important in influencing foreign attitudes, was the over-
whelming confidence of the Egyptians that they knew what they were
doing. It was expressed in many ways, from the public remarks of their
leaders to the attitude of the man in the street, from Nasser to the newspaper vendor. Such confidence must have come from something. As the
U.S. Embassy reported on one occasion, it was as though the Egyptians
had a secret weapon. All of these observations led the embassy to send

its telegram no. 8080 of May 26 referred to earlier (see text in the appendix, document 12) saying the Egyptians appeared to have been prepared for that moment for some time, perhaps as far back as the previous summer, and that the decision to move when the occasion arose was probably taken sometime after the breakdown of the U.S.-Egyptian wheat agreement in February 1967. Also as noted earlier, this view was not shared by the intelligence community in Washington, which concluded that Nasser was reacting to misinformation about Israel's intentions mistakenly supplied to him by the Soviet Union.

There were other indications which, had they been known, might have made the concerted plan theory more convincing at the time. These include the fact that, as Heikal noted, both Nasser and 'Amr had been thinking for some time about removing UNEF and restoring Egypt's control over the gulf. General Fawzi gives some different details in his memoirs.

> Since 1957 the political and military leadership had wanted to remove UNEF in order to control Egyptian territorial waters. . . .
>
> Both President Gamal Abd al-Nasir and Marshal 'Amr made it clear to me before 1967 that they wanted to seize on any international or regional situation which would permit doing away with that force. That opportunity came when Egypt declared that it was ready to enter battle against Israel if the latter attacked Syria. . . .[26]
>
> In 1965, when the first division came back from Yemen . . . Nasser and 'Amr were on the pier to meet it at Port Tawfiq. There was a discussion between them, in the hearing of others, about the possibility of sending this unit from Suez to Sharm al-Shaykh at that time, which would be a big surprise to the world. The conversation ended with hope only, and the division returned to Cairo as previously planned.
>
> Another time this hope was mentioned when Marshal 'Amr went to Pakistan at the head of a military mission in 1966. From there he sent a telegram to Nasser proposing to send troops to Sharm al-Shaykh, and to threaten Israel with closure of the Strait. Until now no one knows the reason for that message. Nothing was done about it.[27]

The importance of these comments is that they run counter to the accepted wisdom among foreign observers at the time, including Israelis and Americans, that Nasser was happy to have UNEF between Egypt and Israel because it spared him the necessity of being belligerent. It also protected him against Israeli adventurism and allowed him the luxury of his own adventurism, as in Yemen, but the increasing virulence of attacks by conservative Arabs accusing him of hiding behind UNEF had given him second thoughts about UNEF by the spring of 1967, if not before.

Another, and possibly false, indicator that there had been some sort of prior planning was the remarks addressed to General Rikhye by the Egyptian general officers who delivered the request to him from General

Fawzi to pull UNEF back from its observation posts. Rikhye asked Brigadier Sharkawy, chief of staff of the UAR liaison team with UNEF, if the Egyptian authorities had considered all the factors involved and the consequences of the withdrawal of UNEF and were prepared for any eventuality. He describes Sharkawy's response:

> "Oh, yes sir!" Sharkawy replied beaming now that the cat was out of the bag and he could talk. "We have arrived at this decision after much deliberation and are prepared for anything. If there is war we shall next meet at Tel Aviv." By the tone and enthusiasm of his reply it was apparent to me that Sharkawy had received some forewarning of the Egyptian intentions but had not found it possible to share them with me.[28]

Yet another reason for suspecting that the Egyptian reaction was planned was that Nasser was known to be in a corner because of the worsening economic situation and his continued involvement in Yemen. As early as the beginning of the year the U.S. Embassy had been expecting trouble because of increasing deterioration in the state of relations between the two countries and had begun quietly to make contingency plans for an eventual break in those relations, including the choice of Spain to be the protecting power if that eventuality arose. Ambassador Battle, in his farewell call on Nasser on March 4 and in a dinner conversation that evening with ʿAmr, Sadat, and Heikal, was impressed by the general gloom they radiated and left with the feeling that Nasser would have to do something dramatic to restore his prestige and rally support. Battle recalls that he posited three possibilities: Nasser would stir up trouble with Libya, would heat up the Yemen war, or would allow the Arab-Israel issue to heat up. Battle thought the last was the least likely, particularly since Nasser had told him that Egypt was not ready for war with Israel.[29] It was nevertheless clear to the Americans that Nasser was going to do something, that he was likely to do it in the summer, and that the United States would be a principal target of whatever he did.

Finally, the speed of the Egyptian reaction—the fact that Egypt moved some 70,000 men into Sinai in ten days—implies a good deal of advance preparation. The detailed staff work which preceded the operation must have been done well in advance, because there was no time for it on May 14, when the troop movements started. While this may have been no more than the normal contingency planning that all armies must do, the choice of contingencies for which to plan says something about the range of choices which are thought to be realistic.

Nasser's own testimony is conflicting. On several occasions he said, both publicly and privately, that Egypt had not planned it that way but had been carried along by events. Thus on May 22 at Bir Gifgafa he said:

News agencies reported yesterday that these movements must have been the result of a previously well thought-out plan. I say that it was the course of events that determined the plan. We had no plan before May 13, because we did not believe that Israel would dare to make such an impertinent statement [a reference to the alleged Rabin statement], or take action against any Arab country.[30]

According to Rikhye's account, Nasser said essentially the same thing to U Thant the following day, i.e., that the UAR had been propelled into a situation where a military confrontation with Israel had become inevitable. Similarly, in opening remarks at his May 28 press conference he described the progression of the crisis in these words:

There was a plan to invade Syria. . . . we could not stand idly by while Syria was threatened with invasion. Therefore the UAR armed forces had to move to positions from which they could effectively deter aggression. Many natural developments followed our action.[31]

Two days earlier, speaking to a group of Arab trade unionists, however, he gave a somewhat different picture.

One day two years ago, I stood up to say that we have no plan to liberate Palestine. I spoke at the (Arab) summit conferences. The summit conferences were meant to prepare the Arabs to defend themselves. Recently we felt we are strong enough, that if we were to enter a battle with Israel, with God's help, we could triumph. On this basis we decided to take actual steps. . . . Once we were fully prepared we could ask UNEF to leave. And this is what actually happened. The same thing happened with regard to Sharm al-Shaykh. We were also attacked on this score by some Arabs. Taking Sharm al-Shaykh meant confrontation with Israel. Taking such action also meant that we were ready to enter into a general war with Israel. It was not a separate operation. Therefore we had to take this fact into consideration when moving to Sharm al-Shaykh. . . . Actually, I was authorized by the Supreme Executive Committee to implement this plan at the right time. The right time came when Syria was threatened with aggression.[32]

Nasser was more truthful than many of his colleagues around the world, but too much weight should not be put on his public words, particularly when they are mutually contradictory. He was often carried away by the spirit of the moment and by audience reaction and was prone to say things he did not really mean or things whose impact on others he had not anticipated. In this case, the contradiction may be more apparent than real, however. It seems clear that 'Amr and his associates had been thinking about this particular contingency for some time and that they had some ideas about what to do if the occasion arose. They had not planned to confront Israel in May, but the occasion arose and they responded to it according to some previously laid plans, plans which may have been half-baked but were sufficiently detailed so that unit commanders could start moving their troops quickly into positions previously assigned to them.

What is not clear is the extent to which Nasser was privy to 'Amr's plans before the crisis broke. It would have been inconceivable for diplomats in Cairo in 1967 to imagine that he was not informed about what 'Amr was up to. It no longer is. Read with his relationship with 'Amr in mind, Nasser's statements can all be interpreted as ad hoc covering for actions over which he was not totally in control. At the same time, the various accounts given by the participants indicate that the entire operation was characterized by improvisation and sudden changes of view on the part of the High Command. The memoirs of Generals Fawzi and Murtagi are particularly rich in details about that. Plans and personnel were being changed up to the last minute, and there was incredible confusion among the forces in Sinai, a confusion increased by the lack of effective command, control, and communications. The result was that the Egyptians defense plan was gutted as units were detached from their assigned posts and sent off on other missions, in part because of 'Amr's obsession with the idea that Israel was going to attack primarily from the south rather than the north.

Fawzi and Murtagi were both seeking to justify their own performances, and their accounts must be read with that in mind; but that there was confusion was also evident from Israel's interrogation of Egyptian prisoners of war. Many Egyptian officers and men said they had been sent to Sinai with no clear idea where they were going or what they were supposed to do. The supply situation was chaotic, troops were being pushed across the canal willy-nilly, and some national guard units arrived with neither weapons nor uniforms. Here is a description from a book by the deputy director of Egyptian military intelligence, Abd al-Fattah Abu Fadl.

> The next day, May 22, on my way back to Suez, we stopped at al-Qantara to wait for a convoy to pass through the canal. During the wait . . . the mayor of Qantara . . . asked that we go with him to the railroad station to say some encouraging words to some reserve troops who were expected at the station en route to the Sinai front. I was shocked to see the state of disorder these troops were in, impossible for one to describe. All were dressed in their civilian clothes, mostly in rural gallabiyas, carrying their rifles and not a uniform among them. They had been summoned hastily from their villages and without any support arrangements having been made for them. They had received only their weapons, while still in civilian clothes, and been put on the train like cattle with no provision for food or drink or rest. They rushed to buy food from the itinerant vendors at the station in a state of complete

anarchy. Their aspect was like that of country watchmen, if not lower in level. A great heap of men and boys lost because of the negligence and recklessness of the armed forces leadership, which did not treat them as respected human beings. As an ex-soldier and combatant, I reflected on this and said, "Is this the status of our forces which will face our enemy Israel? When our enemy Israel mobilized its troops did it operate in this inhuman fashion?"[33]

The operation which looked so smooth to foreigners in Cairo was any-thing but, once the troops arrived in Sinai. If the Egyptians had a plan, it was not being followed or implemented properly.

One final piece of evidence, if it can be called that, indicates that Egypt had decided to exploit the Soviet warning and that the truth or falsity of the report soon became irrelevant. Again we revert to the testimony of Generals Fawzi and Murtagi in their memoirs. Continuing the account of his trip to Damascus on May 14 and 15, Fawzi says:

I returned to Cairo May 15 and presented my report to General ʿAmr. It denied the presence of any Israeli concentrations on the Syrian front. I did not notice any reaction from him about the negative report. . . . from here began my belief that the question of Israeli concentrations, from his point of view, was not the only or chief reason for the mobili-zation and deployments we were undertaking so quickly.[34]

Similarly, we find this passage in General Murtagi's book:

Strangely, Egyptian intelligence felt that it had made a mistake and changed from a state of conviction to one of doubt and lack of confi-dence in a matter of hours. At about noon on May 14 there was a tele-phone conversation between the Director of Military Intelligence and the Commander of the Eastern Military Region, the gist of which was that the Israeli enemy had concentrated seven brigades on the Syrian front and was expected to increase the number to fifteen, and that the enemy would start military operations between the fifteenth and sev-enteenth or the seventeenth and twenty-first.

By nightfall the same day the Intelligence Directorate sent an analy-sis of the situation to the High Command in which it stressed the prob-ability that the crisis was the product of a fabricated plan and advised waiting for more certain information.[35]

If these accounts are true, they mean that Egyptian military officers, at least, had begun to suspect the accuracy of the Soviet report by the evening of May 14 and knew it was not true by the fifteenth, at which point they had taken no irrevocable steps in the Sinai and still had flexi-bility. There was an option to cool things down which was not exercised. It is not clear whether or when the "political leadership," i.e., Nasser, realized the report was untrue. Nasser was still referring to it as a fact two months later. On the other hand, according to Salah Bassiouny's version of the Soviet warning, discussed in chapter 1, people in the Foreign Ministry were aware of Fawzi's report early on, which meant that it did not end with ʿAmr, as Fawzi's description implies. Again, according to Bassiouny, the Foreign Ministry received reconfirmation of the report from the Soviets a few days later. If that is correct, did the Egyptians continue to believe it during the interval? Muhammad Shoukri's version of events contradicts Bassiouny's, but he says the foreign minister was skeptical of the report from the beginning. If so, was any effort made to slow down the rush to Sinai? Pieces of this puzzle are still missing.

In any event, that ʿAmr pushed on after this point implies that with the pretext for a confrontation having arisen, he was not interested in the truth. He had set a goal and was out to reach it. Was Nasser dragged along, or did he go willingly? We may never know.

THE NATURE OF THE MISCALCULATION

If we accept the argument that ʿAmr deceived Nasser about the readiness of the armed forces, it is clear that the primary miscalculation was made by ʿAmr, whose incompetence was shown by his apparent belief that his forces were indeed ready to confront Israel's. That he was thinking in such terms at the time is evident from Nasser's remarks to U Thant about the military's desire to strike first, by a report that ʿAmr had intended to strike at Eilat despite his agreement with Nasser not to, and by the sortie flown over Israel on May 28 mentioned by Mahmoud Riad. Within the military, however, belief in Egypt's readiness was confined to the clique of officers around ʿAmr, if we accept the accounts of Generals Fawzi and Murtagi. If that was indeed the case, it is strange that no one told Nasser.

The secondary miscalculation was Nasser's misjudgment in accepting ʿAmr's evaluation of the military. That he would do so without having independent confirmation of what ʿAmr said seems hard to believe at first, but given what we know of their relationship, it is perhaps understandable. As mistakes go, it was enormous.

The counterargument, that Nasser knew how weak his forces were but was engaged in a gigantic bluff, implies that he was confident he could get away with it either because Israel was afraid to fight or because the international community would not let it fight. His illusions in this respect would be fed by early reports of panic in Israel when the crisis broke and strengthened by his belief, judging by his words at Bir Gifgafa on May 22, that in 1956 Israel had been afraid to take on Egypt without French and British air cover and had not taken a single Egyptian position that had not already been abandoned as part of a redeployment. He also thought he had a commitment from the Soviet Union to come to his aid if he got in trouble, and while he may have dismissed U.S. assurances of opposition to aggression, he may also have counted on them as being of some value if there was a fight.

Belief that he would be saved from disaster by outside forces seemed to be what Nasser had in mind in 1970 when he spoke to Dennis Walters, a British member of Parliament. Walters reported that Nasser told him

> he had never intended that there should be a war. What he felt at the time was that Israel's provocations against Syria and Jordan could not be left unchallenged; if they were then Israel would unleash even more and bigger raids against its Arab neighbours. So he had to do something. But he had been assured that the Americans and Russians had reached an understanding, and that just as the Russians would not allow him to make a pre-emptive strike, in the same way the Americans would restrain the Israelis from doing so. Admittedly the war of words had reached an alarming level, but it was never meant to escalate into a shooting war. So he was forced to conclude that either the Americans had broken the pledge they had given to the Russians (and he implied this is what the Russians had passed on to him), or they had been unable to control their satellite.[36]

It is possible that Nasser actually believed what he said to Walters, but since neither the Soviet Union nor the United States could in fact guarantee the behavior of their respective clients, it is highly unlikely that he was given any such assurance. Certainly the United States did not give him one, although he may have misread U.S. capabilities and assumed that it could and would restrain Israel indefinitely. In the absence of some documentation of the alleged assurance, however, his remarks sound like an after-the-fact rationalization.

A more convincing description of Nasser's state of mind in June 1967 is provided by Anthony Nutting in *Nasser:*

> a few hours before the Six Day War . . . [Nasser told him he was] convinced that the Israelis would not be prepared to fight a war on two fronts, if only for fear of the striking power of Egypt's Russian-equipped air force. . . . his intelligence service . . . had assured him that his Russian Sokhols [sic] were more than a match for anything possessed by Israel. He later told me that, as a result of our conversation, he had gone immediately to ʿAmr's headquarters and told his army commanders to expect an Israeli attack within a matter of hours. But by that time it was too late.[37]

If Nutting's account is accurate, it is yet another illustration of Egypt's impromptu approach. Both Nasser and ʿAmr seem to be influenced by the remarks of the last person they talk to; retired members of the old Revolutionary Command Council wander in and out of meetings and give their opinions; Nasser butts in and nobody pays much attention to him; he takes journalists seriously and revises his intelligence estimate on the basis of their remarks; he is influenced by the casual conversation of diplomats. In a society which relies for its survival on a degree of discipline and cooperation unique in the Arab world, there seems to be no organization or functioning command structure which can come up with an objective assessment. Everything seems to be politicized and unsystematic.

Also striking is the degree to which the Egyptians were responding to phantoms. The crisis was precipitated by a report of nonexistent troop concentrations, given credence by a nonstatement by Israel's Chief of Staff, and made more credible by belief in a nonexistent U.S. plot against the Egyptian revolution involving an Islamic pact which was largely a journalistic figment. Receptivity to these illusions was increased by real events and circumstances, such as the Samuᶜ raid and the April 7 air battle over Syria, tension along the Israel-Syrian border, Egypt's difficult economic situation, the burden of Yemen, and the Nasser-ᶜAmr rivalry. All contributed to a need to do something and a willingness to accept uncritically the arguments supporting a radical response when the stimulus came.

CHAPTER

5

THE AMERICAN ROLE

> At times of great affliction . . . it is impor-
> tant to determine clearly . . . what has really
> happened. . . . We say truthfully that what
> we saw during those five dreadful days was
> the extreme degree of violence in which the
> Arab nation has confronted the U.S. gov-
> ernment.
>
> Mohamed Heikal, *Al-Ahram*, June 16,
> 1967

Nasser's obsession with the role of the United States in the Middle East in general and with its policies toward Egypt in particular was an important factor in his miscalculation. Reading Rikhye's account of the May 24 conversation between U Thant and Nasser, for instance, one is struck by the importance in that exchange of Nasser's denunciation of the United States. On reading the accounts provided by Mohamed Heikal and Abdul Majid Farid, his obsession with the United States becomes even more striking. Judging by his comments, he sincerely thought that his real opponent was not Israel but the United States, which was out to destroy him and the Egyptian revolution.

A similar impression is given by Nasser's 1967 May Day speech, which is devoted largely to an attack on the United States, Saudi Arabia, and Jordan, the latter two being described as tools of the first. On hearing it, Americans in Cairo knew they were in for a hot summer. Nasser could do various things to make life difficult for them, but war with Israel did not loom as a likely possibility. Certainly no one predicted it, although Ambassador Battle mentioned it as a possibility in his farewell telegram.

The stage for Nasser's remarks was set by a series of weekly articles by Heikal in *Al-Ahram* attacking U.S. policies. Heikal appeared to have convinced himself that the United States was unalterably opposed to the Egyptian revolution and committed to bringing it down. He had indicated to Battle before the latter's departure in March that he had been planning such a series but had held it off out of respect for Battle. Heikal's articles and Nasser's speech sounded like exercises in paranoia then and still do today, but there had been enough U.S. involvement with anti-Nasser elements to make the suspicions understandable.

There was indeed considerable anti-Nasser sentiment among certain senior officials in Washington and their views had an impact on policy decisions, but the official government attitude toward the Egyptian revolution was one of indifference. The concern was not the revolution; it was Nasser's adventurism abroad, particularly his activities in the Arabian Peninsula and his habit, as seen through Washington's eyes, of biting the hand that fed him. Both Israel and the conservative Arab regimes played on these concerns and found allies in the U.S. bureaucracy. Nevertheless, there was no U.S. plot to bring down Nasser.

The United States and Egypt had been friendly during the Kennedy era, and the United States still had an active aid program in Egypt in 1967, but the relationship had turned sour after 1963. The essential verity was that it was impossible for Lyndon Johnson and Gamal Abdul Nasser to do business together. In Malcolm Kerr's words, doing business with Nasser was like trying to change a tire on a moving automobile. Johnson was not the man to cope with that. And even if he had been, his known pro-Israeli sentiments would have made it difficult for Nasser to accept him as a friend.

Johnson was not the only U.S. leader to have problems with Nasser. The course of U.S.-Egyptian relations throughout the Nasser period was like an irregular sine curve. Erratic lows and highs betrayed a basic instability arising from irreconcilable conflicts of interest regarding issues involving third countries, notably the conservative Arab states and Israel. Nasser was forever trying to upset the status quo while the Americans were trying to maintain it. Each party realized the importance of the other, and each made efforts to paper over their differences. They succeeded from time to time, but sooner or later the imp of discord poked its head through.

The United States had cautiously welcomed the Egyptian revolution in 1952 and had hoped, as the Israelis had initially, that the young military officers who were behind it would prove more able than the corrupt King Farouk to reach a modus vivendi with Israel. The first U.S. contact with the revolutionaries was made by a young Foreign Service officer at the embassy, William C. Lakeland, and not by the CIA, as claimed by some. According to Lakeland, the CIA was in touch with another group, not Nasser's Free Officers. Lakeland's contact was through Heikal, who had been sought out by the young officers as a responsible and untainted journalist who might be useful to them. His rise to fame was about to begin.

The CIA, once it discovered it was backing the wrong horse, quickly regrouped and established its own contact with Nasser and his colleagues, appealing to their love of conspiracy and their belief that the real power lay with the CIA, not the Department of State. Lakeland was nevertheless the principal U.S. contact with Nasser regarding the agreements on British evacuation of the Canal Zone and on the future of the Anglo-Egyptian Sudan. Meanwhile, Nasser's CIA contacts had led him to believe that the United States would be more forthcoming on the supply of arms than proved to be the case. The resulting misunderstanding was a factor in the collapse of U.S.-Egyptian negotiations over arms in 1954, which led to Egypt's 1955 arms deal with the Soviets. That was the beginning of Soviet penetration into the area.

Given the importance of Egypt, the Americans decided to swallow the arms deal and entered into discussions in the fall of 1955 about financing the Aswan High Dam, which was universally regarded as essential to the development of Egypt. The offer to help was abruptly withdrawn, under circumstances which are still being argued, in July 1956. Various factors had led Secretary of State John Foster Dulles to conclude that Nasser was no gentleman and that he could not work with him. The final straw is popularly believed to have been Egypt's decision to establish relations with Communist China in spite of an oral undertaking from Nasser that he would not do so without first consulting the Americans. Perhaps more important were Egypt's subversive activities against the regimes in Iraq, Libya, and Jordan and Nasser's fierce opposition to the Baghdad Pact, which had become an important instrument of U.S. policy in the area even though the United States was not a member. The deterioration of the situation between Israel and Egypt following the Gaza raids in 1955 was another factor, although in this case Israel's inflexibility and adventurism were as much or more to blame than Egypt's. In any event, early hopes for an Egyptian-Israeli accommodation had been dashed.

Withdrawal of the Aswan Dam offer led to Nasser's nationalizing the Suez Canal Company, which led in turn to the tripartite invasion of Egypt by Israel, Britain, and France in October 1956. President Eisenhower was angered at the collusion between friends, particularly because the British had lied to him about it, and he and Dulles were also distressed by the resort to war. Eisenhower spoke out clearly against the invasion (his speech of October 31, 1956, on the eve of his second-term election, makes remarkable reading today), and U.S. pressure was the major force which halted the invasion and eventually made Israel disgorge the Sinai Peninsula.

U.S. opposition to the invasion momentarily put the United States on the side of the angels as far as Egypt was concerned, but the halo was tarnished quickly by the Eisenhower Doctrine, proclaimed in a presidential message to Congress on January 5, 1957. The doctrine was then embodied in a Joint Congressional Resolution of March 9, 1957. It authorized, in addition to economic and military assistance, "the use of armed forces to assist any nation or group of such nations requesting assistance against armed aggression from any country controlled by international communism." For "country controlled by international communism," read

Egypt. Strange as it may sound today, many influential people in Washington and abroad in those days accepted, or at least did not argue with, the proposition that Nasser was a Soviet puppet.

One outgrowth of the Eisenhower Doctrine was a series of efforts by the United States to bring Nasser down, including covert support for opposition elements and imposition of an economic boycott similar to the boycotts applied against Cuba and Libya today. A symptom of the folly then gripping Washington was that the Office of Near Eastern Affairs in the Department of State was given the task in 1957 of preparing a study, ordered by Dulles, of the feasibility of diverting the Nile to the Red Sea in order to cut off Egypt's water. Fortunately, there was ample data to indicate that it would not work.[1]

U.S. support for conservative Arab regimes, a policy that was less directly anti-Nasser, became increasingly important, and much of it was justified under the rubric of the Eisenhower Doctrine. Thus serious U.S. financial and military support for Jordan began in 1957, and it was initiated to help King Hussein forestall a takeover by radical elements who were thought to be pro-Nasser. Similarly, the United States was involved in financing the defeat of pro-Nasser candidates in the Lebanese parliamentary elections of 1957. The resulting upset of traditional political leaders was a major factor leading to the Lebanese crisis of 1958. U.S. fixation on Nasser was such that the revolution in Iraq of July 14, 1958, was immediately typed as Nasser-inspired when in fact Egypt was not involved. The U.S. landing in Lebanon the following day was intended to forestall another "Nasserist" revolution there.

In the last eighteen months of the Eisenhower Administration the anti-Nasser fervor dimmed somewhat with the departure of Dulles from the Department of State and with the realization that the policy of confrontation was leading nowhere. A policy of gradual easing away from boycott toward accommodation, dubbed the "three-stage rocket," was adopted, and the United States even shipped some food to Egypt under Public Law 480.

This policy was greatly expanded under the Kennedy Administration, which decided to provide massive amounts of surplus agricultural commodities under PL 480 to help finance economic and social development in Egypt. The hope was that in addition to helping with the country's economic problems, it would persuade Nasser and his colleagues to focus on internal development rather than foreign adventure. The program was accompanied by a private exchange of letters between Kennedy and Nasser, initiated by the former. These developments ushered in an age of cooperation and warmth in U.S.-Egyptian relations, much to the discomfort of the conservative Arabs, to whom Nasser was a menace because of the wide following he enjoyed in the Arab world. In that latter respect he was unique, and it gave him considerable capacity for mischief.

But U.S. hopes were set awry. In the first place, Nasser continued to support radical and anticolonial movements in the region and the world at large. In spite of the U.S. aid, which offered Egypt a chance to do something fundamental about its economy, he did not turn inward. In particular, he became deeply involved in supporting the 1962 revolution in Yemen. By 1967 Egypt maintained that it had stabilized the situation, largely by means of air strikes against royalist villages, but one-third of its army was committed there.[2]

That was most distressing to the Saudis, for whom Yemen was a sensitive problem. They were supporting the royalists. It also upset the British, who saw Nasser's involvement in southern Arabia as a serious threat to their position there, in Oman, and in the gulf. This view was shared by enough U.S. officials to make it a serious policy consideration in Washington.

In the early 1960s the United States made a serious effort (the Bunker mission) to broker a graceful exit from Yemen for Egypt, but it was unsuccessful and Yemen became a principal issue souring U.S.-Egyptian relations. The United States eventually found itself in a position where it had to choose between supporting the Egyptians or the Saudis under Faisal, who had developed an implacable hostility toward Nasser, and it chose the Saudis. That had become clear by 1967 and was part of Nasser's reason for concluding that the United States was trying to undo the Egyptian revolution. Yemen looms large in Nasser's 1967 May Day speech.

Another factor in his conclusion was the abortive Islamic pact, mentioned earlier. It was an informal grouping of conservative Islamic states sponsored by King Faisal and including Morocco, Jordan, and Iran. Dedicated to combating radicalism, i.e., Nasserism, it was reportedly discussed in the corridors during the Casablanca summit in 1966 and was the forerunner of today's Islamic Conference. It never became a pact and had little substance in 1967. It was very real for the Egyptians, however, who saw it as a successor to the Baghdad Pact and thought the United States was behind it, since they saw Faisal and the others as U.S. tools. The Islamic pact also figures prominently in the May Day speech and in other comments of the period by Nasser.

Although, as noted earlier, the United States and Egypt had agreed to keep the Arab-Israeli issue in the icebox, a weakening of U.S. resolve not to become a major supplier of arms to Israel had a serious corrosive effect on this agreement. It started with an announcement of a decision to sell Hawk antiaircraft missiles to Israel in 1963, was followed by the sale of tanks by West Germany at U.S. urging in 1965, advanced to a decision to supply A4 Skyhawks in 1966, and was reinforced by U.S. unwillingness to do anything serious about Israel's development of nuclear arms. The United States thus moved from a position of principled restraint to one of expedient openhandedness as far as arms for Israel were concerned.

Egypt saw that as confirmation of President Johnson's fundamental hostility toward the Arabs and toward Nasser in particular, which they dated back at least to 1957, when Johnson opposed sanctions against Israel over the Sinai issue. The Arabs saw changes in U.S. Middle East policy as soon as Johnson came to power in 1963, and they had dark suspicions about his role in Kennedy's assassination, which some of them were calling a Jewish plot within twenty-four hours of its occurrence.[3]

Indeed, Kennedy's assassination meant the end of U.S. cooperation with Nasser, but that was not apparent immediately. Johnson made an effort to continue Kennedy's policies, including the personal correspondence, but Johnson's letters did not have the grace of Kennedy's and Nasser apparently did not like the new president from the beginning. Although it is wrong in a number of factual details, a good account of the Egyptian view of Johnson is given in Heikal's *Nasser: The Cairo Documents* (pp. 205–23). A much fuller and more accurate account, with supporting documents, runs through Heikal's *1967—Al-Infijar.*

In many respects the two men were too much alike. Both were sensitive to slights and harbored suspicions that bordered on the paranoid. Both were born conspirators without undue concern for the truth, although Nasser was considerably more upright in his private life and a good deal more courteous than Johnson. Both were subject to what sounds like narcissistic rage, and they were forever taking offense at each other's remarks. Neither inspired trust in the other, with reason.

The bureaucrats and diplomats might have succeeded in keeping the men far enough apart so that their personality conflict would not interfere with cooperation between the two governments had not a series of untoward events occurred in 1964 and 1965. The first was a Thanksgiving Day attack on the U.S. Embassy in Cairo organized by African students protesting U.S. involvement in the rescue of white hostages in Stanleyville in the Congo. Whether the Egyptians organized the protest or merely permitted it is still being debated. What was clear was that the Egyptian police did nothing to prevent the mob from entering the embassy and burning two buildings: the marine quarters and the Information Service library. The library fire was spectacular; photographs of it were seen widely in Washington and remembered vividly.

Egypt was slow to offer an apology. The chief of police came by after the fire was over and said he was sorry it had happened, but no one came from the Foreign Ministry, whose chief of protocol should have been on the scene immediately, and there was never an explicit official apology, although Heikal claims Nasser ordered Dr. Fawzi to make one. The incident was an embarrassment to Nasser, but he was not the sort to admit it. He did make amends several weeks later, but at the very hour he was telling Ambassador Battle that Egypt would replace the library (which it did in time), the Egyptian air force was in the process of shooting down a U.S. aircraft which belonged to John Mecom, a Texas oilman who was a close friend of President Johnson. The incident was the result of the air crew's failure to reinstate a flight plan, and Egypt was not at fault; but no one knew that at the time, and it looked like an unprovoked attack.

While the Americans were still stewing over that and the bodies of the crew had not yet been recovered, the minister of supply, Kamal Ramzi Stino, made a tactless request of Battle for an increase in PL 480 wheat commitments before the end of the year. Battle, who knew that after the library fire and the plane incident there was not a chance of getting such a request approved in Washington in the few weeks remaining in the year, told Stino it was not the time for such a request. At this meeting Battle was offered orange juice, which he drank. He then left before the traditional coffee was served.

The meeting was described to Nasser by Ali Sabri, the prime minister, while they were on the train to Port Said, where Nasser was to deliver a speech on December 23. Sabri, who was considered anti-American, put the burden of tactlessness on Battle, saying he had been rude, had refused to drink the orange juice offered to him, and, more important, had threatened to cut off wheat supplies. Nasser, infuriated, delivered his famous drink-from-the-sea speech, to an enthusiastic crowd. This excerpt gives the tone of his remarks:

> the American Ambassador yesterday called on the deputy prime minister for supply and sat with him for a few minutes, looking glum and sulky. He was supposed to talk to him about supply material we are obtaining from America in accordance with the products law. The ambassador told the deputy prime minister that he cannot at present talk about this matter at all. Why? Because he does not like our conduct, that is, conduct here in Egypt. I would like him to know that whoever does not like our conduct can go drink up the sea. If the Mediterranean is not sufficient, there is the Red Sea too. We can give him that as well. What I want to say is that we cannot sell our independence for the sake of 30 or 40 or 50 million pounds. We are not ready to accept a single harsh word from any person. He who speaks a single harsh word to us will have his tongue cut off . . . this smacks of an attempt to exert pressure on us. We are sorry. We cannot tolerate any pressure or accept insolent words and vileness. We are short-tempered people. We are born like this. We are a people with dignity. The people have their dignity and are not prepared to sell it, not even for one billion pounds, much less so for 50 or 40 or 30 million pounds.[4]

Few utterances could have been better calculated to upset a Washington already infuriated by the attack on the embassy and the shooting down of Mecom's plane. (Mecom, incidentally, was not on it, as Heikal asserted in *Nasser: The Cairo Documents*. Heikal corrected his error in *Al-Infijar*.) The Americans never got over it, and it continued to rankle in spite of the efforts of diplomats on both sides.

The United States soon began trying to use its wheat and other forms of aid—debt rescheduling, Commodity Credit Corporation rollover, PL 480 financing of development projects, support for Egypt in world monetary circles and New York banks—as well as diplomatic initiatives, such as the Yemen mediation, as political levers. While wheat supplies were continued at normal levels through 1965, by that summer a decision had been taken to keep Nasser on a short leash and to give him no more long-term commitments with respect to aid of any kind. It would be made clear that further aid would be linked to Egypt's behavior on such matters as Yemen. One of the first indications of the new hardline posture was a decision taken not to finance a grain storage project which would have saved Egypt millions of dollars a year in lost grain. It was a victory for the anti-Nasserists in the Washington establishment who increasingly influenced U.S. policy toward Egypt, thanks in part to the timidity displayed by the Bureau of Near Eastern and South Asian Affairs.

By the beginning of 1967 the situation was as follows. During the first half of 1966 the United States had supplied Egypt with 755,000 tons of wheat worth $55 million, but no wheat had been supplied after June 1966 and a request for further wheat and other agricultural products to the value of $150 million had been pending after February 1966.[5] The Egyptians, who had come to regard the wheat as theirs by right, were outraged.

To complicate matters further, by the fall of 1966 Nasser was convinced, or said he was, that the United States was plotting to assassinate him. He let Washington know of this belief through an American lawyer, whom he invited to Cairo for the express purpose of telling him about the plot. Although a high-level effort was made to persuade him that there was no truth to it, he probably did not believe the denials. That was his frame of mind when Ambassador Battle took leave on March 4, 1967, to return to Washington to become assistant secretary of state for Near Eastern and South Asian affairs.

As noted in the previous chapter, Battle was impressed with Nasser's gloomy state of mind and thought he would try to do something dramatic. *Al-Ahram* reported the Nasser-Battle conversation in its issue of March 17, noting that

> when Ambassador Battle took leave of President Abdul Nasser . . . [the latter] asked him to tell President Johnson that "while appreciating and thanking you for all the facilities accorded to us in the wheat question, we want nothing now. In February 1966 we requested you to supply us with wheat. Since then we have neither renewed the request nor reminded you of it. When we want American wheat in the future we shall buy it at market prices and conditions. We have been very patient with all the pressure you have applied to us because of the wheat, but our patience has run out. Please also know that the value of this country

and of its struggle lies basically in its capacity in all conditions to with-
stand all sorts of pressure—economic, military or psychological."[6]

Battle confirms that Nasser withdrew the Egyptian aid request in the
meeting, but says he replied, "I want you to know that you gave up
before I did." Battle says that the Egyptian request had still been under
active consideration on February 22 when Nasser had made yet another
speech attacking the United States and saying Egypt had decided to sacrifice the aid. That killed it, Battle says.[7] The following day, *Al-Ahram* had
carried a Reuters report from Washington which said the United States
had not refused the UAR's request but had delayed replying because of
its "displeasure with President Abdul Nasser's nationalistic politics in the
Middle East, his involvement in the unresolved Yemen dispute, his encouragement of terrorism in Aden and his hostility towards Saudi Arabia
and Jordan." *Al-Ahram* described this as an "unashamed confirmation by
Washington officials of the most cynical charges" to the effect that the
United States was manipulating food shipments "to intervene directly in
internal Arab affairs."[8]

EGYPT'S VIEW OF THE U.S. ROLE

With these events in mind, it is easy to understand why the United States
had no credibility with Egypt when the June 1967 crisis came. The problem was compounded by the fact that Battle's successor, Nolte, did not
arrive until May 21. He arrived in the midst of the crisis and never caught
up. That was unfortuate for him personally, but it was also unfortunate
for U.S. interests, because personal communication at the top was impossible and sending special representatives out in such cases is no substitute
for having a chief of mission on the ground who knows the local leaders
and can have access to them.

The United States, then, was in Coventry when the trouble started.
All its actions were regarded with particular suspicion and its embassy
had no direct contact with the autocratic chief of state. It is easy to understand in these circumstances why Egypt would dismiss U.S. denials
of Israeli troop concentrations (even though some Egyptian officials knew
the report was untrue even before the Americans denied it), and why
Cairo came to believe the United States was guilty of collusion with Israel,
particularly when it became necessary to explain Egypt's defeat. Egypt's
accusations can be grouped under two headings: the United States
participated in the fighting on Israel's side, and it deceived and misled Egypt into thinking it would oppose whoever started hostilities;
while it was encouraging Israel to attack rather than restraining it as
claimed, it led Egypt to believe that Israel would not attack for at least
another week.

U.S. Participation in the Fighting

The first allegation surfaced on the morning of June 6, when Egyptian radio and television began broadcasting a report that U.S. and British aircraft had participated in the attack on the previous day. As indicated earlier, this charge apparently was Marshal 'Amr's excuse for the unexpected destruction of the Egyptian air force. Nasser later admitted publicly that the accusation was not true, but he did so in a manner which did not constitute an apology for what some Americans called "the big lie"; nor did he restore diplomatic relations, which he had broken over the accusation. (They were not renewed until more than three years after his death.) Nevertheless, the accusation was laid to rest as far as informed Arabs were concerned.

The story was left at that for seventeen years, until the publication in 1984 of *Taking Sides: America's Secret Relations with a Militant Israel*, by Stephen Green. Green asserts that aircraft of the 38th Tactical Reconnaisance Squadron of the 26th Tactical Reconnaisance Wing of the U.S. Air Force flew daily reconnaisance missions for Israel over Egypt from June 5 to June 11 or 12. His account includes many details. Green does not name his source, who claims to have been a participant in the operation, and notes that he was not able to get confirmation of the story from officials in Washington.

I have queried a number of people who were in senior positions in the intelligence community, the Department of State, and the White House at the time and have likewise been unable to obtain confirmation. Various former senior officials of my acquaintance suspect that there is something to the story, but it remains unproven. One former CIA official commented that if the story was true it was the best kept secret in Washington. He also admitted, however, that it could have been done by officials in the White House and the Pentagon and be concealed from the CIA. The example which comes to mind is the Iran-Contra affair, which shows that there is no inherent limit on the bizarre at the White House. It is difficult to believe, however, that an operation such as that described by Green would not have left a trail among the bureaucrats and that some of the details would not have leaked authoritatively by now. While Green's account sounds factual because of the wealth of details provided, these details cannot be checked in public sources and other portions of the book are sufficiently marked by carelessness to make one treat all of it with reserve.

U.S. Deception

This allegation is given perhaps its fullest exposition in Riad's *Amrika waal-Arab*. Belief in it is widespread. For instance, Heikal's chapter on the war in *The Sphinx and the Commissar* is called "The Trap," and many Egyptian officials are still convinced that Nasser walked into one.

According to Riad's thesis Johnson was seeking the downfall of Nasser. When economic measures and subversion failed, his only recourse was external aggression, and Israel was the chosen instrument. Johnson provided Israel with priceless intelligence about the Arabs obtained from aircraft and satellite intelligence. He also

> set out to deceive Egypt in order to help Israel win the war by assuring her the element of pre-emption. This was done through assuring Abdul Nasser that the United States would stand against any aggression. He sent a letter which the American Ambassador, Richard Nolte, gave to me on May 23.[9] In it Johnson spoke of the importance of avoiding war and referred to the armistice agreements as providing the exemplary basis for peace along the borders [that was the UAR position, too] . . . confirmed his support for U Thant's peace-keeping mission . . . and promised the following at the end of his letter: "The UAR Government and the other Arab governments can rest assured and depend on the U.S. Government's opposing firmly any aggression of any kind in the region, whether it be open or hidden, whether by regular military forces or by irregulars and this has been the policy under four successive administrations, both in the United Nations and outside it, and our actions on two previous occasions make this point very clear."

Riad writes that Nasser scoffed at this assurance, because of Johnson's pro-Israeli record, but Riad seems to have been impressed by it. Johnson then sent Robert Anderson and Charles Yost with similar messages for Nasser. Meanwhile, Riad asserts, Johnson was meeting with Eban and giving Israel a green light to strike at Israel. Johnson also relied on other parties to carry out his deception. In his letter of May 23 he referred to U Thant's proposals (that is an anachronism; Thant had not yet made his proposals when Johnson's letter was sent) and asked Nasser not to start hostilities, which Nasser agreed to in his meeting with Thant. Riad states that Johnson even succeeded in involving the Soviet Union in his deception scenario when the Soviet ambassador brought a message from the Soviet leaders on May 27 asking that Egypt not initiate hostilities. This message apparently was precipitated by a U.S. message that said Egypt was planning to attack that day. (As noted earlier, there seems to have been a basis in fact for this alarm.) Nasser assured the Soviets he would not attack. The Americans thus secured for Israel an assurance that Egypt would not strike first. Once the Israelis struck, Riad writes, Secretary of State Rusk declared that the United States did not know who fired the first shot in order to justify supporting Israel militarily if its attack failed.[10] The United States supported Israel by sending the Sixth Fleet to the eastern Mediterranean and by sending the electronic surveillance vessel *Liberty* to monitor and jam Egyptian communications. In the United Nations the United States supported Israel's aggression and threatened to veto any cease-fire resolution that called on Israel to withdraw.[11]

Riad's account, written twenty years after the events, suffers from the inevitable corruption of hindsight and from incomplete understanding. For instance, the allegation that the *Liberty* was sent to monitor and jam Egyptian communications is widely believed in Egypt, but the ship, which had been recalled but failed to receive the message telling it to turn back, did not have a jamming capability and by the time it arrived off Gaza on June 7 the war in Sinai was all but over. Few Egyptian communications were left to monitor. Israel torpedoed and strafed the ship, allegedly because it wanted to prevent the monitoring of its communications as it prepared to attack Syria. (Few senior American officials believed Israel's explanation that the attack was an accident. Neither Johnson nor Rusk was among the believers.[12] Ironically, this incident has been transformed into evidence of evil U.S. intentions toward Egypt.)

Riad's thesis also rests on the assumption that the United States and Israel either cooked up the whole thing, manipulating the Soviet Union and Egypt into reacting as they did, or that they exploited a target of opportunity for which they had been waiting. Essential to the argument is the belief that the United States and Israel both wanted to provoke a war. To anyone familiar with either country's government at the time, that is absurd. Ample evidence in the memoirs of participants and the official record shows that war was the last thing either the United States or Israel had in mind at the beginning of May 1967, but it is unlikely to convince those who are addicted to the conspiracy theory and are prepared to believe that the United States could somehow have divined in advance how the Soviets and the Egyptians would react.

The Riad thesis further rests on a denial of Soviet and Egyptian responsibility for provoking the crisis, a denial which does not accord with facts we have been able to establish. If it is established that the Soviet report was stimulated by an Israeli disinformation effort, then Israel would clearly share responsibility for the provocation, but so far we have not proved that.

The allegation that the United States sought to mislead Egypt in order to assure Israel the element of preemption rests in the first place on a misreading of Johnson's letter and statement of May 23. These were meant to warn the Egyptians, not reassure them, because at that point the Americans thought the Egyptians were more likely to start hostilities than the Israelis.

On the other hand, the United States was guilty of some misleading, not to say dishonest, rhetoric about its opposition to aggression and support for the Tripartite Declaration, which it did not honor when the time came. Johnson's original statement of May 23 said the United States was firmly committed to the territorial integrity of all nations of the area and strongly opposed aggression by anyone in the area, in any form. Opposing aggression should have meant opposing whoever was guilty of it, including Israel.[13]

The argument was made at the time by officials of the Department of State that the closure of the Strait of Tiran constituted an act of aggression. Eugene Rostow made this argument to the Egyptian ambassador, Mustafa Kamel, on the evening of May 22, for instance.[14] If this argument was accepted, it followed, according to its proponents, that the Israeli response which took the form of a general attack on Egypt, not an effort directed against reopening the strait, was justified as an act of self-defense and was not an act of aggression. Therefore the United States was not obligated to oppose it.

The Department of State's legal adviser, Leonard Meeker, disagreed, however, and in a memorandum of May 29 to Rusk argued that there was grave doubt that international law would give Israel the right to initiate the use of armed force against the UAR in the absence of an armed attack by the UAR on Israel. Closure and mining of the strait did not of themselves constitute an armed attack, and self-defense did not cover general hostilities against the UAR.[15] Like so many other pieces of paper produced by the bureaucracy at the time, this one seems to have been lost in the shuffle.

As further evidence of U.S. opposition to the use of force in the area, Johnson also made an effort to get Britain and France to reaffirm their support for the Tripartite Declaration of 1950, but both disavowed it, as they had done in 1956 when they and Israel violated it with their attack on Egypt.[16] Nevertheless, Ambassador Goldberg at the United Nations assured U Thant before his departure for Cairo that the United States, at least, still stood by it,[17] and the tripartite-sounding phraseology about U.S. opposition to aggression in any form appeared in so many messages that it was the understanding of the posts in the field that this was indeed the U.S. position. Here is the relevant passage in the Tripartite Declaration:

> The three Governments take this opportunity of declaring their deep interest in and their desire to promote the establishment and maintenance of peace and stability in the area and their unalterable opposition to the use of force or threat between any of the states in that area. The three Governments, should they find that any of these states was preparing to violate frontiers of armistice lines, would, consistently with their obligations as members of the United Nations, immediately take action, both within and outside the United Nations, to prevent such violation.[18]

Nasser was well advised not to take these words seriously as applying to Egypt. But if he did not, it weakens the claim that Egypt was misled by these assurances.

In fact, the record shows that the United States made a serious effort to restrain both Israel and Egypt. Given a little help earlier on, it might have succeeded, but Egypt's inflexibility on the UNEF and Tiran issues, coupled with the increasingly threatening tone of Egyptian pronouncements, made it evident that Israel would be forced to react militarily or accept a serious political defeat. It would have been uncharacteristic for it to take the latter course, as stated explicitly in the famous Heikal editorial in *Al-Ahram* of May 26:

ARMED CLASH WITH ISRAEL IS INEVITABLE

. . . I think there is no escaping an armed clash between the UAR and the Israeli enemy. This clash may occur at any time and at any place along the confrontation line . . . from north of Gaza to the southern tip of the Gulf of Aqaba. . . . I say it for a number of reasons, the most important of which is the psychological factor . . . it does not permit equivocation . . . it is the imperative of security—of existence itself. . . . The closure of the Gulf of Aqaba . . . means . . . that for the first time the Arab nation, represented by the UAR, has succeeded in overturning by force an Israel-related fait accompli which had been imposed on it by force.[19]

The Americans made no attempt to hide their belief that Israel would strike if the UAR persevered in its hard-line policies. That was made clear to Egyptian officials at various levels in Cairo, but they seemed not to be worried by that eventuality. Their response was typified by the remark of a Foreign Ministry official when told that the removal of UNEF would mean the loss of Egypt's insurance policy: "Maybe we no longer need the insurance." Today that official underlines the *maybe* and says he really did not know what to believe at the time. The impression given to the Americans, however, was one of calm confidence that Egypt would prevail.

There is no question that, as noted in chapter 2, the June 3 agreement to send Muhieddin to Washington brought about a palpable relaxation of tension in Cairo. That, along with various efforts of the United Nations and the Soviet Union as well as a misreading of the signals from Israel, may have given Egypt's political leaders a false sense of security, but any chief of state who relaxed his vigilance in the circumstances then prevailing and in light of remarks of the sort Nasser was making about destroying Israel was asking for trouble.

In any event, if Nasser thought there would be a two-week cooling-off period, so did others. President Johnson has this to say on page 294 of *The Vantage Point*:

On May 30 Prime Minister Eshkol sent me a message confirming that there had been a meeting of the minds on May 26. Eshkol's cable assured me that Eban's conversation with me had had "an important in-

fluence on our decision to await developments for a further limited period." He went on to say: "It is crucial that the international naval escort
should move through the Strait within a week or two."

As my advisers and I interpreted it, the phrase "within a week or
two" meant that we had about two weeks to make diplomacy succeed
before Israel took independent military action. This judgment was
strengthened by information from other diplomatic sources.

Early in June we sensed that the Israelis might be moving towards a
decision to reopen Aqaba on their own, but we still believed that we
had time to reach a settlement through diplomacy. On the morning of
June 2 a high-ranking Israeli diplomat [presumably Israel's deputy chief
of mission, Ephraim Evron] called on Walt Rostow. He [Rostow] sent
me a report immediately afterwards containing the following information: "I then asked . . . how much time did they think they had? He
replied that they had made a commitment to hold steady for about two
weeks. He would measure that from the Cabinet meeting last Sunday
[May 28]. Therefore, he was talking about things that might happen in
the week after next; that is, the week beginning Sunday, June 11—although he indicated that there was nothing ironclad about the time period being exactly two weeks."

On the same day, before leaving for Israel, Ambassador Avraham
Harman told Rusk that the test in the Gulf of Aqaba would be made in
the course of "the next week."

The remarks of these Israeli diplomats reflect a decision taken (although not formally inscribed as such) by Israel's cabinet on May 28 to
wait at least another two weeks before striking at Egypt.[20] That decision
was reversed on June 3 at a meeting at Eshkol's house. Although Ambassador Harman, who was present at that meeting, expressed the view that
Israel should wait another week because of its commitment to the United
States, the opposing view carried the day.[21] Johnson may have been told
of this decision, but other US officials were not.

The Americans did not have great confidence that Israel would honor
the two-week commitment, but they had no realistic alternative to taking
it seriously and hoping that it would hold long enough for them to work
out a diplomatic solution. The agreement for Zakaria Muhieddin's visit
was the first sign that such a solution might be possible, although Muhieddin himself was not confident that anything would come of it.[22]
Meanwhile, the Americans had given no commitment of their own to
Egypt that Israel would hold off for two weeks, or any other period. Their
protestations that the United States did not control Israel were lost on the
Egyptians, however, who found it difficult to believe Israel would act on
its own. Perhaps they had heard Ben-Gurion's views in this regard, i.e.,
that Israel should wait until it had an ally who would go into the field
with it.

The question remains. If Nasser thought he still had ten days or two
weeks, why did he give a warning on June 2 of a strike on June 5?

THE GREEN LIGHT

Part of the mythology in both Egypt and Israel is that the United States, and specifically President Johnson, gave Israel a green light to attack Egypt. The standard source quoted by Egyptians today in support of this belief is William Quandt's aforementioned description of the Eban-Johnson meeting of May 26[23] which quotes Johnson as saying, after Eban left the room, "I've failed. They'll go." Or, alternatively, "The Israelis are going to hit them." When I spoke to Mahmoud Riad about that in 1989, he commented, "It seems Johnson wanted them to strike."[24]

In *The Vantage Point*, Johnson focuses on remarks he made to Eban in the May 26 conversation: "The central point, Mr. Minister," I told him, "is that your nation not be the one to bear the responsibility for any outbreak of war." Then I said very slowly and very positively: "Israel will not be alone unless it decides to go alone."[25] Twenty years ago I was told by a well-placed Israeli official that Eban and his political secretary, Moshe Raviv, discussed this language on the way home from Washington and decided that it meant that if Israel struck first it would be on its own, but that did not mean the United States would oppose it. What Israel was particularly afraid of was a repetition of 1956, when the United States compelled it to give up Sinai and Gaza. While some Israelis were arguing that it was militarily risky to go it alone, Israel's military establishment was confident of its ability to do the job by itself. The principal Israeli concern was not the military equation but the diplomatic. Israel did not want to be deprived of the results of its victory by an angry United States. That is a recurring theme in Israeli writings on the period.[26]

A more recent evaluation by the same Israeli source is that the Israelis understood from Johnson's remarks that he thought war was probably inevitable but that he was seeking a way to avoid it and wanted time to try for a peaceful solution. As a result of his urgings, Israel delayed attacking for a week, but war was indeed inevitable. Heikal had said it all in *Al-Ahram*. Israel could not accept the threat Egypt was posing and could not keep its troops mobilized indefinitely. It had to respond to Egypt's buildup in the Sinai, where 100,000 men had been concentrated by June 5. In these circumstances, Israel had regarded Johnson's words not as a green light but as a cautionary one, i.e., not a red light.

The Americans, on the other hand, thought they were giving Israel an unequivocal message not to strike the first blow. It is hard to see how Johnson could have put it in plainer English, and those officials closely involved with the process thought the message had been clear. In pursuit of this issue I talked to, among others, Ambassador Battle; Harold Saunders, who was then Walt Rostow's assistant on the National Security Council staff; and Richard Helms, then director of the CIA. Battle told me: "To the best of my knowledge there was no other conversation. I took it at the time as a warning not to go. That's what I believe. So many different interpretations have been placed on it now."[27] Saunders commented that as far as he could tell, it certainly was not Johnson's intent to flash a green light. He felt that Johnson was quite sincere in not wanting Israel to attack. Saunders had written a memo to Rostow during this period in which he pointed out that no one was even thinking about unleashing the Israelis. Rostow had replied that there was no way the president could consider the option of turning the Israelis loose. Saunders noted that Johnson was preoccupied with Vietnam and terribly worried Israel would get into trouble and have to be rescued. That was one reason he was so insistent in asking that the initial estimate of Israel's military superiority be reexamined by the Pentagon and the CIA. His statement to Eban about Israel not being alone if it did not go it alone was a reflection of this concern. After the war Johnson told a number of Israelis that they had made a terrible mistake, complicating life for others.[28] Helms commented that the allegation that Johnson had given a green light to the Israelis was "baloney." Neither Johnson nor the people around him had interpreted Johnson's attitude as permissive.[29]

Support for the "baloney" view comes from the fact that by my count the Americans sent at least nine high-level messages to Israel telling it not to start the fighting. These messages are described in Brecher's *Decisions in Crisis,* among other places. Here is a summary.

May 18—The Israelis receive a message from Johnson to Eshkol dealing with Syrian situation and warning against retaliatory action. "I want to emphasize strongly that you have to abstain from every step that would increase the tension and violence in the area. You will probably understand that the United States cannot accept any responsibility for situations that are liable to occur as a result of actions in which we were not consulted."[30]

May 21—Eban receives a message from the Department of State saying that the U.S. position is that the problem should be handled in a peaceful manner, preferably through the U.N.[31]

May 22—The Israelis receive a letter from Johnson to Eshkol saying the U.S. would support suitable measures inside and outside the United Nations and suggesting Israel work toward renewal of the Tripartite Declaration.[32]

May 23—Eban read out to the Ministerial Defense Committee a telegram from Minister Ephraim Evron in Washington which contained a formal request by Under Secretary of State Eugene Rostow, on President Johnson's behalf, that Israel take no decision for the next forty-eight hours and that it consult with the United States. Again the president warned that he would not take any responsibility for actions on which he was not consulted.[33]

May 25—Secretary Rusk, following Eban's request for a declaration that an attack on Israel would be considered an attack on the United States, and after consulting with the president, informs Eban that the president did not have the authority to do that without full coordination with Congress. Rusk assured him the president would live up to American commitments, but it was essential that he act with the approval of Congress and public opinion. In the meantime, Israel should not take preemptive action.[34]

May 26—President Johnson receives Eban. The Johnson version is given above. The Israeli report of the conversation, as reported by Evron, has a somewhat different cast to it. He reports Johnson as saying that Israel was a sovereign government, and if it decided to act alone, it could of course do so, but in that case everything that happened before and afterwards would be upon its responsibility and the United States would have no obligation for any consequences which might ensue. He refused to believe that Israel would carry out unilateral action which was bound to bring her great damage. But, he added, that was Israel's affair.[35] Eban's account adds that the president constantly referred to a piece of paper which he gave Eban as an aide-mémoire and which contained the following language: "I must emphasize the necessity for Israel not to make itself responsible for the initiation of hostilities. Israel will not be alone unless it decides to do it alone. We cannot imagine that Israel will make this decision."[36]

May 28—Eshkol receives Johnson's message of May 27 saying that Moscow claimed to have information about Israel's preparations to provoke a conflict and that "the Soviets state that if Israel starts military action, the Soviet Union will extend help to the attacked states." The president repeated his concern about the safety and vital interests of Israel and continued: "As your friend, I repeat even more strongly what I said yesterday to Mr. Eban: Israel must not take pre-emptive military action and thereby make itself responsible for the initiation of hostilities."[37] Also on May 28, Secretary Rusk transmitted through Ambassador Barbour in Tel Aviv the following addendum to a message giving the U.S. résumé of the Johnson-Eban conversation: ". . . With the assurance of international determination to keep the Straits open to the flags of all nations, unilateral action on the part of Israel would be irresponsible and catastrophic."[38]

June 3—Eshkol receives another message from Johnson which emphasized the "vital national interests of the United States" in the right of free and innocent passage through international waterways including the Gulf of Aqaba and repeating his warning: "I must emphasize the necessity for Israel not to make itself responsible for the initiation of hostilities; Israel will not be alone, unless it decides to go alone." It is not clear from the record whether Eshkol had received this message by the time he and his kitchen cabinet met that afternoon and decided to strike.[39]

ISRAEL'S DECISION

The formal decision to strike was not taken by Israel's cabinet until June 4, but in effect the decision had already been taken at an informal meeting of what Brecher calls Israel's political and bureaucratic elites at Eshkol's apartment in Jerusalem on the evening of June 3. Brecher describes the meeting:

> Harman and Amit arrived from Washington in the afternoon. Harman's full report about his contacts with the American Administration again showed that measures to be taken by the maritime powers were still under consideration but that nothing had been firmly decided. The evening meeting was held at Eshkol's Jerusalem home, beginning at 23:00. Present were Allon, Dayan, Eban, Dinstein, Rabin, Yadin, Amit, Yariv, Herzog, Levavi, and Harman. The central issue was whether or not the United States and the Soviet Union would be aligned on the same side, against Israel, if hostilities began. Although Harman expressed the view that Israel ought to wait another week, because of the US belief that they had been given that much time to complete their plans, there was a broad consensus that nothing further could be gained from additional waiting. Amit concurred and the day's events tended to support this assessment. Further, Amit's judgment was that if Israel decided to act alone, the US would not resist. Those present agreed with Eshkol's and Eban's view that the US would extend diplomatic support in the aftermath. There was also agreement that the Soviet Union would not intervene militarily. . . . The meeting ended with unanimous agreement to recommend to the Cabinet the next day the decision to go to war."[40]

A number of factors were moving Israel in the direction of this decision, and these officials saw time as working against them. Prolongation of the mobilization, which had begun on May 19, was costly, and each passing day allowed Egypt to consolidate its position in Sinai. Israel's military leaders were anxious to move sooner rather than later, and had it not been for President Johnson's urging, the cabinet probably would have voted for war on May 28. Pressures to act had been reinforced by events since May 28, notably the unexpected trip of King Hussein to Cairo and the signing of a defense agreement between Jordan and Egypt.

At the same time, the Israelis were disturbed by U.S. insistence on exhausting multilateral channels, including the United Nations, and by the absence of an unequivocal U.S. commitment to force the Strait of Tiran and confront Egypt militarily on Israel's behalf. They noted, for instance, that a message from Johnson received on June 3 was vague on the possibility of naval action.[41] Although they received repeated assurances that the Americans were serious about their commitment to freedom of navigation and were making progress on mobilizing a multilateral naval force to uphold that commitment, the Israelis kept scanning these assurances anxiously and critically, looking for an ironclad commitment that was not there. The United States was in a difficult position. It did not want to confront Egypt militarily, not only because it was tied down in Vietnam, but also because it did not want to risk the Arab animosity which would result. It hoped for a political compromise of some sort, but that was something the Israelis feared would be at their expense. Their concerns in this respect were probably heightened by the information that Muhieddin was going to Washington. Rusk informed Ambassador Harman of this on June 2.[42]

The objective factors were all pushing Israel in the direction of war. There remained the critical question of the American, and specifically Johnson's, attitude. Two Israelis, Eban and Amit, played a prominent role in convincing Prime Minister Eshkol that the United States would not actively oppose Israel if it struck.

Eban

Eban's report of his conversation with Johnson had been instrumental in the May 28 decision to wait two weeks, a decision which was controversial at the time and which Eban goes to some pains to defend in his autobiography. On May 30 Eshkol and he decided that they should re-evaluate the U.S. attitude, and Eshkol decided to send Meir Amit, the chief of Mossad, to Washington for another sounding of high-level views. He left on May 31 or June 1, returning June 3.

Meanwhile, Eban himself underwent a change of heart on the afternoon of June 1 when he received "a document which had a decisive effect on my attitude." He writes:

> An American, known for his close contact with government thinking, had described the situation to one of our friends in Washington as follows:
> "If Israel had acted alone without exhausting political efforts it would have made a catastrophic error. It would then have been almost impossible for the United States to help Israel and the ensuing relationship would have been tense. The war might be long and costly for Israel if it broke out. If Israel had fired the first shot before the United Nations discussion she would have negated any possibility of the United States helping her. Israelis should not criticize Eshkol and Eban; they should realize that their restraint and well-considered procedures would have a decisive influence when the United States came to consider the measure of its involvement."
> What I found new in this information was the absence of any exhortation to stay our hand much longer. . . . At the same time there came over the wires a report of one of Secretary Rusk's press comments. He had been asked whether, in addition to American plans for action in the United Nations, any efforts would be made to restrain Israel from pre-

cipitate action. The Secretary brusquely replied, "I don't think it is our business to restrain anyone."

When my senior officers had assembled, I requested a meticulous scrutiny of all the cables and conversations that had taken place with the United States in the past forty-eight hours. It emerged that since the communication which had reached us on the morning of May 28, no responsible American leader had assumed the authority to urge Israel to wait. . . .

I now came to the conclusion that I must take a decisive step that very day. It seemed that the diplomatic and political exercise on which we had been engaged since May 23 had reached its maximal result. The United States was less confident about its own action and less inclined to take responsibility for restraining Israel than a few days ago. . . .

I returned to our Tel Aviv office and asked the Director General, Aryeh Levavi, to accompany me across the lawn to a meeting with the Chief of Staff, General Rabin, and the chief of military intelligence, General Yariv. I told them that I no longer had any political inhibitions to such military resistance as was deemed feasible.[43]

To put it kindly, it would have been disingenuous of Eban to base his interpretation of the communication from the unnamed American on the fact that he had not had a message of restraint from the Americans for four days (this was not true in any event—Secretary Rusk had again cautioned Ambassador Harman against initiating hostilities on June 2—State Department telegram 297977, June 2) and on a press quote attributed to Rusk. He must, or should, have had more on which to base a decision this important.

Since publication of the Eban book there has been speculation as to who the unnamed American might have been. We now know that it was Supreme Court Justice Abe Fortas. These events are discussed in detail in an article by William Quandt in the spring 1992 issue of the *Middle East Journal*, "Lyndon Johnson and the June 1967 War: What Color Was the Light?" In that article Quandt refers to a July 26, 1990, letter to him from Eban on the subject. The key paragraphs of that letter read:

While I was under pressure from our army chiefs to relax my provisional veto on military action, I received a message from Minister Evron of a talk that he had with the late Justice Abraham Fortas. Fortas, despite his judicial function, often acted as an unofficial emissary in the international field. The Justice said that "Eshkol and Eban *did* great service to Israel by giving the U.S. a chance to explore options other than Israeli force. If they had not done so, it *would have* been difficult to secure the President's sympathy.

I observed that all this was formulated in the past tense. It was not accompanied by any further appeal for patience. This seemed to me to be as near a green light as a President could safely give. I called the Generals [Rabin and Yariv] and told them that as Foreign Minister I no longer asked for any military restraint in the name of diplomatic necessity.

The result was that the United States helped Israel to reject Soviet and Arab proposals in the U.N. Security Council for total withdrawal of Israeli forces without the establishment of peace. This was the result of the restraint and the diplomatic activity undertaken in the period May 24 to June 1, 1967.

Amit

Amit made a very quick round trip between Tel Aviv and Washington. According to the official record, he saw only Helms and his subordinates at the CIA and McNamara and others at the Pentagon. Johnson's June 3 letter to Eshkol mentions that "we have completely and fully exchanged views with General Amit" (Department of State telegram 207955, June 3) but there is no indication in the record that Amit had direct contact with the White House.

No official account has been published of what Amit said to the kitchen cabinet on his return. In *Dangerous Liaison*, Andrew and Leslie Cockburn quote the memoirs of Israel Lior, Eshkol's military secretary, which have Amit saying that there were no significant differences between U.S. and Israeli intelligence assessments, that the United States was not going to use its navy to break the blockade of the Strait of Tiran and, most important, that he had been given to understand that the United States would bless the Israelis if they were to "break Nasser to pieces."[44] I have been given a similar account by another Israeli who was present. According to my source, Eshkol had asked if the United States would interfere and Amit had replied that according to what he had heard, they were ready to help with arms, money, and political support. My source and Lior's account agree that Amit's report was decisive for Eshkol, who had been waiting for a green light from Johnson.[45]

WHAT TO BELIEVE

What can we believe out of all this? We must be careful about accepting any account which is not documented, but several things seem clear.

First, the Israelis heard what they wanted to hear and ignored what they did not.

Second, while Johnson's strictures sound unequivocal, there is a certain ambiguity to them. He did not want Israel to attack but realized that his ability to restrain it was limited. He and the Washington military establishment were concerned that Israel would get in trouble and have to be rescued. He wanted at least to be on record as having tried to dissuade the Israelis, but he did not want to put himself in a position of being defied. If he had wanted to be categoric, he could have threatened to use sanctions or to move against Israel in the United Nations if it moved to preempt. Instead, what he told the Israelis was that they would be on their own, and the Israelis interpreted this correctly as meaning there would be no repeat of 1956. (William Quandt, in the *Middle East Journal* article referred to earlier, argues convincingly that in fact there was a change in the tone, if not in the substance, of Johnson's urgings by June 1, and the Israelis were correct in sensing it.)

Third, although there was no suggestion of it in official records in Washington, except for Walt Rostow's famous reference to the first day of fighting as "the turkey shoot," many members of the U.S. establishment would not have minded if Israel gave Nasser a bloody nose. Johnson probably shared that sentiment.

Fourth, Johnson nevertheless realized the problems war would pose, and he did not give Israel a green light. Unless the Stephen Green allegation that the United States flew reconnaissance missions for Israel is true, there was no collusion. But American opposition to an Israeli first strike was not as unequivocal as it could have been, and Johnson's performance after the fighting started showed a clear and lasting bias in favor of Israel and a disregard for the public commitments he and his administration had made to oppose aggression from any quarter. The Arabs have a legitimate complaint on that score, but there was no deliberate U.S. attempt to mislead them in the period leading up to the war. Rather, a serious effort was made to restrain all the parties and prevent a resort to arms. It failed because the Arabs were not really interested in restraint. They thought they were on the road to victory. When they lost and cried aggression, the response in Washington was to say that Israel had struck in a legitimate act of self-defense and that the Arabs had asked for what they got.

There is a remarkable message (State 207956; see text in the appendix, document 14) which summarizes the position in which the United States found itself on the eve of the war. Sent by Secretary Rusk to his ambassadors in Arab capitals on the evening of June 3, 1967, it is remarkable both because of its content and because it was drafted by Rusk personally and evidently not shown to anyone else before he sent it. (He was perhaps the last secretary of state capable of drafting such a message by himself.) The message was in response to a number of telegrams from the ambassadors, the gist of which was that the United States should restrain Israel and avoid confrontation with Egypt.

Rusk's message said that the ambassadors should not assume that the United States could order Israel not to fight for what it considered its most vital interests: "We have used the utmost restraint and, thus far, have been able to hold Israel back. But the 'Holy War' psychology of the Arab world is matched by an apocalyptic psychology within Israel. . . . Each side appears to look with relative equanimity upon the prospect of major hostilities and each side apparently is confident of success. Which estimate is correct cannot be fully known unless tested by the event, but someone is making a major miscalculation." Rusk claimed that in application of its commitments to support the political independence and territorial integrity of all the nations of the area, the United States had supported Egypt at the time of the 1956 tripartite invasion, had supported Lebanon when threatened by Syria, Jordan when threatened by Egypt, Saudi Arabia when threatened by Egypt, Libya against Egypt, and Israel against terrorist attacks. It had censored Israel in the strongest terms for the attack on Samuᶜ. There was a strong case for the idea that the United States had been evenhanded with respect to the political independence and territorial integrity issue. A major issue in the present crisis was the commitments made at the time of Suez, when the United States obtained the withdrawal of Israeli forces from Sinai in exchange for assurances about the right of passage through the Strait of Tiran. Egypt was aware of these positions, and although it did not endorse them at the time, it was the beneficiary of the arrangements made. The United States had given pledges on the matter and must give the most sober attention to all the implications of such pledges and any failure on its part to insist upon them. The message concluded: "It will do no good to ask Israel simply to accept the present status quo in the Strait because Israel will fight and we could not restrain her. We cannot throw up our hands and say that, in that event, let them fight while we try to remain neutral."

That was the last major message from the department before the fighting started. It reflected Rusk's personal thinking, and perhaps the president's as well. It made clear the limits of Washington's ability to restrain Israel and its unwillingness to wash its hands of the affair. The message also expressed in polite terms Rusk's impatience with the unhelpful messages he was receiving from his ambassadors in Arab capitals such as Cairo, Beirut, and Amman, each of whom, as seen from Washington, was too focused on local considerations and insufficiently cognizant of the big picture. But it also contained a repetition of the U.S. commitment to the independence and territorial integrity of the states of the area. Twenty-five years later, the territorial issue remains the principal unresolved consequence of the war.

PART TWO

———

THE WAR OF ATTRITION

CHAPTER
6

WAR AND NONWAR

A man would have to be blind, deaf and
dumb not to sense how much the administration favors our military operations. .

Yitzhak Rabin, September 19, 1969

The War of Attrition between Israel and Egypt in the period 1967–70 was
a sideshow in a world arena where Vietnam was the main event. Yet it
was a deadly serious confrontation between a defeated Egypt striving to
reassert itself as a regional power and a victorious Israel which saw little
need to compromise with the vanquished.

It was an expensive contest, although the losses seem small on a world
scale. The most comprehensive and authoritative account of this conflict
is David Korn's *Stalemate: The War of Attrition and Great Power Diplomacy in
the Middle East.* Korn puts Israel's casualties on all fronts at 3,500, of whom
750 were killed. Egypt's casualty figures have never been released. Korn
says the Israelis estimated them at 10,000.[1] Egypt's losses were propor-
tionally lower than Israel's, but they were a serious political and military
burden for both countries, even though the governments of both concealed the damage being done from the public and the international community.

This minor war laid the groundwork for the Egyptian offensive in 1973,
led to the first Soviet commitment of troops to the defense of a state
outside the East bloc, and posed a major, and eventually frustrating, challenge to the Israeli Defense Forces, whose apparent military triumph had
unforeseen consequences.

Most important for our purposes, this war was marked by a major
miscalculation of Soviet intentions by the United States and Israel. Neither took seriously a warning from the Soviets that they would have to
do something if Israel did not stop its deep penetration raids into the
Egyptian heartland in early 1970. When the Soviets subsequently made a
major commitment of men and equipment to defend Egypt against these
raids, it came as a shock to both the Americans and the Israelis, both of
whom were victims of their perceptions regarding Soviet behavior and,

at least in the case of the Israelis, their obsession with bringing down Nasser.

Little of the official record for this period is in the public domain. The narrative I present here is based largely on personal notes made when I was director of UAR affairs in the Department of State from August 1967 to May 1970, on published sources, and on interviews with survivors.

ROUND ONE: THE CEASE-FIRE OBSERVED

The cease-fire between Egypt and Israel went into effect on June 8, 1967. Marshal ʿAmr had left general headquarters the night before,* telling the chief of staff, General Fawzi, not to worry about the army and to ask Badran, the war minister, if he needed help. On the eighth, Badran told Fawzi the Soviets would help the Eygptians and that he and ʿAmr were resigning. On the ninth the Soviet military attaché came to see Fawzi and asked for a report on materiel lost and destroyed. A massive Soviet airlift of supplies began two days later, and the rebuilding of the UAR armed forces was under way.[2]

On the same day that the Soviet airlift began, Nasser, who had resigned on June 9 and then reversed himself under popular pressure, appointed Fawzi as commander of the armed forces and began discussing with him the reform and rebuilding of the military establishment. General Abdul Mun'im Riad, who had been head of the United Arab Command during the war, was made chief of staff. According to Heikal, Fawzi was picked because he was a stern disciplinarian who was the sort of man needed to whip the army into shape. It was a daunting task. The command structure was in total disarray. The air force had lost all of its fighter aircraft and the army 85 percent of its equipment; 17 percent of army personnel were casualties, not to mention the many soldiers who had deserted to their villages following their retreat from Sinai.

Egypt's immediate concern was that Israel would mount another offensive across the Suez Canal, and the first task was to organize a defense. The Egyptians were helped in this task by the Soviets, who brought in 1,500 advisers and trainers as well as equipment. By mid-November 1967, Marshal Zakharov, the Soviet chief of staff who oversaw the Soviet effort, could tell Nasser that the defenses could stand up to anything Israel could deliver.[3]

Israel meanwhile was enjoying its new conquests and the novelty of being on the bank of the Suez Canal. A visit there was on all the best itineraries, Israeli soldiers went swimming in the canal, insults were hurled across the water by both sides, and Egypt's humiliation was complete. Its

*According to Fawzi; Baghdadi's memoirs mention a meeting with ʿAmr at headquarters on the night of the eighth.

military capabilities were rated at zero, and although Israel's cabinet decided on June 19 to give back all of Sinai in return for a peace treaty, Israel soon began to have second thoughts about the need for doing that, particularly since Egypt was helpless.

The diplomats and politicians were at work, and on June 19 President Johnson announced his five-point approach to a peaceful solution: a recognized right of national life for everyone, justice for the Palestine refugees, freedom of innocent maritime passage (i.e., for peaceful as opposed to combatant traffic), limits on the arms race, and political independence and territorial integrity for all. These principles were the basis for a draft resolution presented to the U.N. General Assembly in special session on June 20. It was never brought to a vote, however.

Johnson met with Soviet Premier Kosygin at Glassboro on June 23 and 25. Johnson reported that they agreed on some basic principles—every state has a right to live, there should be peace in the Middle East, and there should be withdrawal under the right circumstances—but that there was no agreement on the details. Kosygin was more explicit, saying that the Soviets believed an immediate Israeli withdrawal was the first prerequisite while the Americans were insisting on first considering a complex set of questions relating to the Middle East. The lines drawn here remained more or less fixed thereafter, the Soviets insisting on withdrawal and the Americans insisting that it must be in the context of a peace agreement. Thus began the process that led to the U.N. Security Council's Resolution 242 and to a series of abortive efforts at a peaceful settlement, culminating years later in the partial success of Camp David.

Things did not remain static on the canal. Firing across it began in August and escalated to the point that Israel began targeting Egypt's economic installations, such as the Suez oil refinery, in September. By October an estimated 60 percent of the civilian population in the canal area had been evacuated to the Nile Valley, causing enormous human problems there.

On October 21, Egyptian missile boats firing Soviet-supplied Styx missiles sank the Israeli destroyer *Eilat* at a location not far from that occupied by the *Liberty* at the time it was attacked on June 8. Egypt may have been seeking revenge for one of its missile boats the Israelis said they sank on September 4. Israel claimed the *Eilat* was in international waters, while Egypt said it was within the twelve-mile limit. The report of U.N. observers who had been stationed along the canal since June 1967 supported Egypt's claim, but it was not clear where they got their information. In any event, in addition to marking the introduction of missiles into modern naval combat, it was a serious loss for Israel. On October 23 it estimated casualties at fifteen known dead, thirty-six missing, and forty-eight wounded. The final death count was forty-seven.

Israel responded immediately with air attacks on UAR missile boats in

Egyptian ports. The Soviet Union responded to that by returning eight of its naval vessels to Egyptian ports, where their presence served to inhibit further Israeli air attacks.

A period of relative calm followed. Both sides seemed to be consolidating their positions. The passage of Resolution 242 on November 22 held out the promise of a peaceful settlement, which would obviate the need for further fighting. Gunnar Jarring, the U.N. mediator, began his travels, and there was an initial expectation that he would work out a modus vivendi under which Israel would withdraw in return for an Arab commitment to peace. These expectations were dashed by Arab unwillingness to give the sort of commitments Israel was demanding as the price of withdrawal and by decreasing Israeli interest in exchanging land for commitments of any kind from the Arabs. As Rodger Davies, then deputy assistant secretary of state for Near Eastern affairs, remarked, their appetite had grown with the eating. The ensuing diplomatic stalemate was to last for eleven years.

Egypt did not have great faith in the efficacy of the United Nations, which it saw as being dominated by Israel's patron, the United States. Egypt hoped that Jarring would be able to arrange an Israeli withdrawal but suspected that in the final analysis that would come only as the result of military pressure from Egypt. After hearing from Marshal Zakharov that Egypt's new defenses could stand up to Israel, Nasser instructed General Fawzi to start planning for what became the War of Attrition. On November 29 Nasser told his military commanders they would have to train for five years before taking the offensive. That there would eventually have to be an offensive was already an Egyptian conviction.

With the new year came a new Egyptian cabinet, announced on January 24, 1968. General Fawzi became minister of war. The canal remained quiet, although there was constant talk of how the Egyptians were going to liberate their territory. Nasser told the armed forces in March that having regained its defensive capability the army was being prepared for offensive tasks. In April he said that plans were being made for the Arabs to pass from the stage of *sumud,* or steadfastness, to *nasr,* or victory. Few observers outside Egypt took these remarks seriously, however, because Egypt's capabilities were still rated very low.

The lull ended in June. On the first anniversary of the June War, Ashraf Ghorbal, chief of the UAR Interests Section in the Indian Embassy in Washington, paid a formal call on Lucius Battle, the former ambassador to Cairo who was now assistant secretary of state for Near Eastern and South Asian affairs (NEA), to complain that an entire year had passed since the June War began and that there had been no movement on the withdrawal issue.[4] Resolution 242 had been passed, Jarring had been appointed, and there had been no results. How long would this stalemate be permitted to go on? Battle sympathized and said the United States was working on the problem. (In fact, it was not actually doing anything serious about it, particularly given the absence of a clear UAR commitment to a negotiated settlement.) Ghorbal's representation seemed to be personal and not on instructions. The attitude of the UAR government toward the United States at the time did not encourage diplomatic dialogue. It was typified by a message which Anwar Sadat, chairman of the National Assembly, sent to North Korea complimenting it on the seizure of the U.S. electronic surveillance vessel *Pueblo*.[5]

A few days later, on June 14, an artillery duel broke out along the canal. The U.N. observers were uncertain who started it. On June 18 an Egyptian patrol was intercepted by Israel near Rumana, in the northern sector. Egypt denied involvement. On June 22 there was another artillery exchange for which the U.N. observers blamed Egypt. It was evident that Egypt was taking a more active posture, but Israel was unworried. Swimming in the canal continued, and Israeli officials with whom I discussed the situation on June 19 and 20 in Jerusalem and Tel Aviv appeared to believe that Egypt could not inflict any serious damage on Israel. That view was shared by Washington.

The first really serious incident after the sinking of the *Eilat* was an artillery duel in the Suez–Port Tawfiq area on July 8. Israel shelled the town of Suez, and Egypt reported that forty-three civilians were killed and sixty-seven wounded. Both sides protested to the Security Council, but the U.N. observers did not commit themselves as to who started the firing.

Nasser was in Moscow at that time to discuss military aid and other problems. In great pain, he was diagnosed as having hardening of the arteries in his legs, brought on by diabetes. A month's cure at the Tskhaltubo spa was recommended. Nasser returned to Cairo for the July 23 Revolution Day celebrations with the intention of returning to Russia thereafter, but he postponed going back because of the situation along the canal. On September 10 he had a heart attack, probably brought on by too much work in the wake of the Libyan revolution, and the Russians said he was too weakened to take the Tskhaltubo treatment. He remained in Cairo, disobeyed doctor's orders to rest, and eventually paid for it with his life.[6]

In late summer Egypt was reported to be planning a limited offensive against Israel, and on August 26 an Egyptian military unit crossed the canal, ambushed an Israeli jeep, wounded two Israeli soldiers, and captured a third. The UAR denied responsibility, saying it was observing the cease-fire scrupulously. Israel noted that no one else was capable of undertaking such activities east of the canal.

On September 8 a major artillery duel erupted along the canal from Suez north to al-Qantara. It was the first of what became a regular series in which Israel was clearly outgunned by Egypt, which had massed large numbers of artillery weapons behind the canal. On September 14 Nasser spelled out what he said were the three steps from steadfastness to victory: steadfastness, liberation *(tahrir)*, victory.

ROUND TWO: THE CEASE-FIRE SCORNED

On October 26 the UAR opened heavy fire on Israeli positions. Two commando platoons totaling thirty to fifty men crossed the canal and attacked Israeli units. Fifteen Israelis and five Egyptians were reported killed. The Israelis had been caught napping. One unit had been playing football when the firing started. Each side accused the other of starting it, but the U.N. observers said the UAR began the firing. This attack signaled the end of the swimming-in-the-canal period. At about this time Egypt began talking about "preventive defense."

On the same day, Parker T. Hart, the new U.S. assistant secretary for Near Eastern affairs, and I called on Mahmoud Riad, Egypt's foreign minister, in New York. Riad was there for the General Assembly meetings. The United Nations was one of the few venues in which Egypt and the United States continued to have contacts at a senior level, in spite of the lack of diplomatic relations. Hart told Riad that the firing along the canal was complicating Jarring's mission and making progress on a peaceful settlement difficult. Riad said Hart had not seen anything yet. There would be increasing incidents as long as Israel occupied Arab territory. If Israel went to the Security Council about these incidents, the Arabs would file their own complaint and the council would have to decide which took preference, cease-fire or national sovereignty. Egypt had adhered to the cease-fire with the understanding that Israel would withdraw within a reasonable period. When Resolution 242 was passed, everyone thought withdrawal would be arranged within two or three months. A year had passed and nothing had happened. Egypt would not acquiesce in the indefinite occupation of its territories, and no one had the right to raise firing incidents with the UAR unless the question of aggression and occupation was taken care of first.

With some slight changes of nuance, that remained the UAR's position until the summer of 1970. The UAR had decided not to be bound by the cease-fire as long as there was no progress on implementing Resolution 242, and although it is customary to consider the beginning of the War of Attrition as March 1969, the opening rounds actually were fired on October 26, 1968, if not on September 8.* That was not understood by U.S. officials at the time. Hart and I were impressed by Riad's firmness and apparent lack of interest in the political process, but we were puzzled

*In *The Crossing of Suez: The October War* (p. 15), General Saad Shazly says the War of Attrition began in September 1968.

about Egypt's intentions because we did not think it was capable of inflicting serious damage.

In Israel's Knesset, General Dayan responded on October 29 to Egypt's raid of the twenty-sixth with a statement that Egypt must expect countermeasures. Israel had lost 101 killed and 300 wounded since June 8, 1967. This warning was followed on the night of October 31–November 1 by an Israeli commando raid on bridges and power facilities at Naga῾ Hammadi and Qena, in Upper Egypt. This was the first strike beyond the Canal Zone, and there was satisfaction in Israel, although the press expressed some reservations. *Haaretz* saw short-run advantage but long-run damage because such actions would lead Egypt to strengthen its defenses. *Maariv* argued that such initiatives should become systematic; otherwise they would become a two-edged sword.

Egypt was sensitive to such a threat to its lifeline and filed a complaint in the Security Council. But it eased up on its own firing, and a period of relative calm ensued. At the same time there were reports that the Soviet Union was letting it be known that it would intervene to protect the Aswan Dam if it were threatened. For its part, Israel, which had been taking too many casualties, began building the so-called Bar Lev line, a string of fortresses along the east bank of the canal designed for two purposes: to render it difficult if not impossible for the Egyptians to cross it and to reduce the risk of casualties from artillery shelling and sniping. The decision to opt for a static as opposed to a mobile defense was a fateful one for the Israelis, since it tied them to a fixed line along which Egypt could deliver more fire than Israel could deliver in return. Given their greater tolerance for casualties, the Egyptians were momentarily one-up, although no one seemed to realize it at the time. Certainly I did not.

While the military situation was undergoing a transformation, there was also action of a sort on the diplomatic front. On September 4 the Soviet Union presented a note to the United States proposing a settlement based on three points: the Arabs and Israelis would accept Resolution 242, a timetable would be worked out for Israeli withdrawal, and both sides would sign a multilateral document committing them to respect all sections of Resolution 242. A few days later, Yitzhak Rabin, Israel's chief of staff in the June War and now its ambassador in Washington, called on Secretary Rusk to urge rejection of the Soviet proposal, reaffirming Israel's insistence on a bilateral, contractual peace agreement. The United States subsequently turned down the proposal, adhering to the principles in Johnson's five points, saying that peace must be based on an agreement that is directly binding on the sides and maintaining that the language of 242 did not necessarily mean a return to the 1967 lines. Rabin learned of the reply on October 1 and was pleased with it.[7]

Rabin was less pleased when Rusk took an initiative on his own about a month later. Rusk was scheduled to call on Mahmoud Riad in New York late in the afternoon on November 2. At my suggestion, the Egyptians offered Rusk a drink of bourbon, which he liked to have late in the day. The meeting was more relaxed than usual as a result. Much to everyone's surprise, Rusk fished out of his pocket a piece of paper which contained what has come to be known as Rusk's seven points. (Actually there were eight points, but only seven of them were written on the paper.) According to my notes, they were Israeli withdrawal from the territory of the UAR; a formal termination of the state of war; the Suez Canal then to be open to all flagships; the answer on refugees to be found on the basis of the personal and secret choice of the refugees on where to live (Rusk later clarified this to say it included the choice of return to Israel as one of, say, fifteen countries, but that this meant Israel, and not Palestine, since the latter did not exist, having been replaced by Israel and Jordan; I understood the fifteen countries to include the United States); an international presence at Sharm al-Shaykh which could not be removed without the consent of the Security Council or the General Assembly; a general understanding about the level of arms in the area so as to avoid an arms race (although this point would not be required in the first instance); and the UAR should sign something in writing to which Israel was also a signatory (there was much backing and filling in those days about finding a formula under which the Arabs would agree to sign the same instrument as the Israelis; we have come a long way since then).

After Riad read the paper, Rusk said there was another point: the UAR would not agree on a settlement unless something was worked out for the other Arab states; if something was worked out for the others, the UAR would agree to settle. This point was designed to assuage Egypt's apprehensions that the United States and Israel were trying to get the UAR to sign a separate peace and ditch the other Arabs, which would have had serious political repercussions for Egypt. That is what happened at Camp David ten years later, but it was unthinkable in 1968.

In the event, the eighth point seems not to have registered with Riad, because the Egyptian response, dated December 4, indicated that Cairo still thought the United States was trying for a separate peace. The response was legalistic and negative. A large offer had been made; Egypt should have accepted it quickly in principal and then argued about details. As it was, the United States considered the reply a rejection, much to the distress of Ghorbal, who maintained that it had really been positive. The United States, however, concluded that Egypt was hoping for a better offer from the Nixon Administration, which would be assuming power in a month, and was not interested in making any deals with the lame-duck Johnson Administration.

In 1980 I discussed this incident with Secretary Rusk during the latter's visit to the Air War College at Maxwell Air Force Base on a speaking engagement. I asked him where he had gotten the piece of paper he gave Riad, which had been a complete surprise to the Near Eastern affairs bureau. Rusk said he had thought up the points himself and had not consulted anyone about them—not the White House and not NEA. The paper was his own initiative, and the Egyptians had been fools not to take him up on it because the United States would have been committed to an outcome considerably more favorable than Egypt was likely to get by any other means.

Andrei Gromyko, the Soviet foreign minister, visited Cairo December 22–23, and the Soviets presented their own plan to the Americans on December 30. The plan called for formal acceptance of Resolution 242 by all parties and a commitment by Israel to withdraw from the territories it had seized by a fixed date in exchange for an Arab declaration of readiness to reach a peaceful settlement. Negotiations or "contacts" would then lead to agreement on secure and recognized borders, freedom of navigation in international waterways, and a just solution of the refugee problem. After withdrawal had begun, Egypt would clear the Suez Canal, which had been blocked by sunken ships in 1967. At a later date Israel would withdraw to the 1967 borders and Arab control would be reestablished over the occupied territories. U.N. forces might return to Sinai, the Security Council would guarantee freedom of navigation in the Gulf of Aqaba, and the borders agreed upon would be guaranteed by the Big Four powers (the United States, the USSR, Britain, and France). There might be demilitarized zones between Israel and its neighbors. Documents containing this agreement would be deposited with the United Nations on the day the Israeli withdrawal began.[8]

The United States filed a twelve-point counterplan on January 15, 1969. It included cessation of Arab terrorism; clarification of the belligerents' position on 242; Israeli withdrawal as part of a general solution; the 1949 armistice lines did not constitute definite political boundaries and could be modified; 242 did not state Israel must withdraw from the "occupied territories" but from "territories occupied during the conflict" (the pettifogging diplomatic mind at work); all aspects of implementing 242 must be agreed to before measures were taken to carry it out; the Soviet plan implied Israel would withdraw before the Arabs entered into a binding agreement; peace could only be reached by agreement and could not be imposed; all precautions must be taken to ensure free passage through the Strait of Tiran, including the stationing of U.N. troops if necessary; partial demilitarization of Sinai would not suffice; and there should be an agreement on the level of armaments in the area.[9]

The Soviet Union was still urging a timetable for withdrawal without direct negotiations between the Arabs and the Israelis and before a peace agreement had been signed, while the United States was calling for a contractual peace first and saying that Israel would not withdraw to the 1967 lines even then.

The Phantoms

Running through the U.S.-Israeli relationship at this period was a strong current of insistence by Israel on acquiring the F-4 Phantom, at that point the most potent war plane in the world. It surpassed anything the Soviets had to offer in terms of range and armament, and its introduction into the area would represent a significant escalation in the arms race. The U.S. administration, reluctant to supply it because of the implications it had for relations with the Arab states, had been trying to drag its feet on a response. It was subject to considerable pressure from Israel's supporters in the United States, but the coup de grâce was given by Senator Stuart Symington of Missouri, in whose state the Phantom factory of McDonnell Douglas lay. In the fall of 1968 he threatened to hold up indefinitely the military sales bill, which was very important to the administration, unless President Johnson agreed to sell Israel the Phantoms. Johnson gave in and announced on October 8 that the United States would supply the aircraft in question, but the Pentagon still hoped to extract some quid pro quo and tried to put conditions on the sale which the Israelis refused.[10]

Finally, under urging from Ambassador Rabin that the Democrats would lose credit for the sale unless they moved quickly, Johnson ordered on January 16 or 17, 1969, that the deal be concluded without further delay.[11] Although officials of the Department of State concerned with the Middle East were largely of the opinion that this sale would have unfortunate consequences for the United States, they were unable to be precise as to what those consequences would be, given the apparent inability of the Arabs to get together and do anything effective about either the United States or Israel.

The Nixon Administration

There were important changes in the dramatis personae with the entry of Richard Nixon into the White House. Parker Hart, who had been dragged unwillingly from his post as ambassador to Turkey to replace the retiring Lucius Battle as assistant secretary for Near Eastern and South Asian affairs and had been in the job only a few months, was replaced by Joseph Sisco. Sisco, who had been assistant secretary for international organization affairs, was a renowned bureaucratic infighter. He was an effective assistant secretary but was identified in the minds of Arab diplomats with what they considered false assurances of U.S. intentions to make Israel withdraw from the territories it had seized if they accepted Resolution 242. Sisco had difficulty convincing the Arabs of his sincerity as a result.

At the same time, William Rogers replaced Dean Rusk as secretary of state and Henry Kissinger replaced Walt Rostow at the White House as national security adviser. The Kissinger era had begun.

Across the water, Prime Minister Levi Eshkol died on February 22 and was succeeded shortly thereafter by Golda Meir, a considerably less peaceable person than he was.

Violations of the cease-fire continued along the canal. President Nixon may have had that in mind when he stated in a January 27 press conference that "I believe we need new initiatives and new leadership . . . to cool off the situation in the Mideast. I consider it a powder keg, very explosive. It needs to be defused. I am open to any suggestions that may cool it off and reduce the possibility of another explosion, because the next explosion in the Mideast, I think, could involve very well a confrontation between the nuclear powers."

Israel objected, saying the situation was under control, because it did not want to have the United States getting excited about the risks of an explosion in the region and pressuring it to make concessions.[12] That became a recurring theme and led Israel to minimize, at least to its audience in the United States, the importance of Egyptian shelling and of the casualties it was taking. It was only later that the United States became aware of the real numbers and importance of those casualties. Israel's diplomats in Washington gave the impression at the time that they were pinpricks, and it was not until I read Korn's *Stalemate* that I understood just how badly Israel's soldiers in the Bar Lev line were being pounded by Egypt's artillery.

Serious fighting resumed in March, shortly after completion of the Bar Lev line. On March 4 Israel's chief of staff, General Bar Lev, warned that Israel would respond if Egypt did not stop its sniping. On March 8 the Israelis shelled the Suez oil refineries again, and Egypt's chief of staff, General Abdul Mun'im Riad, was killed during an artillery exchange.

On March 12 the UAR official spokesman, Dr. Muhammad Hassan al-Zayyat, announced that, in effect, the UAR would no longer be bound be the cease-fire. He reiterated the Mahmoud Riad argument of October 26, saying, "The cease-fire cannot be exploited to legalize aggression." The situation which had prevailed since the previous October had now been made official. Egypt resumed heavy shelling and its media drew a picture of continued high tension and worldwide fears that war was inevitable. In the spirit of the moment, the undersecretary of foreign affairs, Salah Gohar, told the Canadian ambassador that the UAR felt it was necessary to maintain tension along the canal in order to disprove the U.S.-Israeli thesis that there was no immediate crisis in the area.

At the same time Egypt began talking about "active defense" as opposed to "preventive defense," the term it had been using. The difference between the two terms remained obscure to most observers, but Israel eventually concluded that it meant that Egypt was preparing the way for a cross-canal operation to recover Sinai. That was not regarded as a very credible possibility in Washington at the time, given the military superiority of Israel.

On March 20 the chief of the U.S. Interests Section in Cairo, Donald Bergus, called on Hassan Sabry al-Kholy at the UAR Presidency on instructions to convey U.S. concern over Zayyat's statement. Al-Kholy had for some time been a designated presidential contact for the Americans on subjects of inter-Arab and national security interest, such as Yemen and the Palestine problem. Al-Kholy indicated an interest in stopping the artillery duels. He said the UAR had lost $100 million worth of industrial plant in the previous few days.

There was no letup in Egyptian firing along the canal, however, and on April 1 Nasser announced the unilateral abrogation of the cease-fire. Zayyat reiterated this position on April 3, 9, and 23. On April 29 Israel staged another raid on Naga' Hammadi, but it did not interrupt the cycle of violence as a similar raid had done in 1967.

In mid-May Bergus made another representation on instructions. He had the impression there was a cleavage between civilians and military on the issue and that the former welcomed American urgings for a cease-fire. This was followed by a momentary marked decrease in incidents along the canal (which may have been coincidental), but heavy firing resumed in early June. Bergus again made representations but got the idea they were not welcomed. It appeared that if there had in fact been a cleavage, the military had won.

ROUND THREE: ISRAEL ESCALATES

In response, Israel too adopted a more active posture. It began aggressive air patrols over the Gulf of Suez, launched commando raids along the Egyptian shore of the gulf and into upper Egypt, and showed an intention to interdict maritime traffic into Suez by shelling two Greek tankers in port there.

On July 8 Israel captured Green Island in the Bay of Suez. It had been heavily garrisoned by Egypt and housed important radar and communications installations. Israel claimed to have killed all the defenders, while Egypt claimed to have driven the Israelis off with heavy losses. The Israelis remained on the island only long enough to demolish the installations, and that was the basis for the Egyptians' claim they had been driven off.

At the same time, Israel mounted heavy air attacks against UAR radar and SAM missile sites along the canal, and the Sweet Water Canal to Port Said was breached. This was the prelude to a new policy, which began on July 20, of systematically attacking Egyptian air defenses along the canal, using aircraft instead of artillery.

In late September Israel inaugurated what it called a "daily policy" of attacking Egyptian positions along the canal whether or not there was provocation from the Egyptian side. Advertised as retaliation, these attacks were an intensification of the campaign which began on July 20, and by December they had reduced Egypt's first- and second-echelon air defenses to rubble. All Egypt lay exposed before the Israelis. They still said publicly that their purpose was to force Egypt to respect the cease-fire, but they had already begun to express the hope privately that they would bring Nasser down.

Israel's campaign did not prevent Egypt from continuing to shoot, however, although the frequency of incidents was reduced. Israeli casualties remained high in spite of the Bar Lev line, or perhaps because of it. Here are figures from Israeli sources on Israeli casualties for March–December 1969:[13]

	Killed	Wounded
March	7	29
April	21	34
May	15	30
June	7	34
July	25	68
August	13	55
September	16	30
October	11	47
November	12	29
December	13	19
Total	140	375

These figures do not include casualties resulting from Israeli-initiated "reprisal attacks." It is not clear whether the latter term refers only to commando raids, of which there were ten in the period July 1 to December 27, or whether it also includes losses among attacking air crews.

The most important of the commando raids took place along the Gulf of Suez coast on September 9. Israel used tanks, aircraft, and ships to attack coastal defense and economic installations and reportedly killed 100 to 300 Egyptians, depending on one's source. The Egyptian performance was so incompetent that Nasser fired the chief of staff, General Ahmad Ismail Ali, and replaced him with General Muhammad Sadiq, who had been the director of military intelligence. Nasser was reported to have been so upset that his diabetes flared up, preventing him from making a scheduled visit to Moscow.

This raid came ninety-six hours after the delivery of the first Phantoms. The U.S. Embassy in Tel Aviv had reported the arrival in dramatic detail. Prime Minister Meir was at the airfield and told those present that some day they would be able to tell their grandchildren that they had helped bring peace to the Middle East. The embassy commented that the arrival of the aircraft would strengthen the hand of those who wanted to play it cool and avoid rash acts.

The September 9 raid was heavily publicized by Israel. One of the first questions asked by news correspondents was whether the Phantoms had been used. In Washington the Department of State spokesman, Robert McCloskey, said he did not know. In Israel an unidentified general staff officer responded to the same query by saying, "All kinds of planes were used." That was interpreted as meaning the Phantoms were included, and the use of these planes against Egypt was a recurring theme in the Arab press thereafter.

There were six more commando raids, on a much smaller scale, with a total body count of eight Egyptians killed and fifteen taken prisoner.[14]

To summarize, 1969 witnessed an Egyptian escalation of violence that was serious but containable by Israel. The Israelis responded by upping the ante considerably, and the result was not containable by Egypt. As early as December 1969 Egypt was seeking advanced equipment from the Soviet Union to help deal with its loss of air cover, a loss which was due more to pilot inadequacy than to the nature of the Soviet equipment being supplied. Israel believed that by its escalation it had frustrated Egypt's plans to try a major canal crossing in the summer, but to drive home the lesson Israel went well beyond that to render Egypt defenseless against air attack. It had shown Nasser the real meaning of attrition.

The process of escalation and response was paralleled by a series of diplomatic initiatives growing out of two sets of talks which had begun under the Nixon Administration, one between the four powers mentioned earlier and one between the two powers (the United States and the USSR). The four-power talks, entered into at the urging of France's President Charles de Gaulle and U Thant, amounted to diplomatic window dressing and led nowhere. The two-power talks were essentially between Sisco and the Soviet ambassador to Washington, Anatoly Dobrynin. They were more substantive than the four-power talks, and the abortive Rogers Plan of October 28, 1969, grew out of them.[15] It was on that date that Sisco gave Dobrynin the full text of an American plan which called for indirect negotiations on the pattern used in the 1949 armistice negotiations on the island of Rhodes. The plan also called for Israeli withdrawal from Sinai, for an agreement signed by both parties ending the state of war, and for agreement on demilitarized zones and the return of 100,000 Palestinian refugees to Israel over ten years. The Israelis called it a disaster and rejected it as soon as they learned of its contents. The Egyptians did the same, and the Soviets followed suit.

The Rogers Plan was a sincere effort to find a proposition the Arabs and Israel could both accept, but it was so watered down in the name of realism that there was not enough in it for either side, although in retrospect the document looks considerably more favorable to the Arabs than to Israel. The latter saw in the plan the seeds of a U.S.-Soviet attempt to impose a settlement which would force Israel to withdraw without a firm Arab commitment to formal peace and would undercut Israel's position on borders, making negotiation pointless. This was not to mention the proposal to permit the repatriation of 100,000 refugees, which was anathema to Israel. The Egyptians, who were not ready to consider real peace with Israel, rejected it as an attempt to put unacceptable conditions on

Israeli withdrawal. The Soviets, more dependent on their clients than the American were, went along with the Egyptians.

At this point Israel began talking openly of erosion in the U.S. position, which had moved from "not excluding" complete withdrawal in Sinai to agreeing to it without reservation in the Rogers Plan. Israel had sensed that this erosion was taking place during a visit to the United States by Golda Meir in late September and early October.

Yitzhak Rabin thought he knew how to stop the erosion—by escalating the bombardment of Egypt. He has some interesting things to say in this regard to his memoirs. On September 19, well before the Rogers Plan was unveiled, he had written to Jerusalem:

> There is a widespread feeling here that the Soviets are not willing to make concessions in order to reach agreement with the United States about the conflict in the Middle East. The National Security Council is considering the impact of Israeli military operations against Egypt, and the Americans are giving careful consideration to their possible effect on the stability of Nasser's regime. The following lines of thought are beginning to emerge: Continuation of Israeli military operations, including air attacks, is likely to lead to far-reaching results. Nasser's standing could be undermined, and that would in turn weaken the Soviet position in the region. Some sources have informed me that our military operations are the most encouraging breath of fresh air the American administration has enjoyed recently.
>
> A man would have to be blind, deaf and dumb not to sense how much the administration favors our military operations, and there is a growing likelihood that the United States would be interested in an escalation of our military activity with the aim of undermining Nasser's standing. Some circles were considering the possibility of Israel destroying the Egyptian army in a large scale offensive action; and certainly no one here is dismayed by such a prospect. Right now, such thoughts have not been expressed formally. But I have the impression that as circumstances evolve, it is a possibility that the United States will take into serious account. Thus the willingness to supply us with additional arms depends more on stepping up our military action against Egypt than on reducing it.[16]

After the Meir visit and after learning from Sisco of the change in the U.S. position on the Sinai border and other aspects, Rabin concluded:

> The key to the erosion in American policy lay in the United States' declining status in the Middle East, which in turn was directly linked to our handling of the war of attrition. In a cable to Jerusalem on October 25, I therefore proposed that we alter the course of the war, and I stressed that our objectives could not be attained by limiting our counter bombardments to the area of the Suez Canal. We had to undertake deep

penetration raids and strike at military targets in the Egyptian heartland. That was the only way to induce the Egyptians to halt the war. Moreover, delivering a sharp blow to Nasser would help shore up American status in the region and thus block its retreat in talks with the Soviet Union."[17]

Rabin thus saw two goals to be attained by bombing targets in the Nile Valley. First, it would force Nasser to halt the War of Attrition, which bombing along the canal had not accomplished. Second, it would halt the erosion in the U.S. position on a settlement. It is easier to see how he arrived at the first conclusion than the second. Rabin had a wide circle of contacts in the foreign policy establishment in Washington, and he undoubtedly encountered many people who would not have minded, and not a few who would have been delighted, if Israel delivered a blow sharp enough to shake or unseat Nasser, but U.S. interest in a settlement was independent of Nasser. He was obviously a major factor in the equation and his removal might make settlement easier (it did in fact), but the U.S. position was based on a desire for a settlement that would work, and that meant withdrawal, in the context of peace, to the old borders with only minor, agreed changes, whoever was in charge in Egypt. Israel had in mind at the time a compromise which would permit it to control the Gulf of Aqaba coast down to Sharm al-Shaykh, and no Egyptian regime could accept that. The idea that Israel could get the Americans to reverse themselves on borders by making the situation on the ground worse, particularly after they had conveyed their position to the Soviets and thus had committed themselves, betrays a profound misunderstanding of human nature.

After Rogers made his plan public on December 9, Israel protested vigorously and Rabin was authorized to launch a public campaign against it. He threw himself into this effort and on January 5 recommended again that Israel escalate its military pressure on Egypt. He seems to take credit for what followed, commenting, "This time I got through."[18]

Other sources, however, say the idea for the deep penetration raids originated with the military. According to Yaacov Bar-Siman-Tov, it was Ezer Weizmann, head of the Operations Division in the General Staff, who proposed it in September 1969.[19] Whoever was responsible, Rabin was an enthusiastic advocate and seemed sincerely to believe what he was saying about American attitudes. During a visit to Israel in December 1969 he lobbied actively to convince Israelis that the United States wanted Israel to strike harder. He spoke along these lines, for instance, to the editorial staffs of both *Maariv* and *Haaretz*.[20] Although Abba Eban apparently had reservations, Rabin seems to have convinced the people who counted, including Moshe Dayan.

ROUND FOUR: THE DEEP PENETRATION RAIDS

On January 7, 1970, Israel opened a new chapter in its struggle with Egypt and with the Arab world. It began heavy air strikes at targets in the heavily populated Nile Valley. Before the strikes were over in April, Israel had made thirty-four such raids by its own count, inflicting heavy casualties, both military and civilian. On at least two occasions it hit civilian targets, a metal factory and a primary school. Both times Israel claimed that the targets were military, but it was all but impossible to find a military target in the Nile Valley or the Delta where civilians would not also be hit.

Amnon Rubinstein commented in *Haaretz* on January 9 in an article entitled "Against Nasser—for a Campaign to Overthrow the Egyptian Ruler":

> Whether we like it or not, the "little war" on the Egyptian border has reached large proportions. The World, which is mainly fed laconic communiques from Israel and lies from Cairo, has still not comprehended the change. . . . This development makes it possible to bring about the collapse of Abdul Nasser's regime. This is a practical possibility for two reasons. First, Israel can strike deep into Egyptian territory and hit the big urban centers even without a massive invasion. Second, in recent times we have heard hints that the United States would not complain—to say the least—if Israeli blows increase (so long as there is no real invasion and occupation).

I commented in a memorandum at the time that the purpose of the raids seemed to be to bring the war home to the Egyptian people, who had been largely insulated from the events along the canal, with a view to putting pressure on Nasser in the hope of bringing him down; making it impossible for him to accept a compromise settlement, which Israel also did not want; and eliminating any chance of a rapprochement between the Americans and Nasser. Both Israelis and Arabs took the continued supply of Phantoms as evidence of U.S. approval of the raids. These planes did the bombing in the Nile Valley and were essential to the deep penetration strategy.[21]

While the Israelis were careful to say publicly that bringing Nasser down was not their purpose, private remarks by Israeli officials indicated that Nasser's downfall was very much what they had in mind. They also hoped that military success "would free the United States from the need to give way to Soviet-Egyptian pressure to impose a political solution in favor of Egypt."[22]

Israel also hoped that the bombing would bring about a halt to the War of Attrition, but that did not happen. Indeed, total casualties in January and February 1970 were slightly higher than they had been the previous two months:[23]

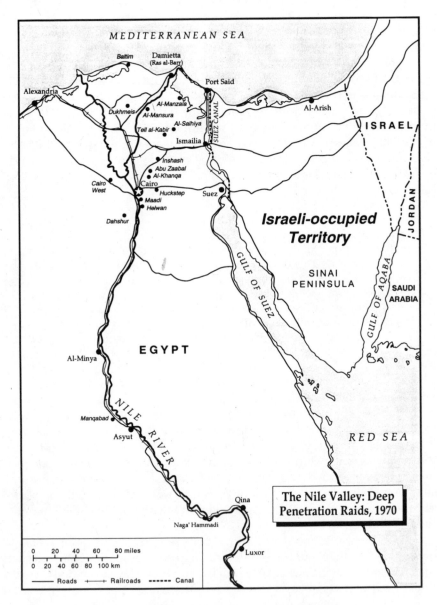

MEDITERRANEAN SEA

Baltim
Damietta
(Ras al-Barr)
Port Said
Alexandria
Al-Arish
Al-Manzala
Dukhmeis
Al-Mansura
ISRAEL
Tell al-Kabir
Al-Salhiya
Ismailia
SUEZ CANAL
Inshash
Abu Zaabal
Al-Khanqa
Cairo
West
Cairo
Huckstep
Suez
JORDAN
Maadi
Helwan
Dahshur

*Israeli-occupied
Territory*

GULF OF SUEZ

SINAI
PENINSULA

GULF OF AQABA

SAUDI
ARABIA

EGYPT

Al-Minya

NILE RIVER

Manqabad

RED SEA

Asyut

Qina

The Nile Valley: Deep
Penetration Raids, 1970

Naga' Hammadi

Luxor

0   20   40   60   80 miles
0   20 40 60 80 100 km
——— Roads   +—+—+ Railroads   ------ Canal

MAP 4

	Killed	Wounded	Total
November 1969	12	29	41
December	13	19	32
January 1970	4	26	30
February	19	38	57

The raids nevertheless brought enormous pressure to bear on Nasser. Heretofore the regime had been able to feed the populace communiques about imaginary Egyptian victories along the canal, but it could not hide the fact that Israel was hitting targets around major population centers. The first raids, on January 7, for instance, struck at three targets: a training camp as Dahshur (site of the Bent Pyramid) just south of Cairo, a military airfield at Tell al-Kabir in the eastern Delta, and the atomic energy research facility at Inshash, eighteen miles northeast of Cairo (see map 4). Dahshur is only eight miles from the industrial suburb of Helwan. That the UAR air force was powerless to stop such incursions could not be concealed for long, particularly when there were large numbers of casualties. In the bombing of a facility at Camp Huckstep, a few miles east of Cairo's international airport, on January 18, for instance, 150 people reportedly were killed. This was soon known to the public. In the words of a senior Israeli air force officer, Israel was "putting the UAR into a corner, forcing them to realize the facts. The situation for them is bad."

On January 22 Nasser, who had understood the message, went to Moscow for a secret three-day visit. We have a firsthand account of it from Heikal, who accompanied him. He says Nasser told the Soviets that Israel had failed to force Egypt to surrender in 1967 and was trying to do so now by breaking the morale of the home front. If the Soviet Union did not somehow provide the wherewithal to defend Egypt effectively against these raids, he would have no alternative but to resign: "We are not asking you to fight for us—we want to keep our independence. But as far as I can see, you are not prepared to help us in the same way that America helps Israel. This means that there is only one course open to me: I shall go back to Egypt and tell the people the truth. I shall tell them that the time has come for me to step down and hand over to a pro-American president."[24]

According to Heikal, the Soviet officials were shocked by these remarks. After hasty deliberations they summoned the Politburo and took a collegial decision to, in effect, take over the air defense of the Nile Valley. They would provide SAM-3 missiles with crews to operate them as well as advanced aircraft with pilots to fly in conjunction with the missile defense.[25] They eventually supplied 12–14,000 military personnel, including 150 pilots and 10,000 missile personnel, and 150 aircraft. It was a major commitment on their part and changed the military equation radically.

In Washington it had been expected that Nasser would go to the Soviets for help. That he had gone to Moscow was suspected very soon after he went, but the details of his conversations there and of the Soviet commitment were not known. Since the problem was one of personnel as much as equipment, there was little the Soviets could do which would have any immediate effect unless they sent pilots to fly against Israel. That was generally regarded by American Soviet specialists as too risky for the Soviets to undertake. Based on past behavior, the Soviets would commit equipment but not military forces.

My view at the time was that the Soviets had been driven into the corner along with Nasser. They had so much at stake that one could not rule out the possibility they would send Soviet pilots. If that occurred, the United States would immediately face frantic pressure from Israel for more Phantoms in a hurry.

Donald Bergus in Cairo had suggested that the United States and the Soviet Union work together to reestablish the cease-fire. It was not clear, however, that the Soviets would be interested, nor whether the two powers could impose a cease-fire if they tried. There was little enthusiasm for the idea in the Department of State. The Bureau of European Affairs suggested that Sisco make a general expression of concern next time he met with Dobrynin, but the embassy in Moscow did not think much would come of that except Soviet charges that it was all Washington's fault. The embassy thought that the Soviets would not be interested unless it appeared Israel was about to unseat Nasser. They probably thought in the meantime that the principal casualties of the raids were U.S. interests in the area.

The Department of State's Directorate of Israel-Arab Affairs argued that it probably would be impossible to get Israel to accept the cease-fire, which would make it awkward if the Egyptians and Soviets agreed. Furthermore, to make such an approach would give the Soviets and Egyptians the impression the Americans were worried, when the best procedure was to convince them to the contrary.

On January 28 Israel bombed a military installation in Maadi, a southern residential suburb of Cairo where many Americans and other foreigners lived. The raid apparently killed several senior Soviet officers. It also blew out windows and terrified students and faculty at the Cairo American College, also in Maadi, which was attended by some 200 American and 100 other foreign children. (When this was mentioned to Shlomo Argov, Israel's minister-counselor in Washington, he suggested that the school be moved.)

Bergus responded to this incident with a message, sent via the CIA channel to avoid upsetting his staff, saying that he was distressed by the lack of reponse to his various messages urging that the United States take steps to restore the cease-fire. He was increasingly worried not only about the morale of his own small staff but also about the security of Americans in Egypt, of whom there were perhaps 500. I recommended sending a firm message to Israel, making a public statement dissociating the United States from the attacks on civilian targets, and asking the Soviets if they were interested in restoring the cease-fire. The second and third recommendations were not accepted, but messages were sent to the missions in Cairo and Tel Aviv instructing them to approach the host governments to urge a cease-fire.

In Israel, Ambassador Barbour called on Moshe Bitan, the assistant director general for North American affairs at the Foreign Ministry, on January 29. He expressed concern that the raids were jeopardizing the lives of Americans and that U.S. silence regarding them had been taken as evidence of approval. He thought the raids were ill-advised in terms of the effect on the prospects for peace and Israel's ultimate ability to live with its neighbors. Bitan said he could not agree that the raids were not having a positive effect on UAR policy. He said Israel believed its tactics would contribute to peace.

In Cairo, Bergus saw Muhammad Riad at the Foreign Ministry and suggested that the Egyptians agree to respect the cease-fire. My notes do not indicate how Riad responded, but clearly the Egyptians did not act on the suggestion.

Meanwhile, Moshe Dayan made a statement on January 29 saying Israel had a triple purpose: to oblige the Egyptians to respect the cease-fire, to prevent them from preparing for another war, and to weaken the Nasser regime by showing the Egyptian masses that their leaders were deceiving them about the real situation in the Arab-Israeli conflict.[26]

The Soviet Warning

On January 30 Soviet Ambassador Dobrynin delivered to Kissinger's office in the White House a letter from Kosygin to Nixon. Similar letters reportedly were sent to Prime Minister Wilson in Britain and President Pompidou in France. After discussing the danger to peace posed by Israel's military actions and its refusal to withdraw from Arab territories, the key paragraph read:

> We would like to tell you in all frankness that if Israel continues its adventurism, to bomb the territory of the UAR and other Arab states, the Soviet Union will be forced to see to it that the Arab states have means at their disposal with the help of which due rebuff to the arrogant aggressor could be made.[27]

The immediate questions posed were what did the Soviets mean and how serious were they? While I am unable to offer documentation without access to classified files, I recall clearly that the almost universal reaction among the Soviet specialists in the Department of State and the CIA was that the Soviets were bluffing and would not in fact go beyond supplying more equipment to Egypt. It would be uncharacteristic of them to send troops; they had not sent any outside the Soviet bloc before. The lone dissenter was an analyst in the Pentagon, who shared my belief that the Soviets would probably commit personnel to the defense of Egypt as well as advanced equipment. The majority finding was congenial to both the White House and the Department of State. The *New York Times* on February 3 reported that Nixon had received a "low-keyed" message which did not explicitly threaten to speed deliveries of advanced weapons to Egypt but hinted broadly at such a move while urging the United States to curtail Israel's thrusts at Arab states. Kissinger commented in a memorandum to Nixon: "Now that he [Nasser] has turned to Moscow to lean on us to press Israel to stop the bombing, he is about to demonstrate Soviet inability to get him out of his box." [28]

By agreement between the White House and the Department of State, the U.S. reply of February 4 took a firm line. In Kissinger's words,

> it rejected the Soviet allegations. It pointed out that the cease fire was being violated by both sides; it had been Egypt that early in 1969 deliberately initiated the cycle of escalation by beginning the war of attrition. Nixon's reply warned that the Soviet threat to expand arms shipments, if carried out, could draw the major powers more deeply into the conflict: "The United States is watching carefully the relative balance in the Middle East and we will not hesitate to supply arms to friendly states as the need arises." The message concluded by rejecting the Soviet position that Israel would have to withdraw before any other peace issues could be settled.

That seemed to be that. Israel continued its raids without letup. An Israeli Embassy officer told me that the Israelis thought the Soviet note showed the raids were having an effect and the Soviets were worried. They were therefore proposing a cease-fire in return for which the Soviets would continue to erode the U.S. position. Various other Israelis expressed the view that the Soviets were paper tigers who would hesitate to take on Israel's highly skilled air force.

The first components of Soviet SAM-3s began arriving in Egypt in late February, and some were operational by mid-March. It soon became evident that Soviet crews were operating them, and by mid-April it was known that Soviet pilots were flying air defense missions over Egypt. Israel, after its first encounter with them over the Delta on April 13, abruptly terminated the deep penetration strategy. It did not want war with the Soviet Union.

Egypt responded by stepping up its own activities along the canal and going on the offensive. That created a situation which led eventually to a U.S.-proposed cease-fire (the second "Rogers Plan"), one result of which was the emplacement of SAM-2 and SAM-3 missiles along the canal, where they were an important factor in the success of an Egyptian attack in 1973, but that is another story.

In April Joseph Sisco met Moshe Dayan in Israel. Dayan asked if the Americans had known the Soviets would respond as they did. Sisco replied to the effect that they had considered the possibility. Dayan said he wished the Americans had told him, because he thought they were backing the deep penetration raids and may even have thought Israel was not doing enough.[29]

CHAPTER

7

MISJUDGMENT ON THE NILE

> From a short term point of view, the Israeli deep penetration raids contained a certain logic; but from a long term point of view, it would appear to have been a major error.
>
> Haim Herzog, *The Arab-Israeli Wars*

Shocked reaction to the Soviet dispatch of troops to Egypt was not long in coming. Both the United States and Israel were quick to cry foul. Abba Eban on April 30 called the use of Soviet pilots "an almost revolutionary change in the military situation" and asked for quick international aid to Israel to compensate for it.[1] Nixon Administration officials were "known to believe the Soviets had altered the balance of power,"[2] and Arthur Goldberg, who was running for governor of New York, said President Nixon "must make it absolutely clear to the Russians that they must not meddle in the Near East and they must keep their men out."[3]

These responses avoided the question of U.S. and Israeli responsibility in the affair and of why, if U.S. officials were going to be so worried about the augmenting of the Soviet presence in the area, they had not taken the Soviet note of January 30 more seriously. Very briefly, Israel made a serious miscalculation, rationalizing an adventuresome policy that was attractive militarily and politically but was based on a misreading of its opponents, Egypt and the Soviet Union. The facts were made to fit the policy. The Americans went along with that policy, within limits, and did not make their reservations felt. The Israelis read U.S. complaisance (correctly, in my view) as approval and overreached themselves. When they got in trouble, they and the Americans blamed the Egyptians and the Soviets for not reacting as predicted.

THE RATIONALE

According to Bar-Siman-Tov, Israel's decision to begin the deep penetration raids had not been taken hastily or lightly, although he says it did not get the full review it deserved. As noted earlier, the idea was first put forward by the military in September 1969, but it was not adopted until December, after the formation of a new government of "national union." It was clear that the "daily policy" of bombing in the canal area had not brought Egypt to observe the cease-fire, and Israel's policy makers reached the conclusion that the best way to put an end to the war and to secure an acceptable political settlement was to make Israel's strategic superiority "really felt." Since land operations to demonstrate this superiority would be too escalatory, air raids were chosen as a less escalatory option.[4]

Ending the War

The idea that Israel could bomb Nasser into either giving up the fight or leaving office was not a new concept. Bombing had been used effectively by the British in South Arabia in the 1930s, and its ineffectiveness in Vietnam had not yet been established. The lesson of World War II was known, but the Egyptians were not the Germans, and their resources were much more limited and confined to narrow areas which were readily accessible. There were, furthermore, signs of internal weakness, which outsiders are forever perceiving in the Arab states. Allowed to run its course, the deep penetration strategy might have worked over time, but judging by the results up until April, it had hardened rather than softened Egyptian attitudes.

The experience of Beirut shows something about the human tolerance for bombardment. There must be some critical ratio of terror and damage to national will which determines whether bombing will work in a given circumstance. Whatever that ratio is, it did not prevail in the time Israel had at its disposal in 1970. It was perhaps reached in Iraq in 1991, but even there it was the land offensive, not the bombardment, that finally brought Iraq to the cease-fire table.

The Israelis seem in the first place to have underestimated Nasser's popular support and staying power. They thought that by bringing the war home to the Egyptian people they would undermine the regime. They certainly placed Nasser in a difficult position, which led him to make his extraordinary demands of the Soviets, and had the latter not come to his aid, he might well have decided to resign as threatened. There is no evidence of which I am aware, however, that popular or elite pressures were building up for him to do so as a result of the deep penetration raids. His personal chagrin rather than political pressures appears to have been what was driving him.

Nor was it at all clear that whoever might succeed him would opt for a cease-fire or be easier for the Israelis to deal with. Israel rejected the idea that anyone who came after him could be worse than Nasser from its point of view, but it was in fact taking a shot in the dark, because who would succeed him was not at all clear. As vice-president since 1968, Sadat was the officially designated successor, but he was not taken seriously and few expected that he would ever be president. Furthermore, Sadat's own past was so checkered that no one could foresee how he would act. (Perhaps the best-remembered episode from his earlier life was his dealing with the Nazis in World War II.) The Israelis were correct, however, in believing that whoever succeeded Nasser would not have his Arab following. He would be weaker and therefore, at least theoretically, more amenable to compromise.

It happened that Sadat did turn out to be easier (but the Israelis were unable to respond to his initial moderation, and he was unable to overcome their territorial aspirations in Sinai until after he had fought a costly war with them). If Nasser had been brought down by public discontent, however, it is unlikely that his successor would have been Sadat, whatever the constitutional provisions. Ali Sabri, a leftist, would have been a much likelier successor because he had impressive political support and Sadat did not.

In the event, Sadat did not come to power on a peace plank. He was committed to waging war more successfully. It was fortunate that Nasser died after the cease-fire of 1970 was negotiated and that Sadat did not have to prove his machismo immediately.

Bombing for Peace

Israel's calculation that bombing was the best way to secure an acceptable peace reflected an absence of empathy. The Israelis were unable to put themselves in the shoes of the Egyptians and the Soviets. What the Israelis considered an acceptable political settlement the Egyptians considered surrender, and they made that clear by their willingness to take heavy casualties. Frustrated by the lack of progress in the implementation of Resolution 242 and convinced that a hostile United States supported Israel's occupation of Arab territory, Nasser seems to have concluded early in the game that there was no hope for a political settlement acceptable to Egypt. His escalation of tension along the canal had been directed at wearing down Israel on one hand and preparing for the eventual reconquest of Sinai on the other, while at the same time convincing the world community the situation was too dangerous to be left unresolved, perhaps hoping this would lead to an imposed settlement.

It is easy to blame Nasser for provoking Israel to respond as it did, but he had limited alternatives. Bound by the famous "three no's" of the August 1967 Khartoum summit—no recognition of Israel, no negotiations with it, and no formal peace—he could not, even if he wanted to, turn around, swallow his pride, and negotiate with Israel without risking serious trouble at home and in the Arab world as a whole.

At the time, many of us dealing with Egypt thought Nasser was interested in a compromise settlement, provided it would return Sinai to Egypt.

This assessment does not seem to be borne out by what has since appeared in the memoirs of Egyptian officials, which indicate that Nasser was no more interested in compromise than Israel was. He let the diplomats play with the possibilities but did not take them seriously, and that is one reason there was no progress on implementing Resolution 242.

If the Egyptian official record is ever published, it may illuminate the question further, but in the meantime all we have to go on is recollections, such as Heikal's in *The Road to Ramadan*. Heikal quotes Nasser as telling his military commanders on November 25, 1967:

> Let me tell you a few facts. Everything you hear us say about the UN resolution is not meant for you, and has nothing to do with you. If you look at what the Israelis are doing in the occupied territories it is perfectly obvious that they are never going to evacuate these areas unless they are made to do so. Please remember what I have said before—what has been taken by force can only be recovered by force. This is not rhetoric: I mean it. I have asked the Soviet Union to let us have bridging equipment, and I have told them I want this as a loan, not a gift or a deal, because after we have crossed the canal I am going to hand back the bridges, so that those who have crossed will have no way of getting back. If I were Levi Eshkol or Moshe Dayan I would do the same thing they are doing; they want to expand and now they think they have the chance to expand. I don't see that even if they wanted to they could withdraw, because they have fed their people with too many hopes and promises. What they are saying now will inevitably harden into official policy and they will become bound by it. So you don't need to pay any attention to anything I may say in public about a peaceful solution.[5]

Nasser might feel obliged to talk to his military commanders in such terms whatever he really thought, but the UAR's foreign policy over the next three years reflected the same lack of interest in compromise. Judging by the negotiating history, if the Egyptians could have recovered Sinai peacefully without negotiating directly with Israel, without concluding anything which could be described as a peace treaty, and with no binding commitment as to future behavior other than to respect the General Armistice Agreement of 1949, they would have accepted it. Israel would not have agreed to that, of course, and the Egyptians saw armed struggle as the only realistic alternative.

For their part, the Israelis, disappointed in their initial hopes the Arabs would sue for peace, were determined to hold out for formal commitments arrived at through direct negotiations, with no prior commitment on withdrawal to the 1967 lines on their part. They kept saying that everything was negotiable, but in fact very little was. They were ready for peace on their terms if Nasser would accept them, but by 1968 they had lost interest in arrangements with Nasser short of a formal peace, and by June of that year they were stipulating an Israeli garrison at Sharm al-Shaykh as a minimal territorial condition.[6]

In the meantime, the Israelis thought that holding on to the territories was preferable to some unreliable Arab half-commitment to peace. Dayan remarked that as between peace without Sharm al-Shaykh and Sharm al-Shaykh without peace, he would prefer the latter, and the Israelis began acting as though they intended to remain in Sinai indefinitely. They built roads and airports, founded settlements, expanded their tourist industry to include Sinai tours, developed a resort at Sharm al-Shaykh and a hotel at Taba, established a fishing industry along the Mediterranean coast, and began exploiting Egyptian oil fields in eastern Sinai. They even attempted, with the aid of a Denver oilman, to try slant drilling into the offshore al-Murgan oil field in the Gulf of Suez, which was being developed for the Egyptians by a subsidiary of Standard of Indiana. To this end they created a dummy corporation in London on behalf of which the oilman hired a Canadian floating drilling rig and began towing it to the Red Sea. Egyptian frogmen attempted to blow it up in the port of Abidjan but botched the job, and it was successfully towed around the Cape of Good Hope. The Canadian crew deserted it, however, after the Canadian government finally brought home to them that the Egyptians were going to shoot at them when they got close to the scene of action.

For their part, Israel's military officials were interested in the strategic advantage Sinai gave them and wanted to defend their continued occupation in the most economical way. When it became evident in late 1968 that Egypt was getting restive, they opted, as we have seen, to build the Bar Lev line, and when even that became too costly in terms of casualties, they felt obliged to take stronger measures. They began using their aircraft as artillery to offset Egypt's advantage in that arm, then systematically destroyed Egypt's air defense capability. That presented them with an opportunity to strike even deeper without serious opposition, and they elected to exercise that option. As Bar-Siman-Tov states, "Israeli air superiority opened the way for still more serious escalation of the fighting."[7] By this time, the military considerations were driving the political.

THE MISJUDGMENT

Israel's most serious miscalculation concerned Soviet reaction to its raids—not that Israel failed to realize there might be a risk of Soviet intervention, but they rated the risk too low. Bar-Siman-Tov describes three appraisals, by Yigal Allon, Moshe Dayan, and Golda Meir.

Allon reportedly believed that Soviet intervention was highly unlikely because the Soviets did not want a confrontation with the United States, because they must have had an accurate appraisal of Israel's strength and knew Israel would go on fighting even if they intervened, because they had avoided intervention outside the Soviet bloc since World War II, and because it would require a large expeditionary force to intervene success-fully.[8]

Dayan, on the other hand, rejected these arguments and thought So-viet intervention could not be ruled out, particularly if the aim of the exercise was to topple Nasser. Nevertheless, he was for the deep penetra-tion strategy. He wanted to use the military option as long as it was avail-able, up to the point of Soviet intervention.[9]

Golda Meir reportedly felt that the possibility that the raids would bring in the Soviets was not great: "Had we known that this could help the Russians to reach the Canal region, would we have considered such a possibility? The answer is that we would have considered it, but it never occurred to anyone then." Meir spoke of "hearing opinions from all the responsible factors" and said that "all information was weighed care-fully." By "responsible factors" she was referring to military intelligence, whose estimate was that limited raids of the sort being carried out would not be enough to produce real military intervention by the Soviets and that if it came it would not endanger the existence of Israel.[10]

On June 16, 1989, I asked General Aharon Yaariv, who was chief of military intelligence at the time of the War of Attrition, for his explanation of Israel's failure to evaluate the Soviet risk more accurately. Yaariv said the Israelis had been mesmerized by the problem of the War of Attrition. It had become their number one national problem. They saw the deep penetration raids as the answer. They did not think it through very thor-oughly, and they made the same sort of mistake the Egyptians had made in 1967. Perhaps their expertise was not good enough. They had had an inkling of what the Soviets might do but were surprised when it hap-pened. Their rationale had been that for the Soviets to do anything seri-ous in support of Egypt would be a challenge to the United States. That would be a big risk for the Soviets to take, and it would involve them in military movement outside the World War II perimeter. The Israelis did not think the Soviets would want to get involved in that.

Ze'ev Schiff, the military correspondent of *Haaretz*, interviewed on the same day, said we must look again to the role of the super powers. If the Americans were not worried, why should the Israelis be? Asked whether he thought the Americans had approved the deep penetration raids, he said the question was *which* Americans had approved. The same question was posed with regard to the Lebanon adventure in 1982. Rabin did not invent what he said about American approval. Schiff had seen him sev-eral times during his visit to Israel in December 1969. Rabin honestly be-lieved it. He said the Americans were waiting for more attacks and thought the Israelis were not using their might.

In an earlier discussion, Schiff said the deep penetration strategy had been a matter of considerable debate within the Israeli establishment and that Rabin had been the principal advocate of it. He had reported to the

cabinet that a number of Americans were backing the idea. Schiff speculated that Henry Kissinger was one of them.[11] Elsewhere Schiff is quoted
as saying "one of the heads of the State Department" was Rabin's source,
and Dan Margalit refers to a "very senior personality" in the American
administration.[12] We will return to the American role later.

It appears from the above and from similar remarks made by other
Israelis at the time that Israel was focusing more on the attitude of the
United States than on the position in which the Soviets found themselves. As Schiff says, if the Americans did not worry, why should the
Israelis? The Israelis' confidence, based on their reading of the Americans, was played back to the latter and, together with Israel's minimizing
of the seriousness of the War of Attrition, was a factor in U.S. overconfid-
ence. This mutual reinforcement of error appears again in 1973 and 1982.
The myth that Israeli intelligence is infallible is one of the givens in Washington, but one would have expected the Israelis to be too smart to buy
the American view without more critical analysis of their own.

SOVIET IMPERATIVES

Nasser was the Soviet Union's most important Middle East client. Some
observers believe that after early 1966 and the leftist takeover in Syria, the
Soviets had been more interested in that state than in Egypt, but that
does not seem to have been the case, judging by the comments of Soviet
officials.[13] According to them, the Soviets welcomed the leftist changes in
Syria and thought they were on the mark domestically, but were concerned by Syria's irresponsible behavior internationally. In spite of their
unhappiness with Nasser's repression of Egyptian communists, they regarded him as someone responsible and stable. They also had a much
larger material stake, the most important aspect of which was the Aswan
Dam, in Egypt than they did in Syria. Perhaps most important of all was
their prestige, which was bound up with Egypt's. Nasser had made them
respectable in the area with the 1955 arms deal, and his approval carried
weight from the Atlantic to the gulf. Syrian approval did not carry beyond the gates of Damascus.

If Nasser was in trouble, so were the Soviets, and the fact that the
Soviet arms which had poured into Egypt since the June War had not
permitted the Egyptians to defend themselves against U.S.-supplied Israel was a serious blow to their prestige. It was a challenge they had to
meet if they wanted to maintain a position of influence in the area. They
showed reluctance to get involved directly, but faced with Nasser's threat
of resignation, apparently felt they had no realistic choice but to come to
his defense. True, it would be a challenge to the United States, but the
latter had indirectly challenged them through its proxy, Israel, and their
response was defensive, not aggressive. It is probable that the Soviet at-

titude hardened following the killing of senior Soviet officers in the January 28 raid on Maadi.

In addition to a failure properly to gauge the situation in which the other side found itself and how it would respond to that situation, there was a degree of fatalistic bravado to the Israeli position. It was expressed in statements to U.S. officials to the effect that the Israelis were not afraid of the Soviets. Israeli air force officers, for instance, were reported to be saying they hoped the Soviets would send in their best planes and pilots so the Israelis could show just how good they were. That bespeaks high morale but limited common sense. Similarly, Dayan apparently knew it was risky but agreed to press on nevertheless, and he was considered to be the most cautious of the decision makers.

THE AMERICAN ROLE

The Americans had a fair idea of the Egyptian position, but they too misjudged Nasser's staying power and the likelihood of a meaningful Soviet response. Their failure to take the Soviet warning seriously seemed to me at the time to be based on too much reliance on past practice as a guide to future behavior, failure to understand the seriousness of the Soviet stake in Egypt, and fascination with the use of force. The first two errors may be classified in the category of lack of imagination. The third is a continuing tendency in U.S. foreign policy, where military force is seen as an easier way out than taking the hard political decisions needed to settle a problem. We saw another striking example of that in the Gulf War of 1991.

While things changed with glasnost, in the period of which we are speaking prediction of Soviet behavior was necessarily dependent more on overt signs such as the official line and changes in it, plus past performance, plus intuition, than on hard intelligence, although there was some of that from time to time. While normal Soviet caution made successful guessing based on the track record easier than predicting Arab behavior, there were risks that behavior would change with circumstances, as in the Cuban missile crisis of 1962.

American Soviet specialists were furthermore hampered by the need to be anti-Soviet, or at least not pro-Soviet. The Arab specialists wanted to avoid being labeled pro-Arab, but that was often impossible whatever they did, and it was not always fatal in any event. Most important, it was not an act of disloyalty to the United States if they felt sympathy for, and occasionally defended, the Arabs, because with some exceptions the Arabs were not declared to be enemies of the United States. To be pro-Soviet was by definition to be anti-American. That made it difficult to express sympathy for the Soviets and to put oneself in their shoes.

Furthermore, with few exceptions, most Soviet specialists knew little about the Middle East. It was a serious failure of the Foreign Service that it had never developed Soviet–Middle East specialization as a major career path. The two areas are closely linked in terms of geography, history, and current interest. From 1955 until the late 1980s, the Middle East was a principal arena of Soviet-American rivalry, but while the Arab specialist needed to know what the Soviets were up to, the reverse was not the case. As a result, the Sovietologists who passed judgment on the intent and meaning of the Kosygin letter to Nixon apparently did not appreciate the seriousness of the situation in which the Egyptians and Soviets found themselves. In particular, they did not seem to appreciate the depth of Soviet commitment to Nasser.

At least, that is my recollection. Among the surviving Sovietologists of that period, the only one I have found who has any detailed memory of the affair is Martha Mautner of the Department of State. She recalls that given a long-established Soviet policy of avoiding the commitment of troops in such cases, she had believed that the Soviets might supply equipment and advisers but not combat forces to Egypt.[14] This was hard to argue with and would have been even more so if we had known that Podgorny had turned down an earlier request from Nasser that the Soviets take over the air defense of Egypt shortly after the June War (described in Abdul Majid Farid's *Min Mahadir Ijtima'at Abd al-Nasir*, pp. 30–31).

The Sovietologists' tendency to believe the Soviets would not intervene with troops in Egypt was strengthened by the globalist attitude of Kissinger and others in the administration who saw the War of Attrition as a contest between U.S. and Soviet arms which the United States was winning. Kissinger's memoirs give eloquent evidence of this attitude. To many of us in the Foreign Service at the time, it was evident that he did not begin to appreciate the regional nature of the conflict between Arab and Israeli until he first went to the area in 1973 and met some Arab leaders. Until then he had seen that struggle as an aspect of the Soviet-American contest. What was important to him and his acolytes was that the United States win the contest, not that it find a solution to the problem on the ground.

FASCINATION WITH THE USE OF FORCE

A more elemental phenomenon was the apparent belief among a number of American officials at various levels that the Israelis might succeed in bringing down Nasser and that doing so was in the U.S. interest. Such thinking was implicit in their lack of interest in doing anything effective to stop Israel from bombing Egypt. The Barbour demarche to Moshe Bitan on January 29, for instance, was not effective because it was made to a midlevel official (which implied that Barbour did not take it very seriously) and was not backed up by a similar demarche, which should have been made at the assistant secretary level or above, in Washington. The lack of action on the Washington end was conspicuous at the time, but it is hard to document because it was something implicit, something not done. As far as I know, it was never spelled out as a formal policy. Responsibility for not acting more forcefully must rest in the first instance with Sisco and Kissinger, but they were not alone.

It is not clear whether the Israelis merely sensed Washington's attitude or heard directly from senior officials that they could safely ignore the Barbour demarche. Rabin, for instance, seems to think that Sisco shared his views on the efficacy of bombing, but he does not have much to go on:

> When Sisco invited me to lunch on January 13 he was not in a position to concede that Israel's air operations were equally welcome to the United States. There was no need for him to say it; he knew that I knew. . . . I now observed a similar trend within the administration, particularly on the part of Attorney General John Mitchell, a key man in the cabinet. . . . In his State of the Union address the president did not even mention the Middle East, and the Rogers plan, if not dead, was in its death throes. Most important of all, against the background of our deep penetration raids, the Administration was soon to adopt a new tone in its give-and-take with the Soviet Union.[15]

The Hebrew version of this conversation is different. Rabin records that Sisco asked for his estimate of the military situation and he replied:

> The more we hit the Egyptians deep inside their territory, the better the situation will be. You know, don't you, that we have already carried out two raids deep inside Egyptian territory. Our planes bombed military targets near Cairo. . . . Sisco is silent. Not even a gesture. Is this concurrence through silence? I thought so then. I'm not sure now.

Rabin engages in interpretation of Sisco's body language on another occasion:

> Joseph Sisco, who informed me of the Soviet note on February 2, also told me that the President had already worded his reply. He described it as a "vigorous and uncompromising answer" that rejected the Soviet version of events and placed responsibility for the military situation on Nasser, who had broken the cease-fire in the first place. . . . This was a tone quite unlike the one I had been hearing from the Americans and it was clear to me that the reversal in US posture vis-a-vis the Soviets was due to our heightened military action. Sisco did not say so outright, but there was no mistaking his tone. As a result I could cable Jerusalem: "We have achieved a marked improvement in the United States' posi-

tion. Continuation of that improvement depends first and foremost on keeping up our air raids into the heart of Egypt." [16]

Given Ambassador Barbour's expression of U.S. doubts to Bitan, Rabin was incorrect in saying later that there had been no approach from the Americans to halt the raids. [17] And as we shall see, not everyone in the Israeli foreign policy establishment believed what he was reporting. Perhaps he meant that no such approach had been made to him, because apparently none was until after the Soviets had begun to arrive in Egypt. In the Hebrew version of his memoirs he says, "It is important to note that in conversations with the Americans there was no criticism of the Deep Penetration Raids. They only wanted to be informed how our campaign was going so they could anticipate future developments."

Rabin was engaging in selective listening, but had I seen his comment at the time, I would have been inclined to agree that the U.S. foreign policy establishment was, at least, not opposing the raids. Indeed, I had the impression at the time that even my colleagues at the working level in Near Eastern Affairs, by and large, were convinced that Israel might succeed in bringing down Nasser and should be given a chance to do so. Certainly I could find little support for any serious effort to reinstate the cease-fire.

Evidently there was some skepticism in Jerusalem about Rabin's reporting of the U.S. position, which may explain the single-minded vehemence with which he pursued it. Eban, in his *Autobiography* (p. 465), comments:

> one of the most decisive debates in Israel since 1967 took place in the late weeks of 1969 and the early days of 1970. At the outset, ministers were divided between those willing to take the risks of a deep penetration of Egypt's air space for massive attacks on Cairo, and those who feared that this would bring the Soviet Union to Egypt's defense with a consequent disturbance of the strategic balance.
>
> A decisive element in this discussion was the advocacy of a militant approach by our ambassador in Washington. Rabin bombarded us with cables urging escalation against Egypt and other Arab states. He clearly believed that there were some people in Washington who might react sympathetically to such a course. I did not believe that this analysis . . . corresponded to international realities. . . . There is no evidence, in my view, that the United States ever wanted us to escalate the war.

Rabin says that when Peter Grose, the *New York Times* correspondent, filed a story in February 1970 saying that continued delay in responding to Israel's request for another twenty-four Phantoms was a sign of U.S. opposition to the raids, Eban called this to Rabin's attention and said he (Eban) was not prepared to accept any more "fabrications" about the reasons for U.S. failure to respond to the arms request. Rabin responded that "since the raids began there has not been a single American statement—or even unofficial hint—that the Americans were displeased with them. And at the risk of belaboring the obvious I pointed out that Mr. Gross [sic] was the *Times* correspondent in Israel, so that his interpretation evidently came from sources in Jerusalem, not Washington."[18] In the Hebrew version, Rabin suggests that Eban was behind the Grose story and says: "There was no connection between the President's indecision concerning the arms and the deep penetration raids."[19]

Rabin seems to have been correct in this latter respect. Grose was referring to a decision by Nixon to delay a decision on additional Phantoms. It was conveyed to Rabin by Kissinger on March 12. The Kissinger and Rabin accounts of this meeting diverge in significant details. Rabin says that Kissinger told him the president's decision on the arms request would include three parts: The first part, to be made public, was that the United States had decided not to decide, i.e., it was putting the decision on supplying the planes in abeyance. It would, however, continue to monitor military developments, and should any change in the situation require a decision on arms supply, appropriate steps would be taken. The second part was that the United States wanted to change the ground rules on the supply of arms. Instead of public statements announcing acceptance, rejection, or postponement, the United States would undertake to maintain the arms balance by replacing Israel's weapons as they were attrited. In the third part, the president would send a personal letter to the prime minister stressing his commitment to Israel's security and assuring her of the arms required to maintain the balance of forces.

Kissinger then told Rabin that the Soviets had proposed an undeclared cease-fire between Israel and Egypt. The terms would require Israel to halt all air activity west of the canal and to refrain for a limited period from responding to Egyptian artillery fire. Kissinger made no attempt to defend this Soviet proposal, which Rabin thought preposterous, but asked that Rabin take it back to Israel for consideration.

Rabin took the cease-fire proposal to Jerusalem and returned with an indignant reply which he gave to Kissinger on March 17. Kissinger responded by giving Rabin a copy of the draft presidential letter reiterating Nixon's commitment to replace the arms Israel needed to maintain the balance and asking Israel to consent to a sixty-day cease-fire.[20] By that time Soviet crews for SAM-3 missiles had begun to arrive in Egypt.

Kissinger's account states that the decision to delay consideration of the arms request was a vindictive response by Nixon to demonstrations against visiting French President Pompidou and his wife, staged by Jewish groups in protest against the sale of French jet fighters to Libya. Demonstrators in Chicago were particularly offensive to Mrs. Pompidou and, according to Kissinger, Pompidou never got over the insult. He does not mention the decision's being a signal of displeasure at the deep penetration raids.

Here is Kissinger's version of the meeting.

> On March 12 I met with Rabin to inform him of Dobrynin's cease-fire proposal and also to convey the President's decision. At the same time I asked that Israel stop its deep penetration raids and agree to an undeclared cease-fire. An aide-mémoire from the President would formalize both the request and the assurance.
>
> Yitzhak Rabin had many extraordinary qualities, but the gift of human relations was not one of them. . . . Not suprisingly, he did not embrace the replacement formula. . . . Rabin was also unenthusiastic about the cease-fire. It would save Nasser. It would settle nothing. Nevertheless he considered the proposal important enough to take to Jerusalem personally. . . . He flew to Israel and returned five days later with the cabinet's reply: Israel would agree to an undeclared cease-fire provided all military activity ceased simultaneously, the replacement figure [for aircraft] was doubled, and there was a public announcement of Nixon's assurance about maintaining Israeli air strength and the military balance in the Middle East. . . .
>
> The very day—March 17—that Israel accepted the cease-fire, Rabin informed me that that a substantial shipment of Soviet arms had arrived in Egypt, including the most advanced Soviet anti-aircraft system . . . accompanied by 1,500 Soviet military personnel.[21]

There is yet another version in the Hebrew edition of the Rabin memoirs that has a clearer description of the Soviet proposal, which would require that Israel stop bombing along the canal as long as Egypt undertook no air action against Israel (something the Egyptians were not capable of doing anyway). Israel could respond to Egyptian artillery fire in kind. Rabin says he rejected this proposal and the decision to delay action on the arms request. He took the proposal to Israel nevertheless and returned to say that the prime minister requested that Nixon reject the Soviet proposal. Israel was ready for an unlimited undeclared cease-fire but not one limited to forty-five or sixty days, and it expected the United States would provide more arms in appreciation of the risk Israel would be running.[22]

In neither version does Rabin say that Kissinger requested Israel to stop the deep penetration raids as Kissinger states. The record may clarify this, and it may not. The point is that by the time Kissinger got around to saying this, if he did, it was too late. The Soviet troops were already under way.

A principal element in Rabin's understanding, or misunderstanding, of American views was the two-tiered system of communications in Washington. While theoretically all official communications should go through the Department of State, there is always much dealing through informal channels which are not monitored by the department. The most egregious of these is the White House–Israel Embassy link, which has functioned on and off since 1948. In Rabin's case, it was reestablished in 1969 by Nixon and Golda Meir. They agreed that Rabin could communicate directly with Kissinger and with Meir, cutting out both the Department of State and the Israeli Foreign Ministry. Kissinger felt free in these meetings to state his own views to Rabin which were often at variance with those of the department (to the extent it had any), and Rabin naturally assumed that the White House was the more authoritative source, although that often was not the case when complicated administrative or legal issues were involved. Sisco warned him not to rely overmuch on the White House, but Rabin seems to have thought he could ignore that warning and proceeded to do so.[23]

SOVIET SIGNALS

Kissinger comments that Kosygin's letter turned out to have been a smokescreen for a decision already taken, not a warning.[24] I was told in Moscow that the decision to send in Soviet personnel as well as equipment was in fact taken before the letter was delivered to Nixon. The letter was intended to establish that the Soviets had made a diplomatic effort and were justified in intervening. The Soviets were interested in maintaining a balance, and they saw it as heavily upset in favor of Israel. The principal shortages on the Egyptian side were in trained pilots and aerial refueling capabilities. The Soviets remedied that.

Can we conclude that the Soviets would not have intervened if the United States had restrained Israel? Perhaps. But if that was what the Soviets had in mind, they could have made a better effort to explain it to the Americans. They did send some signals, but they were indirect and apparently uncoordinated.

One signal was a call on the Pentagon correspondent of a New York newspaper by a Soviet Embassy officer on February 6 to discuss what he called the failure of the United States to appreciate the gravity of Kosygin's message. He said it was intended as a very serious warning to the United States that if it proceeded with the deliveries of aircraft and weapons to Israel, the Soviets would be obliged to deliver "offensive weapons" to the Arabs. The Soviets could not stand idly by while the Israelis bombed the suburbs of Cairo and the Americans delivered "these planes." Nixon's reply had been unresponsive because it invoked rhetoric and did not address itself to the issues raised by Kosygin. Meanwhile, the U.S. press was reflecting American nonchalance about the situation, evidently based on confidence in the UAR pilot shortage.

The Pentagon correspondent, who did not deal with the Middle East, was mystified as to why he had been approached but reported the conversation to the department. Strangely, the Soviets made no similar approach to the department directly, to the best of my knowledge. Sending a junior officer to see a journalist about a subject this important was sufficiently bizarre to make us suspect that he was acting on his own and that the Soviet Embassy was under instructions not to raise the matter officially.

Similar warnings were conveyed through a variety of sources. King Hussein in Jordan told the American ambassador in Amman, Harrison M. Symmes, that the Soviets meant business this time. He said they were furious over the death of Soviet officers at Maadi. A similar message was given to Bergus in Cairo by the Finnish ambassador. At about the same time an unidentified "extremely capable western observer" (Eric Rouleau) reported that Egyptian officers along the canal were confident that Kosygin's letter was the first step in raising the Middle East situation to a major East-West crisis, and they predicted the arrival of Soviet military personnel with the restricted mission of defending the Egyptian heartland against air attack. These phenomena were duly reported but had little effect, although Kissinger claims he used the interval between February 10 and March 12 for "contingency planning in anticipation of some significant Soviet move—almost certainly involving the introduction of military personnel in the Middle East." [25]

Rabin reports, on the other hand, that at lunch in February he suggested to Sisco that the Soviets might introduce military personnel into Egypt but Sisco said U.S. analysts thought that was unlikely. [26] This implies that Sisco was either uninvolved in or unaware of Kissinger's contingency planning. If Kissinger was indeed involved in such planning, there should be evidence of that in the record somewhere.

Soviet accounts of this period may eventually shed some light on Soviet thinking, but it is strange, given the existence of well-worn channels of communication in Washington, that Dobrynin did not pick up the telephone and call Sisco or send one of his counselors to see someone at the deputy assistant secretary level to make it clear that the Soviets were going to act if the Americans did not restrain Israel. Had he done so, Kissinger's smokescreen theory would not hold much water. As it is, the suspicion that the decision to intervene had been taken irrevocably before the letter was sent will remain difficult to refute.

THE NATURE OF THE MISCALCULATION

When the game was all over and the cease-fire was in place in the summer, the Israelis were disagreeably surprised to find that the Egyptians and the Soviets had managed to install an impressive antiaircraft system along the canal. This system was instrumental in the Egyptians' crossing of the canal and breaking through the Bar Lev line in 1973. The deep penetration strategy had been a mistake.

We can distinguish at least three Israeli-American errors which taken together had very unfortunate results: the misjudgment of Egypt's staying power, the misjudgment of Soviet seriousness, and the fascination with the use of force. The fault lay as much with the Americans as with the Israelis. If the Americans at the upper levels had doubts about the Israeli strategy, they should have made them known. That they did not do so gave the impression within the government as well as outside it that they had no doubts. The telegram to Barbour instructing him to make a demarche seems to have been for the record. If it was meant seriously, it was not so taken by the embassy in Tel Aviv.

Rabin bears much of the responsibility for persuading Jerusalem that the raids were essential to protecting Israel's political interests. The fact that this was his first, and probably last, diplomatic assignment may explain his single-minded and somewhat naive interpretation of what he saw and heard. At one point he even convinced himself that Nixon believed Israel had an important role to play in the power balance between the United States and the Soviet Union.[27] He was similarly able to convince himself that Sisco's silence was a sign of approbation. Sisco, of course, was guilty of ambiguity, but one would like to think that a professional diplomat would have known better than to act on the basis of such uncertain signals. Perhaps Rabin was getting less ambiguous signals from people like Kissinger and John Mitchell.

This case is one of four in which the Soviets threatened to take military action in the Middle East: in 1956, 1967, 1970, and 1973. It is the only occasion on which they actually carried out the threat, and it was the vaguest threat of the four. In 1956 they threatened to use missiles against the British and French at the close of the Suez War. In 1967 they threatened to intervene with troops if Israel did not halt its advance on Damascus. In 1973 they threatened to intervene to save the Egyptian Third Army.

The United States government acted to show it was not intimidated by any of these threats. In 1956 it shrugged. In 1967 it ordered the Sixth Fleet to the eastern Mediterranean to show that it would meet force with force. In 1970 it dismissed the threat as a bluff. In 1973 it declared a nuclear alert, the significance and wisdom of which is still being debated. In none of these cases, however, does it seem to have thought that the Soviets were really going to intervene. Similarly the Soviets claim not to have taken any of the American moves seriously. They did not think the Americans would risk a confrontation with them over the Middle East and believed they were merely engaging in their usual posturing.[28]

It was as though we had arrived at that stage described by Arthur Koestler in *The Age of Longing* where the powers exchange ultimatums so routinely that they have reduced the practice to exchanging printed forms of graded severity, and no one pays attention to any of them.

PART THREE

THE ISRAEL-LEBANON PEACE
AGREEMENT OF 1983

CHAPTER
8

THE ISRAELI INVASION OF 1982

Vous avez raison, a dit a Guy Sitbon un
combattant chrétien d'Achrafieh: nous
sommes fous. Mais c'est notre force.

Nouvel Observateur, July 20, 1978

The May 17, 1983, agreement between Lebanon and Israel, setting out
the terms of the latter's withdrawal from the former, signaled what was
to become one of the more important failures of U.S. policy in the Middle
East. Although supported by a substantial portion of the Lebanese population, the agreement was attacked vehemently by the Syrians and their
Lebanese allies and was eventually repudiated by the same Lebanese regime which had accepted it. This process was accompanied by a serious
deterioration of the U.S. position in Lebanon, marked by the blowing up
of the U.S. Embassy and the U.S. Marine quarters at the airport and the
final withdrawal of the marines in early 1984.

Secretary of State George Shultz, who had been instrumental in persuading the Lebanese to sign the agreement, appeared to take its rejection personally. Angered by Arab failure effectively to support it, he turned
his back on the Arab world for most of the rest of his term of office.
By the time he tried again to do something substantial about the Arab-
Israeli peace process, in 1988, it was too late. He had neither the time
nor the political support to make progress on the issue before leaving
office.

The May 17 agreement was the fruit of the Israeli invasion of Lebanon
in the summer of 1982. That invasion was itself a major miscalculation by
Prime Minister Begin, who seems willingly to have let himself be misled
by the minister of defense, Ariel Sharon. Between them they did not appear to understand the imbroglio into which they were immersing themselves or to have much concern about the many innocent lives lost as a
result, although national and international reaction to the Sabra and Chatilla massacre may have been a factor in Begin's decision to resign on
September 15, 1983.

The details of Israel's Lebanon involvement have been well described

MAP 5

by a number of Israeli writers whose books are listed in the bibliography. On reading their accounts one is struck by how little Begin and Sharon knew about the political realities of Lebanon. As officials of a country which has many talented, even brilliant, analysts who spend their lives studying the Arabs, they should have been better informed. Sharon's decision, for instance, to have the Israel Defense Forces (IDF) sponsor the move of the Maronite-dominated Lebanese Forces into the Shuf region of Mount Lebanon (see map 5) showed a deplorable ignorance of the explosive Druze-Maronite rivalry in that area and of its implications for Israel. This may have been due to overreliance on Christian, primarily Maronite, sources of information and advice within Lebanon, but not all Israelis were oblivious to the dangers. Military intelligence reportedly opposed the move, while Mossad supported it.

According to Uri Lubrani, who became Israel's Lebanon trouble-shooter after the event, Bashir Gemayel, the leader of the predominantly Maronite Lebanese Forces militia, had told the Israelis he needed to establish an armed presence in the Shuf and they had agreed to help him do so. Once there, however, the Maronites had behaved badly, setting up roadblocks and terrorizing the Druze population. The Israelis had quickly discovered their error, but by this time Bashir was dead. They tried to get the Lebanese Forces to modify their behavior, but the Maronite leadership was "very sensitive" on the subject. The Israelis had spoken to Bashir's brother Amin Gemayel when he was president about the need to assuage Druze fears, but he had dismissed the Druze as "gypsies" (*nawwar*) who could do nothing.[1]

The Druze, supported by the Syrians, proved to be more effective fighters than the Maronites, and the latter were soon on the defensive. The Israelis then found themselves caught between their Maronite allies in Lebanon and their Druze constituents at home, who were lobbying strenuously on behalf of their Lebanese brethren. They were strongly supported in this effort by the Israel Labor party. By January 1983, according to the Druze, the Israelis were selling arms to them as well as the Maronites, and the Druze were paying for them with Saudi money. The Maronites, meanwhile, were charging the Israelis with favoring the Druze, particularly in the battle for Aley.[2]

Israeli involvement with the Maronites was not a new phenomenon. Its origins were described by Bennie Morris in 1984.[3] Drawing on Israeli archives, he describes in considerable detail the initial contacts in the spring of 1948, followed by Israeli financial support for the Phalanges, or Kataʾib, party of Pierre Gemayel. From the beginning of these early contacts there was discussion of the possibility of military cooperation between the Maronites and Israelis against the Muslims of Lebanon.

Nothing came of that talk, but the idea did not die. In 1954 there was an exchange of correspondence among David Ben-Gurion, the former Israeli prime minister then living in temporary retirement at Sde Boker,

Prime Minister Moshe Sharett, and Eliahu Sasson, Israel's ambassador to Italy, in which Ben-Gurion proposed that the Israelis work to create a Christian state in Lebanon. He argued in a letter to Sharett on February 27 that Lebanon was the weakest link in the Arab League chain around Israel and that the Christians, whom he termed the majority of "historic" Lebanon, had traditions and a civilization completely different from those of the other Arab states. The establishment of a Christian state there would be natural and would find support among Catholics and Protestants, the largest force in the Christian world. It would be nearly impossible to create such a state in normal times, but during a time of confusion, trouble, revolution, or civil war, the matter would be different. He speculated that perhaps the time was opportune for such a project (he apparently was referring to the effervescence in the Arab world following the Egyptian revolution of 1952). It could not be accomplished without Israel's help, and he suggested that this should be one of the principal missions of Israel's foreign policy. To him, it was a historic opportunity which should not be lost. He did not know whether the Israelis had people in Lebanon to carry out the task but thought there were all kinds of methods which could be used, and no expense should be spared. He had in mind a smaller Lebanon, excluding the largely Muslim areas.

In his reply, dated March 18, Sharett argued cogently that the idea was a nonstarter. He noted that if there are instances when such foreign support of an internal political movement is justified, it can only be done when the movement shows some independent activity which points to the possibility of growth and success. There was no use trying to rouse from outside a movement which did not exist internally, and he saw no signs of a viable movement to create a Christian Lebanon within that country. People might have shouted such slogans in the past, and there might be individuals who supported the idea, but the sizable Orthodox community would not fight for such an idea and the vast majority of Maronites followed leaders who had thrown their weight behind a Christian-Islamic alliance. They would not support the idea of a shrunken state, and an initiative to create one would lead to a catastrophe which would drive the Lebanese Muslims into Syria's hands. The end result would be Syrian annexation of Lebanon. Any attempt by Israel to pull off such a scheme would be considered evidence of recklessness and shallowness, and a willingness to sacrifice others for Israel's tactical advantage. The damage to Israel would be incalculable. It was a prophetic statement.

Copies of this exchange were sent to Ambassador Sasson, the leading Arabist in the Foreign Ministry. In his reply of March 25 he takes issue with Sharett's analysis, saying that he does not think all Maronite leaders have forgotten their dreams of restoring the glory of a Christian Lebanon and that the Christian-Muslim alliance was chosen as the lesser of two evils. It could not be a policy for all time. He notes that the population dynamic threw the future of Maronite dominance into doubt. He concludes, however, that he has no hesitation in saying that accomplishment of the goal in question is impossible because in the first place the Israelis do not have qualified people, and particularly Arabists, to carry out the task. Furthermore, they had severed the relations they used to have with the Arab world and no longer knew the local political scenes as they once did, he could not visualize the huge sums of money which would be needed being made available, and he had no confidence in the willingness of the Lebanese to stick it out through a bitter struggle.[4]

Ben-Gurion's grand design was not adopted, but Ariel Sharon, who became minister of defense in 1981, had his own which had in it echoes of the past. According to Ze'ev Schiff and Ehud Ya'ari, his aim was to create a new order in Lebanon by driving out the Palestine Liberation Organization and the Syrians and installing a president who would sign a peace treaty with Israel. Not only would this stabilize Lebanon; it would also force the PLO leadership into a "gilded cage" in Damascus, where it would lose any vestige of influence on the West Bank, and the Israelis would be able to negotiate an agreement on limited autonomy with moderate local Palestinians. He would kill several birds with one stone and would ensure Israel's supremacy for the next thirty years.[5]

An essential element in this scheme was a Maronite leader who would be willing and able to cooperate, who could sign a peace treaty with Israel and turn his back on the Arab world, and who would be strong and resolute enough to impose his will (and Israel's) on Lebanon. To some Israelis, Bashir Gemayel, son of the Phalangist Pierre, looked to be such a man. He had been in touch with the Israelis since 1976, by which time the rather tentative and spasmodic contacts established in 1948 had blossomed into a substantial military relationship, maturing during the 1975–76 phase of the Lebanese civil war, when the Israelis and Syrians cooperated tacitly to suppress the threat to the Maronites from the radical coalition led by the Druze leader, Kamal Jumblatt.[6]

After 1976, Bashir had steadily emerged as the paramount militia leader in Lebanon and had become the principal Maronite interlocutor with the Israelis, although the latter had initially been much more favorably impressed by his rival, Dany Chamoun. In early 1977 the Chamounists were the most prominent clients of the Israelis in Lebanon, but that had changed by the end of that year to the point that Bashir was talking of seizing power with Israeli help, starting with an assault on the presidential palace. He came to call on me at home one evening in December to request American blessing for this project. I discouraged him from trying such an asinine scheme.

Bashir subsequently denied that he had ever had such an action in mind, but he did not give up plotting. In February 1978 the uneasy cease-fire which had been maintained since 1976, thanks to the presence of some 30,000 Syrian troops, was broken by the Maronite militias, who were increasingly restive under the Syrian presence. For some time they had been complaining about the rudeness and insolence of Syrian army personnel at roadblocks and about an attitude which implied that the Syrians were planning to occupy Lebanon permanently.[7] U.S. Embassy contacts at all levels of the Phalanges revealed the prevalence of unrealistic views about Christian versus Syrian military capabilities. The Phalangists were boasting openly of their ability to take on the Syrians and expel them from Lebanon. They were counting on Israeli and, to a lesser extent, American support. Their illusions in the latter respect were reportedly being fed by Charles Malik, the former Lebanese U.N. delegate and foreign minister who had gone to Washington, been received by Secretary of State Cyrus Vance, and returned saying that the U.S. administration understood the Maronites' position and would support them against the Syrians.

On February 7, 1978, there was a dispute between Syrian and Lebanese soldiers at a roadblock near the Lebanese military academy at Fayadiyah, on the Beirut-Damascus road on the eastern outskirts of Beirut. It led to the ambush of a Syrian convoy in which a number of Syrian soldiers were killed. The U.S. defense attaché reported wild elation at Lebanese army headquarters a short distance down the road, and there ensued a generalized campaign of sniping at and ambushing Syrians throughout Lebanon. Both Bashir Gemayel's Lebanese Forces and the Chamounists "Tigers" were deeply involved, but the political leaders of both groups, Pierre Gemayel and Camille Chamoun, refused to do anything to help apprehend the perpetrators, and a tribunal set up to investigate the matter died for lack of defendants.[8]

The Syrians' response was the indiscriminate bombardment of the Christian quarters of East Beirut with rockets. They seemed to have no intermediate tactic between doing nothing and bombardment, although they were also reported to have murdered more quietly a number of people, including at least one American, and to have buried their bodies in the no-man's land along the frontier. This was perhaps more tactful than bombardment, but understandably led to no improvement in Lebanese attitudes.

Fayadiyah signaled the effective end of the period of reconstruction which had begun in late 1976, and although there have been various periods of remission and relative calm since then, the Syrian military presence has been a burning issue and an underlying cause of instability ever since. Prior to Fayadiyah, in the words of Elias Sarkis, then president of Lebanon, Lebanon had been making two steps forward for every step backward on the road to reconstruction and national reconciliation. After Fayadiyah the process was reversed, not to regain its positive momentum long enough to put the country back together until the present.

The full story of Fayadiyah will probably never be known. At the time I thought it was a provocation arranged by Bashir in the hope of starting a general uprising against the Syrians and dragging the Israelis into the fight. Many Lebanese, on the other hand, were convinced that the Israelis had put Bashir up to it, but they have produced no hard evidence of which I am aware to support that contention.

Meanwhile, Bashir concentrated on a drive for the presidency and on eliminating his Maronite rivals. On June 13, 1978, a group of Bashir's men led by Samir Geagea, later Bashir's successor as commander of the Lebanese Forces,[9] assaulted the home of Tony Frangieh, son of the former president Suleiman Frangieh and leader of a Maronite militia, the Marada Brigade, in northern Lebanon. Tony Frangieh, his wife, and their three-year-old daughter were killed in the fight. Bashir's men said the killings had been the result of Frangieh's resisting their attack (it was not clear what they planned to do to Tony Frangieh if he did not resist) and had not been intended. Suleiman Frangieh, however, told the U.S. chargé d'affaires, George Lane, who called to pay condolences, that his granddaughter had been found with her throat cut and a rose between her teeth. She, at least, had been murdered deliberately and viciously. Bashir later paid for this with the death of his infant daughter in February 1979, and perhaps with his own life as well.

On July 7, 1980, militia units under Bashir's command attacked the Tiger militias of Dany Chamoun. They killed an estimated 150 people, largely their coreligionists, and eliminated the last serious rivals to Bashir's own militia. By August 1980 the five independent Christian militias[10] had been constituted or absorbed into the Lebanese Forces and Bashir was their undisputed commander.

Bashir was something of an enigma. Charming and personable, he radiated boyish innocence and frankness but was in fact a ruthless adventurer and a consummate dissembler. Convinced that he could reform and save Lebanon as Ataturk had Turkey, he would stop at nothing to accomplish that task, and for many Lebanese he was the long-awaited man on horseback. We will never know whether he would have succeeded in stabilizing Lebanon had he not been assassinated, but judging by his record, if he did it would have been at great cost in human freedom and lives.

Certainly he was embarked on a collision course with the Druze at the time of his death, and the insensitivity he showed in trying to strongarm them was an omen of trouble ahead. He had tried to portray himself as a leader of all the Lebanese, but he rejected their traditional consensus politics with scorn. He wanted a new garment, not the tattered cloak of the old National Covenant between Sunnis and Maronites. While much about his approach was attractive, it was founded on a deep misunderstanding of the political realities outside the Maronite community. Most important, while many Lebanese shared his goal to a greater or lesser extent, few of them were ready to have his ruthless methods applied to themselves. Those who could oppose him in the Maronite community had been eliminated, but many people outside it still had the means to resist and would do so. Bashir evidently counted on the Israelis to help him impose his will, but he may have miscalculated their willingness to support his running roughshod over everyone who got in his way.[11]

Israeli writers[12] say that, particularly after Begin came to power in 1977, Bashir Gemayel had secured a number of oral commitments to the effect that the Israelis would not permit Syria to liquidate the Christians. (There was never any prospect that Syria would do that, and if Begin actually thought there was and was not just seeking a pretext for intervention, it is indicative of his ignorance of his neighbors.) Bashir reportedly hoped that this could be turned into a more specific commitment to support him in a challenge to the Syrians, and may have been encouraged in this hope by General Rafael Eytan, the Israeli chief of staff and an extreme hawk.

The first real test of Israel's commitment came in the spring of 1981 and centered on the predominantly Christian town of Zahle in the western Bekaa.[13] There are conflicting views on the origins of the crisis. One school of thought, of which Department of State officials responsible for Lebanon at the time were members, argued that Bashir deliberately provoked a clash with the Syrians in order to drag Israel into a fight with them in the hope it would lead to the elimination of the Syrians from Lebanon. According to this version, Bashir moved Lebanese Forces units into Zahle, where they had not previously been active, knowing this would lead to trouble because it was a vital point to the Syrians. In an article in the *Middle East Journal*, Schiff, the *Haaretz* military correspondent, writes:

> Begin was drawn into a ringing declaration [of April 28, 1981] that Israel would not allow the annihilation of the Christians of Lebanon. Israel was thus proclaimed as the protector of the Christian minority in that country. It was a far-reaching commitment, unwarranted by the circumstances. For, as pointed out by intelligence sources in Israel, the troubles with the Syrians in Zahle had been initiated by the Maronites. . . . Intelligence was unequivocal on this score: the Christian elements were bent on provoking a collision between Jerusalem and Damascus.[14]

The relevant passages in *Israel's Lebanon War* by Schiff and Ya'ari are less categoric:

> One Israeli who suspected that the flare-up in Zahle was essentially a Phalange plot to draw Israel into a clash with Syria was the army's chief of intelligence, Maj. Gen. Yehoshua Saguy. Saguy had long been of the opinion that no good would come of the arrangements with the Phalange, but when he voiced his fears to Begin, the prime minister's response bespoke a flinty resistance to any suggestion that the motives of the Phalange were less than pure. . . . the prime minister's other intelligence adviser, Yitzhak Hof, head of the Mossad, was not at first convinced that the Zahle affair could be summed up as sly Phalange maneuver, but before long suspicions similar to Saguy's began to stir in his

mind. Hof also had an inkling that the Phalangists must have received assurances from some high-ranking Israeli that Israel would bail them out if they got in over their heads in Zahle. His chief suspect was Israel's chief of staff, Rafael Eitan, who promptly denied anything of the sort.[15]

Another version provided by William Harris is based on accounts given to him by people in Zahle two years after the event.[16] According to them, the trouble was the result of Syrian pressure on Zahle. They claimed the Syrians provoked incidents in the fall of 1980 in order to justify the stationing of their army units in the town, where they had not previously been.

Harris's sources said that Chamounist elements who had not accepted dissolution of their militia, working with Palestinians who may have had ties with the Syrians, had fomented trouble by attacking Phalangists. Following a clash between Phalangists and Syrians in which four Syrians and three Zahle residents were killed, the Syrians shelled and blockaded the town briefly in December and continued to cut off access to many of the town's vineyards in the new year. Nervous Zahlawis brought in military supplies by foot over Mount Sannin, which lay between them and the Maronite heartland controlled by Bashir, and in March the Lebanese Forces began working to improve the primitive track leading from the western slope over the ridge and down to Zahle.

Whoever started the affair, there seems to be general agreement that the Syrians feared the improved road over the mountain presaged an Israeli-supported Phalangist push into an area they regarded as their preserve. They therefore reacted forcefully, eventually occupying the slopes of Mount Sannin, where they had not been before, and forcing the evacuation of some ninety Phalangist militiamen from Zahle. Responding to Bashir's and Chamoun's calls for help, the Israelis shot down two troop-carrying helicopters full of Syrian soldiers, claiming that they had been gunships. The Syrians responded by installing surface-to-air missiles in the Bekka Valley. The Israelis considered this a violation of the so-called red line agreement of 1976[17] and were preparing to take out the missiles when the United States dissuaded them from doing so, sending Ambassador Philip Habib out to try to negotiate their removal.

Habib did not succeed, but the crisis moved to another area on May 29 when the Israelis began air attacks on Palestinian positions in south Lebanon, without apparent provocation.[18] The Palestinians were hesitant to respond at first, not wishing to expose their positions, but after five days of a second round of air attacks, which began on July 10, they began an artillery and rocket bombardment of towns and settlements in northern Israel. The number of casualties they inflicted was far below those they were taking themselves, but they created an intolerable panic in northern Israel, and Begin, who had initially approved escalating the combat, surprised the Americans by his readiness to accept a cease-fire when Habib went to see him on July 24. The terms of that cease-fire became a controversial issue later on, but it held for almost a year, until the Israelis launched an aerial bombardment on June 4, 1982, followed by the invasion of Lebanon, which began on June 6.[19]

As noted earlier, the invasion had a threefold objective: to destroy the PLO power base in Lebanon, to create a new order in Lebanon which would sign a peace treaty with Israel, and indirectly to undermine the PLO in the West Bank and Gaza. That General Sharon had such ideas in mind had been revealed by him in all or in part to a number of people in advance of the operation. In particular, he discussed his ideas with Ambassador Habib in December 1981 and again with Secretary of State Alexander Haig in May 1982. Habib says he objected strongly to Sharon's argument,[20] and he warned Washington strongly of what was afoot. But the Israelis maintain that Haig, by the feebleness or ambiguity of his remonstrances, in effect gave Sharon a green light (see, for instance, "Green Light, Lebanon" by Ze ʿev Schiff in the spring 1983 issue of *Foreign Policy*). Haig denies this in his memoirs, but as in 1967 and 1970, the Israelis heard what they wanted to hear.

According to David Kimche in *The Last Option* (pp. 144–45), the Israelis had drawn up their invasion plan, had coordinated it with Bashir Gemayel in January 1982, and were "on a course for war; it required only some inflammatory act by the PLO to light the fuse." According to Ambassador Paul Hare, who was deputy chief of mission in Tel Aviv at the time, it was only a question of when and on what scale the Israelis would attack.

The invasion was a military success of sorts but was not noted for brilliance and daring, and the prolonged siege and bombardment of Beirut badly tarnished the image of the Israeli military. It decided nothing politically. Temporarily it removed the PLO military presence from Beirut and the south but not from north Lebanon. And according to Lebanese sources, small numbers of PLO fighters had begun filtering back into the Beirut area by the following January. It also facilitated the installation of Bashir Gemayel in the presidency, but that probably would have happened without the invasion. He was unwilling to sign a peace treaty, however, and after his death the new order rapidly disintegrated into a state of feudal anarchy. The Syrians eventually emerged from the contest more influential than ever in Lebanon, and the Israelis succeeded in alienating a Shia community which had previously been peacefully inclined toward them. This is not to mention the tragedy of the Sabra and Chatilla massacre and the impact it had on Israeli politics and the fortunes of Begin and Sharon, or the thousands of Lebanese civilian casualties which resulted, or the many Israeli, American, and French casualties. By any standard it was a monumental disaster for everyone except the Syrians, and it was costly for them, too.

There was, nevertheless, a brief moment when the Israelis appeared to have won and to be in a position to impose a lasting settlement in Lebanon which would exclude both the Palestinians and the Syrians and in which the followers of Bashir Gemayel would forge a new Lebanese identity in a state closely tied to Israel. Even after Bashir's death the Israelis were in a strong position to influence events and their people were talking of a new Israeli-Egyptian-Lebanese axis, pointing out that Egypt had almost one-third of the Arab world's people and maintaining that such an economic unit did not really need access to the rest of the Arab world to be viable economically. This was nonsense as far as Lebanon was concerned,[21] but that did not prevent pundits from the United States and Israel from promoting that view in the press and elsewhere.

In furtherance of the Israel-Egypt-Lebanon common market idea and the pursuit of profit, the Israelis sent in large amounts of private capital to benefit from the liberal Lebanese banking laws and started selling food, textiles, and manufactured goods at favorable prices. Lebanese businessmen described it as dumping.

On August 12, 1982, the *International Herald Tribune* reported that as early as August 11, while the fighting was still in progress, the Israelis estimated the previous month's exports to Lebanon as $4 million. By December the figure was put at $20 million by the Lebanese. The Lebanese bought Israeli exports even though the quality, particularly of fruits and vegetables, was inferior to their own, because they were cheap and because (according to one U.S. official) the Israelis had forcefully prevented the Lebanese from harvesting and marketing their citrus crop in the south. The Israelis also facilitated the flow of imported goods through the free port of Haifa and into Lebanon without payment of customs, preventing the Lebanese from setting up even temporary customs posts at the border and depriving the government of revenue as well as upsetting trading patterns. (The Israelis used customs control as one of their bargaining points in the later negotiations, refusing to allow the Lebanese to set up a temporary customs post at the border.) A story going the rounds in Beirut in January 1983 may be apocryphal but shows what the Lebanese thought was happening:

> A Beirut appliance dealer took a consignment of refrigerators worth 300,000 Lebanese pounds from Haifa and sold them. He was then visited by two men from the Lebanese Forces who took from him the 150,000 pounds he should have paid in customs dues. The next day he was visited by a third man who asked him what had happened. The dealer told him about the 150,000 pounds. The third man promptly gave him that amount of money and told him to call if it ever happened again. The third man was working for the Israelis, who wanted to keep the Haifa channel open.

A key to the success of the new order, however, was rapid withdrawal of the Israelis. Their invasion had been welcomed by many Lebanese of all religions, but the latter were motivated by anti-Palestinian sentiment, not love of the Israelis. They wanted the latter to do their dirty work for them and remove the armed Palestinian incubus, but they wanted them to leave as soon as they had done it. Many Lebanese, probably a majority, were resigned to the idea of some sort of "normalization" and the movement of people and goods across the border with Israel, as long as it was not called a peace treaty and did not involve them in too much trouble with the rest of the Arab world. In concrete terms, that meant no formal diplomatic relations. Most people I met in a visit to Beirut in late January–early February 1983 were talking in such terms, but the timing of withdrawal was already an important issue and it became even more so with each day that passed.

The Israelis seemed not to have recalled that the Syrians had also been welcomed as liberators from the Palestinians in 1976, and that their prolonged stay had led inevitably to incidents and conflict. The same thing happened to the Israelis, who eventually found themselves in an untenable situation. By the time they realized they were in trouble, it was too late. Their failure to understand how unwelcome they were was due in part to what they were hearing from certain Maronites, many of whom wanted them to stay as protection against the Syrians and some of whom were ready to throw in their lost with Israel. That was what Israelis such as Sharon and Begin wanted to hear, and they apparently let themselves be deluded into thinking the Lebanese really meant it and would be prepared to pay the price it would entail. They were not the first foreigners to be led down that garden path.

CHAPTER
9

THE NEGOTIATIONS

The Israelis wanted everything. They weren't
going to get it. . . . Even the Lebanese
couldn't give them what they wanted in this
agreement.

Philip Habib, May 9, 1990

When the Israelis first invaded Lebanon in 1978, they withdrew partially under heavy pressure from President Carter without any attempt at negotiating a diplomatic settlement with the Lebanese. To the extent that there was negotiation about their departure, it was conducted in the United Nations context with the creation of the U.N. Interim Force in Lebanon (UNIFIL), which was supposed to occupy all of South Lebanon as the Israelis withdrew. (It was not able to do so because of the opposition of the Israelis, who refused to withdraw totally, and who have controlled a "security zone" north of the border ever since through a continued military presence and through a proxy irregular force of Christian fighters who garrison a number of Christian villages in that area.) There were no direct Lebanese-Israeli contacts except for a brief and abortive attempt to revive the Mixed Armistice Commission. This failed because the Israelis wanted to talk about open borders and the fabric of relations, whereas the Lebanese wanted to stick to the original task of the MACs, which was to discuss border incidents and how to prevent them.

In 1982 things were different. A prime political goal of the operation was a formal peace agreement with Lebanon. With time this became an obsession as the Israeli public began to realize what a debacle their victory had produced and the government felt compelled to show some positive result. The process registered its first setback on August 30, a week after Bashir Gemayel's election as president of Lebanon, when Bashir went to meet Begin and Sharon at the Israeli coastal town of Nahariya. According to his own account, as told to Robert Dillon, the U.S. ambassador in Beirut, and Morris Draper, Begin and Sharon treated him like a "bellboy" and tried to pressure him into agreeing then to sign a formal peace treaty before the end of the year. Bashir, mindful of the need to maintain ties with the greater Arab world and of the problems he would have with his constituency, which already thought he was too close to the Israelis, refused, saying he would give them the substance of peace, but not to ask him for the formal trappings yet.[1]

Bashir was assassinated a few days later, on September 4. Had he lived, he probably would have offered Israel a modus vivendi which might eventually have led to a formal peace agreement—but it might not have. He had said repeatedly that he wanted to be president of all of Lebanon and not of some Christian enclave. That meant he had had to placate many people who were unalterably opposed to formal recognition of Israel, and he would have had to be very careful.

With Bashir's death and the election of his brother Amin as president, the Israelis continued to pursue their goal of a formal peace, which they described as "normalization," even though it would seem abnormal to many Lebanese and most Arabs. If Bashir would have been unable to force through such an agreement, Amin was even more so. A member of parliament and an experienced political operator, Amin had none of Bashir's charisma and did not inherit his control of the Lebanese Forces or his support in the Maronite community. He was dependent on the support of the Israelis (who were less forthcoming than they were with Bashir) and Americans and a narrow Lebanese power base which did not give him the sort of personal authority that Bashir was expected to have once he assumed office.[2]

Had the Israelis moved quickly, an understanding might have been worked out which would have given them withdrawal of the Syrians and Palestinians, limited movement of people and eventually goods across the Lebanese border, and reasonable prospect of a stable Lebanon. This would have secured their primary interest—quiet along the border. As it was, three months were wasted in maneuvering about the nature and format of the negotiations which were to lead to an Israeli withdrawal. The Lebanese wanted the Israelis to withdraw immediately and unconditionally, but the Israelis were seeking a package deal in which withdrawal would be tied to permission for the Israelis to maintain a military presence in southern Lebanon in the form of surveillance stations and to maintain a quasi-diplomatic mission in Beirut which would be given diplomatic status even if not formally recognized initially. Withdrawal would be in stages, matched by simultaneous Syrian withdrawal, and the Israelis would have succeeded in imposing peace on their terms. Few remarked on the irony that the Israelis had been fighting the Palestinians and Syrians, not the Lebanese, but the latter were to pay the price at the negotiating table.

By mid-fall two divergent efforts at negotiation were under way. On one hand, the Americans, through Habib and his principal assistant, Morris Draper, were trying to work out a formula consistent with the political realities of Lebanon. They envisaged negotiations in the pattern which Habib had followed successfully in 1981 and 1982, with Habib shuttling back and forth between the parties (or their representatives) and playing an honest broker role. Habib had in mind an informal, working agreement to get all "external forces," meaning the Syrians, Israelis, and PLO, out of Lebanon and to restore Lebanese sovereignty throughout the country. Habib described the process he had in mind:

> What I was going to do was negotiate the kind of understandings that I had negotiated once previously with the Israelis. At that time I actually got the Israelis, the PLO, the Syrians, the Saudis, the Lebanese . . . all to agree to something without having a piece of paper. I was the one who kept the piece of paper. And it was I who announced the understandings. They were always listed as—I have these assurances; I can tell you, Asad, I've got these assurances this will happen. I can tell you, Begin, this is what will happen. You don't have to negotiate with the PLO. The PLO will do this because I'm telling you it will do this. I had done that twice before, I could do it once again.[3]

On the other hand, the Israelis, and Sharon in particular, were trying to reach their own private understanding with the Lebanese without benefit of the Americans, who were likely to influence the Lebanese to resist making concessions.

THE HABIB MISSION

When the 1982 invasion began, Habib had been on his way to the area to try again (earlier efforts in December 1981 had been unsuccessful) to expand on the 1981 cease-fire and to work on the peace process, which had been stalled ever since Camp David. With regard to the cease-fire, he hoped to persuade the Palestinians to move back some of their heavy weapons, particularly their 130-mm guns, with which they could bombard Israel, and to "sanitize" the South Lebanon border, "because we were getting word that the Israelis were deploying forces up in that area. And having known what Sharon had in mind, which I had objected to from '81 on . . . what I wanted to do was to get a better situation along the border to assure that there would be no incidents . . . and there would be no occasion for military action."[4]

The concentration of heavy artillery in PLO hands, which had not been specifically excluded by the 1981 cease-fire agreement, was one of the justifications the Israelis were giving for wanting to attack the Palestinians, even though the guns in question were not firing across the border. Habib had hoped to reconfirm the cease-fire and make it stronger. It had held for eleven months and he hoped it would continue to do so.[5] He had been attending a conference on the Middle East at Ditchley, England, en route to the area when the invasion began and was summoned hastily to Versailles, where President Reagan was attending the Eighth Economic Summit conference. A White House spokesman on June 6 announced that Habib was instructed by the president to offer the assistance of the U.S. government in the cause of peace in the Middle East.[6] Later in the day Secretary of State Haig said the president had decided to send Habib to the area as his personal representative to conduct discussions on an urgent basis with Prime Minister Begin.[7]

Habib arrived in Israel on June 7 and went from there to Damascus, back to Israel, then to Beirut via a brief stopover in Damascus (according to Draper's recollection). He and Draper remained in Beirut, with lightning trips to other area capitals and London, until a successful cease-fire was arranged and the evacuation of Palestinian fighters and some 5,000 Syrian soldiers was completed on September 1. The evacuation had been arranged by dint of strenuous, complex negotiations involving much shuttle diplomacy by Habib and Draper, and Habib then went home for a well-deserved rest, leaving Draper in charge of the mediating effort on the ground.

Habib had expected to return for the inauguration of Bashir Gemayel as president and did return for Amin's election on September 21. He remained in the area long enough to make a visit to Damascus and was back in Washington in time for the October visit of Amin Gemayel to that capital. He was back in the region by mid-December. The day-to-day task of mediation and of getting negotiations started, however, was left to Draper. While he had the personal rank of ambassador (announced by President Reagan on September 8) and was an able diplomat with wide Middle Eastern experience, Draper was considerably junior to Habib and did not have the same authority and personal access. It is by no means certain, however, that even Habib's being there all the time would have made much difference, because a great deal was happening to undercut American objectives in Lebanon. These had been given by Reagan as early as June 30: restoring the authority of the central government, guaranteeing the southern border with Israel, and evacuating all foreign forces—Syrian, Israeli, and Palestinian.[8]

The three objectives were interlocked, of course. The authority of the central government could not be restored unless the foreign armies withdrew, and unless that authority was restored, there could be no guarantee of peace along the border. Bashir's death made restoring the central government's authority even more problematic than it had been when there was an expectation that he would be in charge, but it was still possible if evacuation was arranged quickly and something effective was done in the way of reconciling the armed factions. The Lebanese were ready for reconciliation. They were tired of the fighting. Properly led and relieved of the domination of foreign armies and the interference of foreign intelligence services, they could perhaps have resolved their problems. Unfortunately, none of those conditions was met.

In particular, the Israelis showed no inclination to speed their own departure, which meant, among other things, that the Syrians were under no pressure to leave. While the Americans realized that early withdrawal was important and hoped to have agreement on it before Christmas, they did not succeed in convincing Israel of this. Furthermore, Begin's willingness to cooperate had been affected by the shock of Reagan's September 1 initiative, the U.S. peace plan which among other things called for a return of the West Bank to Arab control. Begin was particularly outraged that it had been announced without prior consultation with Israel. According to Draper, "This was why he went ballistic when he saw Bashir in Nahariya the next day." Begin had been informed of the initiative the night before it was made public, and that was all. This was an example of a constant problem in U.S. relations with the Israelis. If they are consulted in advance and do not like what they hear, they do their best to sabotage it in the U.S. Congress, and they have such influence there that the executive rarely wishes to take the risk. The alternative is to present them with a fait accompli. Their resentment is then doubled and they make even greater efforts to block the action.

Ambassador Draper maintains that Begin deliberately delayed movement on withdrawal from Lebanon because he feared that a successful U.S.-sponsored deal in Lebanon along the lines proposed by Habib would put unacceptable pressure on him to go along with the Reagan initiative. Some other officials who were on the sidelines of the process blame the delay on haggling over details. In either case, while there was no formal linkage, the initiative was tied de facto to settlement of the Lebanon problem—as long as the latter remained unsettled it would be impossible to talk about the former. For one thing, the Arab states would not have participated in such an effort. Egypt, for instance, had withdrawn its ambassador from Tel Aviv in protest over the invasion and did not allow him to return until the Israelis eventually withdrew from most of Lebanon, and linkage of the larger problem to Lebanon had been made explicit by the Jordanians and Saudis.[9]

There was a debate within the U.S. administration on the timing of the September 1 initiative, with officers of the Department of State arguing that it should not be announced until there was progress on Israeli withdrawal. According to one participant, Secretary Shultz insisted on moving forward and was seconded by activists in the White House who thought that the agreement on evacuation of the PLO from Beirut under the protection of U.S. marines and other foreign troops, something no one had anticipated, should be seized upon as the psychological moment for the announcement.[10]

Habib was named by Reagan as his negotiator for the September 1 initiative on October 11, and Habib returned to the area in December, as noted earlier, to start shuttling, regretfully concluding that he had to get agreement on withdrawal from Lebanon before he could start work on the peace process.

The Department of State announced on October 25 that the two sides had agreed to negotiate on Israel's withdrawal. This was denied by the Lebanese government two days later. (Draper describes the denial as "smoke and mirrors.") Three days after that, on October 30, Draper was reported to have announced that the two sides had agreed to assemble negotiating teams to discuss the withdrawal and security arrangements in southern Lebanon. (Draper says he never made a public announcement to that effect.) On November 9, Israeli Foreign Minister Yitzhak Shamir told a visiting congressional delegation that the negotiations could drag on for months, and on the same day the *New York Times* reported that U.S. officials were saying Israel refused to withdraw its forces unless the Lebanese agreed to discuss the normalization of relations. They said Israel had dropped its demand for a formal treaty but insisted on the "trappings of normalization."

SHARON'S END RUN

While the Lebanese, Israelis, and Americans were arguing officially about setting up the negotiations and the Americans were chafing under the delay, secret talks on the Israeli package were conducted between General Sharon and three other Israeli officials, on one hand, and a close associate of Amin Gemayel, Sami Maroun, on the other.[11] At a meeting with Habib, Begin, and others on December 16, Sharon produced a three-page document which he said had been worked out in these negotiations and had been agreed to by Gemayel. It committed both sides to a package deal tying withdrawal to agreement on security arrangements and the normalization of relations.[12]

Habib describes this incident:

> Before I left Washington for my negotiating sessions I had in my pocket my idea of what a draft agreement [on Lebanon] would be like. I had it approved by the Secretary [and by the president as well, according to Draper and then assistant secretary for NEA, Nicholas Veliotes]. . . . I went to Beirut first and met with Amin and explained what I intended to do, and he had no objection. And I went to Israel and I sat down with Shamir and Sharon and the Chief of Staff and I started to lay out my ideas of what could be done now to resolve the Lebanese situation. I hadn't gotten very far in my presentation when Sharon said, "Just a minute, we already have an understanding." And I said I didn't believe it and he said, "Well, I have here a paper which President Gemayel has signed and which lays out the guidelines of an agreement . . . which we will now negotiate." And I said we'd better regroup, and I walked out of the room and got on the telephone to Beirut and said, "I'm choppering up to Beirut and I want to meet immediately with President Gemayel, *alone.*"
>
> I landed on a mountaintop somewhere south and east of Beirut and

went up to see him. He wasn't alone. He had Ghassan [Tueni] and Wadia Haddad with him. [They left the room, according to Draper, who was with Habib and remained for the meeting.] I was so . . . mad. I said, "You didn't tell me about this when I saw you yesterday. What have you done? What is this?"

He said, "This isn't an agreement. These are just guidelines. . . . I didn't sign it. They wanted me to sign it, but I didn't sign it."

Meanwhile, the secret negotiations, when they walked out of the meeting with me the Israelis made them public. Just like that. And of course Amin was horrified. This was a secret understanding, these secret guidelines.[13]

The Sharon-Maroun negotiations were fateful. They seriously undercut the efforts of Habib and Draper, who, while not objecting to the idea of normalization, had been arguing that its immediate implementation was not practicable and that something more modest would have to be worked out if there was to be any hope of an agreement which would last. Their concern at this point seems to have been with general principles they thought the Lebanese could or could not accept rather than the specific threat of a Syrian veto. The Syrians were widely regarded in the fall of 1982 as being in no condition to cause trouble.

As it happened, the agreement had not been signed either by Maroun or Sharon and had no status; nor did Maroun or Gemayel have authority to conclude such an agreement by himself in any event. Sharon further compromised what he had by revealing his secret negotiations to the press. Gemayel promptly denied that he had agreed to anything, but the document Sharon produced strongly implied a willingness on the part of Gemayel to accept the Israelis' normalization package, and amounted to giving the game away without even attempting to play it. The Israelis were apparently convinced by this that if they bargained hard enough, particularly with their troops in a dominant position on the ground, they could eventually get the terms they were seeking. Meanwhile they were enjoying their novel status as occupiers of a relatively friendly population and had rejected an American proposal of late October–early November that they withdraw from Beirut and part of the Shuf to Sidon.

Negotiations actually got under way on December 28, alternating between Khalde, just south of Beirut, and Kiryat Shmona and later Netanya in northern Israel. The Lebanese delegation was headed by Antoine Fattal, a career diplomat who displayed considerable courage in agreeing to take on the task, which proved to be thankless. The Israeli team was headed by Kimche, a man with an intelligence background who was at the time director general of the Israeli Foreign Ministry. His description of the Lebanese problem and the negotiations can be found in his *Last Option* (pp. 125–81), although, it does not give as much detail as one would like. True to Shamir's prediction, the process dragged on and on. Habib distanced himself from the talks,[14] and the role of mediator was left largely to Draper, who showed considerable skill in finding compromises which the two parties could accept on a series of basic issues, some important and some ludicrous. In particular, the Israelis in their desire to secure the Lebanese market for their products consumed an inordinate amount of time discussing the terms under which their goods would be allowed across the border. According to one participant, the nadir was reached in arguing over the pricing of Israeli pickles, although Draper says they were just used as an example to apply to trade generally. The minutes of these meetings have yet to be released, but the principal issues were the question of Israeli-manned surveillance stations, which the Israelis wanted to maintain on Lebanese territory, and the degree of normalization which would be permitted.

By April it was apparent that although the two sides had narrowed their points of difference, the latter remained very difficult to surmount and the negotiations were not going to succeed without some higher-level involvement on the part of the Americans. In the absence of fundamental changes of position, there would be no agreement. Both sides had to be moved, and neither Draper nor Habib could do it. As long as the talks remained at the level of the negotiating teams they would be fruitless, in spite of various signs of high-level U.S. displeasure. Even a U.S. decision on March 31 to suspend delivery of F-16 fighters to Israel until there was agreement on withdrawal failed to budge the Israelis.

The *New York Times* reported on April 13 that on the previous day Habib had participated in a negotiating session for the first time in several months. Perhaps as a result of his observation of the lack of progress in that session, a decision was taken to raise the stakes. On April 21 the *Times* reported that Shultz would travel to the Middle East to push the September 1 initiative and the withdrawal of foreign forces from Lebanon. This was confirmed on April 22 when President Reagan announced that he had decided to send Shultz to the area to assist in negotiating an Israeli-Lebanese agreement on troop withdrawal.

Shultz arrived in Cairo April 24. While there he met with President Husni Mubarak and, on the twenty-fourth and twenty-fifth, with U.S. chiefs of mission and principal officers from Israel and the surrounding states. On the twenty-fifth he was quoted as saying that a Lebanese-Israeli agreement was "doable" and as promising to remain in the area until an accord was reached. He was in Israel on April 27, arrived in Lebanon on the twenty-eighth, and was in Jerusalem on May 1. By a combination of cajolery and arm twisting he brought the two sides close enough together so that on May 4 Begin was scheduling a cabinet meeting to discuss "the U.S.-negotiated Lebanese-Israeli agreement." The agreement was approved in principle by the Israeli cabinet on May 6, but its overall thrust was rejected by President Asad of Syria when Shultz went to Damascus the same day. The Syrian official spokesman called the agreement an "act of submission."

Shultz went from Damascus to Saudi Arabia on May 6, then made quick stops in Israel and Lebanon and returned to Washington. The *Washington Post* of May 12 reported that he told Reagan when he got home that Soviet pressure was keeping the Syrians in Lebanon, although he was confident of their eventual withdrawal. That he was in fact confident of Syrian withdrawal at that point is doubtful, and blaming the Soviets for the Syrian position was apparently the globalist obsession of NSC staffer Peter Rodman and another NSC staffer who had been on the trip, not Shultz. Two senior U.S. officials who were present report that in Jerusalem Rodman seriously proposed anti-Soviet moves elsewhere in the world as a way to put pressure on Syria. Draper speculates that one of the two NSC staffers conveyed their apprehensions about the Soviets to a journalist, who thought they were reflecting Shultz's views.

President Gemayel spoke out against "Arab blackmail" on May 10 and said he was going to seek domestic and international support for the agreement. The Lebanese cabinet unanimously approved it on May 14. The Lebanese and Israeli parliaments both aproved it on May 16, and it was signed on May 17. An unnamed Syrian official meanwhile was reported as saying that the Syrians would do all they could to foil the agreement, and on May 19 the Syrian foreign minister, Abdul Halim Khaddam, said Syria would take measures against the Lebanese state. On June 1 Syria's President Asad said the agreement was dead and predicted a war with Israel. The Lebanese nevertheless proceeded to submit the agreement to parliament, which ratified it on June 14 with a vote of sixty-five to two, with four abstentions. The vote may have been influenced to some extent by moral support from Egypt and Saudia Arabia, as well as the United States.

There obviously was substantial support for the agreement within the Lebanese body politic, particularly among Christians, but some Muslim Lebanese, such as the prime minister, Shafiq al-Wazzan, were deeply unhappy with those aspects of the treaty which constituted a servitude on Lebanese sovereignty.[15] While most Lebanese wanted both the Israelis and the Syrians to leave and many were not overly concerned about the conditions, others were concerned about the impact of the treaty of Lebanon's relations with its Arab hinterland and with Syria in particular, and some of them thought the government's bowing to Israeli and U.S. pressure was shameful.

That the concerns were justified became clear as the Syrians and their allies in Lebanon—principally the Jumblatt Druze, the pro-Iranian Shia, and various radical groups, including the Syrian Socialist Nationalist Party (the PPS), the Communists, and the PLO (both pro- and anti-Arafat factions, between whom fighting had broken out in the Bekaa Valley on May 15, opposed the treaty)—began actively to manifest their hostility to the agreement. While the PLO fighters from South Lebanon and Beirut had been shipped out in September, they remained in considerable numbers around Tripoli and in the Bekaa. As time passed, they began to trickle back into the Beirut area, and as a bewildering series of changing alignments and confrontations between the Palestinian factions and various Lebanese groups, not to mention the Syrians, ensued, they eventually became again one of the factors in the Lebanese equation.

To work up Arab support for the agreement, Shultz returned to the area in early July and remained there four days, visiting Damascus, Saudia Arabia, Israel, and Lebanon. After meeting with Asad on July 6 he said there was no prospect of an immediate Syrian withdrawal, and at the end of his trip, on July 7, he said it had not produced any progress on the withdrawal of foreign forces from Lebanon.

Although the negotiations and the agreement had been over Israeli withdrawal, the Israelis at the last minute had introduced a side letter which made their withdrawal contingent on the Syrians doing the same, thereby giving the latter what amounted to a veto over implementation. Syrian withdrawal was therefore as much an issue as Israeli withdrawal.

Habib and Draper had discussed in detail with the Israelis how a simultaneous IDF-Syrian withdrawal could take place, satisfying military concerns on both sides, and some of these details had also been exposed to the Syrians in the fall of 1982, but there was no clear agreement or understanding on the conditions, if any, under which the Syrians would leave. In the spring of 1983, neither Syria nor Israel showed signs of feeling any great pressure from the situation on the ground to get out of Lebanon, and both saw certain advantages to remaining. Increased domestic opposition to the continued Israeli presence in Lebanon soon became evident in Israel, however, and the Israelis quickly became disenchanted with their position as armed opposition to them, particularly from the Shia, began to manifest itself and internal disorders increased. They eventually withdrew unilaterally, although maintaining a residual presence with the Christian forces in the south, without obtaining a Syrian withdrawal.

CHAOS

There had been intermittent fighting between Maronite and Druze factions in the Shuf area ever since the ill-considered entry of the Lebanese Forces militia into that area in the summer of 1982. As long as the Israelis remained in occupation of the Shuf, the violence was containable most of the time, although it got out of control every once in a while, as when the Druze shelled East Beirut in response to Maronite shelling of their positions in the Shuf in late January 1983.

Not long after the signing of the May 17 agreement, the Israelis began talking about a unilateral redeployment of their troops to southern Lebanon. President Gemayel rejected a proposal by his army commander,

General Tannous, to send army units commanded by Druze officers into the Shuf in return for the departure of the Lebanese Forces outsiders from the region, but was unable to impose government control over the region by any other means. He therefore objected to unilateral Israeli withdrawal, but the Israelis went ahead with their plans and withdrew from the Shuf on September 4. Lebanese Foreign Minister Elie Salem said the withdrawal had "frozen" the May 17 agreement. Meanwhile, heavy fighting between the Lebanese Forces and the Druze to establish dominance in the region had begun and the Americans were soon involved.

In fact, U.S. marines who were members of the multinational peace-keeping force were involved in the fighting as early as August 28, when they fought a battle with unidentified militiamen that lasted ninety minutes. There were no marine casualties. The following day two marines were killed and fourteen wounded. The White House blamed Syria. On August 30 four French members of the multinational force were killed, and on September 1 it was announced that Reagan had ordered another 2,000 marines to the eastern Mediterranean in support of those already in Lebanon.

Things got worse quickly after September 4. On September 6 two marines were killed and three wounded during heavy shelling of the Beirut airport where they were stationed, and two French soldiers were killed by artillery the following day. The U.S. Navy responded by shelling a Druze artillery position on September 8, and on September 12 Reagan authorized the use of "aggressive self-defense" by the marines. The following day he authorized them to call on naval and air support in self-defense.

September 17 was the turning point after which all was lost, according to Draper. On that day the navy fired on artillery positions in Syrian-held areas for the first time, and on September 19 it began firing in support of Lebanese army units in Suq al-Gharb, a small resort town on the ridge east of Beirut commanding the southern approaches to Beirut as well as the airport. Defense of Suq al-Gharb was said by U.S. officials to be vital to U.S. interests. At this point the Lebanese army units whose deployment in the Shuf had been announced by President Gemayel on July 25 had in effect become a faction in the Druze-Maronite dispute, trying to prevent the Druze from taking over the Shuf and thereby protecting the Maronites. The United States had become a part of that faction by coming to the army's aid. The decision to do so reportedly was taken by Robert MacFarlane, who had been sent out as Habib's successor in July. He was allegedly told by a Lebanese officer that all that was needed was a little U.S. intervention to "close the gap."*

---

*One hopes that some young Ph.D. with lots of energy is working on a detailed history of these events and that she or he will eventually get access to the official records and be able to document what occurred. There is much to be dug up. This summary account, based on the *Middle East Journal*'s chronology, is no substitute for a detailed study.

There were more incidents in the last two weeks of September and early October, but both houses of Congress authorized the marines to remain in Lebanon for another eighteen months. Reagan on October 19 said the marines would stay and accused the Syrians of blocking efforts at a settlement. Then on October 23 a truck loaded with explosives crashed into the marine barracks at the Beirut airport and destroyed it with terrible loss of life (241 killed). Another truck bomb destroyed a building housing French troops with the loss of fifty-six lives. Responsibility for these attacks has never been established publicly, but the Syrians and their radical Shia allies are the most likely suspects (as they are for the blowing up of the U.S. Embassy in Beirut on April 18, when forty-six people were killed and some 100 injured). Reagan responded the next day by saying the presence of the marines in Lebanon was "central to [U.S.] credibility on a global scale" and prevented the Soviet Union or its "surrogates" (meaning Syria) from dominating the country. On November 4 it was the Israelis' turn. A truck bomb blew up their headquarters near Tyre, and sixty people were reported killed.

Both the French and the Israelis responded by bombing sites in the Bekaa Valley near Baalbek which were thought to house Iranians and Lebanese Shia involved in the truck bombings. The United States did not join in, for which the administration was criticized by some pundits, but it was never shown that either the French or the Israeli bombings actually had any effect on the level of violence. One can even argue that they probably augmented the violence by increasing animosities.

Meanwhile, on November 3 Reagan announced the appointment of Donald Rumsfeld to succeed MacFarlane, who had been named national security adviser, replacing William P. Clark. Rumsfeld arrived in Beirut on November 14. Neither he nor MacFarlane knew much about the region or its problems (MacFarlane had refused a briefing offered by Habib, according to Draper) and neither was able to make any progress on the Lebanese imbroglio, which had been complicated by bloody fighting between the PLO factions and between the Lebanese army and Shia militants in and around Beirut.

On December 4, U.S. Navy jets attacked Syrian positions, and two jets were shot down. The pilot of one was killed, but the other was taken prisoner by the Syrians, to be rescued eventually by Jesse Jackson. On December 13, U.S. warships shelled Syrian positions after the Syrians fired at U.S. reconnaisance aircraft, and on December 14 the battleship *New Jersey* entered the fight with its sixteen-inch guns, said to be able to drop a shell weighing as much as a Volkswagen into an area the size of a tennis court. The guns were used against Syrian positions in the upper Matn, near the crest of Mount Lebanon, but according to people from the area in question they were not very effective, hitting civilian targets rather than the Syrians.

Meanwhile, also on December 14, Reagan was quoted as saying the marines would remain in Lebanon until the Lebanese government resumed sovereignty over its territory or there was a total collapse of public order. The *Washington Post* on December 20, however, reported that U.S. officials were saying that Gemayel's failure to form a national reconciliation government could lead to withdrawal of U.S. troops. This was followed by a Defense Department report released on December 28 which was very critical of U.S. policy in Lebanon and called for an urgent reassessment of the role of the marines there. The Defense Department had been reluctant to use the marines (or other U.S. forces) in the first place, and pressure began to mount to get them out of Lebanon. On January 4, 1984, House Speaker Tip O'Neill said that without "measurable progress" on the Lebanon problem he would take steps to revoke the congressional authorization for the continued marine presence in Beirut.

As the debate within the administration warmed up, the situation on the ground deteriorated even further, approaching or even exceeding the violence of the first phase of Lebanon's civil war in 1975–76 and threatening the total breakdown of what civil order remained. There was increasingly heavy fighting in and around Beirut between various militia factions and between them and the Lebanese army, and there were various unanswered calls for international intervention to establish a cease-fire. On February 5 the Shafiq al-Wazzan government resigned, and on February 6 Druze and Shia militias took control of much of West Beirut away from the Lebanese army. The U.S. embassy began evacuating nonesssential personnel the next day. On February 2 administration officials had been quoted as saying that a proposed congressional resolution calling for withdrawal of U.S. forces would encourage the forces of radicalism and extremism, but five days later, on February 7, Reagan announced that the 1,600 marines in Beirut would be withdrawn to ships off the coast while naval and air forces would step up their attacks against antigovernment forces operating behind Syrian lines. The move was described by at least one Pentagon official as a strategic redeployment which would increase American ability to react, but it was in fact a retreat which marked the beginning of the end of U.S. involvement. The administration had decided to cut its losses and turn its back on Lebanon, and it did so very quickly. The marine withdrawal began on February 21 and was over by February 26. The positions abandoned by the marines were occupied by Shia militiamen and Lebanese army troops who supported them. The game had been lost, and Amin Gemayel was left holding the bag.

On March 4 the Lebanese cabinet, with Elie Salem as acting prime minister, abrogated the May 17 agreement as part of a Syrian-sponsored reconciliation attempt. The attempt did not work for long in spite of Syrian support, and Lebanon was soon on the road to anarchy again. The Syrians, however, had reemerged as the dominant foreign power in Lebanon, and the Americans were generally perceived as having abandoned the field because they were not willing to take casualties. So much for vital interests. The U.S. retreat, it is argued by some, is one reason Saddam Hussein misjudged U.S. willingness to fight when he invaded Kuwait.

Perhaps more important, the withdrawal from Lebanon signaled the effective end to U.S. efforts to implement Reagan's September 1 initiative. It had been rejected by both Israel and the Palestinians, but Reagan had continued to talk as though he thought it was still worth pursuing. It was, but the administration, and Shultz in particular, seemed to have lost interest. Four years passed before a serious effort was made by Shultz, in early 1988, to revive the peace process, and by then it was too late. During this period, as noted in the previous chapter, he was perceived as having turned his back on the Arabs. He was understood to have lost patience with them and to feel personally betrayed by their failure to support the May 17 agreement. One senior official of the Department of State, when asked at the time why Shultz felt as he did about the Arabs, replied, "Because he thinks they're wimps, and they are."

CHAPTER
10

THE FINAL RECKONING

"Ya Sham al-shuɔm!"*

This chapter discusses the decision by the U.S. administration to press ahead with the May 17 agreement in spite of warnings from ambassadors in the field that it would be opposed by the Syrians and would not hold. The discussion is based on conversations with participants and on documents now available in the public record.

Among those interviewed were Philip Habib, Morris Draper, Nicholas Veliotes, Robert Dillon (ambassador to Lebanon), Robert Paganelli (ambassador to Syria), Richard Viets (ambassador to Jordan), Richard Murphy (ambassador to Saudi Arabia), Alfred Atherton (ambassador to Egypt), Howard Teicher (NSC staffer who participated in the final weeks of the negotiations and remained on the scene afterward as an aide to the president's personal representative), Michael Newlin (consul general in Jerusalem), Ghassan Tueni (publisher of *An-Nahar* newspaper, former Lebanese U.N. delegate, and foreign policy adviser to President Amin Gemayel), Marwan Hammadeh (foreign policy adviser to Walid Jumblatt), and Abdul Halim Khaddam (Syrian foreign minister).

I have supplemented the recollections of the participants with my own observations as adviser to the U.S. Businessmen's Commission on Reconstruction in Lebanon, a group of senior business executives chaired by Lewis Preston of the Morgan Bank who, at President Reagan's request, began in late 1982 to explore the possibilities of aid from the private sector to revive the Lebanese economy. I went to Beirut on behalf of the commission for two weeks in late January–early February 1983. During that stay I met and talked with a wide range of Lebanese, official and private, including the president and three of his predecessors, most of the cabinet, a number of members of parliament, and other political and business figures whom I had known through a total of three tours in Lebanon.

---

*"Oh Damascus, the ill-omened!" Allegedly said in 1085 by Ibn Quraysh, last Arab emir of Aleppo, as he died on the battlefield, abandoned by his Damascene allies; quoted in Kamel Salibi, *Syria under Islam* (Delmar, N.Y., 1990), pp. 143–44.

194 / **The Politics of Miscalculation in the Middle East**

Whatever Haig may have said to Sharon in May 1982,[1] U.S. officials inclined to a pro-Israeli view saw the Israeli invasion as creating a window of opportunity. The Israelis had cut the Gordian knot. They had rid South Lebanon and Beirut of the armed Palestinian presence, which had been an insurmountable obstacle to the resolution of the Lebanese conflict, and had also tamed the Syrians, whose armed presence was another obstacle to resolution of the conflict. Although many in Washington disapproved of Israel's methods, others were prepared to exploit the result.

Haig's resignation had been announced on June 25, and he was succeeded by George Shultz on July 16. While an executive of the Bechtel Corporation, Shultz had met and apparently liked a number of Arabs, including some prominent Palestinians. He came into office disturbed at what Israel was doing in Lebanon and resolved to do something about the overall Arab-Israeli problem—to launch a new peace effort with some muscle in it. He had been thinking about the problem for some time and had discussed his ideas with Philip Habib, among others. The result was the September 1 initiative. According to Veliotes, the actual drafting was done by Veliotes and two other career officers, Wat Cluverius and Charles Hill. It was Shultz, however, who pushed it through and persuaded a reluctant White House to go along with it.[2]

The most important provision of the initiative, drawing on the Camp David formula, was for "transfer of authority from Israel to the Palestinian inhabitants" of Gaza and the West Bank for a five-year transitional period, following which a final peace would be negotiated, borders would be drawn, and Gaza and the West Bank would be associated with Jordan. The talking points given to Begin said the United States believed the Palestinians should be able to decide how they would govern themselves, but it would not support creation of a Palestinian state. In practical terms this could only mean a return to Jordanian control.[3]

The U.S. strategy was based on the assumption that the Lebanon problem was on the way to solution. Reagan said on September 1, "It seemed to me that, with the agreement [on the PLO's departure] in Lebanon, we had an opportunity for a more far-reaching peace effort in the region and I was determined to seize that moment." As noted earlier, there had in fact been disagreement within the administration on timing, with the Bureau of Near Eastern and South Asian Affairs generally arguing that announcement of the Shultz plan should not be timed to coincide with developments in Lebanon. While there was no formal linkage, the president's remarks and the timing clearly established a consequential linkage between the PLO evacuation and the U.S. initiative.

The belief of some in Washington that the Lebanon problem was going to be solved was based not only on the departure of the PLO units from Beirut and the south but also on the fact the Syrians had been badly mauled and pushed back by the Israelis and were thought to be *hors de combat*, as well as the hope that Bashir Gemayel, whose election the United

States had supported, would be able to put the country back together. It also rested on a much weaker assumption that the Israelis, their job accomplished, would withdraw quickly and facilitate restoration of Lebanese government control over all regions of the country.

These hopes and assumptions proved chimerical, and in retrospect it was naive of people to expect otherwise. Had it been possible to work out an informal agreement along the lines Habib had in mind (see the previous chapter) and if the Israelis could have been persuaded to leave by Christmas 1982, which was the informal objective of the Americans, then the strategy might well have worked. As it was, once the United States decided to go along with Israel's insistence on significant normalization and on a role in policing the south, failure in Lebanon was all but inevitable.

It is unclear when the U.S. decision "to go with normalization" was taken.[4] Draper believes it was in October or early November, probably during the visit of Foreign Minister Shamir to Washington, when Shultz said in effect that he could live with the sort of normalization the Israelis had in mind. That was far from being a commitment to press the Lebanese or Syrians to accept it, but the Israelis took it as approval of their strategy. In any event, U.S. participation in the negotiations which began at Khalde at the end of 1982 amounted to acceptance of the principle. Once embarked on that course, it was difficult to turn back.

Even had Bashir Gemayel not been assassinated, and even had the Syrians remained *hors de combat*, it is questionable whether Bashir could have overridden the opposition the May 17 agreement would eventually have generated in Lebanon and in the Arab world. In the event, Bashir did not survive. Nor did the Syrians stay out of the fight. The mystery is why people thought they would. The lesson of the Egyptian resurgence with Soviet help after 1967 should have been in everyone's mind, but was not. The Americans were not alone in their misapprehensions, however. They were joined by the Lebanese and the Israelis, neither of whom were listening very carefully.

THE AGREEMENT

The text of the May 17 agreement less its military annex may be found in *American Foreign Policy*, 1983 (pp. 758–60). The military annex is included in the version in *The Middle East Contemporary Survey* (vol. 7, 1982–83, pp. 690–97). The so-called secret annexes have not been published officially but were leaked to the Arab press quickly. It sounds much like the agreement Sharon worked out with Sami Maroun as described by him to a *Maariv* reporter and carried by that newspaper on December 17. It is a peace treaty in all but name, terminating the state of war in effect since 1948, nullifying the 1969 Cairo agreement and other agreements permitting an armed Palestinian presence in Lebanon, engaging Lebanon not to permit military forces hostile to Israel to use its territory, committing the parties to negotiate an agreement on the movement of people and goods across the frontier, providing for "liaison offices" which would function as embassies and enjoy diplomatic privileges in the two capitals, and committing Lebanon to "security measures" outlined in the military annex that amounted to the Lebanese giving the Israelis a permanent veto over their military activities south of the Awali River. Among other things, the Lebanese agreed to integrate the irregular, Israel-sponsored South Lebanese army into the regular army as a territorial (i.e., national guard) unit, which would be the primary Lebanese army (as opposed to police and gendarmerie) unit permitted south of the Zahrani River. There were also secret agreements to permit Israeli observation flights over Lebanon and to permit operation of Israeli-Lebanese surveillance patrols in southern Lebanon. One of my sources says the agreement permitted an Israeli-manned surveillance station at Jisr al-Qaʿqaʿiya, in effect a permanent Israeli military presence in Lebanon, but I have been unable to confirm this.

The Syrians had been kept informed of the details of the negotiations as they went along, both formally by the Lebanese Foreign Ministry and informally, and more completely, by one or more members of the Lebanese delegation and by a special envoy from President Gemayel, Jean Obeid. The Americans also briefed them from time to time, according to Draper. Indeed, according to one participant, Syrian Foreign Minister Khaddam was better informed about the contents and significance of the final agreement than his Lebanese colleague, Elie Salem, and made this clear on at least one occasion when Salem's understanding of the details was deficient.

As noted earlier, the Syrians publicly described the agreement as a "submission." (A good description of Syrian attitudes toward this affair can be found in Patrick Seale's *Asad,* pp. 366–420.) According to Draper, in his remarks to Shultz, President Asad was not as concerned by the normalization features as he was by the military annex, and what he took particular exception to was the permission for Israeli overflights, even though those had been going on continuously since 1976. Asad was also upset that Israeli withdrawal was tied to Syrian withdrawal. He did not like having his military presence, which had originated at Lebanese request, equated with Israel's, which resulted from an act of war. According to one of the participants, he told Shultz on May 6 that if Israeli withdrawal was linked to Syrian withdrawal, the agreement would not work. But even were the two not tied, it seems doubtful that Asad could have accepted the agreement.

Given Asad's long-winded approach to diplomatic discourse, he may not have gotten around to expressing all his reservations about the treaty to Shultz. Whatever his initial position, the normalization measures would eventually have been important to the Syrians because they would have meant that Israel had succeeded in picking off another Arab state, as it had Egypt, with which to make a separate peace treaty, thus further isolating Syria in its confrontation with Israel. This would have strategic as well as political consequences. Fully implemented, the agreement would have meant an end to the Syrian military presence in Lebanon and would have left the Israelis with an open route to Damascus through the Bekaa.

Furthermore, the agreement meant Lebanon's abandonment of the Arab boycott of Israel. This was something the Israelis wanted very much, and it could significantly weaken the impact of the boycott by other states. The important Beirut entrepôt and widespread Lebanese involvement in the transit trade would provide many opportunities for selling Israeli goods falsely labeled as Lebanese throughout the Arab world. There were plenty of Lebanese who would lend themselves to such trade, and the process had already started before 1982 was over. It had led to Saudi insistence on certificates of origin for products coming from Lebanon, after the Saudis discovered that they were drinking Israeli orange juice.

The existence of an Israeli diplomatic mission, publicly labeled as such (they had had a small, secret liaison detail in the Maronite heartland for years), would also upset the Syrians as further evidence that the Lebanese had surrendered unilaterally, without regard for Syria's interests. Syrian opposition to the agreement was therefore predictable, and was predicted by Paganelli in Damascus, but the popular wisdom in Beirut as late as January and early February was that Syria could do nothing about it and would have to go along. In reality, however, Syria had been rearmed by the Soviets and supplied with a much more advanced antiaircraft missile system and was ready to play an active role in Lebanon by December 1982 or January 1983. When the time came it was able to frustrate the agreement and reestablish itself as the dominant foreign power in Lebanon. Even after it was clear the Syrians were back in the game, however, the Americans, Israelis, and Lebanese continued to act and talk publicly as though they could be safely ignored for the time being and would come around in time. Draper says, however, that he and Habib and Paganelli were deeply concerned about the Syrians by January 1983 and urged Gemayel to make more of an effort with them. The appointment of Jean Obeid, in whom the Americans had no confidence, as an emissary to Asad was the result.

SYRIAN OPPOSITION

When I began interviewing for this study I kept asking whether there was a point at which the Syrians would have accepted an agreement along the lines of the May 17 document and when it had become clear that they

would not go along with what was being negotiated. Ambassador Paganelli, who had been in Damascus, said there was no way to tell, because
the Americans had not consulted the Syrians. If we were to have an
agreement which they would accept we had to sit down with them at
some time and discuss it. He was not arguing that we should try to get
their agreement to chapter and verse, but we at least had to consult with
them. He had harped on this continually but got no hearing in Washington. The attitude there was that the Syrians were finished as a result of
their defeat by the Israelis and would "blow away" or could be intimidated. Paganelli said he could not guarantee that consultation with the
Syrians would work. They were difficult people to deal with, but not
even to make the effort was gross stupidity.[5]

Draper has a very different recollection. He says that Damascus and
other posts in the area were fully briefed on the course of the negotiations
and that Paganelli was authorized to brief the Syrians, circumspectly. Draper
himself went to Damascus several times to talk to the Syrians, and the
Syrians had met with Deputy Secretary of State Kenneth Dam in Washington in the fall of 1982 and promised cooperation.

Ambassador Lewis, who was in Tel Aviv, says that it is wrong to
attack the administration for lack off realism.

> It was all talked out carefully in the fall. Everybody knew the Syrians
> could block it, could make it impossible. The choice was, do you try to
> get it done while the Israeli-Lebanese Christian-American alliance . . .
> was reasonably strong and then either count on the strength of that
> triad, or the alleged commitments which Asad had made to Amin Ge-
> mayel . . . or just pray and hope that it would endure? Alternatively,
> you go first to the Syrians, knowing what the Israeli demands are going
> to be and the degree to which you are going to be able to shape them
> . . . and try to get the Syrians on board for what we assess to be an
> impossible proposition for them to swallow at that time. In which case
> you'd never have an agreement at all. And the judgment was made,
> let's go hellbent for leather and try to get the agreement and then try to
> get the Syrians to swallow it because Amin thinks they will. It was a
> gamble, and I think it would have paid off—I think there was at least a
> fifty-fifty chance it would have worked if we could have done it within
> three months from the time of the [PLO] evacuation. . . . I think it
> could have been signed by the end of November. . . . When you come
> to the conclusion that the Syrians had regained enough self-confidence
> and rearmament that they can't be elbowed aside long enough to get it
> into place, that's when the agreement was no longer going to fly. I don't
> *know* when that was. I think it was probably around the end of the
> year.[6]

Ambassador Dillon, who was in Beirut, agrees with Ambassador Lewis
about timing. What was possible in the fall of 1982 was not possible in
early 1983.

Something that made sense in November or December 1982 certainly by February or March made no sense. . . . In the fall of 1982 the Syrians were flat on their backs. Their air force had been destroyed. . . . It was in no position for offensive action. They were in a very weak position and humiliated . . . in a very weak position in Lebanon. But by some time early in 1983 all that had been reversed. They'd been rearmed. Their confidence had come back, and they certainly were feeling far more confident. . . .

The thing that made it clear to me that it wasn't going to work was the way the agreement had developed. In, let's say, October or November, what people had in mind was a fairly clean agreement with full Israeli withdrawal. By the time, say, February rolled around, it was absolutely clear that it was not going to be that at all. In the first place the Israelis . . . spun out . . . the negotiations. They enjoyed the process of negotiating with the Arabs. They were in no hurry to reach a solution. Secondly, it was clear that they were not talking about full withdrawal . . . what they were talking about was an awful lot of stay-behind activity and agreements that they could come smashing back in under almost any circumstances. . . . I remember what Phil [Habib] told me in the fall when he came back from Damascus. It was something like this. . . . Phil told me that Asad had agreed to respect an agreement but that it had to be understood that the Israelis could draw no political advantages from the invasion. . . . Certainly . . . that meant the Israelis could not stay behind and have a special position.[7]

Ambassador Viets comments that from the perspective of Amman he doubted that any type of agreement negotiated between Israel and Lebanon would have survived, whatever the timing. He felt that "that type of juggernaut imposition of foreign interests . . . on a small, defenseless foreign state simply won't last in this period."[8]

Whether or not one agrees with that assessment, there seems to be general agreement today among the American participants that certainly by January or February 1983 it was too late to get Syrian acquiescence to the sort of agreement then being negotiated. It is not clear, however, to what extent that was understood and reported at the time and to what extent we are dealing with hindsight. Habib agrees that by February it was too late but maintains, "Nobody was telling us the Syrians were going to say no in December, in January, in February, not even in March." Draper on the other hand says that by January he was afraid that it was too late. Paul Hare, the deputy chief of mission in Tel Aviv at the time, told me in a note (mid-October 1991) that "as the weeks went by the Syrian shadow hung heavier over the negotiating table. Everyone was aware of it in a foreboding sense."

The question which arises immediately is why the Americans kept on negotiating an agreement they knew the Syrians would oppose. The answer seems to be a combination of things—a hope the Syrians could be induced to accept the agreement after all, once it was signed and provided they got some inducement, financial or otherwise,[9] a fatalistic determination to push ahead whatever the chances because they were committed politically, and an unwillingness to admit that a mistake had been made in abandoning the Habib formula.

It also is by no means clear that many people realized the agreement was a nonstarter as early as January. Certainly the Lebanese did not seem to. Of some forty politically active Lebanese of all confessions with whom I talked in the period January 28 to February 9, most expressed concern at the pace of negotiations and said time was running out but only three—former President Elias Sarkis, former Foreign Minister Fuad Boutros and Elias Saba, a banker—told me that the agreement then being negotiated would not work because it gave Israel the substance of peace. The foreign minister, Elie Salem, for instance, when I asked him on February 3 whether the Syrians and Palestinians would accept what was being worked out, told me, "They say they will," and seemed quite optimistic. He was under no obligation to be frank with me, of course, and would perhaps not have told me how he actually felt about it. But another Lebanese involved in the negotiations whom I had known for over twenty years, when told that the Lebanese seemed to be negotiating a peace treaty, said, "So what?" I detected little concern at the substance of the negotiations.

A Shia businessman from Nabatiyah, for instance, attempted to persuade me to have the Preston Commission go into partnership with him to buy a piece of land near Damour for a golf and beach development. He said that once peace was signed, the Israelis would be flocking to the beaches of South Lebanon and land values there would skyrocket. He had an option on 3.5 million square meters of land for $30 million. Another $7 million would be needed to develop it. He would sell lots for $50 per square meter and earn $210 million. Our money would return a profit of 300 to 400 percent. He and his associates, one of whom was a cabinet minister, thought peace was coming and had no qualms about it. They were looking forward to the economic benefits it would bring to South Lebanon. They were not concerned with principles or a political need to be hostile towards Israel.

As a result of conversations such as this I returned to Washington convinced that the Israelis had won the game, that provided they moved quickly to sign an agreement that was not too onerous on Lebanon and began withdrawing, they would have succeeded in making peace with another Arab state. I had also concluded that while it was too early to start investing in Lebanon, it was time for companies to start actively exploring the possibilities. Ambassador Dillon and his political counselor (later ambassador), Ryan Crocker, have both expressed disbelief that I could have thought that so late in the game, but they did nothing to disabuse me, and neither did anyone else in the Department of State at the time. I was in regular contact with a number of officials involved in Lebanon, discussing my findings and plans for proceeding with the work of the Preston Commission through May. Indeed, Lewis Preston and I were scheduled to go to Beirut on May 20 to present the commission's preliminary report to President Gemayel, and the visit was canceled only because the U.S. Embassy was blown up on April 18 and we decided, after consulting officials of the Department of State, that Beirut was unsafe for the time being. None of those officials told us the game was over and lost. Draper comments, "You know of course, sometimes we have to keep plugging away."[10]

Without access to the classified reporting for the period in question, it is difficult to determine just how lively the perceptions of imminent failure were among U.S. officials in the area at the time and how clearly they reported them. That both the White House (meaning the NSC staff) and the upper levels of the Department of State had bought the Israeli approach would have served to inhibit criticism of it. Certainly it inhibited any public expression of doubt by departmental officials. Draper comments that the NSC, the Department of State, and the Department of Defense were in great disagreement over other matters at the time, including a drive on the part of some NSC officials to have the U.S. military take over security responsibilities for much of Lebanon, a move opposed successfully by State and Defense.[11] Dealing with one set of ill-advised proposals of this sort often diverts attention from others which turn out to be no less dangerous.

Thus when Shultz arrived in Cairo on April 24, he may not have realized how slim the chances were for success. He appeared to be disagreeably surprised in any event when, on the afternoon of April 25, in a meeting with U.S. ambassadors and principal officers in the region, several of them told him that the proposed agreement would not work and that he should not let himself get involved with it. By all accounts he was visibly upset, abruptly terminated the meeting, and stalked out of the room. It is alleged that he wanted to remove Ambassador Paganelli, who had been the most outspoken, and one account says he wanted to fire everyone except Ambassador Lewis and Consul General Newlin. Habib and Draper deny that Shultz wanted to sack anybody, but there is enough testimony to the contrary to make the story plausible.

According to one participant, Shultz had come to the area with marching orders from the White House to bring home an Israeli-Lebanese agreement. He felt he had done a good job of finally getting the Reagan Administration to focus on the Middle East, and the September 1 initiative was the first policy statement of importance which it had made on the subject. He felt justifiably proud of that effort and was upset to encounter instead of gratitude a great deal of criticism from the ambassadors in the field, most of whom he found overly negative and unsupportive of his efforts.

I have talked to each of the six chiefs of mission who were present (Dillon, Paganelli, Lewis, Viets, Murphy, and Atherton) plus others who were there, including Habib, Veliotes, Draper, and Teicher, and corresponded with Newlin. Recollections vary and are contradictory, of course. If there is a written record of the meeting it has not been made available to me, so we must make do with the oral testimony for the present. Those interviewed, however, agreed that Paganelli made the strongest presentation against the agreement, seconded strongly by Dillon and Viets. Murphy and Atherton both describe themselves as being on the sidelines and not taking positions one way or the other, although Atherton says he may have said that being already committed, we should stay the course. He had found Paganelli's argument persuasive, however, and thought we were whistling in the dark if we believed the Syrians would stand still for the agreement then being negotiated. Murphy says he was not in the loop regarding the negotiations and did not have much to say about them. He did not recall, in fact, that those present had been asked for their advice.

Lewis describes the meeting as unpleasant. He says, and others agree, that there had been a premeeting with Veliotes at which the ambassadors expressed their views and there was a division. He and Atherton had taken one position and everyone else had taken another. The question was not whether the agreement would work; the odds were not good at that point. The issue was "having gone as far as we had gone, should we try to complete it or not? . . . Roy [Atherton] and I were very strongly of the view that we should play out the hand. And in terms of U.S. relations with both Israel and Egypt, and particularly with Israel, to back away from the agreement at that time and admit defeat to the Syrians was a disastrous idea, and that was Paganelli's position." [12]

Viet's recollection is that every chief of mission except Lewis supported Paganelli's position.

> Some of those present were very cautious in how they conveyed their views to the Secretary, but for those of us who were there and knew them, we knew what they were saying. Perhaps Shultz didn't read them as clearly as we did. . . . Sam Lewis was the only ambassador there who spoke out . . . [and] said . . . that we, from our backgrounds and posts in the Arab world had just lost sight of the whole damned game. Such a treaty surely not only was possible, but was badly needed, and it was in the interest of the United States to go flat out to achieve the treaty. The person who was the most outspoken was Bob Paganelli. Bob . . . is a man of no persiflage. He tells it as it is, and he got on his high horse with George Shultz and went at him in an unvarnisherd, straightforward fashion, and just told him it wasn't going to work—it was going to prove a costly error for Shultz. [13]

Newlin recalls that the meeting took place at Ambassador Atherton's residence in Cairo, that Paganelli was upset over press accounts that Israel was a strategic ally of the United States and that the Arab world could not be counted on when it came to serious questions of peace and security. He commented on these reports somewhat emotionally and then asked Shultz how he could hope to succeed in arranging a separate Israel-Lebanon peace over Syria's opposition. Shultz turned red in the face and said, "I hear you, but disagree with you totally," and that was the end of the exchange. Newlin comments that it took no great expert to come to the same conclusion as Paganelli and he had told the latter that he agreed with him. Paganelli had said, "Yes, but you see how he reacted." [14]

Draper's recollection sounds the most precise. He says:

> I flew to Cairo from Israel [on the twenty-forth], arriving there after Shultz's first meeting with the Ambassadors, and met with him, [Raymond] Seitz [then Shultz's special assistant], Habib, and a few others after dinner in his hotel room. He, Shultz, was deeply discouraged, but I had brought good news. The Israelis had caved in on two issues, after months of stubbornness, and Shultz was immensely cheered up. Too much so, Habib later remarked. The next day Shultz met with all of us at Roy's [Atherton's] residence, after seeing Mubarak. Sam Lewis had hammered together among the ambassadors a consensus (along the lines of the Lewis-Atherton views expressed above), and Shultz accepted it, somewhat grumpily but with eventual politeness. He gave Bob Dillon a chance to speak and Bob was pessimistic about Lebanese abilities to hold in the Syrians, but he spoke very carefully and circumspectly by comparison [I was told] with Paganelli's brief of the night before, which I had not witnessed.

Draper paints a picture of a Shultz who was depressed and discouraged by the views of his ambassadors but who saw no alternative to continuing with the course already decided upon and was determined to make it work if at all possible. Although a more tactful approach by Paganelli, supported more systematically by the others, might have been more persuasive, the chances of getting Shultz to change course at that late date were probably nil.

No one seems to remember exactly what Paganelli said, but the tenor of his remarks is perhaps conveyed by Murphy's recollection that Paganelli said he could not see any difference between Shultz's policies and Haig's, whereupon the secretary turned red. Everyone seems to remember that he turned red, but the immediate cause varies. There is general agreement that Paganelli was feeling frustrated by the lack of response from Washington, meaning Shultz, to his telegrams warning of trouble. Paganelli says that the Syrians had never agreed to anything in connection with the negotiations. They kept asking him what the Americans were up to and he kept asking Washington for permission to give them a briefing, but Washington kept refusing. He had been reduced to apologizing for his inability to tell them anything. They had been kept in the dark and their reaction was understandable. [15] Draper questions Paganelli's description. He says that he and Habib kept all ambassadors fully informed of what was going on and that, as noted earlier, Paganelli was authorized to brief the Syrians carefully and selectively. If Washington refused such permission, he never saw the cable exchange.[16]

As we have seen, Shultz went ahead in his determined way to get the two sides to iron out their differences, using his considerable skills as a labor negotiator and the preponderant weight of American influence. He got both sides to make a few concessions, but he accepted Israel's last-minute condition tying Israeli to Syrian withdrawal, the importance of which one observer says Shultz did not understand and which he could have rejected, because the Israelis were so anxious for an agreement at that point they would not have insisted. Another informed observer comments that one lesson Shultz had learned as a labor negotiator was that one first had to clear away the minor irritants in order to put everyone in a positive mood and that, applying this lesson to the current case, he had decided to give the Israelis everything they wanted in order to put them in a positive frame of mind. He did not realize they would interpret this largess as meaning they did not have to compromise. Those involved in the negotiations, however, argue that there was not much which could be wrung out of either party by April and that any last-minute concessions would have been so minor as to have no impact on Syria's attitude.

THE NATURE OF THE MISCALCULATION

In fairness to Shultz, he had no attractive alternatives on April 24. To back out of the negotiations at that point would have been an admission of failure, never a pleasant or rewarding prospect. When asked in 1990 what alternative he would have proposed in 1983, Paganelli said he would have to think about that. Neither he nor anyone else seems to have offered a positive alternative.

It is not clear that Shultz himself had any illusions about the agreement's actually working. His careful public utterances indicated that he thought there was a chance, but they were hardly enthusiastic. The positive views he did express could have amounted to putting a good face on a bad situation for tactical reasons.

Heretofore one of the mysteries, as far as most of the participants were concerned, was what Habib had told Shultz privately. Habib was very discreet about revealing his views. Draper comments that at one point Habib told him they should start all over again and scrap the agreement, but Draper did not know whether he had ever said that to the secretary. Ambassador Viets recalls that while Habib did not speak out at the Cairo meeting, before it began he told the ambassadors to speak frankly to the secretary and not to hold back, because he needed their best judgment. This can be read to mean that he shared their doubts and wanted them to warn Shultz he was headed for trouble. That would be consistent with his having distanced himself from the negotiations. In fact, Veliotes, who was present, says that Habib and he went to California in early January 1983 to see Shultz and that Habib made an impassioned plea to Shultz not to go along with Israel's normalization strategy because it would lead to disaster. Shultz heard him out, made no substantive comment, and did not follow his advice.[17]

There are recurring references in public statements (e.g., by "a senior administration official" in a press briefing on January 27, 1983; by Shultz in a press conference on January 30; and by Shultz to the House Foreign Affairs Committee on February 16) to Syrian commitments to withdraw made in 1982. Two commitments are mentioned. One was reportedly given to Shultz by Khaddam, Syria's foreign minister, on some unspecified occasion in 1982. Shultz's most detailed description of this that I have found was made in a briefing for national Jewish leaders on May 20, 1983:

> Syria has made statements to various people, including me personally, in the form of the Foreign Minister, that they would withdraw as Israel withdraws. They have made that statement to the Lebanese directly, as recently as the Nonaligned Conference in New Delhi, which was about 6 weeks ago, or something of that kind. And the PLO the same. So there are a lot of statements that have been made.[18]

The other commitment was reportedly given to Amin Gemayel by Asad. Ambassador Lewis, for instance, refers to it in his comments noted above, but I have been unable to pin down the date and context. Asad also reportedly told Habib in early October 1982 that he would be willing to accept an agreement between Israel and Lebanon, but as noted above, it must be one that gave Israel no political advantage from its invasion. Lacking the official records of these conversations, it is impossible to know exactly what the Syrians said or how much weight should have been put on their words. For instance, the *New York Times* reported on October 4, 1982, that on the previous day Habib had been informed by foreign ministry officials in Damascus that Syrian forces would leave Lebanon if Israeli forces also withdrew. When I asked if that was true, Habib replied: "Asad's position was always that he didn't have any intention of staying in Lebanon, and so forth. I don't think he ever said precisely, 'You get the Israelis to withdraw and we'll withdraw.' But there's no question that's—I'd have to look at the files to tell you exactly what was said."[19]

Draper says that to his certain knowledge a Syrian commitment to withdraw was given by Khaddam to Kenneth Dam, the deputy secretary of state, in Washington in the fall of 1982. He is not sure whether one was also given to Shultz directly.[20]

What we seem to be dealing with here is a series of statements which have been interpreted by the hearer as sufficiently encouraging or explicit to be taken as evidence that if the Israelis could be gotten out of Lebanon quickly, the Syrians would cooperate and would withdraw themselves. Syria's stipulations for withdrawal were never explored in detail, however, probably for fear their reaction would be too negative and would jeopardize continuation of the negotiations. Draper comments that Syrian stipulations were explored, but not in detail: "He [Asad] told us there would have to be equity in the withdrawal understanding."[21]

By the time the agreement was signed the conditions under which the original commitments, if they can be called that, had been given had changed substantially—Israel had not withdrawn quickly, the Maronite-Druze struggle was preventing a national consensus in Lebanon, and the Soviet Union had rearmed Syria in the interim. More to the point, what had been signed amounted to a peace agreement, and the Syrians say they had given clear signals that they would not accept that.[22]

Although he knew the negotiations would be difficult, Shultz apparently felt in late April that an agreement signed and approved by the Lebanese government and the parliament would impress the Syrians. He may not have realized that if ever there was a time when that was so, it had passed. Shultz's public statements give some clue to his thinking on the matter.

On April 24, at a press briefing enroute to Cairo, Shultz was asked: "How concerned are you that even if you do get an agreement with the Israelis that you will end up with nothing from the Syrians—that they will no longer be willing to leave?" He answered:

Well, anything is possible, but they have said they will withdraw as the Israelis withdraw, as the Government of Lebanon requested them to withdraw. The Arab/Fez statement set that out as an Arab understanding. All of those things were confirmed when the Lebanese met with them in New Delhi at the time of the non-aligned summit [March 7–12, 1983] and so all those statements are there. But we have to have an Israeli agreement to call their card and I hope we'll have it.[23]

On May 7, in a statement to journalists in Damascus, Shultz said that

of course, the Syrians will speak for themselves about it, but I think it is fair to say that they are hardly enthusiastic about the agreement that Lebanon and Israel have worked out. Now, procedurally, as I understand it, what has happened is that Lebanon—which had brought a copy of the draft agreement as of, I think, late Tuesday [May 3], here and discussed it with them—will, after Lebanon acts on the agreement—show them—although that's up to Lebanon—the actual agreement as it has been finally shaped up. Then Lebanon will have the negotiation with the Syrians about Syrian withdrawal and with the PLO about PLO withdrawal, and my guess is that these will be very difficult negotiations, but this is okay. At least from my experience in the Middle

East, nothing happens easily, so no one expected that this one would be. On the other hand, at least in my judgment, there are great incentives built into this situation for people in the end to go along with it, but that's only my judgment.[24]

On May 13, in a speech to the Business Council at Hot Springs, Virginia, Shultz said:

As you may know, Israel is not prepared actually to withdraw its forces until Syrian and the remaining PLO forces also leave Lebanon. There will be a negotiation between Syria and Lebanon on the subject. I know Amin Gemayel well enough to know that he will vigorously defend Lebanon's sovereign right to determine its own future. He and his colleagues are showing courage and statesmanship, and they deserve wholehearted American support. When Lebanon makes its sovereign decision with backing from the main constituent groups in the Lebanese national consensus, that decision will command considerable moral authority.[25]

And on May 20, in the briefing for national Jewish leaders, Shultz said:

We have felt that the best basis on which to go forward with Syria is first to get agreement between Lebanon and Israel completely nailed down—signed, sealed and delivered, so to speak. And, insofar as Lebanon is concerned, to have it endorsed not only by the President and the Negotiating Committee. . . . So the President . . . got unanimous support of his Cabinet. Then he took it to the Lebanese Parliament and got unanimous [sic] support in the Parliament. So our feeling was—and we had this advice as we went around prior to the agreement and talked with our friends in the Arab world that was their advice: Let it be visible that this is something that the Government of Lebanon, supported by the broad sweep of the confessional groups in Lebanon, not just the Christians, and so on, support. That lays down a certain marker, so that's been accomplished now.[26]

A rather different picture is given by one of the Lebanese who participated in the negotiations. According to him, early in the game the Lebanese had understood the Syrians to be saying that they did not object to the Lebanese signing an agreement with the Israelis. Subsequently they had begun to get different signals, and it became clear at the nonaligned meeting in New Delhi in March, where they met with Khaddam, that the Syrians were going to oppose any agreement, whatever the terms. Asad had told Walid Jumblatt as far back as November 1982 that the Syrians opposed any agreement with the Israelis but did not want to put pressure on Amin Gemayel because they were confident he would not sign one. Jumblatt had told Asad he did not know how unreliable Amin was, but Asad brushed that off.

After New Delhi, the Lebanese had told the Americans the Syrians would not go along, but in effect they were ignored. The negotiations had come to an impasse over Israel's insistence on tying its withdrawal to Syrian and Palestinian withdrawal. The Lebanese pointed out that this gave the Syrians and Palestinians a veto over the withdrawal, and what were they negotiating about in that case? The Israelis had responded by sending a rude note to Amin, via the Lebanese Forces, enclosing the text of the Maroun-Sharon agreement and telling Amin that he was obligated to sign it and if he refused the fate of all the Christians in the Middle East would be endangered. The Israelis had furthermore proposed that the Americans be eliminated from the negotiations, which should be between the Lebanese and Israelis.

Shultz had come out at this time. After being told that the Syrians would not go along with any agreement with the Israelis, he had flown to Damascus, where he failed to get Syrian concurrence. He returned to meet with the Lebanese in Gemayel's office at Baabda [on May 8?]. Habib, Veliotes, Draper, and everyone else of any importance were there. Shultz said he had not persuaded the Syrians. The Lebanese said they had already heard that on the radio while Shultz was flying to Beirut. One of the Lebanese negotiators said the Syrians would not go along and the Lebanese therefore could not sign the agreement, which was already drafted, with only a few details to be settled.

Shultz had ignored the Lebanese negotiator and turned to Draper and asked how long it would take to put the agreement into Hebrew, Arabic, and English. Draper had said twenty-four hours. Shultz had then responded, "Then let's have the signing on the 10th." One of the Lebanese had responded that the Israelis still had not answered the Lebanese question about a withdrawal timetable. Shultz had ignored him, too, and turned to Gemayel, who had asked what they would do about the Syrians. Shultz had said not to worry about the Syrians. The United States had a number of tricks up its sleeve. He was going to Europe and he would take care of the Syrians. Gemayel had then said he would sign the agreement. (Draper has no recollection of such an exchange taking place.)[27]

It turned out, according to my Lebanese informant, that what Shultz had up his sleeve was the Saudis, who were to deliver the Syrians through exerting financial pressure on them. The agreement was signed and the Syrians immediately began arming the Jumblatti Druze. The rest was history.

I cannot vouch for the exactitude of the above account, which was given to me more than five years after the events. That Shultz hoped the Saudis would be able to bring the Syrians around has been confirmed by several Americans who were involved in the process. Whether he was actually counting on it is less clear. In any event, Habib and Draper went to Riyadh on May 19, and the *New York Times* of May 23 reported that a Saudi envoy, Shaykh Abd al-Aziz al-Tawajiri, met in Damascus with Asad the previous day to discuss Syria's opposition to the Israeli-Lebanese agreement. Al-Tawajiri was the deputy commander of the Saudi National Guard and presumably was representing the commander of that organization, Prince Abdallah, the member of the Saudi royal family who had the Asad portfolio.

Asked about the trip, Habib replied, "I would presume we were trying to tell the Saudis to be helpful. [The phrase "I would presume" conveys an uncharacteristic uncertainty which is not reflected in the accounts of Murphy and Draper. I presume Habib was just being cautious.] . . . My guess is that they probably did [do something], but it wasn't enough. They didn't put enough behind it. The Saudis are masters of persuasion, not of threats."[28] Ambassador Murphy said he recalled going in to see the Saudis and relaying American concerns about Syrian opposition. The Saudis had promised to do their best, and they meant it, but he imagined that when the Syrians explained to them just what the agreement was and why they opposed it the Saudis had backed off. They would not want to get involved in something like that [a peace treaty rather than a troop disengagement agreement]. (Draper recalls their [Habib, Draper and Murphy] meeting with the Saudis as being awkward. Some Saudi princes were upset that Saudi ideas regarding revival of the 1982 Fez agreement was not getting a fair hearing.)[29]

Shultz evidently hoped the Saudis would use their substantial ($2–3 billion) annual subsidy to the Syrians as a lever to get them not to oppose the agreement. This is reminiscent of a similar fiasco in 1958, when King Saud of Saudi Arabia, who was being touted by Washington as a rival to Nasser, tried to buy the loyalty of the Syrian intelligence chief, Abd al-Hamid Sarraj, and Sarraj publicly displayed the check he had received from Saud before turning it over to the government. It is easy to criticize Shultz for thinking the Saudis would be willing to stick their necks out for something that would be unpopular once its true contents and significance for the Arab cause were known, but misunderstanding the power of Saudi money to affect political changes is common in Washington. In part this is the result of the lack of in-depth experience in Arab affairs of itinerant cabinet members and other high flyers, who make lightning trips to the area, meet a few local leaders, and do not understand what they are seeing and being told. David Newsom described the phenomenon well in an article in the *Middle East Journal* (Summer 1981):

> The American, with his official brief, will want to make sure he has said all he wants to say tactfully but firmly so he can tell his govenment how well he did his job. Each may pause politely to permit the other to speak. The Arab may well seek to say that which will please the visitor. The American is unlikely to understand that he is being told that his host thinks he wants to hear. He usually rejects the attempts by the Ambassador to explain what the host really meant. The result may be that neither will really hear what the other is saying. Each may return think-

ing he has the agreement of the other. Serious misunderstandings can result."

It is easy to understand why people as notoriously insensitive as Begin and Sharon would misjudge the possibilities in Lebanon. It is less easy to see how a man of Secretary Shultz's intellect and discernment would do so, and until we know more about what he actually thought at the time, we cannot conclude definitively that he did misjudge. He may have felt obliged by domestic pressures to keep pursuing something he knew would not work on the off chance it might. Some of those present at the Cairo meeting, however, have speculated that he was driven by a desire to have his own Camp David, or that he had fallen under the spell of the Israelis and their domestic lobby and was misled by their assurances that they would take care of the Syrians. Others add that he was overly influenced by the Christian Zionist sentiments of Charles Hill, who later became his special assistant.

I have been unable to interview Shultz, but the memoirs on which he is working may eventually give us some details. In the meantime, I think we can conclude that he too heard what he wanted to hear and discarded that which conflicted with it.

In retrospect, he had a viable alternative, provided he exercised it in time. It would have been politically expensive to abandon a commitment already given to support normalization, but it need not have been fatal. The administration had already distanced itself from that as an immediate goal a number of times in early 1983 and could have taken a stand then.[30] If the Americans had had the courage to tell the Israelis unambiguously early in the game that they could not support an agreement they knew the Syrians would not accept, it would then have been up to the Israelis to work out a more realistic set of arrangements. Perhaps that would have been impossible for them to accomplish, but at least the Americans would have been spared the loss of American lives and prestige which they incurred by associating themselves with something they were clearly told would not work and, what was worse, luring the Lebanese into it.

Disassociating could, or should, have been done before the personal prestige of the secretary of state was involved. As it was, by not properly evaluating Syria's capabilities and not taking effective steps either to enlist it in the peace process or prevent it from sabotaging it, the Americans shielded the Israelis and the Lebanese from the realities of their situation until it was too late for them to bail out. This was a costly error for all. The Americans and Israelis could walk away from it, however; the Lebanese could not. They would not have signed the treaty if they had not thought the Americans and Israelis would protect them from the Syrians, and it is understandable that they would feel betrayed when that did not happen.

The Israelis and Lebanese were not the only people who were shielded from reality until it was too late. For the Americans to think seriously that they could sell the Syrians when they were strong a disagreeable fait accompli which they would not accept when they were weak may have sounded brave and hard-bitten in the Washington political arena, but it was to indulge in self-delusion as far as foreign policy was concerned. It might have been realistic if the administration had been prepared to enforce the treaty militarily, as the NSC staffers Rodman and Teicher reportedly were urging, but that was hardly a realistic option at the time. Failing a willingness and an ability to impose the treaty by force, the Americans should have realized it was hopeless and withdrawn from the process. Paganelli and Habib were right.

CONCLUSION

Therefore, Egypt was prepared and ready.
This is the foremost fact of the strategy of
Egyptian action during the ten great days
. . . events began to move. One calculated
step followed another.

Mohamed Heikal, *Al-Ahram*,
May 26, 1967

Our definition of *miscalculation*, given in the introduction, is "a policy decision which goes awry because those making it did not foresee properly what the results would be." The term implies a weighing of the odds before deciding on a course of action. That it went awry implies that the policy could have worked. It did not do so because the consequences were not, perhaps could not be, thought through as thoroughly as they should have been, or because actors did not perform as expected, or because of some irrational or random factor such as incompetence or a problem of communication. (The random may not be predictable but can always be expected. Military decision makers seem to understand that better than civilians do.)

The decision may have seemed irrational to others at the time, or it may appear to be so in hindsight, but those making it were reasonable and intelligent people who believed that they were making the optimal choice in pursuance of the national and their own interest. The question is: why or where did they go wrong?

The answer differs in each instance, of course. The three cases we have looked at are all different in important respects, but there are common aspects to all of them.

First is the element of *avoidability*. None of the decisions was imposed by objective imperatives. All could have been avoided. The Soviets did not have to pass their warning to the Egyptians in 1967, and the Egytians did not have to overreact as they did. The Israelis did not have to undertake the deep penetration raids. The United States did not have to dismiss the Soviet warning of January 30, 1970, as a bluff, and it did not have to support the Israeli drive for normalization of relations with Lebanon. The decision makers may plead political necessity in each case, but in fact the decisions were elective. Had they known where they would lead, they would have decided otherwise.

Second is the element of *irrelevant domestic political considerations*. Except possibly in the case of the Soviet warning in 1967, domestic political considerations that were largely irrelevant to the problem being addressed played a major role in the decisions taken. Thus it seems evident from the survivors' accounts that Nasser's concerns about the internal situation and his relations with 'Amr and the army were a major factor in his decisions in 1967. Unwillingness to confront the Israelis because of the strength of the Israel lobby in the United States was an important, perhaps the determining, factor in the U.S. attitude of tacit acquiescence in, if not encouragement of, the deep penetration raids in 1970 and of active support of Israel's quest for normalization of relations with Lebanon in 1983, while domestic political concerns clearly played a major role in determining Israeli policies in both those cases.

A third common aspect is *narrowness of consultation*. In each case, decisions were made by a few people at the top without much consultation with the foreign policy and intelligence establishments. There was little or no meaningful debate, and the decisions were largely personal, not collegial. Those taking them were not open to countervailing arguments, particularly once the decision had been made, but before that as well. It is Nasser and 'Amr who make all the decisions in Egypt, while Brezhnev and Kosygin seem to carry the ball in Moscow. President Johnson and the Rostow brothers make policy in Washington in 1967, and Nixon, Kissinger, and Sisco in 1970. Shultz presumably listens to someone in 1983, but it is not clear who. It was not those directly involved on the ground, however.

A fourth element is the precedence given *intuition over intelligence*. Two of the cases, 1967 and 1983, are characterized by a misunderstanding or flouting of the realities on the ground. In both instances intelligence was available indicating that the decision in question would be a mistake. It was ignored or dismissed in favor of a judgment which was largely intuitive as to what the outcome would be. In the third case, 1970, it is true that the professional Sovietologists generally supported the intuitive reaction of the decision makers that the Soviets were bluffing, but their consensus was based on intuition and precedent rather than hard intelligence, which was not available.[1]

Fifth is the common aspect of *great power backing*. In each case, one or both of the super powers were alleged to have incited their clients to take actions which proved destructive. The Soviets were thought to be encouraging Egyptian intransigence in 1967 and during the War of Attrition. The United States was popularly believed to have given the Israelis a green light to take offensive action in 1967, 1968–70, and 1982. In each case there is enough substance to the allegation to make it credible. In each case, super-power backing contributed to miscalculation by one or both of their client states.

Finally, there is the element of *selective hearing*. The most striking common aspect of all is the extent to which the decision makers heard what they wanted to hear and ignored what they didn't. In 1967 Nasser and ʿAmr apparently ignored General Fawzi's report that there were no Israeli troop concentrations; ʿAmr ignored the advice of his generals not to occupy Sharm al-Shaykh or to close the Gulf of Aqaba; and Nasser chose to accept ʿAmr's assurances about the state of the army when he knew the man was a military incompetent. For their part, the Israelis chose to call what they heard from the Americans a green light and to ignore both American urgings not to strike and their own commitment not to do so for another week. In 1970 the Americans and Israelis dismissed Kosygin's warning as a bluff because that fit with their strategy and beliefs. In 1983 Shultz and the Israelis ignored the warnings of the Americans and others on the ground that normalization would not work because it had become a political necessity for them.[2]

Although I suspect we will find that selective hearing is an almost universal element in miscalculation around the world, it would be wrong to generalize from these examples. The list illustrates the complexity of the phenomenon, however. There is no single, simple explanation for miscalculation. Rather, we have to deal with a complex set of variables that change with each circumstance.

In his presidential address to the American Historical Association in 1982, Gordon Craig, speaking of the decision-making process in foreign affairs, said:

> In this realm of ambiguity the statesman must ask himself repeatedly, How much choice do I actually have? How compelling are the domestic and foreign considerations that I must bear in mind? How much freedom do I derive from, or to what extent am I limited by, the stability and effectiveness, or the unsteadiness and incompetence, of my political system compared with my opponent's, our relative physical and moral resources, and the momentum of events? And he must at the same time remember that the game does not end when he makes up his mind to act or not to act, for once decisions are implemented they assume a life of their own, producing reactions and counterreactions among the other players and creating situations that may confound original expectations.

Craig appears to have had the rational actor in mind. In *Essence of Decision: Explaining the Cuban Missile Crisis*, Graham Allison points out that most analysts tend to think in terms of a rational actor model. They "attempt to understand happenings in foreign affairs as the more or less purposive acts of unified national governments. . . . Predictions about what a nation will do or would have done are generated by calculating

the rational thing to do in a certain situation, given specified objectives."
Elsewhere, he says that "treating national governments as if they were
centrally coordinated, purposive individuals provides a useful shorthand
for understanding problems of policy. But this simplification . . . obscures the persistently neglected fact of bureaucracy: the 'maker' of government policy is not one calculating decisionmaker but is rather a con-
glomerate of large organizations and political actors."[3]

The illusion of an orderly decision-making process, where decisions
are the result of a carefully reasoned and thought out strategy, is held
more often by outside observers than by participants, who may be all too
aware of the disorderly way in which the decision was reached. This is
not always the case, however. Heikal's contention that "one calculated
step followed another," assuming he believed it, shows that even the
insider may cherish the illusion that an orderly process is under way when
the reality is quite different, as it was in Egypt in 1967.

To Gordon Craig's list of essentially rational factors being weighed by
the decision maker one must add a number of factors which we can term
irrational—they shouldn't count, but they do. These include, aside from
bureaucratic and organizational politics, the decision maker's disposition,
self-image and *amour propre*, emotions such as jealousy and infatuation,
the influence of personal rivalry, paranoia and careerism, and the question of who gets credit for what, plus the influence of the liver, spleen,
and thyroid, among other organs.

The executive's disposition, for instance, is often as important as his
or her place in the hierarchy in determining how he or she will react. An
angry or excited decision maker is unlikely to take a cool and rational
approach while in that condition. Similarly, either jealousy or infatuation
can lure the executive to the wrong path, whatever the national interest
objectively calculated. A proposition identified with a rival, no matter how
worthy of consideration, risks being opposed if plausible grounds for doing
so are at hand, while one advanced by a love object or by one's self (often
the same thing) is likely to be supported until well after it is untenable.

Thus, judging by his own account, Yitzhak Rabin had become so fix-
ated on the deep penetration raids, for which he claimed a certain credit,
that he lost perspective. Similarly, Shultz's personal identification with
the May 17 agreement seems to have been an important element in his
determination to push it through.

MISPERCEPTION

Selective hearing is often the result of misperception. People become attached to a certain view of what they perceive as the realities and draw
their conclusions in the light of that view. They accept that which accords
with it and reject that which does not. For instance, while modern histo-

rians are coming to a more nuanced view of John Foster Dulles, to those of us at the working level in Middle Eastern affairs in 1957 he appeared to have concluded that Nasser was a tool of the Soviets because his policies paralleled theirs in certain respects and because he opposed the Western-supported status quo in the region. Egypt thereby became a state "controlled by international communism," in the words of the Eisenhower Doctrine, and a variety of consequences flowed from that. When such a policy is identified with the president and the secretary of state, it becomes difficult for the bureaucracy to question it, at least officially. As Leslie Gelb noted in the *New York Times* of May 5, 1991, commenting on General Colin Powell's reported preference for sanctions over military action, "Presidents unfortunately take dissent for disloyalty."

In his presidential address, Craig cited as an example of confounded expectations the German government's decision in 1890 not to renew its alliance with Russia, expecting thereby to give greater coherence to the German alliance system and to encourage the British to join it. The action had quite the opposite effect, however. It led eventually to an alliance between Russia and France, the automatic response feature of which was one of the elements which made World War I a world war.

In *The Fateful Alliance,* George Kennan points out that one of the stimuli to which the tsar (Alexander III) was reacting in concluding the treaty with France was "an abundant crop of rumors" that Britain was about to join the Triple Alliance between Germany, Italy, and Austria-Hungary. He comments, "Seldom does one find, in the history of diplomacy, serious anxieties, influential in affecting the course of history, for which there was less real substance or justification than these Franco-Russian fears of an adherence by Britain to the Triple Alliance."[4]

Kennan's description of the spread of rumors about British accession and the way in which they became established fact in the minds of Russian diplomats and other officials is a classic illustration of diplomatic mass hysteria of the sort that occasionally goes through the world's chanceries like hoof-and-mouth disease. Although Alexander III was not known for brilliance and was something of a recluse, one does not have to be stupid to be credulous of rumors and allegations, as we saw in the case of Nasser in 1967.

Susceptibility to misinformation is a common affliction of senior executives, who have insufficient time to learn the details of complex problems and who tend to be isolated from reality by their staffs. They are dependent on what is fed to them, and the feeders are often unwilling to convey unpleasant truths, particularly if it means telling the leader he is wrong about something, or does not understand the situation. Clark Clifford, for instance, in his memoirs has given us some fascinating and disturbing insights into Lyndon Johnson's reliance on intuitive judgments on matters of vital importance to the nation and of his attitude toward those who disagreed with him. When a leader of that sort gets his mind set on a particular vision of the situation he confronts, it is difficult to persuade him otherwise. While in that state he will tend to see everything in the light of his own mindset.

The difficulty is often increased by the intellectual limitations of the people around the leader. Presidential aides tend to be picked for their personality, loyalty, and political acumen rather than their sophistication about foreign policy, and what the leader is fed by them inevitably is filtered through their own perceptions and sometimes limited vision. The leader is sometimes able to rise above their perceptions and see more clearly for himself or herself, but often is not.

In all three of our cases the leaders involved were reacting to misperceptions. Nasser and the Soviet leaders had an unrealistic perception of Egypt's military strength and of Israel's likely reaction; the Israelis and Americans believed in a rule of Soviet behavior in 1970 that did not apply to the case at hand; and George Shultz was apparently relying on unrealistic expectations regarding the Saudis and Syrians. He may have been misled in this respect by the active role played by the Saudis in arranging the 1981 cease-fire in Lebanon and by the "can do" approach of Bandar Bin Sultan, the Saudi ambassador in Washington.

Misperception and intelligence failure are not the same phenomenon, but the latter may be the cause of the former, and vice versa. If we classify Soviet and Egyptian acceptance of the intelligence report of Israeli troop concentrations 1967 as an intelligence failure, we can ascribe that failure in part to the two states' refusal to accept American denials because of their perception that the Americans were out to get Nasser. Misperception may also contribute to the intelligence failure by sending people to look for the wrong thing. As Richard Betts comments, "The ultimate cause of error in most cases has been wishful thinking, cavalier disregard of professional analysts, and above all, the premises and preoccupations of policy makers. Fewer fiascoes have occurred in the stages of acquisition and presentation of facts than in the stages of interpretation and response. Producers of intelligence have been culprits less often than consumers."[5]

Whether we decide it is a matter of intelligence failure or misperception or both, these factors are only part of the problem. As noted earlier, we must take account of a wide range of variables, and the only constant is the unpredictability of human reaction—something we cannot measure. In my view, however, there are a few general observations regarding the three case studies which may have some general application.

The principal cause of miscalculation was *myopia*. The decision maker was too focused on the immediate consequences, often analyzed with an expediential calculus, to see the long-term effect of the decision taken. Shortsightedness was exaggerated by a lack of realism about capabilities and intentions. Nasser apparently had unrealistic expectations about his own army, about the Israelis, and about the Soviets and Americans in

1967; the Israelis had unrealistic expectations about the Egyptians in 1970; both the Israelis and Americans had unrealistic expectations about the Soviets in 1970; both the Americans and Israelis had unrealistic expectations about the Syrians in 1983. Had the decision makers in question known how the other parties would react they would have acted differently themselves.

The second cause was *commitment, moral or contractual*. Nasser was hostage to his commitment to the Syrians and to a doctrine of hostility to Israel and the conservative Arab states; the Israelis were committed philosophically and practically to a position on territory and how to deal with the Arabs which left them no alternative but military action for dealing with the War of Attrition; the Americans were hostage to their moral commitment to Israel and in the case of Haig and Shultz to the idea that Israel was somehow a strategic ally. None of the parties was completely free to act in accordance with its national interests narrowly defined.

The third cause was *image*, particularly a fear of appearing irresolute, weak, or indecisive. This fear was based not only on a desire to avoid shame but also on the belief that weakness invites attack or manipulation as well as being politically disastrous at home. In 1967 Nasser reportedly wanted to show that his commitment in Yemen did not prevent him from coming to the aid of Syria, and he increasingly rejected any course of action which would have affected his image as a resolute leader of all the Arabs. The Israelis were keen to maintain their reputation as resolute enforcers of the *lex talionis*. The Americans in 1970 were concerned to show the Soviets they could not be bluffed and in 1983 to show that they could not be buffaloed by the Syrians.

All three of these elements are imponderables. They cannot be weighed and measured exactly but can be felt and witnessed, and they are the stuff of which decisions are made. We can see all of them in operation in the exchanges preceding the second round of negotiations between Israel and its Arab neighbors in December 1991. They have characterized American and Soviet decision making in the Middle East much of the time since 1945. They were at work in Vietnam and the Cuban missile crisis.

WHAT TO DO ABOUT IT

As long as political animals are making the decisions, foreign policy will be marked by intelligence failure, misperception, and miscalculation. Leaders will forever follow intuitive hunches, conventional wisdom, and domestic political imperatives first and intelligence second, and as often as not they will ignore the latter when it conflicts with their perception of what is real and what is practicable. The mindsets with which the decision makers enter the discussion will be the most important single factor in determining what they finally decide, not only affecting their analysis of what they are told but also influencing the choice of factors to consider and what weight to give them. The decision makers will furthermore fight for prestige, national or personal, as though it were more precious than human life. The bureaucracy will facilitate this for them by going along in all but the most egregious mistakes, and even then it may follow all the way to disaster if discipline is good and the circumstances are right, as in Vietnam and Lebanon.

Assuming, however, that if the decision makers had all the facts and understood the situation perfectly they would be less likely to miscalculate, how do we assure that they have that understanding? The idea that you can deal with this by some sort of structural reform of the machinery dies hard, but it has been difficult to implement, particularly in a government which in fact has no long-range policy but follows a day-to-day pragmatic response method that is susceptible to domestic political pressures and the personal idiosyncrasies of its leaders.

That system works no worse and perhaps somewhat better than most others. The Soviet system, for instance, operated for decades under the burden of a Procrustean ideology that smothered dissent and produced an inefficient response mechanism. Its capacity for error was fully as great as that of the American system, as we saw in the Middle East in 1967 and in Afghanistan in 1979.

Undoubtedly the system can be improved in a number of ways, but deciding what those are comes down again to the problem of the mindset of the decision maker, who approaches the problem with certain conceptions about what should be done and how, reflecting his or her own experience and interest. How to overcome that mindset and permit an open discussion is a perennial problem.

The Devil's Advocate

A frequent suggestion is that there should be a devil's advocate—that there should be people designated to argue against policy, whatever it is. As Richard Betts comments, "Establishing a devil's advocate would probably do no harm. . . . But in any case the role is likely to atrophy into a superfluous artificial ritual."[6] Robert Jervis notes that "even when opposition is genuine, decision-makers may expose themselves to it in order to be able to tell others, and themselves, that they have considered all views. They may then gain renewed confidence in their policy from the incorrect belief that they have been especially open-minded."[7]

Part of the problem is that dissenting from established views of the leadership is an unrewarding, not to say perilous, activity. No matter how much people may talk about wanting frank and diverse opinions, they rarely welcome them in fact. They are more likely to resent the person who dissents as someone who has no team spirit or is positively disloyal. The dissenter, if he is good at his task and argues well, will inevitably be labeled a sorehead or crank who has lost objectivity and composure, and this negative image will affect decisions on promotions and postings. More important for our purpose, because the officer is thought to be a sorehead, his or her arguments are not taken seriously. This apparently happened, for instance, to Habib, Veliotes, and Paganelli, among others, in 1982–83. It has been the fate of Arabists in general since 1948.

An interesting experiment in this regard has nevertheless been carried out by the Department of State, which in 1971 established a special reporting system called the Dissent Channel to permit officers in the field or the department to challenge decisions and conventional wisdom either of their colleagues in the field or of the department itself, using a regular reporting format. (Although heralded as an effort at openness, one purpose was clearly to keep dissent within classified channels and out of the press.) These reports are sent directly to the Policy Planning Staff in the department, which determines their distribution and is responsible for the response to them. A serious effort is made to prevent superior officers from suppressing or trying to divert such reporting or from punishing the person who does it.

Policy Planning's handling of the message is monitored by an office known as the Secretary's Open Forum, which is outside the command structure and is directed by an elected chairman who is a serving officer on full pay. The forum was established in 1967, before the Dissent Channel, in part to provide a vehicle for dissent from Vietnam policies. It hosts regular meetings and seminars and publishes a classified journal in which divergent views on current issues are expressed by people within as well as outside the government.

These two devices constitute a dissent structure which is unique in the federal government. It has permitted a certain letting off of steam and has provided a means of registering dissent without undue fear of retribution, but its impact on policy issues has been marginal at best. It is too slow and reactive to have much effect on the daily policy operation, which often moves rapidly on critical issues, as we have seen in the case of the response to the Kosygin letter to Nixon. Furthermore, because imagination and energy fade with age, dissenters tend to be junior and mid-level officers and the senior levels of the department are unlikely to pay much attention to them. Because it is not considered a compliment to the principal officer at a post to have his subordinates disagreeing with him officially in a protected channel to Washington, efforts are often made to discourage the practice.[8] Nevertheless, there is in place a mechanism through which those who disagree with policy can express their views to the policy level and cannot be prevented from doing so by their superiors. That is progress.

This is perhaps as close to a devil's advocate system as the Department of State can get, given the competitive nature of the Foreign Service personnel system, where people are graded and rated against each other every year and must be promoted at certain intervals or selected out. Deviation or dissent from the accepted wisdom is risky in such an environment, whatever measures are taken to insulate the dissenter from retribution, and it takes courage and commitment to do it.

As far as I can tell, this system had no visible impact on the policy process regarding Lebanon in 1982–83, the only one of our three cases that occurred after the system was established. It is conceivable, however, that it could have an impact on some future Middle East issue, provided there were a secretary of state who was interested in the opinions of the Foreign Service, which does not seem to be the case at this writing. And even were it to have an impact in the Department of State, that does not mean it would affect attitudes in the other foreign affairs agencies such as the NSC, CIA, and Defense.

Insulation from Domestic Politics

Were it possible to insulate the foreign policy process from domestic political considerations, the policy maker would have a freer hand and theoretically would be able to treat problems solely on the basis of the national interest in the issue itself, without worrying unduly about its impact on the next election. This would not necessarily reduce the risk of miscalculation in all cases. While the Soviets were able to make Middle Eastern policy relatively free of domestic constraints in the past, such freedom probably increased rather than decreased their rate of error. Their Afghanistan debacle, for instance, might have been avoided had the government been more responsive to domestic considerations in its foreign policy decisions.

The British, who are much less burdened than the Americans are by spoils system personnel at the upper levels of the Foreign Office and have had much longer experience in foreign affairs, are somewhat freer than the Americans to formulate policy in accordance with national interests as perceived by the professional foreign policy establishment. This has not prevented them from making their own monumental errors in the Middle East, their handling of the Palestine issue being the most salient.

In any event, isolation of foreign from domestic politics is impossible in the United States, where policies on such questions as the Arab-Israeli problem, Cyprus, and Poland, not to mention broader issues of attitudes toward the Soviets or on human rights, have long been domestic as much as foreign policy issues. The impact of domestic pressures has been greatly magnified, however, by the dependence of elected officials on campaign contributions from political action groups. Meaningful reform of the election financing process which reduced or eliminated that dependence could permit the national government to act abroad more freely in pursuit of the national interest. That might reduce the risk of miscalculation, but there would be nothing automatic about it.

Education of Policy Makers

Were it possible to educate policy makers more broadly, to give them a better understanding of other cultures and some knowledge of history, about which most of them are quite ignorant, perhaps even to make them learn a foreign language or two, they might be more sophisticated about what they are dealing with and less likely to misjudge the other parties or the consequences of their actions. That would require reform of the system by which political appointees are now chosen for senior positions in the foreign policy apparatus with insufficient regard for qualifications and capabilities. It would also require reform of the entire educational system, either to create a better educated mass from which leaders could be chosen or to create a trained elite, as in France. Unfortunately for this argument, the superbly knowledgeable professional bureaucrats and administrators of France make the same sort of mistakes their loutish colleagues in Washington do.

Reform of the political appointment system and educational reform, and particularly greater instruction in languages and foreign affairs, are surely desirable, but they will not make humans predictable, and the absence of predictability is the principal cause of miscalculation. Science and education may make our guesses more accurate, but we will still be guessing. The most we can hope to do is to improve our score. That is still worth trying.

Before we pass final judgment on the decision makers discussed in this study, we should bear in mind that every decision has within it the possibility that it is wrong, and we should ask ourselves whether we would have done differently in the circumstances.

The decision process is a matter of at least binary choice. The person deciding has at least two possibilities: to act or not to. There may be multiple choices, all equally desirable or equally repugnant, or it may be possible to rate them on a scale of desirability and repugnancy, but the essential act is one of choosing between alternatives, even though it is common to claim that in fact there was no alternative, that only one course was possible. What is meant in such cases is that only one course was accceptable, or viable, or politically realistic, or whatever the decision maker chooses to feel about it. Whether the decision is right or wrong often depends on circumstances and events beyond the control of the decision maker. The choices are often so equal in their undesirability that whatever is decided will be considered wrong by someone, perhaps by everyone.

Furthermore, whether a given decision is actually right or wrong depends on its final outcome, which may not be evident for years. The final verdict is not yet in, for instance, on Moroccan occupation of the Western

Sahara or Israeli occupation of the West Bank and Gaza, but both have proved to be costly acquisitions to date. Nor will the verdict be unanimous in many cases. Judgment about whether a given decision was a miscalculation very often rests on partisan or subjective assessments of benefits and damages, and in particular on whose ox was gored.

Nevertheless, there are enough clear examples of miscalculation to provide a corpus for systematic study, and there are lessons to be learned which can be applied to today's problems. The diplomat or policy maker who is aware of the errors his or her predecessors have made and why they were made is less likely to repeat them. Even a marginal improvement in this respect can improve the human condition, given the stakes involved.

Appendix

With the exception of document 1, which is from the LBJ Library in Austin, Texas, and documents 5 and 6, which are from the United Nations Archives, the documents in this appendix were obtained by the author from declassified files of the U.S. Department of State.

DOCUMENT 1

CIA report, June 1967 (TDCS-314/08242-67)
Subject: Soviet official's comments on Soviet policy on the Middle Eastern War
Source: A medium level Soviet official

1. The Soviet told . . . there had been "miscalculations" by the Soviets and by the Arabs. The Soviets overestimated the Arabs' ability to employ their substantial military strength against the Israelis while the Arabs overrated their own strength and underrated the Israeli military capability and determination to win. When source asked if that meant that the Soviets had encouraged the Arabs in their hostile attitude toward Israel, the Soviet replied affirmatively, stating that the USSR had wanted to create another trouble spot for the United States in addition to that already existing in Vietnam. The Soviet aim was to create a situation in which the US would become seriously involved economically, politically, and possibly even militarily and in which the US would suffer serious political reverses as a result of its siding against the Arabs. This grand design, which envisaged a long war in the Middle East, misfired because the Arabs failed completely and the Israeli blitzkrieg was so decisive. Faced with this situation the Soviets had no alternative but to back down as quickly and gracefully as possible so as not to appear the villains of the conflict.

2. The Soviet thought that Nasser "must go" and that he would "most probably" be assassinated in the near future by his own disillusioned people. He said that Nasser's charge that US and British aircraft had aided the Israeli forces was a desperate attempt to save face in the Arab world after suffering a humiliating military defeat and that no one, certainly not the USSR, believed the charge. In a final comment, the Soviet said the war has shown that the Arabs are incapable of unity even when their vital interests are at stake.

DOCUMENT 2

Department of State telegram no. 194188, from Secretary of State to U.S. Embassy, Cairo, May 15, 1967

1. Chargé should return to FonMin soonest and state USG (U.S. Government) greatly concerned at increase in tension and resulting military movements.

2. Chargé should inform FonMin that we have urged restraint in strong terms at highest level Israel Government. We have cautioned against unsettling effects of threatening statements made by GOI (Government of Israel) leaders. We are

unaware of any major changes in disposition of Israeli forces or of "mobilization" measures. We have impression that if commando activities against Israel should terminate, tension in Israel will diminish.

3. We are also urging restraint with Syrians. As GUAR (Government of the UAR) aware, however, USG influence with Syrians is minimal. We believe that UAR can play useful role in urging Syrians put stop to terrorist incidents which tend to inflame the border situation.

4. We think greatest restraint and resistance to provocation should be exercised by all parties at this critical period. If this is done and if appropriate UN machinery used to fullest practicable extent, we see no reason why a serious crisis cannot be avoided.

DOCUMENT 3

Department of State telegram no. 199704 to U.S. Embassy, Cairo, May 22, 1967
Deliver following through quickest means to President Nasser from President Johnson:

May 22, 1967

Dear President Nasser:
I have spent much of these past days thinking of the Middle East, of the problems you face, and the problems we face in that area.

Various of our common friends, including Ambassador Battle, have told me of your concern that the United States may have indicated an unfriendliness toward the UAR. This, I would wish you to know directly, is far from the truth.

I have watched from a distance your efforts to develop and modernize your country. I understand, I think, the pride and the aspirations of your people— their insistence that they enter as soon as possible the modern world and take their full part in it. I hope that we can find public as well as private ways to work more closely together.

I also understand the political forces at work in your region, the ambitions and tensions, the memories and the hopes.

Right now, of course, your task and mine is not to look back, but to rescue the Middle East—and the whole human community—from a war I believe no one wants. I do not know what steps Secretary General U Thant will be proposing to you; but I do urge you to set as your first duty to your own people, to your region, and to the world community this transcendent objective: the avoidance of hostilities.

The great conflicts of our time are not going to be solved by the illegal crossings of frontiers with arms and men—neither in Asia, the Middle East, Africa, or Latin America. But that kind of action has already led to war in Asia, and it threatens the peace elsewhere.

I had expected that I might ask our Vice President to go to the Middle East to talk with you and other Arab leaders, as well as with the leaders of Israel. If we come through these days without hostilities, I would still hope that visit by my most trusted friend could result immediately.

Each of us who has the responsibility for leading a nation faces different problems shaped by history, geography, and the deepest feelings of our peoples. Whatever differences there may be in the outlook and interests of your country and mine, we do share an interest in the independence and progress of the UAR and the peace of the Middle East.

I address you at this critical moment in the hope that you share that assessment and will find it possible to act on it in the hours and days ahead.

Sincerely,

Lyndon B. Johnson

DOCUMENT 4

Department of State telegram no. 199710, May 22, 1967, note verbale from Secretary of State

FOR DAMASCUS, TEL AVIV, AMMAN, BEIRUT, JIDDA, ALGIERS: The following telegram is being sent to Cairo. You should make appropriate substitutions and deliver identical note to your government.

FOR LONDON, ROME, PARIS, OTTAWA, ANKARA, MOSCOW, TEHRAN: You should inform your host government of our action, and request that we remain in closest contact in light of reports of UAR decision to close Strait of Tiran.

FOR CAIRO:

1. You should request urgent meeting with Foreign Minister Riad to convey following note verbale:

2. In recent days, tension has again risen along armistice lines between Israel and Arab states. We agree with view of Secretary General of United Nations that situation there is matter of concern to international community as whole. It is our earnest wish to support efforts in which he is taking lead to reduce tensions, and to restore conditions of stability and trust.

3. We have no reason to believe, in present situation, that any of parties to Armistice Agreements between Arab States and Israel has intention of committing aggression. Danger, and it is grave danger, lies in misadventure and miscalculation. There is risk that those in authority in area may misapprehend or misinterpret intentions and actions of others.

4. Three aspects of situation cause us particular concern. First is continuing terrorism being carried out against Israel with Syrian approval, and at least in some cases, from Syrian territory. This is directly contrary to the 'General Armistice Agreements which call on signing governments to assure that no warlike act or act of hostility shall be conducted from territory of one against other party or against civilians or territory under control of that party. We believe General Armistice Agreements remain best basis for maintenance of peaceful conditions along borders. We hope that UAR will join us as well as other governments in urging all parties to Agreements to observe scrupulously their provisions.

5. Secondly, we are concerned that a precipitate withdrawal of the United Nations Emergency Force may make the problem of maintaining peace along the UAR-Israeli border more difficult. In our opinion, the presence of UNEF has been an important aid in preserving basic security along this border. USG supports Secretary General Thant's mission to Cairo and earnestly trusts that the UARG will explore fully with him possibilities for continued UN peacekeeping presence in some form along UAR-Israel border.

6. Third, USG considers it particularly important that the present cycle of troop build-up on both sides be arrested and reversed. We have noted statements of

United Arab Republic and Israel indicating that their military movements are defensive in purpose and we would hope that both parties, as well as other states in the area which have taken military precautions, will return their forces to their normal dispositions. In doing so, they could perform an important service toward relieving the present tense situation.

7. We would also take this opportunity to reaffirm our continued adherence to principle of free access to Gulf of Aqaba for ships of all nations. The right of free and innocent passage of these waters is a vital interest of the international community. We are convinced that any interference whatever with these international rights could have the gravest international consequences.

8. In present situation UARG, as well as other Arab governments can rely on certainty that USG maintains firm opposition to aggression in the area in any form—overt or clandestine, carried out by regular military forces or irregular groups. This has been policy of this government under four successive administrations. Record of our actions over the past two decades, within and outside the United Nations is clear on this point.

9. In conclusion USG expresses its sincere hope that UAR will join it as well as numerous other nations in their efforts, both within UN and outside of that body, to bring about a lessening of tension and restoration of area stability.

DOCUMENT 5

U.N. memorandum of meeting between Secretary General U Thant and UAR Foreign Minister Mahmoud Riad, May 24, 1967, Cairo

1. The meeting opened at 9:45 hours on Wednesday 24 May 1967 at the Ministry of Foreign Affairs Office, Giza. The SG started the conversation by recounting developments which had led to his ordering the withdrawal of UNEF. He said that he had consulted the UNEF Advisory Committee and representatives of governments contributing contingents to UNEF before the final action was taken. Brazil, Canada, Denmark, and Norway were opposed to withdrawal and wanted him to refer to the General Assembly at an Emergency session. Sweden also did not appear to approve of the action of withdrawal. Only India, Pakistan, and Yugoslavia fully supported his action. Outside these consultations France's attitude seemed to be neutral. UK and US were opposed to withdrawal, and the Soviet Union wanted the Secretary General to comply with UAR request for immediate withdrawal. SG also added that member states could ask for the convening of an Emergency session of the General Assembly under the existing rules, but no member state indicated to him any desire to take such an initiative.

2. SG then discussed Ambassador Goldberg's letter given to him and gave a copy to FM for his personal information. This letter stresses US policy regarding its commitments to Israel in the event of aggression against Israel.

3. FM, in a lengthy discourse, gave details of events which led to UAR's request for withdrawal of UNEF from Sinai and later completely from this area. He said a few days ago the area was peaceful. There had, however, been a legacy of escalation of aggression by Israel against Arabs, especially against Jordan and Syria. There had been attacks against Jordan water projects, many incidents involving increasing use of weapons, i.e., exchange of fire, guns, tanks, and the latest use of air force was most serious. The Israelis had the upper hand here because other

Arab countries did not possess comparable air forces. Israel followed this pattern of boasting after 1956. Recently Eban and Rabin threatened to invade Syria and master Damascus.

4. UAR had made no move before receiving reports of Israeli concentrations. They had received information of a plan of invasion by Israel against Syria. Only on 15 May US Chargé d'Affaires in a meeting with FM, when referring to the situation in Syria, had said, "We take it most seriously."

5. "Strangely," the FM continued, "after we had decided to move against Israel, US Chargé told us that there were no concentrations but would not give us any guarantees. We were back in a similar situation as existed in 1956 when the US Ambassador gave us similar information, and yet we were attacked."

6. "We understand that Israel does not intend to annex Syria, and Damascus is not part of their plan. Their plans are confined, however, to south of Syria where bulk of Syrian Army is deployed, which they wish to destroy as well as the military and economic installations. Israel could achieve this with its Air Force and invade south Syria. By the time Security Council would meet, it would be possible for them to have inflicted serious punishment on Syria. Israel then, supported by its friends, would agree to having a new UNEF on Israel-Syrian frontier."

7. "Israel's positions on the Syrian border are weak. Syria holds dominant positions and can open fire on a number of settlements in north Israel. Israel is determined to alter this situation. UAR had a parallel experience in 1956 with the difference that they did not have any large installations in the Sinai. Therefore, when US Chargé told me that 'we are against aggression,' it means little to us. I told US Chargé that they were supporting and encouraging Israel. US will share responsibility of any attack. UAR had no choice but to move into the Sinai for we had no time to make any moves. Our deterrent action would make Israel think before they attack now."

8. FM said that he agreed with SG on total withdrawal of UNEF without leaving one single soldier. Withdrawal of consent to placing peace-keeping forces must be the last word according to the agreement between his government and the late SG. "I told the Canadian Ambassador that if there was any delay in the withdrawal of Canadian Contingent we would send them away by force. The SG had saved the UN flag and the idea of peace-keeping."

9. SG said that US still maintains that we were wrong in withdrawing UNEF. FM stated that for political reasons often personal ambition has led many in US to lose their balance on the question of Israel. SG said that in his view there was little support against withdrawal in the GA.

10. FM, continuing with his discourse, said that "when UNEF withdrew, we moved into the Sinai, including Sharm el Sheikh. We had decided to continue our actions as they were before 1956. Israeli propaganda before 1956 had stated that Gulf of Aqaba was not important to them, but after 1956 Israel claimed that they had succeeded by opening the Gulf. By re-establishing UAR positions in Sharm el Sheikh and closing the Gulf of Aqaba, the UAR has pulled the last curtain on the Israeli aggression of 1956. Israel will not profit from that aggression any more."

11. FM stated that Eilat was not too important economically. "The question is of prestige with Israel as it is with us. We realize that Israel considered question of Sharm el Sheikh a serious one. It had posed as a powerful country, and the end of such an atmosphere as a result of our recent actions would be detrimental

to their interests. Israel is losing prestige inside and outside that country, which would affect their future financial support and rate of immigration."

12. "Our move was important from our point of view. We are defensive in posture; we had no plans to attack Israel. We realize that any attack by us would create a great international crisis. If US intends to support Israel and exploit the situation, we are ready. The extent of such support is open to question."

13. The SG inquired whether the US Ambassador had told the FM of its past commitments to Israel concerning the Gulf of Aqaba. The FM replied that the US Ambassador had only said, "We are against aggression."

14. FM then informed the SG regarding developments in the Arab world. He said that they had received offers of co-operation from all the Arabs but had refused any aid from Jordan and Saudi Arabia. Tunisia was too unimportant even to consider.

15. The SG said that Israeli delegation had told him that they attached the greatest importance to Straits of Tiran and that they would be prepared to go to war. Before President Nasser's statement of 22 May, Ambassador Goldberg and the Canadian delegate had advised him of similar Israeli reaction. There may be a Security Council meeting today. The SG had to submit a report after his visit to Cairo. Some delegations had suggested that he invoke Article 99, but he declined to do so for several reasons including the position of USSR and France. Hammarskjold had done it only once, during the Congo crisis. At that time the entire membership supported his initiative. SG stated that the UAR case had to be presented in the light of Big-Power play. Ambassador Federenko had told him that he thought that the UAR would not do anything to precipitate a crisis over the Gulf of Aqaba. SG requested FM not to take any precipitate action.

16. FM said that their stand on the Gulf of Aqaba was firm. They had anticipated all possible moves, including possibility of war with Israel. Only yesterday he was present at talks with the President and with the PM and COS of Syria. They had agreed to be firm. They were ready to attack Israel if it became necessary. If the US attacked the UAR, what could they do? "UAR is a small power. When President Nasser makes a statement, he does so after a great deal of deliberation. He cannot withdraw from that position." The prestige of the UAR and all Arabs was involved. This point had not been discussed by the FM with the US Ambassador. If the US wished to avoid war, they should consider making a balance. In the case of Gulf of Aqaba, US alleges that UAR has violated international law. These were legal arguments, and the UAR was prepared to discuss them.

17. FM further said that there was the question of the GAA (General Armistice Agreement). Israel would not accept to implement and return to the GAA. If US was serious, they should help in this respect. Implementation of GAA means to Israel (a) no border; (b) that Israel does not finally exist; (c) there exists a state of belligerency; (d) reinstatement of El Auja situation prior to 1955. Although Israel had violated GAA in respect of El Auja, UAR had agreed to continue relations with EIMAC (Egypt-Israel Mixed Armistice Commission) to indicate its willingness to co-operate with UN. US has talked about presence of UN in the area. FM had asked new US Ambassador for clear proposals. FM had said that UN was already present with the GAA. SG remarked that Israel's position was clear on EIMAC. FM agreed because Israel had said "EIMAC is dead and buried." Israel was also not co-operating with ISMAC. FM said that expansion of EIMAC would be discussed if Israel accepted GAA. Israel's national policy was to occupy De-

militarized Zone area. That is why they were after DZ is Syria. If MAC attempted to prevent cultivation of DZ on Syrian border, Israel would not agree. UAR had patiently waited, but then attack on Gaza on 28 February 1955 had been the turning point.

18. SG inquired about UAR's attitude on question of repatriation and compensation. FM indicated that since this arose out of a GA resolution, they would not raise it at this point.

19. SG informed FM that Ambassador Goldberg had told Bunche of US advice to Israel not to send ships through Gulf of Aqaba, but Israel's reaction was negative.

20. SG asked UAR position on Security Council meeting being called today. FM replied that there was no complaint. They would not object if Ambassador El Kony were called to meeting.

21. SG sounded FM as to possible UAR reaction if he made an appeal to freeze the situation in the Gulf along lines during Cuban crisis. SG mentioned moratorium for two to three weeks to give him time for consultation and discussions. FM replied that his Government did not wish to show any weakness to its people, and especially the Army. If Security Council attempted a resolution against UAR action in Gulf of Aqaba, it would surely be vetoed by Soviet Union. The question might then perhaps go to GA, which would not be able to do much.

22. The SG said that we should look for a solution to calm down the present crisis. He would appeal to Israel not to send ships through Gulf of Aqaba for a certain period, for if a ship were sent and the UAR acted against it, the situation would explode.

23. The SG asked FM's reaction to possibility of SG's appointing a personal representative in the area who could base himself in Gaza and have access to Israel and UAR. The FM wanted clarification on his functions. The SG said these could be discussed.

24. The SG informed FM regarding Canadian initiative to persuade Israel to accept UNEF on their side. He asked FM's reaction, and latter replied that it would be all right from their point of view, if Israel agreed. However, UAR would not agree to re-establishment of UNEF on its territory.

25. SG then raised matters relating to EIMAC and asked if UAR would agree to their patrolling and establishing OP's in Gaza Strip and Sinai. FM replied that in the Gaza Strip the UAR would agree to the same situation relating to EIMAC as existed before 17 May 1967. They would not permit UNMOs (UN military observers) to enter the Sinai.

26. The SG inquired whether UAR would object to construction of a barbed wire along ADL. FM said that this was an old question, unacceptable to the UAR. However, if Israel wished to construct wire on their side and away from the ditch, they would not object. UAR was against sign-posting or any permanent marking which would indicate that the present armistice lines had changed into an international frontier.

27. The SG then discussed some broad aspects of disposal and dumping of UNEF property. He informed FM that it was UN's intention to transfer some equipment to Pisa and Jerusalem for use by UN peace-keeping operations, present and future. Some of the surplus equipment would be disposed of locally. FM said that their Army had everything but like every other army were always greedy to obtain more. He understood the SG's position.

28. The SG, in taking leave of the FM, reiterated his two main lines of approach to resolve the present crisis: firstly, a moratorium for a two- to three-week period to allow time for discussions; secondly, to attempt to obtain Israel's agreement to reactivate GAA, for which he would seek US support. Lastly, if GAA cannot be fully implemented as it applies between Israel and UAR, to discuss the possibility of his recommending to Security Council the appointment of a special representative to this area.

29. The FM agreed to consider these questions and also to arrange for the SG to meet the President.

30. The meeting closed at 1230 hours.

DOCUMENT 6

U.N. memorandum of meeting between Secretary General U Thant and UAR President Nasser, May 24, 1967, Cairo

1. The President received the SG at his residence for dinner and discussion at 2000 hours on 24 May 1967. The SG opened the conversation by saying that he was required to make a report to the Security Council on his visit to Cairo. He would therefore like to have the President's reaction to his proposal on declaring a moratorium in the Gulf of Aqaba. SG also told the President that on his way to Cairo, he got information at Paris airport regarding the closing of the Gulf of Aqaba. To be frank he was very much surprised, since in his view war was inevitable, for that action.

2. The President briefly stated the position of the UAR along the same lines as the Foreign Minister during SG's meeting with him earlier in the day. Regarding the closing of the Gulf of Aqaba, President said that the decision had been made some time earlier. The question was the timing of the announcement of the decision. If the announcement were to be made after SG's visit to Cairo, it would be widely interpreted that SG had been snubbed. So it was decided to announce it before SG's arrival. President said that already two ships entering the Gulf had been searched by the UAR; however, he wished to help the UN in restoring peace, especially when it was threatened by the attitude of Israel which had given every indication of invading Sharm el Sheikh. UAR forces were prepared to defend themselves. President would, however, accept SG's proposal for a moratorium for a period of two weeks. It was no longer possible for him to physically withdraw his blockade but he would issue orders that his people in the Gulf would be "good boys" as long as Israel on its part complied with SG's request.

3. SG stated that he would cable Bunche tonight if possible to carry out consultations to persuade Israel not to send shipping through the Gulf for some time and to refrain from sending strategic materials to Eilat as required by the UAR.

4. The question of UN supervising compliance of this agreement during the two-week moratorium period was considered and rejected by the President on the grounds of breach of armed forces' security involved with any UN presence.

5. The President said that UAR had achieved its goal by returning to pre-1956 position, with one difference: that they were now in a position to defend their country and their rights. He had accepted offer of troops from Algeria, Kuwait, and Iraq. UAR did not require military assistance from any other Arab country, but it was important to agree to accept token contributions in the interest of the

morale of the Arab world. The populace of these countries had received a great fillip in their morale, and many volunteers were offering themselves for the fight against Israel.

6. President covered the position of the major Powers and blocs on the question of the Gulf blockade. He said that the US had always supported Israel. The Russians have declared their support for the UAR. France was neutral, and the UK followed the US line. The line-up was typical of the present division amongst the major Powers. UAR relations with US have deteriorated over the years because of a clash of mutual interests. US had applied economic pressure and stopped assistance last year. UAR had to reduce its industrial production and to limit importation of raw material to provide sufficient hard currency to buy food. The economic position had improved for this year. The President had declined, however, any offers of assistance from US, UK, and West Germany. His position also was that if credits were made available, interest on past loans would be paid. He had therefore refused to pay interest on loans to US, UK, and West Germany. The International Monetary Fund had also applied some pressures as had the World Bank. But his position was, if no more credits, no payment of past dues and interest. France and Italy had renegotiated medium loans to long-term loans. They had also been able to obtain some credit elsewhere, and the UAR economic position had somewhat improved. He concluded by stating UAR's determination to retain its independence of action and to defend its sovereignty and its rights.

7. The SG asked President's comments on the possibility of appointment of a special representative to the area with possible location at Gaza. The President said that US and Canada had in 1957 attempted to place Gaza Strip under UNEF administration. This was unacceptable to UAR then as would be any appointment which might indicate international presence after withdrawal of UNEF by anyone other than EIMAC. The President offered, however, to accept any UN diplomatic presence in Cairo and assured the SG of his fullest co-operation.

8. During a discussion on possible developments during the Security Council meeting, FM said that the item inscribed was the Middle East. There were lots of trouble spots in the Middle East besides the Gulf of Aqaba, and it would appear that a free-for-all discussion would take place in the Security Council. The SG said that the Security Council was involved in a procedural wrangle and would probably waste time on it. The president said that he had already instructed the FM to open the UN files on the failure on the part of Israel to comply with UN resolutions. On the other hand, Egypt had always supported and co-operated with the UN and would continue to do so.

9. The President then raised the question of removal and disposal of UNEF property. He said that their armed forces would be prepared to buy any items for disposal.

10. Rikhye informed President of the arrangements already made that certain items, including vehicles, radio sets, and other military type equipment, would be transferred to Pisa and Jerusalem as required. Other items for disposal were being sorted out, and the UAR would be informed about availability.

11. The SG confirmed arrangements, especially about the transfer of certain items to Pisa and Jerusalem. The President expressed his acceptance of such an arrangement and promised his fullest co-operation. He said that if any difficulties arose, these should be brought to the notice of the armed forces authorities who had his instructions to co-operate with UN.

12. The President then offered to the SG the highest UAR military decoration for UNEF. At first this was misunderstood; SG and Rikhye thought the offer was for individual officers and men. The President, however, clarified the point by saying that he was offering a decoration for UNEF as a whole along the customary military lines when a whole unit or a formation is decorated. The SG said that he would like to give further consideration to this generous offer of the President and would send him a reply from New York.

13. The President stated his gratitude to UNEF and to UN for helping the UAR in 1956 and since then till now. He conveyed his great appreciation for the assistance rendered by UNEF in keeping and maintaining peace in the area. He asked Rikhye to convey his personal thanks to all ranks for the services rendered to the UAR and for keeping peace in the area.

DOCUMENT 7

U.S. Embassy Cairo telegram no. 8093 to Department of State, May 28, 1967

1. We are increasingly concerned by continuing divergence in assessments of likely UAR positions and actions between dept and this mission.

2. It is inconceivable to us that UAR with full Soviet backing would not rpt not challenge most vigorously any UN resolution tending to contest their Aqaba Gulf position, calling for status quo ante closure or endorsing any sort of UN or other international maritime patrol.

3. As we have said before UAR will in all probability militarily confront any naval or other force which attempts assure "free passage" unless of overwhelming size.

4. UARG's forty-eight hour evacuation ultimatum to UNEF Canadians suggestive of UARG determination.

5. Important not base our plans and actions in coming days on misassessment of probable UAR reactions.

—Nolte

DOCUMENT 8

U.S. Embassy Cairo telegram no. 8349 to Department of State, June 2, 1967

1. Yost made private call last evening on Foreign Minister Riad who was colleague in Syria and at UN. Riad held forth for hour and half with intense and uncharacteristic emotion and bitterness.

2. First hour largely devoted to complaints against US and Israel. He said he had given up hope of US ever dealing impartially with Arab-Israeli issues and had concluded political pressures inside US would always make it impossible for USG to support measures in or out of the UN which Israel opposes. He cited recent statements US senators, "provocative" declarations Commander Sixth Fleet, and "one-sided" presentation US press as latest evidence supporting his conclusions. Yost explained considerations governing US policy in Near East but made little impression.

3. Riad dealt at some length with Israeli refusal to observe armistice agreements and repeated violations UN resolutions, emphasizing particularly seizure of

El Auja in 1955, Ben Gurion's denunciation of demilitarized zones along Syrian and Jordanian borders, disproportionate reprisal raids and so on. He spoke of his own and other Arab efforts at UN to revive EIMAC and alluded to draft resolution just submitted to SC by UAR. He said he had just had phone call from El Kony reporting objection some SC members to derogatory preambular references to Israel and said he had instructed El Kony to drop all such references and limit draft to two operative paragraphs calling for revival EIMAC and report to SYG within two weeks. He added however that he is aware this draft resolution will be unacceptable to Israel and that US will therefore, though it may be embarrassed, find some means of killing resolution.

4. He went on to say that, while Egypt has no quarrel with Israel, heart of Arab-Israel issue is fate of more than one million refugees. This can never be forgotten by Arabs. Treatment of refugees by Zionists is taught every school child and issue will not die.

5. As to present crisis there is extraordinary unity among Arabs which will not be shaken by threats. UARG under heavy pressure from army officers to take more vigorous action. It is resisting this pressure but is mobilizing public opinion in preparation for probable attack by Israel or others. Perhaps only way out of impasse, he declared at one point, may be short war, appeal to UNSC, which would then call for cease fire with which UAR would at once comply. Thereafter more realistic settlement might be possible.

6. Yost explained our apprehension of consequences and possible repercussions of war and our so far successful efforts to persuade Israelis to hold off, citing however Israeli fears of Arab mobilization against them, Nasser's references to return to 1948 status quo, and Israeli conviction of vital interest in free passage through Tiran Straits, as well as US policy on this subject.

7. Riad stated in strongest terms, and reiterated several times during conversation, UARG determination not to alter its decision to close Straits to Israeli ships and strategic materials including oil. He said that twenty days ago UAR had every expectation this would be quiet normal summer. Threatened attack on Syria had taken them by surprise and they had had to react by requesting UNEF withdrawal. However, reoccupation of Sharm el Sheikh had made inevitable return to status quo of 1956 and closure of Straits. UAR certainly has sovereign right to maintain state of war against Israel and hence to exercise belligerent rights in its territorial waters. Minister said he would see no objection to Israel presenting complaint on this issue to ICJ if it so desired. Firm public position has been taken on closure Straits and Nasser's position in Arab world would be destroyed if he should yield. UAR has no alternative but to fight "anyone" who endeavors to force passage of Straits.

8. On other hand, if oil is kept away from Straits, there will be no problem. He noted efforts to persuade Iran to prevent oil shipments over this route, referred to President Tubman's "wise" decision concerning Liberian tankers and added, "If US really wishes to be helpful" it might urge US oil companies to refrain from making shipments over this route. Israel can be otherwise supplied and problem is not economic but purely psychological.

9. After some discussion this issue, Yost said he had heard considerable apprehension expressed that UAR not only insists on closing Straits but will proceed to other demands also unacceptable to Israel. Riad replied that, while as he had said refugee problem is underlying cause of difficulties, UAR has no other demands.

He believes very strongly it would be in general interest for EIMAC to be reconstituted and UNTSO observers reactivated along Israel-IUAR frontier. Otherwise, incidents sure to occur. He cited Israel seizure five man UAR patrol few days ago, fact patrol not yet released and probability that, in absence UNTSO which could effect release, UAR forces will have to seize corresponding Israeli patrol. However, he was practically certain Israel would not agree to revival EIMAC since it would mean they would have to give up El Auja.

10. He also warned that UAR could not tolerate further substantial aggressive Israeli actions on Syrian or Jordanian frontiers such as Es Samu raid or shooting down Syrian planes over Syria and Jordan. Consequences of incidents this kind would be war and great destruction on both sides.

—Nolte

DOCUMENT 9

U.S. Embassy Lisbon telegram no. 1517 to Department of State, June 2, 1967
Eyes only for President and SecState from Robert Anderson

1. There follows a summary of my talk with President Nasser. Unless otherwise indicated, I will be trying to express his point of view to me.

2. After exchange of pleasantries, Nasser said he became worried and afraid of Israeli attack because of speeches and his own intelligence of mobilization by Israel [deletion]. As an example, he stated that 13 brigades were mobilized near Syria.

3. Nasser explained that he did not want repetition of 1956 affair when he was reluctant to believe that an attack had begun and was slow in moving troops to Sinai only to be caught between the Israelis in the north and the British at Port Said. He said he felt he had no choice but to mobilize and send troops to Sinai, which he did, and request the removal of UN forces. While he did not say so, I believe he was surprised at the rapidity of the removal of UN troops because he said they were only a token force and would have created no real obstacle.

4. He was asked specifically if he intended to begin any conflict and he said to please explain to my govt that he would not begin any fight but would wait until the Israelis had moved. This was qualified by saying that he did not know what the Syrians would do and had worried all day (Wednesday) for fear the Syrians might start something out of anger because of the pact which he had made with Hussein. He also stated that, contrary to most public opinion, he did not have control over the radical elements of refugee organizations who were interested only in starting a conflict because they had no real responsibility for the conduct of military affairs. He was asked if this conflict occurred, for example if Syria should attack against his desires, where he would regroup and he answered affirmatively saying that any . . . bring response from him.

5. It was pointed out that if Israel felt she was virtually alone she might be motivated to strike first in order to secure a strategic advantage and that so long as she felt she had friends she might be restrained. Nasser replied that this was a risk which he would have to accept and that he thought the first Israeli target and main thrust of Israeli offensive would be against Egypt and Cairo. He said that elaborate plans had been made for instant retaliation, and that he was confident of the outcome of a conflict between Arabs and Israelis.

6. [deleted by Department of State]

7. With reference to Gulf of Aqaba, Nasser stated that for eight years after 1948 the Straits had been closed to Israeli shipping and was open only by the illegal act of Israel, France and England, and he proposed merely to return to the status of 1956 which had been at least tolerated by all the nations for eight years. He explained that even we had deplored and opposed the act of the Israelis, British and French which changed the status quo in 1956. He stated that the Straits of Tiran were navigable only in a width of three miles which was clearly territorial waters and that he intended to maintain this position. He was asked specifically what commerce he would allow through the Straits under his concept and he replied by saying that the exclusions would be 1) Israeli ships, 2) oil or any refined products, and 3) arms for Israel. Here he stated that all countries claimed territorial waters to a greater distance offshore than he was asserting and further that he was at war with Israel and had been since 1948 with nothing existing between them except an armistice, and that under these circumstances he was entitled to assert jurisdiction.

8. He was asked if he would consider referring this matter of the Straits to either the United Nations or the World Court, in view of the fact that four countries had borders on the Gulf. He replied that he would not submit the question to the UN because the Israelis normally treated resolutions of the UN not favorable to them as "pieces of paper." He said that he did not have sufficient knowledge of the World Court to answer specifically about referring the matter to the World Court for decision but would consult his legal advisers. This was qualified by saying that he did not want to undertake any course of action that would take "years" to decide.

9. He also stated that even if he agreed on some other course of action, any other course of action would be strongly opposed by all Arab countries who were now his allies. On this point he seemed on the one hand adamant about the position he had taken in the Straits and yet he did not rule out completely possibility of a World Court review if it could be done speedily. For the time being I think he will remain firm.

10. He was asked if he was not prepared to accept Israel as a matter of fact, even though he might have emotional and legal feelings concerning the establishment of the country in Palestine. Nasser replied by saying that he did not believe stable and lasting peace could be achieved without disposing of the refugee problem. He was asked if this could be done by compensation as well as some limited return of refugees. He replied that he thought practically all refugees would return if permitted and that even if compensation were paid they would not be satisfied but would continue to agitate for return to Palestine. He went into long discourse on Arab mentality as it affects their feelings toward the place where they were born and reared.

11. Nasser stated that he had been prepared to sign an agreement with the Monetary Fund but had just received a letter saying that the Fund wished to review their relationships with Egypt further. He then stated he was glad he had not signed the agreement with the Fund because they were unreasonable and left him no flexibility. He emphasized that he did not want to be subject to economic pressure. It was explained to him that neither the Fund or local American banks were in fact exerting pressure when they did not comply with national requests

since they were all governed by strict rules that limited their own flexibility in making loans to countries that did not comply with all regulations.

12. Nasser expressed keen desire to have friendship of American people and American govt explaining that under no circumstances was he a Communist. On other hand, he felt that US policy was motivated largely by the large Jewish vote in US and that American govt would be reluctant to oppose this voting strength. He then called attention to the fact that Eisenhower had taken a strong position in 1956 against Israeli invasion and this had not hurt him politically.

13. He seemed anxious to have Zakaria Mohieddin explain his position directly to US govt and said he hoped we would take the long view because the Arab countries stretched from Morocco on the west to Pakistan on the east and that now he even had the support of Pakistan and India. He did not see how a minority in the US could influence US policy to oppose what such a vast region and such large numbers of people believed proper. It was explained to him that the US govt was not motivated by political considerations but was concerned essentially in maintaining peace and the integrity of countries.

14. At this time Nasser said that if the policy was for Arabs and Israelis to live together harmoniously and Israel should allow a million refugees to come back to Palestine, which would solve the refugee problem and still the Israelis would have two million of their own citizens in the same country, this, he said, would be true "living together."

15. He made it clear that he felt US was taking the lead in peace efforts but that these efforts were oriented toward Israel and not toward the Arab point of view. He kept reassuring me that he was not going to start a war but that he was not responsible for all groups and that he would intervene in any actual conflict begun. He stated that under present circumstances Jordanian troops, insofar as the Israeli problem was concerned, were under UAR command. This of course is applicable to other troops such as Iraqis and Algerians who were reporting for duty.

16. This I think summarizes the basic points of our conversation on which I will elaborate further on my return.

17. For your general information I spent three days in Beirut before going to Cairo. During this visit I saw Saudi Arabs, Kuwaitis and Iraqis, as well as Lebanese. They are people who are generally moderate and have a tendency to oppose Nasser. At this time they were all applauding Nasser's action, insisting on the closing of the Gulf of Aqaba and taking a position that the US was supporting a minority for political purposes. I am impressed more because of the quality of the people who made these assertions than the fact that they were made. Under the circumstances it would seem desirable that whatever international arrangements are thought proper it would be helpful if the initiative could be taken by some country other than US and that US be in a position of support of international efforts to secure peace rather than leadership which seems to be construed as favoring Israeli cause.

17 [*sic*]. During our conversation Nasser was relaxed, in sport clothes, and seemed confident both of his intelligence and of his military capability. We had no discussion re Soviets except his assertion that he was not and would not be Communist. I believe he would regard any effort to open the Straits of Tiran as hostile and any act of aggression, whether originating from Israel or resulting from actions in

Syria by the terrorist groups, would bring response. He stated that his target system was prepared and that this time he would be ready.

18. I am proceeding to send message to Cairo through US Embassy to Nasser which will result in Zakaria Mohieddin arriving in New York presumably Sunday or early in week. I will return New York Saturday afternoon and will be available to come to Washington Sunday or thereafter. I can be reached through embassy here today and tomorrow morning, if desired.

19. Upon rereading this text I want to make clear as I understand it UAR has military command over its own troops, the Jordanian troops as related to any Israeli problem, the troops committed by Iraq, Algeria or any country sending troops, but does not include command over Syrian troops. It is because of this latter situation which I think bothers Nasser as to whether or not the Syrians might undertake unilateral action designed to force a confrontation. It was because of his concern on this subject that he was asked if he would intervene even if the Syrians acted against UAR desires and the reply was affirmative.

DOCUMENT 10

U.S. Embassy Cairo telegram no. 8362 to Department of State, June 2, 1967
SecState for Battle from Yost. USUN for Goldberg.

1. There is unanimity among observers I have seen here that UARG at this point cannot and will not relax position on closure Tiran Straits except as result overwhelming application of military force. Opinion in other Arab countries seems practically unanimous in backing UAR on this issue.

2. While this may appear in US as "aggression," it is seen here as entirely legitimate restoration 1956 status quo which was upset by Israeli aggression. In light UAR "belligerency," moreover, legal case is at least open to doubt.

3. As consequence I have reluctantly come to conclusion that there is no rpt no prospect for success our present tactic of mobilizing maritime powers to reopen Straits, except by exercise military force which would be out of proportion to real US interests at stake and would have most damaging repercussions on US position throughout Arab world. If we pursue this tactic much further, I am afraid we may find ourselves in same dead end as British and French in 1956.

4. Proposed declaration by maritime powers would have no effect on UAR stand nor would show of naval strength in neighborhood, though latter would increase Arab agitation, reinforce Arab unity and provoke anti-US demonstrations. Actual use of sufficient military force could presumably open straits but force would have to be maintained there indefinitely and political consequences would be as indicated above.

5. While I realize very great importance Israel attaches to keeping Straits open, I cannot believe this is vital to Israel's existence, especially recalling that Straits were closed prior to 1957. Gain to Nasser's prestige resulting from this victory will be unfortunate and troublesome but post facto attempts by either Great Powers or Israel to reverse it are more likely to prolong than to curtail his currently resurrected leadership of Arab world.

6. I would have thought more productive tactic would be henceforth to concentrate on limiting damage, primarily by finding means acceptable to both parties of strengthening UNTSO machinery all along Israeli frontiers but particularly on

Israel-UAR line. If some action on Tiran necessary, complaint could be presented to ICJ and interim arrangements made to supply Israel with oil through other ports. I would presume Israel would expect and should receive renewed assurances of US support in case its existence or integrity is threatened.

7. If stability is to be preserved in area over long run, it will also be important that US endeavor within reasonable limits to maintain contact and some measure cooperation with UAR. Pressure tactics, such as fleet movements or blocking IMF action and bank credits, will have precisely contrary effect, throw UAR even more into Soviet arms, and make future aggressive action vis-à-vis Israel more likely.

8. There can be no assurance that Arab appetites, whetted by unexpected and intoxication show of unity, will not soon demand further satisfaction, despite Riad statement to me UAR has no such present intention. However, I am convinced we would have much better prospect obtaining world and perhaps even some Arab support against more obvious and brutal threat to Israeli security than closure Straits is generally conceived to be. Either overt or covert sanctions are at this time more likely to provoke than to discourage more aggressive Arab policy.

9. Believe I have felt pulse here as fully as may be feasible or useful in near future and that, unless Department wished me to undertake some negotiation, I might plan to return to Washington to report in two or three days. I should probably see Riad once more before leaving but Ambassador Nolte now has easy access to him and will be fully capable henceforth of carrying on.

DOCUMENT 11

U.S. Embassy Cairo telegram no. 8397 to Department of State, June 2, 1967

1. Following is text UAR Foreign Office "unofficial translation" of letter to President Johnson from President Gamal Abdul Nasser. With reference penultimate paragraph, was explicitly assured by Foreign Minister Riad that it was up to President Johnson to decide whether to send Vice President Humphrey here or invite Vice President Mohieddin to go to Washington, with no expression of UARG preference. While waiting for typing to be completed, enjoyed long pleasant conversation Foreign Minister Riad on non political matters. Will pouch original letter in Arabic and Foreign Office translation. Text follows:

2. Cairo, June 2, 1967. Dear President,

3. I welcome your initiative in writing to me on the current situation in the Arab homeland. For, however distant the point of agreement between us seems from the scope of our outlook at the present stage, I am convinced that any joint endeavor on our part to establish communication of thought, might at least contribute to dissipate part of the artificial clouds intended to depict the exercise of right as a sin and the right of defense as aggression.

4. It would be useful in the assessment of current events, to view them in their chronological and logical entity, to avoid misunderstanding and make a sound, reasonable, and fair evaluation of the facts we face.

5. Hence, I shall try to set forth a number of facts which I would term as preliminary:

6. First: It is essential that we go back to the few days which preceded the measures which the United Arab Republic took of late, and to recall the dangerously aggressive situation created by the Israeli authorities vis-à-vis the Syrian

Arab Republic, the hostile threats proclaimed by a number of Israeli leaders, and the accompanying mass troop concentrations on the Syrian border in preparation for an imminent aggression on Syria. It was only natural then, that the United Arab Republic should assume her responsibilities and take all measures necessary for defense and to deter the planned aggression against our countries.

7. Second: Defense measures taken by the United Arab Republic made it imperative that our armed forces move to their advanced positions on the border to be able to cope with developments and through their very presence foil Israel's premeditated invasion. Urged by our concern for the United Nations Emergency Forces, we found it imperative that they should withdraw: such has become our final position on the matter.

8. Third: Following the withdrawal of the UNEF, it was only logical that the United Arab Republic armed forces should occupy their positions, among which was the area of Sharm el Sheikh overlooking the Straits of Tiran. It was equally logical that we exercise our established sovereign rights on the Straits and on our territorial waters in the Gulf.

9. Here again, I wish to take you a few years back to the tripartite aggression on Egypt: we still recall with appreciation, the fair position adopted by your country with regard to that aggression.

10. Prior to the aggression, the United Arab Republic exercised its established legal rights with regard to Israeli shipping in the Straits and the Gulf. These rights are indisputable. Following the departure of the United Nations Emergency Forces and their replacement by our armed forces in the area, it was unthinkable that Israeli shipping or strategic materials destined for Israel be allowed passage. Our position thereon . . . indeed aims at removing the last vestige of the tripartite aggression, in consonance with the moral principle which rules that no aggressor be rewarded for his aggression.

11. In all the measures we have adopted in defense of our land and our rights, we have underlined two points:

12. First: That we shall defend ourselves against any aggression, with all our means and potentialities.

13. Second: That we shall continue to allow innocent passage of foreign shipping in our territorial waters.

14. These are facts relevant to the direct position proclaimed by the United Arab Republic, and which we feel afford no ground for some to create a climate of crisis or to launch that psychological campaign against us.

15. While this campaign takes on new dimensions and forms we notice complete and regrettable overlooking of a number of other facts which I wish to term as basic. These are the very facts which carry full weight on current events and will continue to have their bearing on the future until all appreciate them fully and assess their dimensions and roots. Here I shall refer to two facts:

16. First: The rights of the Arab people of Palestine. In our view, this is the most important fact that should be recognized. An aggressive armed force was able to oust that people from their country and reduce them to refugees on the borders of their homeland.

17. Today the forces of aggression impede the Arab people's established right of return and life in their homeland, despite the UN resolutions, the last of which was adopted last year.

18. The second fact is related to Israel's position toward the Armistice Agree-

ments: a position represented not merely by the constant violation of those agreements, but which has gone as far as to deny their presence and refuse to adhere to them. It has even gone as far as to occupy the Demilitarized Zones, oust the UN observers and insult the international organization and its flag.

19. Those are two basic facts which should be considered in the assessment of today's events and developments.

20. In your message you referred to two points:

21. First: You urge that we put the past aside and endeavor to rescue the Middle East or rather the whole human community through the avoidance of hostilities. Here, allow me to refer to the policy of the United Arab Republic which does not restrict herself to placing world peace as an objective, but goes beyond that and assumes a positive role on which I do not wish to elaborate lest I should border on the area of self-glorification. As for endeavors to avoid military operations, I have but to emphasize what I have already declared that the measures we have adopted were imposed by the forces of aggression and their conceit as well as by their belief that they have reached the stage where they could impose their aggressive policy. Yet, our forces have not initiated any aggressive act, but no doubt, we shall resist with all our potentialities any aggression launched against us or against any Arab state.

22. Second: Your observation that the conflicts of our time cannot be solved by the crossings of frontiers with arms and men. Here, I share your view. Yet, we have to see how this principle is applied to every case. If you are referring to the crossing of the demarcation lines by some individuals of the Palestinian people I would urge the importance of considering this aspect in the general perspective of the question of Palestine. Here also, I may ask how far any government is able to control the feelings of more than one million Palestinians who, for twenty years, the international community—whose responsibility herein is inescapable—has failed to secure their return to their homeland. The UN General Assembly merely confirms that right, at every session. The crossing of the demarcation lines by some Palestinian individual is, in point of fact merely a manifestation of anger by which those people are naturally possessed as they meet with the full denial of their rights by the international community, and by the powers which side with Israel and assist it materially and morally.

23. Whatever our attempts to divide the aspects of the problem, it is imperative in the end that we return to its origin and fundamentals, namely the right of Palestinian people to return to their homeland, and the responsibility of the international community in securing them the exercise of this right.

24. My letter may seem rather long in a way: yet, it was my wish to explain briefly some of the basic features of the situation we now face in the Arab region.

25. Finally, I wish to assure you that we would welcome listening to Mr. Hubert Humphrey, the United States Vice President, at any time he may choose to visit the UAR. We shall provide him with a picture of the situation as we conceive it amidst the fundamental events faced by the Arab nation today. I am ready to send Vice President Zakareya Mohieddin, to Washington immediately to meet with you and expound our viewpoint.

26. Please accept my regards and considerations.

27. (Sgd) (Gamal Abdul Nasser) President of the United Arab Republic.

—Nolte

DOCUMENT 12

U.S. Embassy Cairo telegram no. 8080 to Department of State, May 27, 1967
EUCOM for POLAD
Subject: Middle East sitrep
Ref: State 203788

1. Reftel notes reports that "tend to raise possibility for first time that some Arab leaders may be in process convincing themselves Arabs can beat Israel in armed conflict." As we reported week ago (Cairo 7760), Nasser is playing for keeps and thinks he can win. He appears sincerely to believe Egyptians can beat Israelis if we do not intervene and his estimate is shared by every official Egyptian we have talked to. It also seems to be shared by Arabs in general. Current state of Arab mind seems to be that of early 1948 rather 1956. In brief, Arab belief in victory is no tentative possibility, but a reality.

2. If Nasser's and Haikal's words are to be believed, Egyptians have been prepared for this moment for some time. In retrospect, it may have been as long ago as last summer, when they reportedly decided their fleet was able to operate without Soviet advisors and could be confident it would be able trouble Sixth Fleet should latter move to assist Israelis. Decision to move when opportunity presented itself probably made sometime after UARG decision last February to withdraw request for wheat and subsequent decision to give up trying cultivate USG following spate unfavorable congressional statements, particularly unfortunate report of Senator Clark. Over past ten years we have comforted ourselves with number myths regarding Egypt's relative indifference to Palestine problem as a factor in our relations and have proceeded on assumption Nasser wished keep issue in ice box. It now clear how much it has rankled and how important it has been to Nasser. He is ready to risk everything for it. He has bided his time and has planned well. His only area of miscalculation may be his estimate of Egyptian military capabilities vis-à-vis Israel, and even there we may be in for some surprises.

—Nolte

DOCUMENT 13

U.S. Embassy Cairo telegram no. 5030 to Department of State, March 4, 1967

1. I made farewell call which lasted one hour and ten minutes on President Nasser March 4. After exchange pleasantries during which he expressed regret my departure, I said I wished reflect on some of my final conclusions and impressions as I left this country where I had made many friends and in which I had had a very rewarding tour of duty.

2. I said I was more convinced than when I came of the rightness of US goals in the area. Seeking peace and stability as we do, we must attempt maintain as friendly relations as possible with as many countries as possible. This is not an easy course. In large measure changes in relations Arab countries to each other frequently resulted in suspicions re US motives and aims. For example, I mentioned sales arms Jordan stemming from UAC (United Arab Command) assess-

ment defense needs that country, an arrangement which Egyptians now appeared in some strange way view with suspicion. On Yemen, Saudis suspected we more tolerant Egyptian attitudes than of their own and Egyptians considered we supported Saudis. In truth we have no material interest in Yemen and wish only see peaceful resolution that problem, which is danger to relations between our friends the Saudis and our friends the Egyptians. In accordance his instructions, Hassan Sabry El Khouly and others his government have kept me fully informed re UAR efforts at various times resolve situation. I still hoped way could be found bring about peaceful resolution this difficult area problem. At various times Egyptians had indicated to me that if US wanted solution Yemen problem we should play more active role that direction. I wanted to ask him today whether on my return Washington to assume broader responsibilities for area relations I should urge my government offer join in one of several offers mediate or take initiative on our own in that direction.

3. President then launched into lengthy discussion Yemen, saying he had gone to Jidda to conclude agreement Feisal against advice his colleagues and had entered agreement "on my own responsibility." As he landed for Jidda meetings, he felt nervous and uncertain, but felt he must make effort resolve conflict. Since that time many actions had entered into situation, including Islamic pact, Aden problem and other difficulties. He could not at present be hopeful solution. Yemen operation not now costly to UAR although has been in past. UAR can remain indefinitely and will do so if necessary. He was always interested offers solution but not hopeful in view Feisal's arrangements Jordan and in view their determination to view his earlier efforts as sign weakness, which Jidda agreement had not in fact reflected.

4. I said I took it from his remarks that he would not oppose any efforts by US if we thought we could be helpful but he did not appear hold out much hope chance success any US efforts. He replied this was his attitude although he appeared pause and be somewhat reflective in his response.

5. Nasser then launched into thirty minute tirade of most emotional character yet displayed in my meetings with him. He said UAR proud, independent country with its own dignity. He had decided in thinking over my call on him to be very frank and he hoped I would not take offense at anything he said, but he must deal lucidly and frankly with issues. UAR would not respond US pressure. It did not want American wheat. During time we had provided wheat he had gone to bed each night disturbed that UAR dependent on US for food and had resented each item in American or world press reminding UAR that five out of each eight loaves of its bread were provided by US. UAR would not accept interference by other countries. It was not influenced by Russia and would not be. Whether he remained or not, attitudes UAR re its own independence would be consistent and those lieutenants he trained would take same position as he took. UAR had no designs other countries contrary our impression and our press but wanted, for example, Aden to be ruled by revolutionary forces and not British stooges. Re Israel, his views are well known. He hoped Arabs could return.

6. He then switched to IMF, asking why he should pay IMF 104 million dollar debt when it would not give him seventy million dollars to which he felt entitled. In meeting in that room a few days ago, when some of his colleagues voiced concern re UAR relations IMF, he had stated UAR must stand on own feet and if IMF and all Western interests refused do business with UAR, UAR would still

survive and make progress. UAR would have been better off if it had not in developing its economic plans based those plans upon continued supply wheat which had distorted development efforts by permitting broader program than justified. If any country attempted hurt UAR, UAR would respond and no doubt could do damage US and other countries.

7. I replied by asking his permission be as frank with him as he had been with me, saying I would not under any circumstances wish offend him in my last meeting but I must answer as frankly as he had on statements he had made.

8. The US had entered into food arrangement, which admittedly had become issue of its own between us, in hope providing help which would accelerate development and be of help to Egyptian people. Based on his speeches, it appeared he had given up hope continuing these arrangements before I had and before Executive Branch had completed deliberations on matter. During recent days, for example, consultations had been under way with congressional leaders, that consultation had not been helped by his own statements and those of Heikal with respect our relations and motives. I mentioned specifically latest Heikal article.

9. He interrupted, saying he had given up hope of wheat several months ago and reminded me that he had never before brought up wheat in conversation with me and that I had always raised matter first. He could not approve efforts his ambassador Washington to obtain wheat in manner that appeared be begging on knees.

10. I went on to say US government and I personally respected need for UAR be independent, dignified country and we wanted see it develop viable economy and we still hoped for success in those goals and in his achievements and aims for his people.

11. He referred to fact that he owned several newspapers in Beirut and that Saudis and Jordanians also had newspaper spokesman in area. Indicated he had been restrained in his response many of their attacks on UAR but could only accept so much and had had to respond to them.

12. I said that I wished remind him as I had in past that he was world figure and that each utterance coming from him was read and interpreted throughout world and that his remarks more important than newspaper stories one kind or another. While this great compliment to his influence in world, it was also responsibility to bear as I well recognized. I said there was no doubt ability many countries hurt each other, including ourselves, but we must find way to build lasting friendship which I was convinced both sides really wanted. I hoped he could find satisfactory relationships IMF and with West. He replied, "If we cannot, we will go on with other countries."

13. In closing I repeated that US policy in area had not changed and that we sought continued friendship UAR and that while I had not succeeded in removing suspicions and doubts and problems from agenda, I had every intention in new assignment continue my efforts and I hoped he would view future as long time indeed in which we would try overcome various problems between us in relations marked by such ups and downs.

14. Nasser was more emotional than I have ever seen him and at moments developed glaze over eyes typical of that we have seen when he makes speeches. He was at all times extremely cordial to me, very friendly and warm and at various moments of tirade against US said not to take it personally. In view his

attitudes re US mediation Yemen, I cannot be hopeful. Suggest we wait few days, however, to see whether idea picked up by lower level officials.

—Battle

DOCUMENT 14

Department of State telegram 207956, memo from Dean Rusk to US Ambassadors in Arab capitals, June 3, 1967.

EYES ONLY FOR AMBASSADOR FROM SECRETARY.

I wish to express my personal appreciation to our Ambassadors in Arab Capitals for their full and timely reporting and for frank expressions of views on the present situation in the Near East. The considerations which you have advanced are being taken fully into account in a situation which is as complex and as dangerous as any we have faced. I should like to put before you some additional considerations and ask you to put your minds to possible solutions which can prevent war.

1. You should not assume that the United States can order Israel not to fight for what it considers to be its most vital interests. We have used the utmost restraint and, thus far, have been able to hold Israel back. But the "Holy War" psychology of the Arab world is matched by an apocalyptic psychology within Israel. Israel may make a decision that it must resort to force to protect its vital interests. In dealing with the issues involved, therefore, we must keep in mind the necessity for finding a solution with which Israel can be restrained.

2. Each side appears to look with relative equanimity upon the prospect of major hostilities and each side apparently is confident of success. Which estimate is correct cannot be fully known unless tested by the event but someone is making a major miscalculation. It does not help that Israel believes that time is working against them because of the continuing Arab build-up and deployment of forces. If anything could be done in the direction of reversing the mobilization on both sides, this would, of course, be a great advantage.

3. You should bear in mind the background of the application of the statement of four American Presidents that (to quote from President Johnson's statement of May 23) "The United States is firmly committed to the support of the political independence and territorial integrity of all the nations of that area." You will recall the actions taken by the Eisenhower Administration when Egypt was attacked by Israel, Britain and France and when Lebanon was seriously threatened by Syria. You will recall our steady and substantial support to Jordan to reinforce its position over and against Egypt. You will recall that President Kennedy sent a squadron of U.S. fighters to Saudi Arabia as a demonstration of support when Saudi Arabia was being threatened by Egypt. Most of you may know that we used a major diplomatic effort in Cairo to cool off subversive and propaganda assaults upon Libya. We supported Algeria's demand for independence and have tried to steady the nerves of Tunisia and Morocco when they felt threatened by Algeria. When Israel has been attacked by terrorist groups we have supported Israel; when Israel resorted to disproportionate actions of retaliation against Samu in Jordan, we publicly and privately censored Israel in the strongest terms. I sug-

gest we have a strong case for the idea that we have been even-handed with respect to the political independence and territorial integrity of Near Eastern countries.

A major issue for us in this present crisis involves the commitments we made at the time of the wind-up of the Suez affair. At that time we were acting on behalf of Egypt. As a part of the settlement which obtained the withdrawal of Israeli forces from the Sinai, including Sharm el Sheikh, we assured Israel that we would support an international right of passage through the Strait of Tiran. We endorsed Israel's statement in the General Assembly (in fact it was drafted in consultation with Secretary Dulles) that Israel would have the right under Article 51 of the Charter to protect its flagships transiting that Strait if fired upon. Egypt was aware of these positions and, although it did not endorse them at the time, it was the beneficiary of the arrangements made.

4. The central principle of international law involved in the Strait of Tiran was encompassed in the Conventions on the law of the sea of 1958. This principle is of vital importance to us all over the world where there are many such narrow passages connecting bodies of international waters. In any event, the United States has given some pledges on the matter and we must give the most sober attention to all the implications of such pledges and any failure on our part to insist upon them.

5. There may be some flexibility in what Cairo would be willing to do before major hostilities. The Strait of Tiran is a key issue. The free passage of crude oil is a major part of that issue. We shall not know details until further explorations of the problem with Cairo or intermediaries. We cannot abandon, in principle, the right of Israeli flagships to transit the Strait. There might be some possibility of a breathing space if in fact passage were permitted for genuinely peaceful traffic, including crude oil. This is not a proposal on our side but an indication of a possible de facto standstill pending further diplomatic effort.

6. I have presented these considerations in order to enlist the best thought of our Ambassadors in Arab Capitals as to profitable approaches to the problem. It will do no good to ask Israel simply to accept the present status quo in the Strait because Israel will fight and we could not restrain her. We cannot throw up our hands and say that, in that event, let them fight while we try to remain neutral. I should be glad to have any further suggestions any of you might have on this situation.

Notes

1. THE SOVIET WARNING

1. Quoted in Ramses Nassif, *U Thant in New York* (London, 1986), p. 75.

2. In *Embassies in Crisis* (Englewood Cliffs, N.J., 1968), p. 1, however, Michael Bar Zohar claims that "early in the evening of May 12, 1967, the highly sensitive receiving apparatus of an information service somewhere in Western Europe picked up a coded message. . . . It was a report from the Soviet embassy in Cairo, signed by Ambassador Dimitri Podyedyeev [*sic*] and intended for the Ministry of Foreign Affairs in Moscow. . . . When first read, the telegram seemed merely another daily report . . . [but] the next to the last sentence read: 'Today we passed on to the Egyptian authorities information concerning the massing of Israeli troops on the northern frontier for a surprise attack on Syria. We have advised the UAR government to take the necessary steps.' " A footnote says the text of the message was obtained by an American whom Bar Zohar had interviewed in New York on November 8, 1967, and asks the reader to consult the bibliography at the back of the book. The bibliography lists five Americans he may have seen in New York: Maxwell Finger of the U.S. delegation to the United Nations; Roderick MacLeish of Westinghouse Broadcasting Company; Richard H. Nolte, former U.S. ambassador-designate to Egypt; William Stricker of the Foreign Correspondents Center; and Leon Volkov of *Newsweek*. Of these five men, only Finger might have been in a position to see a message of the sort described, had it been intercepted. But Finger has no recollection of meeting Bar Zohar or of ever seeing such a message. Queries to a number of persons who would have been in a position to know about such things at the time make me doubt whether such a message was ever intercepted by anyone. On June 14, 1989, I interviewed Bar Zohar, now a member of the Israeli Knesset, and asked him about his source. He said he could not remember and had not seen the report; it had been read to him. Anything is possible, and until we see the official record we cannot be sure that there has not been some confusion about the date in Cairo, but as of now I assume that the May 13 date (not May 12) is correct.

3. Foreign Broadcast Information Service (FBIS) Daily Report, May 25, 1967, p. B-2.

4. Ghorbal says he was not present at this meeting. He was preoccupied with administrative arrangements for his imminent departure for Washington, where he was to be minister counselor at the Egyptian Embassy (al-Feki was to be ambassador), and had not gone to the office for some days. (Author's conversation with Ghorbal, April 24, 1990.)

5. Author's Conversation with al-Feki, Alexandria, June 5, 1989.

6. Anwar al-Sadat, *In Search of Identity* (New York, 1977), pp. 171–72.

7. Nasser was officially designated as commander-in-chief and 'Amr as his deputy, but in fact 'Amr had absolute control over military affairs and was commander in all but name.

8. Mohamed Heikal, *1967—Al-Infijar* (Cairo, 1990), p. 447.

9. Ibid., pp. 444–45.

10. Communication to the author of April 8, 1990, from Salah Bassiouny and author's conversation with him on June 4, 1992. Letter of May 11, 1991, from Ashraf Ghorbal.

11. Heikal, *Al-Infijar*, p. 445. The July 1966 Cairo diplomatic list of the Egyptian Foreign Ministry shows four "counselors" whose functions are not otherwise

identified. None is named Sergei. They are Petr Cheine, Valentin Velikoseltsev, Vladislav Jassenev, and Vadim Sinelnikov. The only Sergei is Sergei Tarassenko, the last and therefore most junior person on the list with the rank of attaché, which could mean anything. The Sergei in question could have been Tarrasenko or any one or none of the above, assuming Heikal got the name right.

12. The officials in question were Georgiy Kornienko, former deputy foreign minister, and Vitaly Naumkin of the Oriental Studies Institute. In a conference on the 25th anniversary of the June War convened at the Center for the Study of Foreign Affairs at the Department of State's Foreign Service Institute, June 3–5, 1992, they said that not only had what seems to have been a preliminary search of the Foreign Ministry archives turned up no trace of an instruction to Pojidaev to make such a demarche, but there was also no record of his having reported doing so. According to them, his first recorded discussion of the matter with the Egyptians was on May 16. As for Semyenov informing Sadat in Moscow, they said Semyenov was notorious for scanning intelligence reports before such meetings and then retailing them as the latest gossip. (This behavior pattern is not unknown among senior U.S. officials.)

By all accounts, Pojidaev was not the sort of bureaucrat who would do something like this on his own, and Kornienko and Naumkin said there was no Soviet "back channel" used to instruct ambassadors without the knowledge of the foreign ministry. On the other hand, my Egyptian sources are categoric that Pojidaev did deliver the warning as described in this text. Further research in the Soviet archives may solve the puzzle.

13. There are so many tales about these invitations that it is hard to keep them straight. I have found references to their being extended and refused on October 12, 1966, in April 1967, and at least three times in May 1967—May 11, 12, and 27. Pending a thorough look at the official Israeli and Soviet records, I am taking it on faith that these references are reliable. The public record is also uninformative about precisely how Israel (and the rest of the world) learned of the Soviet report in the absence of an Egyptian or Syrian complaint to the United Nations. I have so far been unable to find a reference to this aspect of the case in the telegrams of the U.S. Department of State.

14. Author's conversation with Samir Mutawi, Amman, June 13, 1989.

15. General Muhammad Fawzi, *Harb al-Thalath Sanawat* (Heliopolis, 1980), p. 71.

16. Author's conversation with al-Feki, June 5, 1989.

17. Author's conversation with Blasch, January 2, 1990.

18. Heikal, *Al-Infijar,* p. 42.

19. Avigdor Dagan, *Moscow and Jerusalem* (London, 1970), p. 203.

20. Ibid., p. 174.

21. Ibid., p. 187.

22. Moshe Gilboa, *The USSR and Arab Belligerency* (in Hebrew), as quoted in Benjamin Geist, "The Six Day War" (Ph.D. dissertation, Hebrew University, 1974), p. 196 n. 15.

23. Author's conversation with Bassiouny, Cairo, June 4, 1983, and communication of April 8, 1990; author's conversation with al-Feki, June 5, 1989. See also al-Feki's article in *Akhbar al-Yawm* (Cairo), April 28, 1979.

24. Mahmoud Riad, *Amrika wa al-Arab* (Cairo, 1986), p. 42. Author's conversation with Mrs. Levy Eshkol, Jerusalem, June 18, 1989.

25. The Egyptians said repeatedly that the report was "confirmed" (*mu'akkada*), but according to General Abdul Muhsin Kamil Murtagi, who was appointed commander of the ground forces on the Sinai front at the beginning of the crisis, all the intelligence reports that seemed to confirm the Soviet allegation originated with a single source—the Soviet military attaché in Beirut; see Murtagi, *Al-Fariq*

Murtagi Yarwa al-Haqaʾiq (Cairo, 1976), pp. 53–55. He cites no source, and while his claim is plausible, it is not proved.

26. Author's conversation with al-Feki, June 5, 1989.

27. Abba Eban, *An Autobiography* (Jerusalem, 1977), p. 330.

28. Author's conversation with General Aharon Yaariv, Tel Aviv, June 16, 1989.

29. Under the armistice agreements negotiated between Israel and its Arab neighbors and signed on Rhodes in 1949, four mixed armistice commissions (MACs) were set up to monitor and report on border incidents and other matters affecting the armistice. Israel and the Arab state in question appointed delegates to the appropriate MAC, and they met under the chairmanship of an officer from outside the area who was appointed by the United Nations. Military officers from various contributing states, including the United States, Canada, France, and Belgium, were assigned to the MACs as observers whose principal task was to investigate and report on violations of the armistice. The MACs were under the direction of the United Nations Truce Supervision Organization (UNTSO), the successor to the U.N. Truce Commission established during the fighting in 1948. It was commanded by a chief observer, who was a Norwegian major general, Odd Bull, in 1967. The Israelis had boycotted the Egypt-Israel MAC since 1956, but the other three were still functioning in 1967, although both the Syrian and the Jordanian MACs had done so intermittently since 1956. U.N. observers on the Israel-Syrian MAC were living on both sides of the border in May 1967 and were in a good position to monitor troop movements in northern Israel.

30. Author's personal recollection. Some feeling for the atmosphere in Cairo at the time is given by the U.S. embassy telegrams which have been released under the Freedom of Information Act: 7975 of May 25, 8007 of May 26, and 8218 and 8219 of May 30.

31. Author's conversation with al-Feki, June 5, 1989.

32. The assurances were given in a meeting with al-Feki on May 16. Nes told him on instructions that the United States had excellent sources of information in Israel and there were no unusual troop movements or concentrations. Al-Feki said the Egyptians had their own sources, but he relayed Nes's report to Nasser's office, which classified it as "the assurance of an Israeli attack," according to Winston Burdett, *Encounter with the Middle East* (New York, 1969), pp. 212–13. I have recovered the U.S. Department of State's instruction to Nes (State 194188 of May 15) but not Nes's report of the conversation.

33. Indar Jit Rikhye, *The Sinai Blunder* (New Delhi, 1978), p. 73.

34. Author's conversation with Hare, October 16, 1989. Vol. 16 of *Foreign Relations of the United States* dealing with the Suez crisis (1955–57) includes the text of a telegram from Hare in Cairo dated October 29, 1956, on the eve of the Israeli-British-French attack on Egypt. Hare, who called on Nasser to deliver an October 28 statement by President Eisenhower expressing concern about "disturbing reports that Israel was making a heavy mobilization of its armed forces," reported that "Nasser was friendly and relaxed and said [he was] unable to understand what all the turmoil was about." Hare then informed him that the United States had decided to evacuate nonessential Americans from Egypt. Nasser commented that he was still at a loss to understand why such action should be felt necessary. This account would seem to refute the reported insinuation by Nasser and Riad in 1967 that Hare had misled the Egyptians about Israeli intentions. Rather, it sounds as though he had been unable to wake the sleeping giant.

35. Author's conversation with Mahmoud Riad, Cairo, June 3, 1989.

36. Mahmoud Riad, *The Struggle for Peace in the Middle East* (New York, 1981), p. 17.

37. Ernest Dawn, "The Egyptian Remilitarisation of Sinai," *Contemporary History*, July 1968, p. 210.

38. In *Green March, Black September,* John Cooley says he was not present but heard a tape recording of the briefing and it was Yaariv who spoke. On p. 160 he reproduces extracts of the remarks. Knowledgeable Israelis have confirmed that it was Yaariv.

39. Author's conversation with Mustafa Abdul Aziz, Cairo, June 5, 1989.

40. Michael Brecher, *Decisions in Crisis* (London, 1974), p. 36.

41. For an early suggestion of this hypothesis, see Michael Howard and Robert Hunter, "Israel and the Arab World: The Crisis of 1967" (Adelphi Paper no. 41, London, 1967), pp. 15–16.

42. William Quandt has called to my attention a declassified CIA report in the Lyndon Baines Johnson Library from June 1967 that offers a fourth hypothesis (see appendix for text). It quotes an unidentified "medium-level Soviet official" as saying the Soviet Union "had wanted to create another trouble spot for the United States in addition to that already existing in Vietnam. The Soviet aim was to create a situation in which the US would become seriously involved, economically, politically and possibly even militarily and in which the US would suffer serious political reverses as a result of its siding against the Arabs." This hypothesis, too, would explain everything. But we cannot evaluate the report without knowing the identity of the source and the reliability of the person who reported it, which we are unlikely ever to learn. In the absence of such information or of confirmation from other sources, I am reluctant to classify this report as evidence worth considering. I reproduce it in the appendix for the record.

43. Author's conversation with Moshe Zak of *Maariv,* Jerusalem, June 17, 1989.

44. Author's conversation with General Yaariv, June 16, 1989.

2. MOSCOW'S EXPLANATIONS

1. William Quandt in *Decade of Decisions* (Berkeley, 1977) and Nadav Safran in *From War to War* (New York, 1969) say that Nasser called for the withdrawal of UNEF in 1960, but that was not the case. General Rikhye informed me that on two occasions, in late 1959 and in 1960, Egypt moved troops into the border area in response to what it perceived as provocative acts by Israel. On both occasions it agreed to move the troops back as soon as things quieted down. There was no request for UNEF to redeploy. (Author's conversation with Rikhye, April 29, 1991).

2. See, for instance, an article from *Le Nouvel Observateur* republished in *Atlas* (August 1967, pp. 17–20), and Roderick MacLeish, *The Sun Stood Still* (New York, 1967), p. 26. The *Nouvel Observateur* piece is attributed to a high Soviet official, who said, "It was with our approval that Nasser massed his troops on the Sinai frontier to demonstrate to the Israelis that if they launched an offensive against Syria, that country would not fight alone." That approval was probably post hoc, judging by Egyptian accounts and my findings in Moscow.

3. Igor Beliaev of *Literaturnaya Gazeta,* for example, recalls that he went to Algiers on May 22 with a delegation headed by Rotislav Ulyanovsky of the Central Committee, who had been completely briefed by the intelligence people before departure from Moscow and had made no mention of the possibility of war. Beliaev himself had been incredulous when he learned on June 5 that war had begun.

4. *American Foreign Policy, Current Documents,* Department of State, 1967, pp. 493–94.

5. FBIS Daily Report, May 31, 1967, p. B-8.

3. THE EGYPTIAN REACTION

1. The UNEF observation post was actually at Ras al-Nasrani. Sharm al-Shaykh was the base camp location.

2. The U.S. commitment regarding navigation in the Gulf of Aqaba was contained in five paragraphs of an aide-mémoire from Secretary of State Dulles to Israeli Ambassador Eban of February 11, 1957. The key paragraphs read:

> With respect to the Gulf of Aqaba and access thereto—the United States believes that the Gulf comprehends international waters and that no nation has the right to prevent free and innocent passage in the Gulf and through the Straits giving access thereto. We have in mind not only commercial usage, but the passage of pilgrims on religious missions which should be fully respected.
>
> In the absence of some overriding decision to the contrary, as by the International Court of Justice, the United States, on behalf of vessels of United States registry, is prepared to exercise the right of free and innocent passage and to join with others to secure general recognition of this right. (*Documents on the Middle East*, American Enterprise Institute, 1969, pp. 180–82)

3. U.N. Document S/7880, May 11, 1967.

4. Nasser mentioned this Syrian warning publicly on several occasions, and several former Egyptian officials who were in a position to know at the time have confirmed it to me. I have sought confirmation from Syrian authorities with no results to date. It is not clear why, if Syria gave the warning in the first place, it later denied the existence of the troop concentrations, if it did. And why was Syria not in a state of alert when General Fawzi visited on May 14? Something is wrong with one or both of these stories.

5. Eric Rouleau et al., *Israel et les arabes: Le 3ᵉ combat* (Paris, 1967), p. 54.

6. Author's conversation with the CIA's former Beirut station chief, December 5, 1989.

7. Rikhye, *Sinai Blunder*, p. 159.

8. Ibid., pp. 13 and 159.

9. This version is from p. 53 of Murtagi's book. On p. 49 he says that the previous evening Sadiq had reported that an estimated fifteen Israeli infantry and parachute brigades were on the border and were expected to launch an attack between May 15 and 22.

10. Fawzi, *Harb al-Thalath Sanawat*, pp. 69–70.

11. Rikhye, *Sinai Blunder*, p. 159.

12. Rikhye says (p. 73) that this conversation took place with Riad, not al-Feki, and on May 15, not May 16. The telegram of instruction (State no. 194188; see appendix, document 2) was not sent until the fifteenth, however, and Nes would not have had it before the morning of the sixteenth, which is when he called on al-Feki, according to the Cairo press.

13. Brian Urquhart, *A Life in Peace and War* (New York, 1987), p. 20.

14. U.N. General Assembly Document A/6669, May 18, 1967, p. 6.

15. These details are taken largely from Thant's report to the General Assembly (ibid).

16. UNEF's total strength was about 3,400. It included roughly 1,000 Indians, 800 Canadians, 600 Yugoslavs, 500 Swedes, 400 Brazilians, 72 Norwegians, and 3 Danes.

17. *Al-Ahram*, February 26, 1968, p. 1.

18. Dagan, *Moscow and Jerusalem*, pp. 211–12.

19. FBIS Daily Report, May 23, 1967, pp. B-2–B-3.

20. *American Foreign Policy, Current Documents*, Department of State, 1967, p. 494. Riad, in *Amrika wa al-Arab* (p. 40), gives an account of the messages delivered by Nolte which seems to confuse Johnson's personal message of May 22 with his public statement of May 23.

21. Nassif, *U Thant in New York*, p. 89.

22. Rikhye, *Sinai Blunder*, pp. 63–79.

23. Ibid., p. 72.

24. There are various reports of this conversation. Those by Quandt in *Decade of Decisions* (pp. 52–54) and Eban in *An Autobiography* (pp. 354–59) are used here.

25. General Murtagi, in *Yarwa al-Haqaʾiq* (p. 81), says that on May 25 ʿAmr had issued an order for an air strike, code-named Asad (Lion), at first light on the morning of May 27. The order was canceled before it could be executed. General Fawzi, in his memoirs (p. 124), says the strike was canceled on May 25 after a half-hour closed meeting between Nasser and ʿAmr. Heikal, in *Al-Infijar* (pp. 573–77), says the code name was Fajr (Dawn) and that the target was to be Eilat. According to him, Nasser learned of it in a meeting of the High Command on May 26 but waited until May 27 to make ʿAmr cancel it. The implication of his chronology is that the strike was scheduled for May 28. He seems to be a day off, because his chronology does not track with the events. See n. 26.

26. Riad, *Amrika wa al-Arab*, p. 42, and Heikal, *Al-Infijar*, pp. 573–77. Heikal reports that Nasser took the message from Kosygin and the Rostow-Kamel conversation as indicating that Israel had learned of operation Fajr and issued orders immediately to tighten security. Heikal seems to think the message from Ambassador Kamel was received on May 27, but it should have been received on the twenty-sixth, assuming he sent it immediately after seeing Rostow.

27. Dagan, *Moscow and Jerusalem*, pp. 216–17.

28. For example, the account on p. 312 of Safran's *From War to War*.

29. Riad, *Struggle for Peace*, pp. 22–23.

30. Ibid., pp. 19–20.

31. FBIS Daily Report, May 31, 1967, p. B-7.

32. Ibid., p. B-13.

33. Riad, *Struggle for Peace*, p. 23.

34. Mohamed Hassaneih Heikal, *The Sphinx and the Commissar* (New York, 1978), p. 177.

35. For details, see Gideon Rafael, *Destination Peace* (New York, 1981), pp. 147–48. The texts of the two messages are different, but in each U Thant is calling for a two-week moratorium—for the Egyptians on imposition of their blockade and for the Israelis on trying to send a ship through the strait. Nasser evidently was not prepared to accept any limitation on immediate blockading of cargo bound for Israel as well as of Israeli ships.

36. *Middle East Journal*, 1967, p. 390.

37. Details from Riad, *Amrika wa al-Arab*, p. 42, and Anderson's telegram reporting his meeting with Nasser, sent from Lisbon on his way home (Lisbon 1517, June 2). I have also drawn on the account in the "Administrative History" of the crisis at the LBJ Library in Austin, Tex. There is a conflict in the various accounts as to whether Anderson saw Nasser on May 31 or June 1. Anderson does not give the date of the meeting in his telegram, ignoring one of the first rules of diplomatic drafting.

38. Author's conversation with Lucius Battle, October 7, 1989. Battle said his first choice had been David Rockefeller.

39. Riad, *Amrika wa al-Arab*, p. 42.

40. Dagan, *Moscow and Jerusalem*, p. 223.

41. Sadat, *In Search of Identity*, p. 174.

42. Dagan, *Moscow and Jerusalem*, p. 224.

4. FROM DETERRENCE TO DISASTER

1. Author's conversation with Muhiedden, June 3, 1989.

2. Rikhye, *Sinai Blunder*, p. 159.

3. Heikal, *Al-Infijar*, pp. 447–54.
4. Author's conversation with Muheiddin, June 3, 1989.
5. Rikhye, *Sinai Blunder*, p. 72.
6. Heikal, *Al-Infijar*, p. 458.
7. Rikhye, *Sinai Blunder*, p. 19.
8. Ibid., p. 25.
9. Heikal, *Al-Infijar*, pp. 468–69.
10. Secretary General's Report of May 18, 1967.
11. David Kimche and D. Bawley, *The Sandstorm* (London, 1968), pp. 95–97.
12. Author's conversation with Muheiddin, June 3, 1989.
13. *Al-Ahram*, February 26, 1968, p. 1.
14. Rikhye, *Sinai Blunder*, p. 14.
15. Al-Fariq Murtagi, *Yarwa al-Haqaʾiq*, pp. 65–68.
16. Fawzi, *Harb al-Thalath Sanawat*, pp. 76–82.
17. Sadat, *In Search of Identity*, p. 176.
18. Riad, *Amrika wa al-Arab*, p. 38.
19. Abdallah Imam, *Nasir wa ʾAmr* (Cairo, 1985), p. 155.
20. Riad, *Amrika wa al-Arab*, p. 37.
21. Ibid., pp. 38–39.
22. *Al-Hawadith*, September 2, 1977, p. 20.
23. Fawzi, *Harb al-Thalath Sanawat*, pp. 151–52.
24. Author's conversation with Abdul Majid Farid, October 3, 1990.
25. Ibid.
26. Fawzi, *Harb al-Thalath Sanawat*, p. 69.
27. Ibid., p. 73.
28. Rikhye *Sinai Blunder*, p. 21.
29. Arthor's conversation with Battle, October 7, 1989. The text of Battle's telegram (Cairo 5030) reporting his farewell conversation with Nasser is given in the appendix, document 13. It does not contain Battle's comments on what Nasser might do. Battle believes they were in his final telegram from Cairo, the text of which has not yet been released to me.
30. FBIS Daily Report, May 23, 1967, p. B-2.
31. Ibid., May 31, 1967, p. B-11.
32. Walter Laqueur, *The Israel-Arab Reader* (London, 1969), pp. 175–76.
33. Abd al-Fattah Abu Fadl, *Kunt Naʾiban li-Raʾis al-Mukhabarat* (Cairo, 1986), pp. 278–79.
34. Fawzi, *Harb al-Thalath Sanawat*, p. 72.
35. Murtagi, *Yarwa al-Haqaʾiq*, p. 64.
36. Dennis Walters, *Not Always With the Pack* (London, 1989), p. 179.
37. Anthony Nutting, *Nasser* (New York, 1972), p. 398.

5. THE AMERICAN ROLE

1. Ironically, William Lakeland, the original U.S. contact with Nasser, was given responsibility for this study. It was he who reminded me of it.
2. Nasser was quite cynical about the Yemen revolution. He once told Ambassador Battle, "That was no revolution. That was a plot!"
3. Personal recollection.
4. *Documents on the Middle East*, ed. Ralph H. Magnus (American Enterprise Institute, 1969), pp. 104–6.
5. *Middle East Record*, 1967, p. 51.
6. *Middle East Record*, 1967, p. 51.
7. Author's conversation with Battle, February 21, 1990. Battle's recollection of this exchange accords with that given in Cairo's 5030, (see appendix, document 13).

8. *Middle East Record,* 1967, p. 51.

9. As noted earlier, Riad has confused Johnson's address to the nation of May 23 with his May 22 letter to Nasser. Johnson made no private commitments to Nasser in this period, although Robert Anderson may have told Nasser that the United States was trying to restrain Israel. This statement does not appear in Anderson's telegram, however.

10. This statement seems to have been made by White House spokesman George Christian, not Rusk. See *American Foreign Policy,* 1967, Department of State, 1969, p. 505.

11. Riad, *Amrika wa al-Arab,* pp. 40–42.

12. Author's conversation with Richard Helms, October 11, 1989.

13. In his memoirs, *As I Saw It* (New York, 1990), p. 388, Rusk comments:

> For twenty years, since the creation of Israel, the United States had tried to persuade the Arabs that they needn't fear Israeli territorial expansion. Throughout the sixties the Arabs talked continuously about their fear of Israeli expansion. With the full knowledge of successive governments in Israel, we did our utmost to persuade the Arabs their anxieties were illusory.
>
> And then following the Six-Day War, Israel decided to keep the Golan Heights, the West Bank, the Gaza Strip, and the Sinai, despite the fact that Israeli Prime Minister Levi Eshkol on the first day of the war went on Israeli radio and said that Israel had no territorial ambitions. Later in the summer I reminded Abba Eban of this, and he simply shrugged his shoulders and said, "We've changed our minds." With that remark, a contentious and ever bitter point with the Americans, he turned the United States into a twenty-year liar.

14. "Administrative History," Arab-Israel Conflict, LBJ Library, p. 31.

15. Ibid., pp. 77–78.

16. Lyndon Johnson, *The Vantage Point* (New York, 1971), p. 292.

17. USUN (U.S. delegation to the United Nations) telegram 5404 of May 22, 1967.

18. *Documents on the Middle East,* ed. Magnus, pp. 163–64.

19. *Al-Ahram,* May 26, 1967.

20. Brecher, *Decisions in Crisis,* pp. 146–47.

21. Ibid., p. 164.

22. Author's conversation with Muhieddin, June 3, 1989. Muhieddin said he was to explain Egypt's position and make it clear that it did not want war. He was not optimistic about his chances, because the war machinery, already in motion, was impossible to stop at that point.

23. Quandt, *Decade of Decisions,* p. 54.

24. Author's conversation with Riad, June 3, 1989.

25. Johnson, *Vantage Point,* p. 293.

26. See, for instance, Eban's *Autobiography,* p. 354.

27. Author's conversation with Battle, October 7, 1989.

28. Author's conversation with Saunders, December 4, 1989.

29. Author's conversation with Helms, October 11, 1989.

30. Brecher, *Decisions in Crisis,* p. 107.

31. Ibid., pp. 113–14.

32. Ibid., p. 115.

33. Ibid., p. 120.

34. Ibid., p. 133.

35. Ibid., p. 137.

36. Eban, *Autobiography,* p. 359.

37. Brecher, *Decisions in Crisis,* p. 146.

38. Ibid.
39. Ibid., p. 37.
40. Ibid., p. 164.
41. Ibid.
42. "Administrative History," Arab-Israeli Conflict, LBJ Library, p. 97. Donald Bergus, who was then the officer in charge of UAR affairs in the Department of state, recalls that when Rusk told Ambassador Harman of the planned Muhieddin visit, Harman expressed surprise and great interest, and said he would not entrust this important development to a telegram but would carry it personally to Jerusalem. After Harman's departure Rusk said that perhaps he should not have told him about Muhieddin's travel plans. Later Rusk was said to have mused aloud that perhaps this was the spark that touched off the Israeli attack. Bergus comments that that certainly seemed plausible to him. (Bergus letter of April 4, 1991).
43. Eban, *Autobiography*, pp. 384–86.
44. Andrew and Leslie Cockburn, *Dangerous Liaison: The Inside Story of the U.S.-Israeli Covert Relationship* (New York: Harper Collins, 1991).
45. Amit, in the conference on the June War at the Center for the Study of Foreign Affairs, denied categorically that he had received a light of any color from anyone in Washington. He said that he had reported an "impression" after talking to twenty or thirty people in the course of a day and a half.

6. WAR AND NONWAR

1. David A. Korn, *Stalemate: The War of Attrition and Great Power Diplomacy in the Middle East, 1967–1970* (Boulder, Colo., 1992), pp. 208 and 275.
2. Fawzi, *Harb al-Thalath Sanawat*, pp. 161–70.
3. Mohamed Heikal, *The Road to Ramadan* (London, 1975), pp. 43–44.
4. Egypt had broken relations with the United States on June 6, 1967, alleging U.S. participation in Israel's attack the day before. Relations were not resumed until after the October War of 1973. In the interim, diplomatic contacts were maintained through "interests sections," which were legally part of a protecting power's diplomatic mission but were de facto independent of them. The U.S. Interests Section in Cairo was under the protection of the Spanish Embassy, while the Egyptian Interests Section in Washington was under the protection of the Indian Embassy.
5. FBIS Daily Report, March 6, 1968, p. G-7.
6. These details are from Heikal's *Road to Ramadan*.
7. Yitzhak Rabin, *The Rabin Memoirs* (Boston, 1979), pp. 138–39.
8. Laurence Whetten, *The Canal War: Four-Power Conflict in the Middle East* (Cambridge, Mass., 1974), pp. 68–69.
9. Ibid.
10. Rabin, *Memoirs*, pp. 141–42.
11. Ibid., p. 142.
12. Ibid., p. 143.
13. Yaacov Bar-Siman-Tov, *The Israeli-Egyptian War of Attrition 1969–1970* (New York, 1980), p. 97.
14. Ibid., pp. 100–101.
15. For a more detailed discussion of the two- and four-power talks and the Rogers Plan, see David A. Korn, "US-Soviet Negotiations of 1969 and the Rogers Plan," *Middle East Journal* (Winter 1990).
16. Rabin, *Memoirs*, pp. 151–52.
17. Ibid., p., 157.
18. Ibid., p. 165.

19. Bar-Siman-Tov, *Israeli-Egyptian War of Attrition*, p. 118.

20. A *Maariv* reporter disclosed this to a U.S. Embassy officer in Tel Aviv at the time, and Ze'ev Schiff of *Haaretz* confirmed it to me in the summer of 1989. The *Maariv* reporter in 1970 had expressed the hope the Israelis would soon start bombing civilian as well as military targets and said he was confident the United States supported Israel's policy; otherwise it would not continue to supply aircraft.

21. Bar-Siman-Tov, *Israeli-Egyptian War of Attrition*, p. 120.

22. Ibid., p. 121.

23. Ibid., p. 171.

24. Heikal, *Road to Ramadan*, p. 82.

25. The Soviet Union had already supplied SAM-2s, which were of limited use against low-flying aircraft and were baffled by the electronic countermeasure equipment the United States had supplied to Israel. The SAM-3s were more advanced and more effective against the tactics being used by Israel.

26. *International Documents on Palestine*, 1970, p. 24.

27. The full texts of Kosygin's letter and Nixon's February 4 reply can be found in ibid., pp. 26–31.

28. Henry Kissinger, *The White House Years* (New York, 1979), p. 561.

29. Personal recollection.

7. MISJUDGMENT ON THE NILE

1. *New York Times*, May, 1, 1970.

2. Ibid.

3. Ibid., May 3, 1970, p. 70.

4. Bar-Siman-Tov, *Israeli-Egyptian War of Attrition*, p. 120.

5. Heikal, *Road to Ramadan*, p. 47.

6. Author's conversations with Israel officials, Foreign Ministry, Jerusalem, June 1968.

7. Bar-Siman-Tov, *Israeli-Egyptian War of Attrition*, p. 104.

8. Ibid., p. 127.

9. Ibid., p. 128.

10. Ibid., pp. 128–29.

11. Author's conversation with Schiff, April 17, 1989.

12. Quoted in Bar-Siman-Tov, *Israeli-Egyptian War of Attrition*, p. 230 n. 31.

13. For example, the comments made by Vitaly Naumkin of the Institute of Oriental Studies in his conversation with the author, November 22, 1989.

14. Author's conversation with Mautner, March 1990.

15. Rabin, *Memoirs*, p. 165.

16. Ibid., pp. 166–67.

17. Ibid., p. 167.

18. Ibid., p. 168. I have been unable to find the Grose article and he has no recollection of it. He did not arrive in Israel until July 1970, however, and Rabin is incorrect in claiming that his sources were in Jerusalem. (Grose letter of May 3, 1990.)

19. Rabin, *Pinkas Sherut* (Tel Aviv, 1979), p. 279. This is the unexpurgated Hebrew version of his memoirs.

20. Rabin, *Memoirs*, pp. 169–70.

21. Kissinger, *White House Years*, pp. 568–69.

22. Rabin, *Pinkas Sherut*, p. 280.

23. Ibid., p. 274.

24. Kissinger, *White House Years*, p. 562.

25. Ibid., p. 563. At some point after receipt of the Kosygin warning and before early March, when it was evident that Soviet military personnel were involved in the air defense of Egypt, the Americans had hard intelligence that the Soviets had decided to send troops there. According to Harold Saunders, who was then the senior NSC staffer responsible for the Middle East, the contingency planning Kissinger refers to took place after receipt of that information. I cannot fix the date but believe it was in late February at the earliest.

26. Rabin, *Memoirs*, p. 133.

27. Rabin, *Pinkas Sherut*, p. 277.

28. I am indebted to Janice Stein of the University of Toronto for this insight into the Soviet attitude.

8. THE ISRAELI INVASION OF 1982

1. Author's conversation with Lubrani, February 28, 1984. According to Morris Draper, much of the blame goes to Amin Gemayel for refusing to cooperate with his own army chief of staff, General Tannous, who wanted to replace the Lebanese Forces units in the Shuf with Druze units (communication of May 22, 1991).

2. Author's conversations with Druze and Maronite personalities, Beirut, January–February 1983. See also Thomas Friedman, "Duplicity Charges Traded by Israelis and Phalangists," *New York Times*, February 13, 1983.

3. Bennie Morris, "Israel and the Lebanese Phalange: The Birth of a Relationship, 1948–1951," *Studies in Zionism* 5, no. 1 (1984). Most nonspeakers of French seem not to realize that the name of the party is a plural: Phalanges (phalanxes), or Kata'ib (battalions) in Arabic, not Phalange.

4. This version of the correspondence is translated from an Arabic translation of the Hebrew that appeared in a Beirut newspaper in 1978. More extensive quotations from the Ben-Gurion and Sharett letters but not Sasson's are in Livia Rokach, *Israel's Sacred Terrorism* (Belmont, Mass., 1980), pp. 24–28.

5. Ze'ev Schiff and Ehud Ya'ari, *Israeli's Lebanon War* (New York, 1984), pp. 42–43.

6. Whether Israeli expectations in this regard were realistic is conjectural. Morris Draper comments that based on the many talks he and Philip Habib had with Bashir, he was sure Bashir would never have signed a real peace treaty. Whatever his private views, he knew Lebanon could not divorce itself from the Arab world (communication of May 22, 1991). For an informed account of Bashir's equivocation on this issue in his conversations with the Israelis, see David Kimche, *The Last Option* (London, 1991), pp. 153–58.

7. Among other activities, Syrian officers were reported to be doing a brisk trade in stolen automobiles and hashish. A tour in Lebanon had allegedly become a sought-after perquisite.

8. Pierre Gemayel, for instance, when I went to see him at the request of President Sarkis to ask that he turn the culprits over to the Lebanese authorities, said that he could not be responsible for finding some stupid *con* of a Phalangist who had shot at the Syrians.

9. For a description of the evolution of the Lebanese Forces from the disparate Christian, largely Maronite, militias in the period 1976–80, see Lewis W. Snider, "The Lebanese Forces: Their Origins and Role in Lebanon's Politics," *Middle East Journal* (Winter 1984), pp. 1–33.

10. The Kata'ib or Phalanges, the National Liberal party (the Chamounist Tigers), the Tanzim, the Guardians of the Cedars, and other fighters not affiliated with any party.

11. The comments on Bashir's character and political views are based on nu-

merous contacts and conversations with him during the period February 1977–October 1978, when I was ambassador to Lebanon.

12. For example, Schiff and Yaʿari in *Israel's Lebanon War*, pp. 11–37. and Yair Evron in *War and Intervention in Lebanon* (Baltimore, 1987), p. 92.

13. Zahle's population of 130,000 was estimated to be 50 percent Greek Catholic, 25 percent Maronite, and 15 percent Greek Orthodox. An important market and service center, the town is famous for its arak and restaurants and was a noted resort in former times. It lay well outside the Maronite heartland and had largely been spared the fighting until Bashir came along. It had never been part of his turf. The Lebanese Forces claimed they had always been active there, but that is denied by other Lebanese.

14. Zeʿev Schiff, "Lebanon: Motivations and Interests in Israel's Policy," *Middle East Journal* (Spring 1984), p. 224.

15. Schiff and Yaʿari, *Israel's Lebanon War*, p. 33.

16. William Harris, "The View from Zahle," *Middle East Journal* (Spring 1985), pp. 270–86.

17. The terms of this agreement, if it can be called that, have never been published. As far as I could determine in Beirut in 1977, there was no document and no map with a red line on it, only a Syrian commitment, conveyed through Henry Kissinger, not to undertake actions in Lebanon threatening Israel's security. Several years ago I was informed by a responsible official of the Department of State that he had been unable to find a document which described the terms of such an agreement, that there was in fact no map and no agreement on an actual line, and that Kissinger did not recall the details. My efforts to check with knowledgeable Israelis have been unsuccessful. Meanwhile, the Israelis have felt free to interpret the agreement rather broadly, invoking a movable red line to suit evolving requirements. There does, however, seem to have been Syrian acquiescence in 1976 to Israel's demand that no surface-to-air missiles be introduced into Lebanon and that Israel be free to make military overflights. Morris Draper, who was director of the office dealing with Lebanon in the Department of State (NEA/ARN) at the time, comments that this was a "fairly explicit" element in the agreement and that the term *red line* really came into effect late in 1976 when the Israelis made it clear that they would not allow the Syrians to move troops as far south as Nabatiyah. For more details about the Nabatiyah question, see Naomi Joy Weinberger, "Peacekeeping Options in Lebanon," *Middle East Journal* (Summer 1983), pp. 341–69.

18. The Israelis claimed they had destroyed "Libyan anti-aircraft missiles guarding Palestinian positions." The last Palestinian-initiated incident along the border had been on April 20, when rockets were fired into western Galilee from Lebanon. (*Middle East Journal* chronology).

19. The proximate justification offered at the time was the attempted assassination of Israel's ambassador to London, Shlomo Argov, on June 2. The real justification, according to David Kimche, was the shelling of forty towns and villages in upper Galilee by Palestinian gunners following an Israeli air attack against PLO ammunition dumps in Beirut (*Last Option*, pp. 145–46).

20. Author's conversation with Habib, May 9, 1990.

21. Ninety to 97 percent of Lebanon's pre-1982 exports went to the Arab world, and remittances from workers in Arab states were estimated at $130 million a month, accounting for 45 percent of the national revenue, according to the *Middle East Economic Digest* in January 1983. There was no likelihood that similar sums could be generated from Israel and Egypt, both of which were heavily dependent on American financial support. On the other hand, the Lebanese might have been able to introduce some free-market rationality into the Egyptian and Israeli economic systems. Certainly the Israelis and Egyptians would have found the liber-

tarian climate of Beirut and the trading acumen of the Lebanese challenging, perhaps too much so for comfort.

9. THE NEGOTIATIONS

1. Author's conversation with Ambassador Dillon, March, 22, 1990. For a fly-on-the-wall account of the Gemayel-Begin-Sharon meeting which may or may not be accurate, see Schiff and Ya'ari, *Israel's Lebanon War*, pp. 233–36. The meeting, which was supposed to be secret, was reported by Israel radio on September 3, the day before Bashir's assassination.

2. Amin had the initial support of the Sunni establishment, some members of which had boycotted Bashir's election, but had not made an accommodation with the Shia as Bashir apparently had. His rivals in the Maronite community began undermining him soon after he was elected and may have had some Israeli support in that effort. Particularly troublesome was his failure to reach an accommodation with the Druze led by Walid Jumblatt. He deprecated the importance of the Druze on one hand and tried to undermine Walid's relationship with the Americans on the other. Amin thus ended up with no support from the radical elements in either the Muslim or Christian communities, and they were the people who controlled the streets.

3. Author's conversation with Habib, May 9, 1990. Draper comments that "Habib finally got Washington to support his 'piece of paper' fully, but it was too late. Sharon had already reached an understanding with Gemayel's secret emissary, and the Israelis would not back away from a *de facto* peace treaty. Unfortunately, Shultz had accepted in September-October the Israeli concept of 'normalization' and the need to formalize understandings" (communication of May 22, 1991).

4. Author's conversation with Habib, May 9, 1990. Draper comments that Habib and he had presented their concept of pullbacks on both sides to the Israelis in December 1981. The Israelis had rejected it but Habib had wanted to keep trying. Draper went to Saudi Arabia in May 1982 to ask the Saudis to restrain the PLO and keep them in line with the 1981 cease-fire (communication of May 22, 1991).

5. There was serious disagreement between the Israelis and Habib over interpretation of the 1981 cease-fire agreement, with the Israelis maintaining that an attack on Israelis or Jews anywhere, e.g., on a synagogue in Europe, was a violation of the cease-fire. The PLO maintained that the agreement was limited to attacks across the Lebanese border. The United States took a position in between, arguing that the agreement applied to all attacks across Israel's borders, including the sea frontier, if they originated from Lebanon. The Israelis also viewed with concern the much enhanced military capability the PLO was building up in Lebanon under shelter of the cease-fire. (Author's conversation with Ambassador Samuel Lewis, May 16, 1990).

6. *American Foreign Policy*, 1982, p. 804.

7. Ibid., pp. 804–5.

8. "Policy Goals in Lebanon," presidential press conference, June 30, 1982, in *American Foreign Policy*, 1982, Document 366.

9. Draper communication of May 22, 1991.

10. Author's conversation with Draper, January 26, 1989, and with Howard Teicher, June 8, 1990.

11. Maroun is described by both Americans and Lebanese as a businessman with no diplomatic experience. David Kimche, who was the leader of the Israeli negotiating team, describes him as "a handsome, intelligent Maronite patriot, whose polite and winning manner charmed the Israelis with whom he was dealing. . . . his creative mind never tired, examining one plan after another, trying them on

for size before discarding them and picking another . . . the ideal negotiator." That the Israelis would find him ideal is understandable, since he seems to have given them everything they wanted. Knowledgeable Lebanese were incredulous that Gemayel would have entrusted an affair of this importance to him. Contrary to the allegation of Schiff and Yaʿari (*Israel's Lebanon War*, p. 290) that Gemayel kept the Americans informed of the nature of the talks Maroun was having, Draper says that they knew Gemayel was establishing a private channel to the Israelis but had not known that he had gone so far as to begin negotiating an agreement with Sharon through Maroun. The revelation on December 16 came as a severe shock to Habib, to the obvious delight of Sharon and others. Draper describes the meeting with the Israelis as "a terrible scene. One Israeli kept giggling while Habib talked, and Rubenstein didn't even bother to take notes. Unforgettable." (Author's conversation with Draper, June 19, 1990, and communication of May 22, 1991.) One of Gemayel's Lebanese advisers told me in January 1983 that Gemayel and Maroun had not understood the significance of what they were doing, i.e., that they were negotiating a peace treaty and giving the game away.

12. Schiff and Yaʿari, *Israel's Lebanon War*, p. 291.
13. Author's conversation with Habib, May 9, 1990.
14. Ibid.
15. Conversation with Ambassador Dillon, March 30, 1991.

10. THE FINAL RECKONING

1. Accounts differ, but U.S. officials present at the first part of the Haig-Sharon meeting in May 1982 were so concerned about Sharon's interpretation of Haig's remarks in that meeting and in their subsequent private meeting that they drafted a letter from Haig to Begin warning the Israelis against overreacting in Lebanon. Ambassador Lewis, who delivered the letter to Begin, notes that it did not say "or else," i.e. it was not categorical and did not warn of consequences. He comments, "Now, when Sharon got back, we know what happened. . . . He told Begin, 'Bah! Nothing to worry about. They'll have to make a little noise, but they'll swallow it.' And the letter was read in the light of that comment and of Sharon's own report [of what Haig had said to him]." (Author's conversation with Lewis, May 16, 1990.)

2. Author's conversation with Veliotes, May 17, 1990.

3. The text of the Reagan statement of September 1 and the talking points can be found in William Quandt, *The Middle East Ten Years after Camp David* (Washington, 1988), pp. 461–70.

4. Patrick Seale, in *Asad* (Berkeley, 1989), p. 405, says "the debate between advocates of informal soundings and direct talks was then [after December 16] resolved by Kenneth Dam, deputy Secretary of State, but it is inconceivable that he could have acted without Shultz's support." Seale does not cite a source but presumably obtained this bit of bureaucratic lore from one of the officials involved. It sounds as though Dam cleared an instruction or finding which directed the bureaucracy to support normalization, but Seale is correct that Dam would not make a decision on a subject of this sensitivity without Shultz's prior agreement. Without access to the specific pieces of paper involved, it is difficult to know what Dam authorized and what it meant in practice. For one thing, the language used in the papers was often ambiguous because an intense bureaucratic battle was going on in Washington between advocates of differing approaches to the problem, according to Veliotes. In his view, sometime between early December, when Habib departed for the area with Shultz's approval of his "piece of paper" concept, and early January 1983, Shultz had decided either that the Israelis

were right in seeking normalization or that he could not beat them at the influence game in Washington. (Veliotes believes that if the latter was the case, congressional passage of a supplemental appropriation to fund the Israeli invasion, which Reagan and Shultz had opposed, was instrumental in the decision.) That does not mean, however, that Shultz was convinced of the necessity of a formal, written agreement of the sort the Israelis were seeking. That seems to have come later. (Author's conversation with Veliotes, December 4, 1991.) Note that Shultz's press conference statement of January 30 (see n. 29) implies that while he saw normalization as a legitimate objective, he had doubts about the parties reaching agreement on it. Similarly Reagan expressed doubts about the legitimacy of Israeli demands eight days later. Shultz's conversion to the full Israeli view must have come after that.

5. Author's conversation with Paganelli, May 16, 90.
6. Author's conversation with Lewis, May 16, 1990.
7. Author's conversation with Dillon, March 22, 1990.
8. Author's conversation with Viets, March 30, 1990.
9. Draper comments that to some extent American thinking about Syria's willingness to cooperate was influenced by the alacrity with which Syria accepted ("in 12 hours and without a single nit-pick") the U.S. proposal for its evacuation from Beirut. Communication of May 22, 1991.
10. Ibid.
11. Ibid.
12. Author's conversation with Lewis, May 16, 1990.
13. Author's conversation with Viets, March 30, 1990.
14. Newlin letter of April 2, 1990.
15. Author's conversation with Paganelli, May 16, 1990.
16. Communication of May 22, 1991.
17. Conversation of May 10, 1991.
18. *American Foreign Policy*, 1983, p. 761.
19. Author's conversation with Habib, May 9, 1990.
20. Draper recalls that Khaddam said that Syrians would withdraw when requested officially to do so by the Lebanese government, but Lebanon would have to remain an independent Arab state and the Israelis would have to withdraw fully. This was the standard, omnibus position of the Syrians, the exact meaning of which was never explored fully.
21. Communication of May 22, 1991.
22. Author's conversation with Abdul Halim Khaddam, Damascus, June 8, 1989. Khaddam said the Americans thought they were so strong they could ignore weaker states. The Syrian position had been made very clear. It was no secret. Paganelli had been very precise and correct. Khaddam would dictate and Paganelli would take notes.
23. *American Foreign Policy*, 1983, p. 752. Note that Shultz's version of the Syrian attitude at Delhi does not jibe with the Lebanese description given later in the chapter. Given the Syrian track record, the Lebanese account is more plausible.
24. Ibid., p. 755.
25. Ibid., p. 757.
26. Ibid., p. 761.
27. Communication of May 22, 1991.
28. Author's conversation with Habib, May 9, 1990.
29. Author's conversation with Richard Murphy, May 1990.
30. The following examples, among others, are found in *American Foreign Policy*, 1983, on the pages indicated: P. 734—Shultz press conference of January 30, 1983. "There is a pretty wide gap between the conditions that Israel feels she needs in order to withdraw and the conditions that Lebanon feels are consistent with the

emergence of a new Lebanon . . . sovereign and in control of its territories. . . . I believe there is a genuine convergence of views on finding appropriate security arrangements for southern Lebanon . . . that is accepted as a legitimate objective. . . . Beyond that are the issues surrounding so-called normalization, and that's a different kind of issue entirely and was not part of the announced rationale for going into Lebanon in the first place, but nevertheless it is an objective." P. 736—Veliotes appearance before House Foreign Affairs Committee, February 2, 1983. Congressman Weiss: "Why do we seem to be critical of policies for normalization of relations between Lebanon and Israel?" Veliotes: "I don't accept the premise . . . we not only favor normalization, but we favor peace treaties. . . . the question has been judgment as to what is possible in the short term, which . . . must take account, above all, of Lebanese judgment of what is possible, given their own internal issues and Lebanon's relations and, frankly, economic dependence on the Arab world." P. 738—Reagan interview with TV anchormen, February 7, 1983, responding to a question about his relations with Begin. "It's true we disagree on this particular issue about getting out of Lebanon. . . . Israel is delaying, we believe unnecessarily in that . . . there's a certain moral point we think the Israelis are neglecting. . . . For them not to leave now puts them technically in the position of an occupying force."

CONCLUSION

1. The decision makers gave themselves little time for serious consultation in any event. Kosygin's letter was received on a Friday and my recollection is that the decision to treat it as a bluff had been made by the time I got to the office on Monday morning. This meant that there was time only for a rapid consultation among a handful of people. The reply was expeditious, but more thought could have been given to it.

2. Robert Jervis, in *Perception and Misperception in International Politics* (Princeton, N.J., 1976), p. 382, describes the selective hearing phenomenon as the result of cognitive dissonance, which means that when there is a conflict, or dissonance, between the rationale for a decision and the realities of the situation, the decision maker, seeking justification for his or her behavior, will "rearrange his beliefs so that they provide increased support for his actions." This is what Shultz seems to have done in early 1983, after he became committed to the normalization concept and in effect rejected Habib's argument that it would not work.

3. Graham T. Allison, *Essence of Decision* (Glenview, Ill., 1971), pp. 3–5.

4. George Kennan, *The Fateful Alliance*, pp. 82–87.

5. Richard K. Betts, "Analysis, War and Decision: Why Intelligence Failures are Inevitable," *World Politics* 31 (October 1978), p. 39.

6. Ibid., p. 48.

7. Jervis, *Perception and Misperception*, p. 417.

8. For a critical description of how the Dissent Channel has worked, or not worked, see "The Decline of Dissent" by Kai Bird in the February 1985 *Foreign Service Journal* (pp. 26–31). For an insightful study of the results of tinkering with the foreign affairs structure in the U.S. government, see John Franklin Campbell, *The Foreign Affairs Fudge Factory* (New York, Basic Books, 1971).

Annotated Bibliography

ON MISCALCULATION IN GENERAL

A large body of writings relates to miscalculation, usually under a title which speaks not of miscalculation but of intelligence failure, misperception, the decision process, or the case being studied. I have found the following works useful and informative, but they are only a subjective sample of a much larger number.

Intelligence Failures

Agranat, Shimon (president of the Commission of Inquiry into the Yom Kippur War), *Report of the Commission of Inquiry* (April 2, 1974). A partial text can be found in the *Jerusalem Journal of International Relations* 4, no. 1 (Jerusalem: Magnes Press), pp. 70–90. This is the basic document describing Israel's failure to evaluate properly the Egyptian preparations for attack in October 1973.

Hughes, Thomas, *The Fate of Facts in a World of Men: A Nontheological Approach.* Headline Series no. 233, Foreign Policy Association, New York, December 1976. A former director of intelligence and research in the Department of State and president of the Carnegie Endowment discusses the problems of intelligence gathering and assessment and what happens to information in the bureaucracy. Readable and informative.

————, "Present at the Escalation." In *Secrecy and Foreign Policy*, ed. Thomas Franck and Edward Weisband (Oxford, 1974). More insightful comment on the intelligence process.

Knorr, Klaus, "Failures in National Intelligence Estimates: The Case of Cuba." *World Politics* 16 (April 1964). An early study of the phenomenon of intelligence failure.

Shlaim, Avi, "National Intelligence Failures: The Case of the Yom Kippur War." *World Politics* 28 (April 1976), pp. 348–80. The best single description of why the Israelis were caught napping in 1973, based largely on the Agranat Report.

Stein, Janice Gross, " 'Intelligence' and 'Stupidity' Reconsidered: Estimation and Decision in Israel, 1973." *Journal of Strategic Studies* 3, no. 2 (September 1980). A revisionist look at the "simplistic explanation of surprise and failure offered by the Agranat Commission and widely accepted by participants and critics alike" (including Avi Shlaim).

Whaley, Barton, *Codeword Barbarossa.* Boston: MIT Press, 1973. A fascinating study of the impact of mindset on intelligence: why Stalin refused to take seriously the warnings that Germany was about to attack the Soviet Union in 1941.

Wohlstetter, Roberta, *Pearl Harbor: Warning and Decision.* Stanford, Calif.: Stanford University Press, 1962. The classic study of why the United States was unprepared for the Japanese attack on December 7, 1941.

————, "Cuba and Pearl Harbor: Hindsight and Foresight." *Foreign Affairs* 43 (July 1965). A useful comparison of the Cuban missile and Pearl Harbor crises.

Decision Making

Allison, Graham T., *Essence of Decision: Explaining the Cuban Missile Crisis.* Glenview, Ill:, Scott, Foresman, 1971. A ground-breaking study of the decision-making process in the Cuban missile crisis, positing three models for explaining government behavior: the rational actor, the organizational process, and the bureaucratic politics models.

Blight, James G., and David A. Welch, *On the Brink*. New York: Farrar, Straus and Giroux, 1990. An account of the series of discussions in which the Americans and Soviets, and eventually the Cubans, reexamined the Cuban missile crisis twenty-five years later.

De Santis, Hugh, *The Diplomacy of Silence: The American Foreign Service, the Soviet Union and the Cold War, 1933–1947.* Chicago: University of Chicago Press, 1980. A study of the attitudes and reporting of American Foreign Service officers working on Soviet affairs in the 1930s and 1940s, and why they were not more prescient about what was happening in Europe.

Etheredge, Lloyd S. *Can Governments Learn: American Foreign Policy and Central American Revolutions.* Elmsford, N.Y.: Pergamon Press, 1985. Judging by Etheredge's findings, the answer seems to be "hardly ever."

Garthoff, Raymond L., *Reflections on the Cuban Missile Crisis.* Washington: Brookings, 1989. A former intelligence officer looks at this example of miscalculation and seeks rational explanations.

Janis, Irving L., *Stress, Attitudes and Decisions.* New York: Praeger, 1982. An interesting study of the effects of stress and mindset on the decision-making process. Some surprising findings.

———, *Victims of Groupthink: A Psychological Study of Foreign Policy Decisions and Fiascos.* Boston: Houghton Mifflin, 1972. A well-known study of the impact of group dynamics on the decision-making process. Two heads are not necessarily better than one.

Jervis, Robert, *Perception and Misperception in International Politics.* Princeton, N.J.: Princeton University Press, 1976. Cognitive dissonance and other concepts described and explained.

———, *The Logic of Images in International Relations.* Princeton, N.J.: Princeton University Press, 1970.

———, "Hypothesis on Misperception." *World Politics* 20 (April 1968), pp. 454–79.

Rusk, Dean, *As I Saw It.* New York: Norton, 1990. Rusk's frank description of his role in foreign affairs is revealing for what it says about the occasionally casual nature of the decision process as well as the often conflicting interests that must be taken into account.

Stein, Janice Gross, "Can Decision-Makers Be Rational and Should They Be? Evaluating the Quality of Decisions." *Jerusalem Journal of International Relations* 3, nos. 2–3 (1981). A discussion of the concept of rationality in decision making as viewed from the different perspectives of various schools of human behavior.

Verba, Sidney, "Assumptions of Rationality and Non-Rationality." *World Politics* (October 1961), pp. 93–118. An earlier discussion of rationality in decision making—to what extent models using nation states as the prime actors can give us an adequate explanation of international relations.

ON THE JUNE WAR

Abu Fadl, Abd al-Fattah, *Kunt Naʾiban li-Raʾis al-Mukhabarat* (I was deputy to the director of intelligence). Cairo: Dar al-Hurriya, 1986. Contains description of the state of unpreparedness in Sinai on the eve of the war.

Badran, Shams al-Din, "ʿAlanu Masuliyati al-Kamila" (I declare my full responsibility). *Al-Hawadith* (London), September 2, 1977, pp. 18–23. An interview in which Badran describes his visit to Moscow and his discussions with Soviet officials in late May 1967.

Baghdadi, Abdul Latif, *Mudhakkirat* (Memoirs). Cairo: Al-Maktab al-Hadith, 1977. A member of the original Revolutionary Command Council gives his frank account of conversations with Nasser and other RCC members about what was happening in Egypt. Many details about the Nasser-ʿAmr rivalry.

Bar Zohar, Michael, *Embassies in Crisis: Diplomats and Demagogues Behind the Six Day War*. Englewood Cliffs, N.J.: Prentice-Hall, 1968. Written shortly after the June War and based in part on interviews with participants. Bar Zohar, a journalist, later became a member of the Knesset.

Brecher, Michael, *Decisions in Crisis*. Berkeley: University of California Press, 1980. A well-documented and carefully researched study of a series of crises, including the June War. Perhaps the most serious single published account of the process leading up to Israel's decision to strike.

Brown, Leon Carl, "Nasser and the June 1967 War: Plan or Improvisation?" In *Quest for Understanding: Arabic and Islamic Studies in Memory of Malcolm H. Kerr*, ed. Seikaly, Baalbaki, and Dodd (Beirut: American University of Beirut, 1991). A carefully reasoned essay which argues that Nasser stumbled into the war.

Burdett, Winston, *Encounter with the Middle East: An Intimate Report of What Lies Behind the Arab-Israeli Conflict*. New York: Atheneum, 1969. Includes a long section on the June War. A serious piece of journalistic research. Burdett was extensively briefed by officers of the Department of State on their views of what happened.

Burns, William J., *Economic Aid and American Policy toward Egypt, 1955–1981*. Albany, N.Y.: SUNY Press, 1985. A carefully researched and documented study of the ups and downs of U.S.-Egyptian relations and the role of economic aid therein.

Dagan, Avigdor, *Moscow and Jerusalem*. London: Abelard-Schuman, 1970. An account of Soviet-Israeli relations and their exchanges prior to the June War.

Dupuy, Trevor, *Elusive Victory: The Arab-Israeli Wars, 1947–1974*. New York: Harper and Row, 1978. Perhaps the best known of the American military commentators who write on the Israeli military machine, Dupuy has been given unusual access to Israeli military information. He is less informative about the Arab military.

Eban, Abba, *An Autobiography*. Jerusalem: Steimatsky's, 1977. Eban was the Israeli foreign minister in 1967. His memoirs have a useful account of events leading up to the war and of Israel's exchanges with the Americans.

Ennes, James M., Jr., *Assault on the Liberty*. New York: Random House, 1979. Ennis was the executive officer of the *Liberty*, and this detailed account of what occurred makes chilling reading. This book has played an important role in keeping the controversy about whether the Israelis knowingly attacked an American ship alive.

Farid, Abdul Majid, *Min Mahadir Ijtima ʿat Abd al-Nasir* (From the Minutes of the meetings of Abdul Nasser). Beirut: Muʾassassat al-Abhath al-ʿArabiyya, 1979. Farid was the secretary of the Supreme Excutive Council of the Arab Socialist Union, the highest executive authority in Egypt. This book is based on the minutes of certain meetings of the council. It unfortunately does not include the details of the meetings at which the decisions leading to the June War were taken, but it was useful information on the Nasser-ʿAmr relationship.

Fawzi, General Muhammad, *Harb al-Thalath Sanawat* (The three years war, i.e., from the June War to the cease-fire in 1970). Heliopolis: Dar al-Mustaqbil al-Arabi, 1980. Fawzi was chief of staff in 1967 and replaced Marshal ʿAmr as deputy commander-in-chief when the war ended. Much important military detail by a professional.

Al-Feki, Ahmad Hassan, "Muhimma Siriyya fi Musku" (Secret mission in Moscow). *Akhbar al-Yawm* (Cairo), April 28, 1979. Al-Feki, the senior diplomat accompanying Shams Badran on his visit to Moscow, told me he wrote this article as a corrective to the account given by Badran to *Al-Hawadith*. The microfilm copies of the article are all but unreadable.

Geist, Benjamin, "The Six Day War," 2 vols. Ph.D. thesis, Hebrew University, 1974. The most comprehensive study in English of the Israeli sources. Geist contributed importantly to the Brecher book mentioned above.

Gilboa, Moshe, *The USSR and Arab Belligerency* (in Hebrew). Referred to by Geist but not found in his bibliography and the Library of Congress cannot provide publication data. I am told it was an ephemeral publication of the Israeli Foreign Ministry.

Green, Stephen, *Taking Sides: America's Secret Relations with a Militant Israel*. New York: Morrow, 1984. A readable but somewhat polemical account of the special relationship with Israel. Provides fascinating details of alleged intelligence cooperation on the eve of and during the June War, but Green does not identify his sources and so far his details have not been corroborated by others.

Hamrush, Ahmad, *Kharif Abd al-Nasir* (The autumn of Abdul Nasser). Cairo: Maktabat Madbuli, 1984. One of a number of books dealing with the decline of Abdul Nasser following the June War.

Heikal, Mohamed Hassanein, *Nasser: The Cairo Documents*. London: New English Library, 1972. Heikal is always readable, either in Arabic or English, but this is a disappointingly thin set of recollections, some taken from documents, published soon after Nasser's death. Pages 205–24 describe the relationship between Nasser and Johnson and the deterioration of U.S.-Egyptian relations under the latter.

―――, *The Sphinx and the Commissar*. New York: Harper and Row, 1978. An informative account of the Egyptian-Soviet relationship, with anecdotes about Khrushchev and others. Contains the first published account by an insider of the details of Soviet-Egyptian contacts on the eve of the June War.

―――, *1967—Al-Infijar* (1967—The explosion). Cairo: Al-Ahram, 1990. A massive (1,089 pages) and often fascinating insider's account, supported by 149 pages of documents, of the events leading up to the June War. Heikal's selective use of sources to support his contention that Egypt was the victim of a U.S.-Israeli conspiracy throws doubt on other aspects of his narrative, and one does not know what to believe. Few other Egyptians know as much as he does, however, and at this point he is the only one who is talking.

Howard, Michael, and Robert Hunter, "Israel and the Arab World: The Crisis of 1967." Adelphi Paper no. 41, Institute for Strategic Studies, London, October 1967. A first-crack-out-of-the-box study of the events leading up to and the consequences of the June War. Worth reading as a reminder of how much detail we have forgotten.

Hussein, Ibn Talal, *My War With Israel*. London: Peter Owen, 1969. King Hussein of Jordan's account of his side of the June War.

Imam, Abdallah, *Nasir wa ʿAmr* (Nasser and ʿAmr). Cairo: Ruz al-Yusuf, 1985. An account of the Nasser-ʿAmr relationship, with many details, some not original.

Kimche, David, and D. Bawly, *The Sandstorm: The Arab-Israeli War of 1967, Prelude and Aftermath*. London: Secker and Warburg, 1968. Another early work in popular style which has been given more weight than it deserves by some authors because of Kimche's intelligence background.

Laqueur, Walter, *The Road to War, 1967*. London: Weidenfeld and Nicolson, 1968. A serious study by a well-known student of the area.

MacLeish, Roderick. *The Sun Stood Still*. New York: Atheneum, 1967. MacLeish, a reporter and a well-known commentator on National Public Radio, was one of the few early writers on the June War who actually talked to a Soviet official about the Soviet role.

Marei, Sayyed, *Awraq Siyasiyya* (Political Papers), vol. 3. Cairo: Al-Maktab al-Misri al-Hadith, 1978. Recollections of Sadat's deputy in the Egyptian National Assembly in June 1967. Pages 522–48 have interesting details of postwar recriminations and Nasser's reaction to the death of ʿAmr.

Murtagi, General Abdul Muhsin Kamil, *Al-Fariq Murtagi Yarwa al-Haqaʾiq* (General Murtagi narrates the facts). Cairo: Dar al-Watn al-Arabi, 1976. The commander of the Sinai front gives his version of events. A useful account of the problems of command and decision under Marshal ʿAmr.

Mutawi, Samir A., *Jordan in the 1967 War*. Cambridge: Press Syndicate, 1987. Dr. Mutawi was given access to documents in the Jordanian military archives relating to the war. A carefully researched and responsible book which gives Jordan's side of the question.

Nassif, Ramses, *U Thant in New York*. London: C. Hurst, 1986. Nassif, who accompanied U Thant on his trip to Cairo in May 1967, describes their discussions there. Includes the memorandum of U Thant's conversation with Nasser.

Neff, Donald, *Warriors for Jerusalem*. New York: Simon and Schuster, 1984. Probably the best single account of the June War published to date. Based on extensive interviews and declassified documents as well as the public record.

Nutting, Anthony, *Nasser*. New York: Dutton, 1972. A sympathetic account of Nasser's role in Middle East politics from the 1952 revolution to his death.

Quandt, William B., *Decade of Decisions: American Policy toward the Arab-Israeli Conflict, 1967–1976*. Berkeley: University of California Press, 1977. A former NSC staffer's well-researched and authoritative study of U.S. policy based on declassified documents, interviews, and personal knowledge.

———, "The United States and Egypt." Washington, D.C.: Brookings, 1990. A philosophical look at U.S.-Egyptian relations focusing on the period after 1970.

———, "Lyndon Johnson and the June 1967 War: What Color Was the Light?" *Middle East Journal* (Spring 1992). A thorough and authoritative reexamination of the U.S. government's attitude toward Israel in the June War crisis, based on facts learned since *Decade of Decisions* was published.

Rafael, Gideon, *Destination Peace*. New York: Stein & Day, 1981. Israel's former U.N. delegate's recollections of a long and distinguished diplomatic career.

Riad, Mahmoud, *The Struggle for Peace in the Middle East*. New York: Quartet Books, 1981. The first volume of memoirs of the former Egyptian minister of foreign affairs.

———, *Amrika wa al-Arab* (America and the Arabs). Cairo: Dar Mustaqbil al-Arabi, 1986. The third volume of Riad's memoirs. His interpretation of events leading up to the June War and of American responsibility for it come in the first forty-three pages.

Rikhye, General Indar Jit, *The Sinai Blunder*. New Delhi: Oxford and IBH, 1978. The commander of the U.N. Emergency Force describes the critical events of May and June 1967 from his perspective.

Rouleau, Eric, with Jean-Francis Held and Jean and Simonne Lacouture, *Israel et les arabes: Le 3ᵉ combat*. Paris: Editions du Seuil, 1967. Knowledgeable French journalists give their version of events.

Al-Sadat, Anwar, *In Search of Identity*. New York: Harper and Row, 1977. Sadat's autobiography. Not as many details about the Soviet warning delivered to him in Moscow as one would like.

Safran, Nadav. *From War to War: The Arab-Israeli Confrontation*. New York: Pegasus, 1969. A well-known student of the area writes on Israel's wars up to 1969.

St. John, Robert, *Eban*. New York: Doubleday, 1972. A sympathetic biography of Abba Eban.

Sam'o, Elias, ed., *The June 1967 Arab-Israeli War*. Wilmette, Ill.: Medina University Press International, 1971. A collection of articles on the June War.

Schleifer, Abdullah, *The Fall of Jerusalem*. New York: Monthly Review Press, 1972. An eyewitness account by a journalist.

Springborg, Robert. *Family, Power and Politics in Egypt*. Philadelphia: University of Pennsylvania Press, 1982. A study of Sayyed Marei and his family.

Stein, Janice, and Raymond Tanter, *Rational Decision Making: Israel's Security Choices 1967*. Columbus: Ohio State University Press, 1980. An in-depth study of the factors affecting Israel's decisions in the 1967 crisis.

Urquhart, Sir Brian, *A Life in Peace and War*. New York: Harper and Row, 1987. Urquhart was Ralph Bunche's principal deputy in 1967. These are his memoirs, with a brief account of the June War crisis as seen from New York.

Walters, Dennis, *Not Always with the Pack*. London: Constable, 1989. A member of the British Parliament, Walter met with Nasser well after the June War and has an interesting account of Nasser's explanation for his miscalculation.

Yost, Charles W., "The Arab-Israeli War: How it Began." *Foreign Affairs* 42, no. 2 (January 1968), pp. 304–20. Perhaps the most insightful single article explaining the circumstances which led to the June War, by a senior retired diplomat who was sent to Cairo as a special envoy during the crisis.

Al-Zayyat, Muhammad Abd al-Salam, *Al-Sadat, al-Qina' wa al-Haqiqa* (Sadat, the mask and the truth). Cairo: Kuttab al-Ahali, 1989. Zayyat was Sayyed Marei's deputy in the National Assembly. Described as his memoirs, this book is largely an attack on Sadat. Interesting details about the latter's behavior during the June War.

ON THE WAR OF ATTRITION

Bar-Siman-Tov, Yaacov, *The Israeli-Egyptian War of Attrition 1969–1970*. New York: Columbia University Press, 1980. A serious Israeli scholar's study.

Farid, Abdul Majid, *Min Mahadir Ijtima 'at Abd al-Nasir* (From the Minutes of the meetings of Abdul Nasser.) Cairo: Mu'assasat al-Abhath al-'Arabiyya, 1979. Contains minutes of a number of important meetings in the post–June War period, including the Nasser-Podgorny meeting immediately after the war in which Nasser asked the Soviets to provide air defense of Egypt.

Heikal, Mohamed Hassanein, *The Road to Ramadan*. London: William Collins, 1975. Devoted to events after the June War and leading to the Egyptian assault across the Suez Canal in 1973. The first ninety-four pages deal with the War of Attrition.

———, *1967—Al-Infijar*. Cairo: Al-Ahram, 1990. Latter portions deal with the post–June War period and the War of Attrition.

Herzog, Haim, *The Arab-Israeli Wars*. New York: Random House, 1982. By a former general, military commentator, and Israel's delegate to the United Nations, who became president of Israel in 1983. Contains a sobering chapter on the War of Attrition.

Kissinger, Henry, *The White House Years*. New York: Little, Brown, 1979. Fascinating counterpoint to Yitzhak Rabin's description of U.S. policy on the War of Attrition.

Korn, David A., *Stalemate: The War of Attrition and Great Power Diplomacy in the Middle East, 1967–1970*. Boulder, Colo.: Westview Press, 1992. Korn was a political officer in the U.S. Embassy in Tel Aviv during the War of Attrition. Drawing on Hebrew and Arabic as well as English sources, he has written the best account of that war to date. Full of interesting facts and insights not hitherto revealed to English-only readers.

Rabin, Yitzhak, *The Rabin Memoirs*. Boston: Little, Brown, 1979. Invaluable for its account of Rabin's contacts with the administration in Washington during his tenure as ambassador.

Shazly, General Saad, *The Crossing of Suez: The October War*. San Francisco: American Mideast Research, 1980. Pages 11–12 put the beginning of the War of Attrition in September 1968.

Whetten, Lawrence L., *The Canal War: Four-Power Conflict in The Middle East*. Cambridge: MIT Press, 1974. One of the few serious, book-length studies of the War of Attrition.

ON LEBANON, 1983

Evron, Yair, *War and Intervention in Lebanon: The Israeli-Syrian Deterrence Dialogue*. Baltimore: Johns Hopkins University Press, 1987. A serious work by an Israeli scholar.

Haig, Alexander, *Caveat: Realism, Reagan and Foreign Policy*. New York: Macmillan, 1983. The former secretary of state's frank and often opinionated account of his tenure in the Reagan Administration.

Kimche, David, *The Last Option*. London: Weidenfeld and Nicolson, 1991. A personalized discussion of various issues in Israel's foreign policy by the head of Israel's team in the 1983 negotiations with Lebanon. Pages 125–85 deal with Lebanon. Lots of atmospherics but not much useful detail.

Rabinovitch. Itamar, *The War for Lebanon, 1970–1985*. Ithaca, N.Y.: Cornell University Press, 1985. Rabinovitch is rector of Tel Aviv University and a well-known scholar of Middle Eastern affairs. A serious account that has been overshadowed by the Schiff-Ya'ari book.

Rokach, Livia, *Israel's Sacred Terrorism*. Belmont, Mass.: Arab-American University Graduates, 1980. A partisan, some would say polemical, account of Israeli activities abroad. It contains part of the Ben Gurion–Sharett correspondence about creating a Christian state in Lebanon.

Schiff, Ze'ev and Ehud Ya'ari, *Israel's Lebanon War*. New York: Simon and Schuster, 1984. Schiff is the military affairs correspondent of *Haaretz* newspaper and Ya'ari is Middle East affairs correspondent for Israel Television. This best-seller is full of insider accounts of Israel's decision process and its strategy in Lebanon.

Seale, Patrick, *Asad: The Struggle for the Middle East*. Berkeley: University of California Press, 1989. Seale, a long-time student of Middle Eastern affairs, had unparalleled access to Asad, about whom little had been known by the Western world before this book. A basically sympathetic biography, it gives the Syrian view of the Lebanese affair.

Index

Grechko, Andrei, 8, 29-34, 50, 52, 54
Green, Stephen, 108, 121
Gromyko, Andrei, 29, 50, 57, 133
Grose, Peter, 158-59, 256n18
Gulf of Aqaba, 3, 11, 30, 38, 40, 48-51, 53-58, 61, 65, 72-76, 90, 112, 113, 116, 133, 140, 214, 227-33, 236, 237, 251n2

Habib, Philip, 175-76, 180-86, 188-90, 193-95, 197, 199, 200, 202-205, 208, 211, 220, 257n6, 259n3, 259n4, 260n11, 260n4, 262n2
Haig, Alexander, 176, 182, 194, 203, 218, 260n1
Hare, Paul, 176, 199, 249n34
Harman, Avraham, 113, 117, 119, 255n42
Hart, Parker T., 130, 134
Heikal, Mohamed Hassanein, 5-6, 10, 27, 29-36, 50, 51, 54-56, 59-66, 68-73, 75, 80-82, 91-92, 99-100, 104-105, 108-109, 112, 114, 126, 143, 151, 212, 215, 242, 244, 247n11, 252n25, 252n26
Helms, Richard, 114, 115, 120
Herzog, Haim, 117, 148
Hill, Charles, 194, 210
Hof, Yitzhak, 174-75
Humphrey, Hubert, 48, 55, 225, 239, 241
Hussein, King Ibn Talal, 52, 55, 64, 76, 102, 117, 162, 235
Hussein, Kamal al-Din, 75, 86
Hussein, Saddam, x, 192

Ibrahim, Hassan, 75, 86
Institute of Oriental Studies, 21, 25
International Court of Justice, 49, 56, 73, 76, 90, 251n2
Iran, x, 103, 169
Iraq, x, 4, 85, 101, 149
Israel-Syrian Mixed Armistice Commission (ISMAC), 14, 41, 44-45, 229, 249n29

Jarring, Gunnar, 128, 130
Jassenev, Vladislav, 248n11
Jervis, Robert, 219, 262n2
Johnson, Lyndon B., 37, 48-52, 55, 56, 61, 100, 103-104, 106, 109-18, 120-21, 127, 131, 132, 134, 213, 216-17, 225-26, 239-41, 245, 254n9
Jordan (country), 4, 40, 41, 64, 99, 101, 102, 103, 107, 122, 132, 194
Jordan (river), x, 4, 38
Jumblatt, Walid, 193, 207, 259n2

Kamel, Mustafa, 51, 69, 111, 252n26
Katz, Katriel, 11, 57
Kennedy, John F., 102, 104, 245
Kerr, Malcolm, 40, 100
Khaddam, Abdul Halim, 187, 193, 196, 205, 207, 261n20, 261n21
al-Kholy, Hassan Sabry, 135-36, 243

Kimche, David, 176, 185, 257n6, 258n19, 259n11
Kissinger, Henry, 134, 145, 146, 154, 156, 157, 159-63, 213, 257n25, 258n17
al-Kony, Muhammad Awad, 45, 46-47, 69-70, 230, 234
Korn, David A., 125, 135
Kornienko, Georgiy, 21, 23, 27, 32-33, 248n12
Kosygin, Aleksei, xi, xiii, 8, 10-11, 13, 29, 32-34, 50, 51, 54, 56-57, 127, 145, 156, 161, 213, 214, 220, 252n26, 257n25, 262n1
Kuwait, x, 4, 192

Lakeland, William C., 100-101, 253n1
Lebanese Forces militia, 169, 173-75, 180, 188, 189, 258n13
Levavi, Arye, 10, 57, 117
Lewis, Sam, 198, 201-203, 205
Libya, x, 92, 101, 122

MacFarlane, Robert, 189, 190
MacLeish, Roderick, 247n2, 250n1
Mahmoud, Sidqy, 12n, 57, 85
Marei, Sayyed, 13, 36, 80, 88
Maronites, 169-74, 178, 180, 188, 189, 197, 206, 258n13, 259n2
Maroun, Sami, 184-85, 195, 208, 259n11
Mecom, John, 104-105
Medvedko, Leonid, 22, 28-29
Meir, Golda, 134, 137, 139, 152, 153, 161
Miscalculation, ix, 212-14, 218-19
Mitchell, John, 157, 163
Mixed Armistice Commission (MAC), 179. *See also* Egypt-Israel Mixed Armistice Commission; Israel-Syrian Mixed Armistice Commission
Mubarak, Husni, 37, 186, 203
Muhieddin, Zakaria, 13, 55, 57-59, 62, 63, 70, 72, 79, 80, 112, 113, 118, 237-39, 241, 254n22, 255n42
Mukhtar, 'Izz ad-Din, 67, 68
Murphy, Richard, 193, 201-203, 209
Murtagi, Abdul Muhsin Kamil, 23, 36, 42, 43, 59, 62, 73-75, 85, 88, 94-96, 248n25, 251n9, 252n25

Nasr, Salah, 6, 14, 89, 90
Nasser, Gamal Abdul, 5-6, 12, 14, 15, 18-20, 36, 59-61, 126, 209, 231-33, 242-45, 247n7, 249n32, 249n34, 251n4, 252n25, 252n26, 252n35, 253n2; and the closing of the Strait of Tiran, 48-51, 70-76, 229, 234, 238; his miscalculation, 96-98, 213, 214, 216-18; and the move into Sinai, 42, 43, 61-63; and the removal of UNEF, 46-47, 63-67, 250n1(1); his rivalry with 'Amr, 28, 78, 80, 83-89, 98, 213; and the Soviet Union, 5-6, 12, 14, 22-23, 26-34, 154-55, 216, 217-18, 224; and the theory of a planned confrontation, 89-96; and UAR's military capabilities, 76-82; and

RICHARD B. PARKER, a former Foreign Service Officer who spent most of his career in the Middle East and North Africa, served as United States ambassador to Algeria, Lebanon, and Morocco in the Ford and Carter administrations. He was editor of the *Middle East Journal* from 1981 to 1987 and is the author of *North Africa: Regional Tensions and Strategic Concerns*.